Orientalism and Islamic Studies

Orientalism and Islamic Studies

Religion, Science, and Colonialism in Nineteenth Century Europe

Dietrich Jung

SHEFFIELD UK BRISTOL CT

Published by Equinox Publishing Ltd.

UK: Office 415, The Workstation, 15 Paternoster Row, Sheffield, South Yorkshire, S1 2BX
USA: ISD, 70 Enterprise Drive, Bristol, CT 06010

www.equinoxpub.com

First published 2026

British Library Cataloguing-in-Publication Data
A catalogue record for this book is available from the British Library.

ISBN-13 978 1 80050 866 8 (hardback)
978 1 80050 867 5 (paperback)
978 1 80050 868 2 (ePDF)
978 1 80050 869 9 (ePub)

Library of Congress Cataloging-in-Publication Data
Names: Jung, Dietrich, 1959- author
Title: Orientalism and islamic studies : religion, science, and colonialism in nineteenth century Europe / Dietrich Jung.
Description: Bristol, CT : Equinox Publishing Ltd, 2026. | Includes bibliographical references. | Summary: "Applying both macro- and micro level perspectives, the book investigates the complexities of the relationship between religion, science, and colonial politics in the late nineteenth and early twentieth centuries. In this way, it revisits and challenges the questionable truism of an almost complete alignment of Islamic studies with colonialism"-- Provided by publisher.
Identifiers: LCCN 2026007074 (print) | LCCN 2026007075 (ebook) | ISBN 9781800508668 hardback | ISBN 9781800508675 paperback | ISBN 9781800508682 pdf | ISBN 9781800508699 epub
Subjects: LCSH: Orientalism--History | East and West | Islam--Relations
Classification: LCC DS61.85 .J85 2026 (print) | LCC DS61.85 (ebook) | DDC 320.55/7--dc23/eng/20260220
LC record available at https://lccn.loc.gov/2026007074
LC ebook record available at https://lccn.loc.gov/2026007075

Typeset by S.J.I. Services, New Delhi, India

Contents

Acknowledgements

After a long academic career, there are many people to whom I wish to express my gratitude. Colleagues, family, friends, students, teachers, and many others contributed in one way or the other to making me what I am. Remembering the big and small contributions of all of them is as impossible as it would be to mention them all. This applies equally to all the institutions at which I was able to further develop my thoughts. The engagement with researchers during longer fellowships and visiting professorships in Ankara, Hamburg, Kuala Lumpur, Leipzig, Munich, Princeton, Singapore, and Victoria left formative imprints on me. Last but not least, thanks to project grants from the Carlsberg Foundation and the Danish Research Council for the Humanities, I was able to extend my research efforts far beyond what would have been possible in ordinary university life. So, although not directly mentioned here, my summary of gratitude will hopefully reach you all.

This is not to say that nobody was directly involved in the writing of this book. I would like to thank in particular four individuals for their specific help. First of all, my gratitude goes to the late Richard Martin (1938–2019). From the time my book *Orientalists, Islamists and the Global Public Sphere* (2011) was published, Richard wholeheartedly supported me in my research efforts in disciplinary history. He insisted that I should continue with this work. Presumably, this book would not exist in this form without the many conversations we had on the history and nature of Islamic studies. Second, but not in any hierarchy, I am grateful to my previous colleague Kirstine Sinclair. Kirstine attentively went through all the chapters of this book and provided me with the most helpful incisive comments on the text. There is no doubt that her engagement with my manuscript made it a better book. Third, Jan Busse read the first chapter on Edward Said when I started this book project during a fellowship at the University of the Bundeswehr in Munich in May 2024. I thank him for his remarks on my critique of *Orientalism* and its postcolonial followers. Finally, my friend Catherine Schwerin has subjected the manuscript to her critical eyes in terms of language. She has corrected my texts over the past decades, meticulously eradicating my Germanization of the

English phrases. So, thank you Cathy for your sustained efforts to polish my written language.

The necessary institutional support came from my publisher Equinox in Sheffield. When asked for a revision of *Orientalists, Islamists and the Global Public Sphere*, I suggested instead that I write a new monograph placing the emphasis on the interrelationship of politics, religion, and science in the formative period of Islamic studies. I am extremely pleased that the managing director, Janet Joyce, and her colleague Val Hall responded positively to this idea. Thank you for encouraging me in this project from the very beginning. Moreover, I would like to thank Amanda Nichols and Ayla Çevik for their excellent jobs in copy editing and indexing my manuscript. Finally, I must express my sincere gratitude to an institution and its people who have nothing to do with my studies as such. However, the writing of a book is also subjected to the contingencies of life. In September 2024, I underwent major open-heart surgery at the Rigshospitalet in Copenhagen. The incredible team in the Department of Cardiac Surgery did an outstanding job repairing me. Thanks to their professional care and attention, my body and mind were ready to get to work again—which meant I was able to finish this book!

Copenhagen, summer 2025

Introduction: Why *Orientalism* Again?

"Revise and resubmit!" This was the verdict on a draft article which I submitted once to an international journal. Under the working title "Islamic Modernities. Religion and Modernization in the Muslim World," this essay critically engaged with Shmuel N. Eisenstadt's (1923–2010) thesis of multiple modernities (Eisenstadt 2000a, 2000b). Eisenstadt emphasized the formative role of religious and imperial traditions in shaping culturally different modern projects. In this way, he brought religion back into the sociological discussion on modernity. Yet Eisenstadt did not really address the historical fact that these multiple modernities can differ enormously not only between, but also within what he called "civilizational complexes." In his theory, multiple modernities hardly exist within Islam. Employing a combination of theoretical elements from classical sociology with theories of social emergence, I tried to account for the historical fact of the rise of multiple modernities within Islam. This mix of theories did not find the consent of the reviewers. To put it bluntly, the review report trashed my essay from a presumably postcolonial studies angle. In applying the term of the "Muslim world," I was even accused of thoughtlessly using outdated concepts of an "orientalist" provenience.[1] Most significant, the reviewers critiqued my lack of engagement with Edward Said's *Orientalism* (1978). The report explicitly stated that without discussing Said's classic, my article would not live up to the required scholarly standard.

Anyone who has undergone academic peer-review processes knows what feelings a report like that can trigger. A distinct sense of injustice first occupies the author's mind. Did I not just engage in discussing *Orientalism* for more than two decades? Including the confession that my way into Middle East and Islamic studies was—in Said's wording—triggered by the romanticist "orientalism" of my youth? How do they have the audacity to presume that a scholar of modern Islam had not read Said's book? Though, of course, the basic rationale of a double-blind peer-review process is that the answers to these questions are unknown to the reviewers. After digesting this harsh and in my eyes unjustified criticism, I accepted the verdict. The report even motivated me to have a fresh look into *Orientalism*. As a matter of fact, this encounter with the anonymous reviewers of my article resonates with the purpose of the present book. In analyzing the rise of the modern discipline of Islamic studies, this monograph aims to tell a different story about orientalist scholarship than the oh so prominent one told by Said. The predominant aim of this book is to enhance our understanding of the complexities in the relationship between religion, science, and colonialism in Europe. Yet my engaging once again with Said's polemic book is also embedded in another reason.

In his afterword to *Orientalism* from 1994, Said emphasized that he had written a partisan book in which he had unilaterally taken part (Said 1994, 339). The book was apparently written "with a palpable anger" (Brennan 2000, 580). Moreover, in the debate about *Orientalism*, Said continuously pointed to the autobiographical starting point of his book. The writing of *Orientalism* was inseparably connected to his own biography. The personal investment in writing this book came from his "awareness of being an 'Oriental' as a child growing up in two British colonies" (Said 1978, 25). For Said, it was the book of an American literary professor with Palestinian roots (1978, 27). Thus, *Orientalism* is also a "profoundly American book" (Brennan 2000, 560). In addition, it was written and published at a time in which "disdain of philology" was widespread in the American intellectual environment (Trüper 2020, 25). Against this background, *Orientalism* is not so much an academic treatise as a personally motivated indictment. It is the polemic of an academic and public intellectual from the United States written amid the Cold War. Against this background, *Orientalism* first and foremost was directed to an American audience. Due to its polemic nature, Said's argumentation has been exposed to a host of diverse criticisms. Again and again, his selective use of sources and his inconsistent recourse to theoretical approaches found the criticism of many of his colleagues. In an interview from 1986, Said replied to these accusations with the succinct indication that the inconsistencies in *Orientalism* were intended (Salusinszky 2002). His selective usage of scholarly work and literature, therefore, was necessarily reductive. Said's normative concern, his anger, always had priority over the scholarly correctness of his argument.

This biased and polemical thrust of *Orientalism* would not have been a problem if its reception remained that of the sophisticated and probably at this point of time necessary polemic of an American public intellectual. But this is not the case. Less than 25 years after its appearance, translations existed in 36 languages. *Orientalism* quickly left its American context and had an "iconoclastic effect" on the international scholarly environment. As a fierce critique of Western knowledge about the East it "remains unmatched" (Prakash 1995, 200–201). Over decades, Said's book has played an almost hegemonic role in the debate about the Eurocentric character of the social sciences and the humanities. *Orientalism* made a paradigmatic contribution in the development of a diverse body of work generally subsumed under the label of "postcolonial studies" (Ashcroft et al. 1995, 141). The publication of Said's book "opened the floodgate of postcolonial criticism that has breached the authority of Western scholarship of Other societies" (Prakash 1995, 199). Consequently, it shattered the self-understanding of established academic disciplines such as Islamic studies and anthropology. According to the late Richard C. Martin, for example, no single book changed the meta-discourse in Islamic studies as much as this one did. Since the publication of *Orientalism*, according to Martin, training by orientalist mentors was "no longer a negotiable credential in one's professional portfolio" (Martin 2010, 903). In the field of anthropology, Said's polemic even triggered "the so-called crisis of anthropological representation" (Leistle 2010, 211). Contemporary anthropology had to systematically interrogate the historical circumstances and its link to colonialist governmentality out of which the discipline once emerged (Pels 1997).

I agree with the historian Sebastian Conrad that postcolonial studies have made a major contribution to a more complex understanding of modern history. Postcolonial theories are particularly relevant when it comes to the historical entanglement of the colonial centers with their assumed peripheries (Conrad 2024). However, when we look at the reception of *Orientalism*, many of the followers and epigones of Said did precisely what he wanted to avoid: They turned *Orientalism* into a "theoretical machine" (Said 1994, 339). In this process, the complexities, details, and inconsistencies of his argumentation gradually became submerged. Many representatives of postcolonial studies tend to conceive of colonialism in terms of a "totalizing structure." As David Scott argued, "postcolonialism has uncritically taken over this Fanonian image of colonialism" (Scott 2004, 6). Consequently, postcolonial scholars often tend to assign colonialism the role of an independent variable in their historical interpretations. At the same time, *Orientalism* has been taken out of the profoundly American historical and cultural context in which it was once written (see Brennan 2000). Today's textbook knowledge on *Orientalism* has reduced Said's polemic thesis to the meanwhile axiomatic wisdom of the close collaboration of orientalist scholarship with the colonial domination of the East by the West (Quinn 2017, 11). Against this background, the evolution of Islamic studies has been described in normatively denigrating terms too. Modern scholarship on Islam has often been narrated as an inherent, if not even necessary, part of the imperialist tradition (McCarthy 2010, 73). It is this reductive oversimplification of a historically complex process that I intend to challenge here. Though sympathetic with Edward Said's wake-up call, I will develop a different narrative to the questionable truism of an almost complete alignment of Islamic studies with colonialism that so many have taken from his work.

In this endeavor, I partly rely on previous research efforts for my book *Orientalists, Islamists, and the Global Public Sphere: A Genealogy of the Modern Essentialist Image of Islam* (2011). The publisher of the book initially suggested that I produce a revised edition. Revising the old book, however, did not find my interest. Rather, I was keen to write a new book that takes its point of departure in the research from *Orientalists, Islamists, and the Global Public Sphere*. Published in 2011, the motivation to write that genealogy was the observation that many intellectuals and scholars, both Muslim and non-Muslim, have described Islam as something more than a religion. They declared Islam to be a social unity, if not a comprehensive way of life. The revealed sources of Islamic law, the shariʿa, and the example of the Prophet and the early community of Muslims in Medina served them as a basis for the claim that Islam has a holistic nature. In this understanding of Islam, it is not difficult to find the basic traits of what Said described as the essence of the "orientalist" representation of Muslim culture. According to Said, in "orientalist" thought, Islam stands for society, morals, law, religion, and politics at the same time. Yet, how can we understand the parallels in the holistic image of Islam in the works of both "orientalist" and Islamist thinkers?

This is a question Said never posed. Already in the year 1983, the Syrian philosophy professor Sadik al-Azm (1934–2016) criticized Said for this crucial blind spot in his book. In the journal *Khamsin*, al-Azm pointed out that the ideas of Arab nationalism and those of Islamist ideologues contain similar stereotypes about the Orient. In their ideological constructs al-Azm discerned a kind of "orientalism in reverse." Arab nationalists and Islamists, so his argument, referred to a kind of self-contained "Arab" or "Islamic" spirit too. However, they did so in a different way. They did not regard the purportedly holistic culture of Islam as inferior to European culture. On the contrary, if only lived in its original purity, Islam was clearly superior to Western culture (al-Azm 1981, 234). Ten years later, Mahmut Mutman again emphasized this reciprocal relationship in the "orientalist" discourse. He criticized Said for tracing back the essentialist representation of Islam to imperialist interests alone (Mutman 1992–1993, 174).

Taking up this thread of argumentation, I organized *Orientalists, Islamists, and the Global Public Sphere* around the central question as to why "orientalists" and Islamists have defined Islam similarly as an all-encompassing social system (Jung 2011, 7). In my answer, I traced the modern essentialist image of Islam back to the intertwined emergence of the academic discipline of Islamic studies and the broad intellectual movement of Islamic modernism. The modern image of Islam, as was my core thesis, evolved throughout the nineteenth and twentieth centuries in a complex historical process of cross-cutting (self-) interpretations of Muslim and Western life experiences based on the reinterpretation of Islamic traditions through the lenses of modern social concepts (Jung 2011, 8). In short, the essentialist image of Islam is the result of a complex entanglement of Islamic and Western thought.

In the six chapters of that book, I wrote a genealogical but selective reconstruction of the historical trajectory that modern knowledge on Islam had taken. In so doing, my temporal focus was on the period between 1850 and the First World War. I analyzed the ways in which collective and individual actors were shaping and consolidating the discursive structures on which this essentialist image of Islam rests. In chapters four and five of the book, I examined this historical path from a European perspective, while chapter six explored it in the history of ideas of the Islamic Reform Movement. In this way, I pursued the aim of reconstructing the origin and evolution of the modern essentialist image of Islam. The book took issue with the ways in which European scholarship on Islam and the ideas of Islamic modernism crosscut in the construction of Islam as a modern religion. In the present book, I take up the thread from chapter four and chapter five of *Orientalists, Islamists, and the Public Sphere*. However, now I aim to more carefully examine the complex relationship among religion, science, and national and international colonial politics out of which Islamic studies emerged. In again taking my point of departure from the debate around Said's *Orientalism*, I pose the question as to which role European imperialism played in the making of a modern academic discipline.

In finding answers to this question, I am following one of the suggestions of Said in *Orientalism*. In contradistinction to Michel Foucault's focus on the structural impositions of a discursive formation, Said emphasized the important role of individual writers in shaping the "orientalist" discourse. He therefore called for a close textual reading of individual authors (Said 1978, 23). Likewise, I will put the focus on the life and work of a few individuals who played significant roles in shaping the coordinates in which the formation of modern Islamic studies as an academic discipline took place. These individual case studies comprise scholars with whom I had already made myself familiar in the context of the previous book and who played an important role in the rise of modern Islamic studies. My analysis of the life and work of these individuals, however, is embedded in a structural environment that is characterized by the emergence of the modern social systems of religion and science in Europe. As an academic discipline, Islamic studies largely developed as an inherent part of the formation of the religious and scientific realms of modern society and of nation states. In terms of power relations, European imperialism provided the historical context for these social developments. Therefore, the study of each of the representative scholars must take into account both this emerging process of modern social structures and the very different national contexts in which each of them lived.

Part I of the book has the task of providing the necessary analytical and historical framework for the later chapters. Theoretically, it will answer two pertinent questions: What is the conceptual nature of the three terms modernity, religion, and science? How are structure and individual agency combined in the analysis? Empirically, it is necessary to historically qualify what we understand by the term "colonialism." In this context, both Said and postcolonial studies have often delivered a very reductionist framing of European colonialism. Chapter one therefore combines a discussion of some core assumptions of postcolonial studies and *Orientalism* with a brief description of the complexities behind European colonialism by taking the historical example of the colonial latecomer Germany. Then, chapter two presents my theoretical frame of reference with a focus on religion and science as modern social systems. This theoretical framework makes selective use of Niklas Luhmann's Modern Systems Theory and theories of social emergence. I illustrate this excursion into macro-sociological theory with a brief historical description of oriental studies in nineteenth-century Germany. The first part of the book ends with a chapter on the life and work of the German sociologist Max Weber (1864–1920). As a classical figure in sociology Weber is often referred to in the critical writings of postcolonial scholars who try to discredit his work on normative grounds—similar to Said regarding European orientalists. Moreover, in empirical terms, Weber's sociology of religion relied on the studies of his contemporary orientalist scholars. The chapter takes its point of departure in the postcolonial critique of "Max Weber as an imperialist" and leads to a discussion of Weber's ideas on modernity, religion, and science in the context of German imperialism.

In Part II of the book, I deal with three scholars who mark the transition from classical orientalism, with its close connection to Christian theology, to the study of Islam and the Middle East in modern academic disciplines: Julius Wellhausen (1844–1918) from Germany, the British theologian and Arabist William Robertson Smith (1846–1894), and the French public intellectual Ernest Renan (1823–1892). The purpose of this part is to analyze the life and work of these three individuals in light of both the Saidian accusations and my own central question about the relationship between colonialism, religion, and science. The predominant aim here is to discuss their studies and biographies in the context of societal boundary negotiations between science and religion. In these chapters, the impact of Biblical criticism on their life and work is center stage. Therefore, the readers should not expect a detailed critical assessment of the content of the scholarship of these three orientalists. In particular regarding their studies on the Old Testament and pre-Islamic Arabia, such an undertaking would also be beyond my own scholarly expertise. In Part III of the book, then, I move on to three founding fathers of modern Islamic studies: the Hungarian orientalist Ignaz Goldziher (1850–1921), the Dutch scholar and colonial adviser Christiaan Snouck Hurgronje (1857–1937), and the German Arabist and later Prussian minister of culture Carl Heinrich Becker (1876–1933).[2] To what extent do the biographies of those scholars resemble the stereotypes of Saidian "orientalism"? Did these scholars really work in the service of European imperialism? What role did they play in the formation of Islamic studies?

Notes

1 In this book I write "orientalist" and "orientalism" in inverted commas when referring to Edward Said's meaning of these terms. *Orientalism* in italics is reserved for Said's book, while other usages of the term and its derivates related to the academic discipline are applied in a normatively neutral sense.

2 Quotes from non-English texts are all my own translations unless otherwise indicated.

Part I

The Scholarly Field: Common Questions and Diverging Answers

1 Setting the Scene: Postcolonialism, *Orientalism*, and the Colonial Mindset

"No Postcolonialism without *Orientalism*" (Williams 2013, 48). Whether this is true or not, I do not know. Yet, there is a broad consensus in scholarly literature about the pathbreaking role of *Orientalism* in the rise of postcolonial studies. To quote Gayatri Chakravorty Spivak, herself an iconic figure in the field of postcolonial critique: "When we begin to teach marginality the source book in our discipline is *Orientalism*" (Spivak 1997, 200).[1] Said's thesis became almost paradigmatic for subsequent new generations of scholars in comparative literature studies as well as for some historians and many younger anthropologists (Ashcroft et al. 1995, 141). These scholars have clearly been following the directions once given by *Orientalism* in their normative concern, to make visible the ongoing subordination of the peoples of the global South (Young 2003, 4). This influence of Edward Said is further corroborated by the fact that the field of postcolonial critique first evolved within literature studies, the academic discipline Said himself once represented. The creation of postcolonial theory has largely been the domain of comparative literature studies and of scholarly émigrés from the global South (Nash 2022, 228).

The publication of *Orientalism*, however, did not only contribute to the development of postcolonial studies. Due to its polemic nature, Said's book also triggered a long-lasting and often fierce controversy among scholars of different proveniences. This controversy is documented in the numerous reviews of the book which appeared in more than 60 international journals in the first eight years after its publication (Mani and Frankenberg 1985, 178). Legendary among them were the exchanges between Edward Said and Bernard Lewis (1916–2018). In his responses to Said's thesis, the late Professor of Islamic history at Princeton University was no less polemic than the author of *Orientalism*. Lewis accused Said of causing "intellectual pollution" of the debate on oriental studies, eventually making any rational discourse about the discipline impossible (Lewis 1993, 251). The German historian Jürgen Osterhammel seconded this point of view with his critique of Said's ideological position.

In Osterhammel's reading, *Orientalism* denied any advances in knowledge in the work of European scholarship on the Middle East and Islam (Osterhammel 1997, 599–600). According to Lewis, Said supported this conscious denial of the achievements of orientalist scholars by his arbitrary choice of sources and a deliberate "transmutation of events" (Lewis 1993, 259). For the Princeton professor, therefore, Edward Said subordinated scholarly knowledge to the profound anti-Westernism that in Lewis' eyes characterized *Orientalism's* core argument (Lewis 1993, 264).

In this chapter, I will take up the role of Edward Said in the emergence of postcolonial studies. I briefly look at the ways in which postcolonial scholars refer to *Orientalism*, have expanded Said's approach, and meanwhile have moved away from him. Then, I return to Edward Said and his critics, recapitulating the major points of critique on *Orientalism* in the scholarly community with a focus on those points which are important in the research for my own book. The purpose of this discussion is therefore not to present something like the state of the art. The heterogeneity and diversity of postcolonial studies and the broad reception of *Orientalism* in general make it elusive to aim at such a comprehensive review. As the editors of a *Postcolonial Studies Reader* indicated, postcolonial studies refers to an "amalgam of critique" meanwhile lumping together very diverse kinds of scholarship (Ashcroft et al. 1995, 141). Consequently, it is not my intention to engage with this multifaceted postcolonial discourse more deeply. The purpose of this book is not to offer a detailed critique of postcolonial theories as such, nor to take part in the meanwhile extremely polarized and politicized public debate between adherents of postcolonialism and their opponents. I simply want to tell a different story about the rise of Islamic studies in Europe.[2] Discussing postcolonial literatures and Said's thesis, therefore, only serves the aim of situating my own approach within ongoing scholarly debates. Furthermore, my literature review will indicate the ways in which my study has been stimulated by Said and his successors. The chapter will end with some remarks on the concept and the "historical reality" of colonialism. For this purpose, I will look closely at the example of Germany. The country's short colonial history serves me as a means of critique for the rather reductive ways in which both *Orientalism* and postcolonialism, as well as many of their critics, have dealt with the complexities of European colonialism.

Orientalism, Postcolonialism, and the Quest to Decolonialize the Humanities

For the rise of postcolonial studies as an academic discipline, *Orientalism* was a paradigmatic text in several ways.[3] Edward Said's book was instrumental in establishing a kind of "new orthodoxy," grounding anti-imperialist critique in the interpretative study of colonial discourses in literary texts (Osterhammel 1997, 597). The reading of these texts with a focus on the production and dissemination of knowledge became a core topic for many scholars in the field of postcolonial analysis (Mongia 1996, 4). Constitutive thereby was "an undifferentiating disavowal of all forms of nationalism and a corresponding exaltation of migrancy, liminality, hybridity, and multiculturality" (Lazarus 2002, 771). With his "preoccupation on the West" and the nexus of power and knowledge, Said left deep marks on postcolonial studies (Sylvester 1999, 714). In *Orientalism*, Said claimed to examine this nexus through the textual analysis of the authorities, canonical texts, doxological ideas, exemplary figures, and organizational features of the "orientalist" discourse (Said 1978, 22). In this way, his book offered the new field of study templates for the future development of its own research agenda. Moreover, Said introduced a whole range of concepts—ambivalence, identity, knowledge, power, representation, resistance, stereotypes—which rank high in postcolonial discourse analysis (Ashcroft et al. 1995, 141). In theoretical terms, Said's rather idiosyncratic usage of the work of Michel Foucault (1926–1984) contributed to the engagement of postcolonial theorists with the work of poststructuralist French scholars. Through the writings of French poststructuralists, postcolonial theorists also adopted the thought of German anti-Enlightenment philosophers such as Friedrich Nietzsche (1844–1900) and Martin Heidegger (1889–1976), despite the Eurocentric and discriminating elements we can find in their writings (Brennan 2014). Symptomatically, in postcolonial studies the reading of these theoretical works has often also followed the eclectic, idiosyncratic, and unsystematic application of social theory that characterized *Orientalism*.

Edward Said's influence on postcolonial studies, however, was not limited to concepts, methods, themes, and theories. It is also present in the strong normativity and accusatory writing style of many postcolonial critics. Said's anti-imperialist drift and anti-Western tendency clearly left deep traces in postcolonial studies. Yet, postcolonial scholarship not only aims to deconstruct European thought, but has also turned against the nationalist political narratives of indigenous postcolonial state elites. Many of the anti-colonialist utopias turned into social and political nightmares after independence. In short, "the bankruptcy of postcolonial regimes is palpable" today (Scott 2004, 1). In its critique of the political elite of the global South, postcolonial studies goes beyond *Orientalism*. This is explicitly the case in the writings of the Subaltern Studies Group, another inspirational source for the new field. This group of scholars of Indian origin, once initiated by Ranajit Guha (1923–2023), vehemently criticized the nationalist history writing of India's postcolonial modernizing elite. Faced with the hegemony of colonial and Indian-nationalist narratives, Guha called for the writing of an alternative history of modern India, for a history from below. In his view, this history should be based on the rediscovery of the voices of the subaltern, the voices of the "anonymous poor peasantry in colonized worlds" (Sivaramakrishnan 1995, 418). This call to write an alternative historiography to that of India's "bourgeois nationalists" found one of its foundational texts in Spivak's essay "Subaltern Studies: Deconstructing Historiography" (Spivak 1985). Her approach was then also adopted by many scholars in postcolonial literature studies. In its call for alternative knowledges from below, postcolonial studies clearly incorporated the perspective of Ranajit Guha and other scholars of the Subaltern Studies Group.

The writings of Spivak were also important for postcolonial scholarship when it comes to the category of gender (Hassan 2002, 48). In her presidential address to the annual conference of the North American Middle East Studies Association (MESA) in 2008, then MESA president Mervat Hatem criticized the absence of women in Said's book. In her opinion, *Orientalism* was still following "the gaze of 'dead white men'" (Hatem 2009, 5). Generally speaking, in its gendered discourse, *Orientalism* either ignores sexual difference or understands it as an "issue which belongs to a different field" (Yegenoglu 1998, 2). When it comes to questions of the construction of the other and gender, Said could have learned a lot from previous feminist scholarship, such as Simone de Beauvoir's (1908–1986) seminal book *The Second Sex*.[4] Published thirty years before *Orientalism*, the French author analyzed the historical status of women from an existentialist philosophical perspective. In the othering of women, she identified a more general dualism in Western thought concerning the construction of minorities (Rich 2007, 16). Women, according to de Beauvoir, are the other of men. They are the "negative of the absolute masculine human type," representing the fundamental alterity to men (de Beauvoir 1949, 25, 28). In fact, in 1949, de Beauvoir had already applied Said's model of othering. In her book, it was not Europe but men who "gained in strength and identity" by setting themselves off against women (see Said 1978, 3).

Since the 1990s, gender "as a multi-dimensional structure of inequality" has increasingly informed the social sciences and humanities and consequentially also postcolonial studies (Scarborough 2018, 4). In taking the intersectional character of othering into account, the mutually constitutive roles of class, gender, sexuality, and race, postcolonial theory clearly expanded the analytical frame of reference of *Orientalism*. In this process, the role of race, in its ideological representation in racism, became a prime concern of the field. For some scholars, searching for traces of racism in classical and contemporary scholarship became the core endeavor in their normatively guided research. Sara R. Farris, for instance, identified in Max Weber (1864–1920) one of the "most important systematizers" of the "prejudicial view" that Said assigned "orientalist" scholarship (Farris 2010, 266).[5] Andrew Zimmerman even considered the German sociologist to be the pioneer of "a racism of exploitation and subordination" (2006, 54).[6] Regarding contemporary scholarship, one of the more recent cases of such zealotic writings was the accusation of racism made against the Danish scholar of international relations, Ole Wæver. In an utterly polemic and prosecutorial piece, Alison Howell and Melanie Richter-Montpetit contended that they had discovered the foundational role that racist thought has played in the development of the theoretical framework of the so-called Copenhagen School of Security Studies (Howell and Richter-Montpetit 2020). This school is closely linked to scholars such as Ole Wæver, Barry Buzan, and Jap de Wilde, who met in the 1990s at the Copenhagen Peace Institute (COPRI). My impression here is, however, that Howell and Richter-Montpetit simply want to deny the scientific legitimacy and analytical relevance of the theory posited by the Copenhagen School. In my eyes, we can observe in this case internal struggles for power and positions within the academy that are based on moral-normative accusations alone.

These examples are, on the one hand, in the tradition of *Orientalism*. Like Said, in talking about "distorted knowledge" (Said 1978, xxii), postcolonial scholars try to deny the validity of so-called Western or racist scholarship through the lenses of their own normative predispositions. This profound suspicion and hostility against "Western thought" meanwhile became an integral part of the interdisciplinary and intradisciplinary discussions of various disciplines within the humanities and the social sciences. However, even if these accusations were right, Mansoor Moaddel's argument against Said applies equally to the postcolonial critique. In an assessment of the study of Islamic culture and politics, Moaddel argued that the mere fact of "ideas produced in the context of domination" does not render them invalid *per se* (Moaddel 2002, 366).[7] In its more extreme positions, on the other hand, postcolonial studies clearly deviated from Said's humanism. *Orientalism* is not a manifest against the humanist and emancipatory legacy of the European Enlightenment. On the contrary, Said staunchly defended this legacy and accused orientalist scholarship precisely of having eliminated these humanistic values from its research (Said 1978, 110). Against this background, he did not call for a departure from humanism, but he demanded its radical reformulation to live up to its universalist claims (Williams 2013, 49). In postcolonial theorizing, this dimension of Said's work has gradually been replaced by identitarian argumentations, increasingly creating a kind of antagonism between *Orientalism* and postcolonial studies (Brennan 2000, 575). The majority of scholars in postcolonial scholarship have chosen the track of the "anti-Enlightenment tradition" with its "cult of difference" (Sternhell 2010).

Timothy Brennan rightfully argued that we should read *Orientalism* as a profoundly American book, despite its anti-Westernism (Brennan 2000, 560). The author of *Orientalism* was without doubt himself a part of the scholarly world against which his critique was directed. In a similar way, postcolonial studies are firmly rooted in European theoretical traditions such as Feminism, Marxism, Poststructuralism, Psychoanalysis, and more recently Queer studies (Hassan 2002, 47; Young 2003, 114). Due to this "Eurocentric" heritage, postcolonial theory has meanwhile itself become the target of a more radical critique, demanding a complete departure from so-called Western epistemologies. Operating under the label of "decoloniality," this new movement accuses scholars in postcolonial studies of still following Eurocentric epistemological frames of reference that themselves contain major elements of coloniality (Rodríguez 2010; Gu 2020). Scholars such as Walter D. Mignolo and Ramón Grosfoguel therefore call for a decolonization of postcolonial studies and advocate a fundamental rupture with the Enlightenment legacy of social science research (Colpani et al. 2022, 3). They consider the heritage of European social theory as necessarily dispensable and want to radically do away with what they consider the all-encompassing "colonial matrix of power" (Mignolo 2020, 613). In contradistinction to the concept of decolonization as the formation of independent, sovereign nation states, the movement of decoloniality aspires to a radical transformation of institutions and intellectual thought (Gu 2020, 597). Against this approach, Spivak defended postcolonial studies as theoretically acknowledging the entanglement of Western and non-Western thought. She described decoloniality as a kind of "liberal-radical fantasy" based on the "romanticization of a past-riddled power play" (Spivak et al. 2022, 138).

Since the publication of *Orientalism*, the debate has moved to a point at which postcolonial and decolonization studies mark an utterly heterogeneous discursive field. The common grounds of these strands of literature are often nothing more than a staunch opposition against an imagined West. Europe or/and the West became "a fetish with 'no credible referent'" (Mannathukkaren 2015, 311). Seemingly they represent something like an amorphous set of the "evils of modernity," a way of confusing colonial domination with modernity as such. Postcolonial scholarship often reduces the reading of texts into a translation of dense literary textures, "into the meager thematizations of its own esurient vocabulary, repetitively, and predictably" (Patke 2002, 695). Ironically, the postcolonial call for alternative bodies of knowledge and epistemologies seems to be informed by a dichotomizing system of stereotypical concepts and taken-for-granted narratives similar to that which Said once detected in the "orientalist" discourse of the nineteenth century (Pouchepadass 2004). Like the Orient in Said's book, the West of many postcolonial critics is a homogenizing fiction, a dynamic but normatively grounded idea rather than an analytically meaningful category.[8] Not least, my own narrative also works against this fiction of a homogeneous West.

The judgment on postcolonial discourse analysis by Aijaz Ahmad appears to be as relevant today as it was more than thirty years ago. In 1991, Ahmad argued that postcolonial studies had "gathered force through a system of mutual citations and cross-referencing among a handful of influential writers" (Ahmad 1991, 281). The number of writers has meanwhile grown considerably, turning the study on colonial discourse into a huge discursive system of its own. As the work of the German sociologist Niklas Luhmann (1927–1998) convincingly showed, it is the nature of self-referential systems that they are not able to communicate with their environment. Consequently, it would not make sense to attempt to develop my own story about the formation of Islamic studies in close conversation with the debates in postcolonial studies. This conversation would end in the very same mess as the review process of my article mentioned in the introduction to this book. The following chapters therefore attempt to present a narrative of their own, yet a narrative that complements Edward Said's. My work is also concerned with colonial power structures and is theoretically informed by intersectional approaches regarding the power relations of social life. Not entering the discursive system of postcolonial studies does not mean disregarding the contributions of this field of scholarship nor does it mean not taking some of its major questions seriously. Therefore, I will start my narrative, too, with the critical debate about *Orientalism*. It is the task of the next section to recapitulate this crucial debate.

Orientalism and Its Critics

Edward Said grounded his thesis in *Orientalism* on a collection of texts about the Orient that were mainly literary and seldom scholarly. In this literature, he discerned ontological and epistemological differences that supposedly distinguish an unchanging Orient from a dynamic West (Said 1978, 96). In setting itself off from the Orient, according to Said, Europe gained strength in its own identity construction (1978, 3). From this perspective, Said claimed that Western orientalists, from Ernest Renan to Bernard Lewis, constructed Islam in the form of a cultural synthesis that could be studied separately from the economics, sociology, and politics of Muslim peoples (Said 1978, 105). In Said's analysis, European writers produced a hegemonic discourse about the Orient through which they legitimized the colonial oppression of the East by Western powers. Inspired by his idiosyncratic reading of Michel Foucault, Said saw the birth of the "Oriental" as the result of a specific nexus of power and knowledge. According to the American professor of literature, European orientalists and novelists invented an "imaginative geography" that provided the necessary knowledge for "the mapping, conquest, and annexation of territory" (Said 2000, 181). Said therefore declared orientalist scholarship to be an imperial institution with the purpose of facilitating and justifying colonial domination.[9] In this way, he extended the previous notion of orientalism enormously. Once the designation for the philological discipline of an academic avant-garde, Said turned the concept of an "orientalist" into a pejorative label for stereotypical Western thinkers who claim the absolute superiority of the West over the East.

I first read *Orientalism* as a student. This confrontation with Said's thesis went hand in hand with my courses in Islamic studies at Hamburg University in the late 1980s. The curriculum there at that time incorporated works of important classical orientalists such as Carl Heinrich Becker, Ignaz Goldziher, Theodor Nöldeke, Julius Wellhausen, and Arendt Jan Wensinck. Said only mentions these authorities in the field very superficially in just a few lines (Said 1978, 207). Apparently, he himself had never read them.[10] Said's knowledge of orientalist scholarship was extremely reductive and almost entirely based on secondary sources (Trüper 2020, 13). The orientalists with whom Said engaged more closely in his book—Edward William Lane, Ernest Renan, and Silvestre de Sacy—were not part of my course readings in Islamic studies. In my university curriculum, they never appeared as the "inaugural heroes" who ostensibly built the field (Said 1978, 122). Nevertheless, Said's sweeping generalizations in *Orientalism* made an impact on my academic career too. His polemic gave my studies the then necessary critical edge. The anti-imperialist tone of *Orientalism* deeply resonated with me. The balancing of his thesis with my knowledge of the orientalist classics became a challenge to me in the course of many years. Both *Orientalism* and orientalists contributed to the development of my thought. Moreover, this antagonism of knowledge also influenced my reading of Said's critics.

In my own understanding, the multifaceted critique of *Orientalism* has revolved around five major themes: Said's inconsistent application of social theory, his a-historic thesis of a continuity of "orientalist" stereotypes in Europe since antiquity, the neglect of orientalism in reverse, his arbitrary selection of sources, and the self-evident and instrumental combination of imperialism with orientalist scholarship.

The first critique, Said's inconsistent use of social theory, is to a certain extent elusive when we take the polemic nature of *Orientalism* seriously. Even more important, as already mentioned in the introduction to this book, Said had no problem admitting to his theoretical inconsistency. He considered it not as a weakness but rather as a strength of *Orientalism*. When it comes to the second critique, the narrative of historical continuity, this was again a deliberate construction by the author. To claim that there is a linear path from Homer to Henry Kissinger is certainly an anathema to any historiographic research. Said's anachronistic continuity thesis solely served the purpose of supporting and strengthening the overall argument of his book. Historical accuracy does not boost the polemic nature of a book.[11] Third, the critique made by Sadik al-Azm that Said had a blind eye for the various forms of "orientalism in reverse" was the core concern of my *Orientalists, Islamists, and the Global Public Sphere* (Jung 2011). Thus, there is no need to take up these three critical questions once again in the context here.[12] Only the question of sources and Said's complete confusion of oriental scholarship with imperial politics remain interesting for this book.

Historians of the Middle East have been particularly vocal in their critique of Said's sources. Bernard Lewis and Richard Irwin, for instance, even accused him of deliberately following a deceptive strategy in writing his book. In Irwin's eyes, the "distortion of the subject matter" would render any form of working with Said's approach a waste of time. However, I do not think that the almost complete omission of orientalists who were not nationals of the colonial powers of Great Britain and France, or of the later international hegemon of the United States, is proof of Said's "malignant charlatanry" (Irwin 2006, 4). Rather, it is the obvious strategy of somebody who first and foremost wants to construct a polemic argument with an American audience in mind. Consequently, orientalist scholars from countries such as Austria, Germany, Hungary, and Italy hardly play a role (Kerr 1980, 545). Against the background of Said repeatedly emphasizing his Palestinian-Arab background, it seems to me more surprising that he totally omitted an investigation of the considerable literature on European orientalists in Arabic (Winder 1981, 617). Ironically, Said himself also did not give the "orientals" a voice. Additionally significant, Said refers only very briefly and superficially to one of the founding fathers of modern Islamic studies, the Dutch scholar Christiaan Snouck Hurgronje. After teaching at the college for colonial staff in Leiden, Snouck Hurgronje served from 1889 to 1906 as a colonial adviser in the Dutch East Indies, present-day Indonesia, before holding several professorships at Leiden University. What better choice than Snouck Hurgronje would there have been as the exemplary scholar for an investigation of the close complicity between oriental scholarship and imperial politics?

In terms of sources, Said's data taken from the life and work of orientalist scholars is utterly weak if not fully inadequate. He picked and chose whatever underpinned his polemic interest. In fact, when it comes to orientalist scholarship, the basis of his data does not provide the necessary evidence for his generalizing thesis. It may be true that "Said was seeking to prove that academics had, in effect, collaborated in the West's domination of the East" (Quinn 2017, 11). Yet the author of *Orientalism* never really put forward enough evidence to justify this thesis. His reference to Theodor Nöldeke's and Julius Wellhausen's denigrating comments on Islam, for instance, are good examples of Said's lack of knowledge about major figures in oriental studies. Dedicating only a few superficial sentences to them, he suggests understanding the two scholar's negative attitudes toward the Islamic religion as being a result of the "fact of substitution and displacement" of the Orient in the work of European orientalists (Said 1978, 209).

Said apparently did not know that Nöldeke was an openly declared agnostic rationalist whose contempt was directed at all religions and not only at Islam (Sellheim 2007). In Nöldeke's eyes, religion as such was an obstacle to humane progress (Maier 2021, 190). In his correspondence with other orientalists, Nöldeke often declared himself to be an "orthodox heathen" (Simon 1986, 253). Carl Heinrich Becker mentioned that Nöldeke wrote to him about his doubts on whether religions had actually benefited humanity, positing instead that they had tended to harm it (Becker 1932, 515). From his anticlerical position, Julius Wellhausen sided with Germany's Chancellor Bismarck (1871–1890) in the struggle against the Catholic Church during the so-called German *Kulturkampf* (1871–1887). Bismarck had a deep mistrust of the political loyalty of Germany's Catholic population, who found their political representation in the German Catholic Centre Party. Triggered by the Vatican's declaration of papal infallibility in 1870, Chancellor Bismarck began to move against Catholic priests who were voicing political opinions. Furthermore, he put religious schools under state supervision, dissolved the Jesuit order in Germany, exerted state control over ecclesiastical appointments, and made civil marriage compulsory in 1875 (Mann 1992, 441–444). Even more significant, Prussia severed its diplomatic ties to the Vatican in 1872. In 1875, Pope Pius IX responded to these measures with the *Encyclica quod numquam*, in which he declared the Prussian legislation void, and by calling on the German bishops to lead active resistance (Besier 1990, 216–217).[13] In this period, Wellhausen wholeheartedly supported the secularist demands of the Prussian state (van Ess 1980, 42). Theodor Nöldeke and Julius Wellhausen were typical representatives of the anticlerical intellectual elite that inhabited German universities toward the end of the nineteenth century. In fact, although raised in a "Christian culture," Germany's liberal Protestant university professors did not normally have external relationships with the churches (Swatos and Kivisto 1991, 352). The pejorative views on Islam shared by these two orientalists were part and parcel of their secularist worldviews and anticlerical attitude in general.[14] In their correspondence and writings, Nöldeke and Wellhausen were equally denigrating of orthodox Christians, Jews, and Muslims.

When looking at Nöldeke's work—almost 700 academic publications in various orientalist sub-disciplines and based on primary sources in

Arabic, Persian, and Turkish—it is difficult to imagine that this opus was driven by complicity with Europe's colonial ambitions (Sellheim 2007, 142). He even admitted that in his youth he only accidentally committed himself to Qur'anic studies (Simon 1986, 191). In 1856, Nöldeke wrote his dissertation on the history of the Qur'an in Latin, which was then later published in German in 1860 as *Geschichte des Qorāns* (Sellheim 2007, 135). The young Nöldeke's first book became a standard reference for the critical analysis of the historical chronology of the Qur'an (Fück 1955, 218). Could any colonial endeavor have motivated a twenty-year-old scholar who already acquired excellent knowledge of classical Arabic to publish an academic treatment of the Qur'an in Latin? What about the first complete edition of the historiographical writings of the famous Persian historian al-Tabari (839–923)? The editor in chief of this voluminous work was Nöldeke's Dutch friend and colleague Michael Jan de Goeje (1836–1909). De Goeje, professor at the University of Leiden, conducted this editing project over the course of 22 years until its publication in 1871. Funded by external sources "from both East and West," and strongly building on access to Ottoman archives, this scholarly work could hardly serve the interests of Dutch or other European colonizers (see Vrolijk 2001). This conclusion equally applies to the recordings of music and speeches which Snouck Hurgronje made on wax cylinders in the years 1905 to 1909 at the Dutch consulate in Jeddah. Recorded in the 1990s on DAT-tapes, this collection of music played in religious, folk, and urban contexts remains one of the oldest and largest collections of Arab music in the world (van Oostrum 2012).

These examples profoundly underpin the critique of the sources used by Said in his book and cast doubt on his general thesis of the neat complicity between orientalist scholarship and colonialism at the micro level. Moreover, they are sound proof of a number of lasting scholarly accomplishments achieved by European orientalists. What does the edition of al-Tabari's historiographic works have to do with the justification of colonial domination? In *Orientalism*, Said's choice of texts was governed by the overarching normative and polemic purpose of his book. The linear linkage between power and knowledge made by Said, however, also found numerous critics who argued beyond the source critique made by historians of the Middle East. They emphasized Said's very reductionist understanding of colonialism. David Kopf, a British scholar on the modernization of India, criticized Said's focus on the Middle East while leaving out Turkey and the whole of Asia (Kopf 1980, 496). This preoccupation with the Arab Middle East was further criticized with respect to the historical fact that the region experienced a shorter, more indirect, and mediated form of colonial domination when compared to large parts of Asia (Lewis 1993, 261). Indeed, Said's geographical bias clearly reflects Brennan's argument concerning the fundamentally American character of *Orientalism*. Said's focus on the Arab Middle East closely matched both his own biographical narrative and the geopolitical gaze of the United States in the late 1970s, the two converging in the Camp David Accords (1978) and the signature of a peace treaty between Israel and Egypt (1979).[15]

In looking at orientalist works by European scholar of Japan, Richard Minear, convincingly argued that the academic discourse on Japan closely resembled some of the "orientalist" stereotypes which Said detected in the discourse on Islam. Moreover, European Japanology applied a similar historical differentiation between an oriental greatness in the past and its complete degradation in the present (Minear 1980, 507). In the case of Japan, however, this stereotypical representation of Japanese history and culture happened in the complete absence of overt Western domination (1980, 515). Even more important, the degrading attitudes of European scholars toward Japan found their cross-cultural counterpart in Japan's historically entrenched racist and ethnocentric traditions (1980, 516). This argument of the cross-cultural presence of ethnocentric, racist, and often hostile stereotypes of the other beyond the West hardly appears in the postcolonial writings of the Saidian tradition. A different example is the study of Sanna Dhahir on fictional literature from Saudi Arabia. Dhahir clearly demonstrates the ways in which black people in Saudi public parlance are represented by "pejorative stereotypes and racial slurs" (Dhahir 2023, 150). Contemporary Saudi novelists regularly describe expressions of racial discrimination, marginalization, and oppression which are otherwise impossible to articulate critically in Saudi public discourse (2023, 115). Evidently, pejorative and racist representations of other cultures are omnipresent social phenomena and not a characteristic limited solely to the colonial imaging of Europe.

It is certainly true that Said made a lasting impact on generations of scholars after the publication of his book. Since *Orientalism*, the thesis that orientalist scholarship was an "inherent part of the imperialist tradition" gained the status of conventional knowledge and has been disseminated through numerous textbooks to generations of students and scholars (McCarthy 2010, 73). The two previous sections tried to make this link between Said and postcolonial scholars transparent by indicating the deviations of postcolonial studies from Said's approach at the same time. These deviations pertain, among other things, to those limitations of *Orientalism* which Said himself admitted to. Already in the Introduction to *Orientalism*, he acknowledged that due to his focus on the "Anglo-French-American experience," he did not do justice to the important contributions to orientalism as an academic discipline by other nations, in particular Germany. Moreover, he expressed his awareness that the "revolution in Biblical studies" gave "important impulses toward the study of the Orient" (Said 1978, 17). In a nutshell, these admitted limitations are at the heart of my book. I do not intend to present an "archaeological critique" of Edward Said's thesis. My study focuses instead on what he has not done. This book deals with the crucial deficiencies of his thesis which have been almost completely submerged in the postcolonial discourse. One of them is Said's rather simplistic understanding of the colonial power matrix, which I will address in the last section of this chapter.

Colonialism and the European Colonial Mindset: The German Experience

Instead of doing away with it, *Orientalism* and postcolonial studies have largely confirmed the dichotomic worldview of East versus West—colonialized versus colonizers—though in different ways. This is the accusation of many of their critics. Indeed, in Said's book, colonialism is synonymous with the so-called West. Even more important, this West appears in terms of some kind of powerful and unified actor. The colonized people, by contrast, do not appear in *Orientalism* as agentive actors in their own right. The colonized do not act. In this sense, Said reproduced the "orientalist" topoi of the "silent East" in his own work. In contradistinction to Said, postcolonial theories have tried to give the people of the global South a voice.[16] Moreover, postcolonial theorists addressed the relationship between colonizers and colonized in new ways. Gurminder Bhambra, for instance, proposed studying this relationship based on an approach of "connected sociologies." This approach aimed to integrate the entanglement of the historically not so clear-cut dichotomy between colonial center and periphery into social theory-building (Bhambra 2014). Postcolonial scholars have participated in the creation and distribution of the analytical concept of entanglement that refers to the historical interconnections and mutual dependencies of colonizers and colonized. From this perspective, we should understand the present as the result of formative processes to which diverse cultural traditions have contributed, yet within shifting and often utterly asymmetric power relations (Randeria 2002). The concept of entanglement gives agency back to the colonized, whose social actorhood was largely absent in *Orientalism*.

This introduction of the agency of the subaltern has increasingly been complemented with the application of intersectional approaches in postcolonial studies. Intersectional approaches reveal the mutual reinforcement of multiple systems of oppression such as "race, class, gender, sexuality, and nation" (Scarborough 2018, 6). Viewing them as a cultural phenomenon, scholars analyzed the colonial power structures as the intersection of different but mutually reinforcing schemes of discrimination. I fully endorse this theoretical and methodological extension of the Saidian view. Unfortunately, however, this laudable appreciation of social complexities is almost exclusively applied regarding the observation of the oppressed in European colonies. The representation of the oppressor—the West—often remains, as in *Orientalism*, that of a holistic actor. Understanding colonialism, in my eyes, demands an intersectional view of the colonizer too. This does not only mean differentiating between different nations in the colonizing West, but also investigating and taking intersectional tensions within European nation states seriously. The multiple systems of colonial oppression closely connected "center and peripheries." Simplistic dichotomic designations such as East/West or global South/North contribute little to the understanding of the social complexities of colonialism.

In this final section, I look more closely at the complexities of the colonial situation in a specific colonizing country. I do so by taking the example of Germany for two reasons. First, Germany has a different colonial history in comparison to Great Britain and France. In terms of territorial colonialism, Germany was a latecomer among the European powers. The case of Germany, therefore, has been a core issue in the debate on *Orientalism* due to Said's omission of scholars and novelists with a German background. Yet despite the prominent role of this issue in the debate, even in postcolonial studies one searches almost in vain for a serious discussion of the history of German imperialism (Fuhrmann 2006, 21). In what ways—if at all—would the German experience make a difference to great colonial powers such as Britain and France? Second, in German state formation, national integration coincided with colonial expansion in the late nineteenth century. Therefore, the country is a good example for discussing the intersection of global, national, and local social levels in the epoch of European imperialism. In what ways were German colonial policies characterized by mutually reinforcing schemes of discrimination in the colonies and at home?

Several critics of *Orientalism* pointed to the role of German orientalists in shaping the discipline while not having been citizens of one of the major colonial powers (Fähndrich 1988; Fowden 2011; Kerr 1980; Lewis 1993; Sivan 1985). This critique makes sense with respect to the scholarly significance of German orientalism. I agree with Suzanne Marchand's opinion that German scholars were pacesetting "in virtually every field of oriental studies between 1830 and 1930" (Marchand 2009, xviii). Indeed, it is problematic to make generalizing judgments about oriental studies in Europe without knowing the life and work of the German scholars who were leading representatives of the field. When it comes to the colonial cultural context, this argument of Said's lack of regard for Germany, however, misses the point. The economic, political, and social development in Germany was closely knit into the structural settings of European imperialism: the development of industrializing societies and the rising power competition among Europe's nation states (Wehler 1970a, 11). In its territorial dimension, German colonialism was certainly less significant and relatively short-lived in comparison to that of Great Britain and France. The Berlin Conference (1884–1885) set the starting point of Germany's colonial expansion. With the declaration of South West Africa as a German protectorate in 1884, the period of German colonial rule overseas began, though it only lasted until the end of the First World War (Gründer 1991, 71).

This short period of direct colonial rule in the times of "high imperialism," however, was preceded by a history in which German companies, adventurers, and noble rulers were seeking to gain control over colonial territories (van der Heyden 2011, 219). Already long before the foundation of the modern German state in January 1871, colonialism was an inherent part of both the German experience and the German mindset (Langbehn and Salama 2011, 31). Public discourse in the then plurality of German states was characterized by "colonizing phantasies" which had appeared in books, essays, scholarly articles, novels, and political treaties since the sixteenth century (Zantop 1999, 9–10). As early as the 1840s, the Prussian general Helmuth von Moltke (1800–1891) propagated the idea of German settlements in the Middle East (Gründer 1991, 19). In the foundational phase of the German state, public culture was already permeated by colonial discourse (Honold and Simons 2002, 14). In the second part of the nineteenth century, then, Western Anatolia and

Greece became popular destinations for German scientific missions by archologists, biologists, and geographers (Fuhrmann 2006, 27). In public discourse, these German claims to the Eastern Mediterranean were justified by a crusader's myth according to which Germany has historically grounded rights to power in this region (Fuhrmann 2003). The German excavations in Asia Minor and the Baghdad railway project were also central issues in Emperor Wilhelm II's oriental journey in 1898 (Honold 2002). After the proclamation of the state in 1871, German colonialism in its territorial and cultural dimensions was the attempt to enter the world imperial system (Berman 2011, 170). Berlin's colonial strategies were an inherent part of "German efforts to compete with England, France, and Russia on the world stage" (2011, 182). The "colonial mindset" was as dominant in Germany as it was in Great Britain and France.

Though comparatively short-lived in its territorial dimension, as a cultural frame colonialism had been firmly established long before the factual colonial expansion of Germany began. Guided by this mindset, German colonialism was also governed by the racist belief in the "white man's superiority" that was ubiquitous in Europe (von Strandmann 2011, 207). German racism was terribly proven by the genocidal nature of the colonial war against the Hereros (1904–1907) in South West Africa. This war included random killings, extermination schemes, and concentration camps on the side of the German colonial troops (Eckl 2008). Like other European powers, Germans treated indigenous cultures with the "creed of inequality, segregation, paternalism, and condescension." In addition, ruthless exploitation and slave labor also characterized Germany's colonial economy (Kundus 2011, 34). However, as Isabel Hull in her study on the German conduct of war between 1870 and 1918 shows, we should be careful not to trace a linear line from racist attitudes to colonial atrocities. Complicity in mass slaughter was not a general phenomenon and, therefore, the "ubiquity in racialist thinking in Europe" does not tell us the reason "why Europeans went to extremes in some situations and not in others" (Hull 2005, 331). In the German example too, colonialism took on very different forms in Africa, Asia, and in its special relationship with the Ottoman Empire. In stark distinction to South West Africa, the German Empire was following a strategy of "peaceful penetration" of the Ottoman state according to which Berlin aimed to gain as much influence as possible by maintaining the political *status quo* (Fuhrmann 2006, 12). In conclusion, German colonialism was not fundamentally different from that of other European powers (Gründer 1991, 241). The German expansion was an inherent part of European imperialism "driven by nationalism, social Darwinism, racism, imperial competition and a civilizing mission" (Wehler 1995, 978). Therefore, it would be a clear mistake "to dissociate German colonialism from the broader European context" (Langbehn and Salama 2011, x).

Looking at colonialism as a public discourse of othering, Germans were without doubt part of a European "interpretative community" for which colonialist patterns of thought represented a kind of "common sense" (Stoler 2009). This interpretative community, however, did not comprise the whole of Europe. While we can detect this colonial common sense in European thought, not all Europeans were on the side of the colonizers. The German colonial discourse is once again a good example of this. Chancellor Bismarck's policies of "inner colonialization" paralleled the country's territorial expansion.[17] Employing the very same topoi of a civilizing mission, these policies "fashion[ed] the Polish as uncivilized in order to legitimate German domination" (Kopp 2011, 148–149). Even more significantly, the middle class discussed the situation of the urban poor in European countries in terms of frequent "analogies between European and non-European 'savages'" (Dejung 2019, 181). The philanthropic missionary movements, for example, employed the categories of class and race as discursive tools in their examination of the relations between colonial subjects and European underclasses. The home mission movements frequently compared "colonial 'savages'" with the domestic population in urban slums (Dejung 2019, 173). Consequently, the European colonial mindset had global, regional, and national dimensions.

The above phenomenon of the "orientalization" of European people at regional and domestic levels does not play any role in *Orientalism*. Given this colonial mindset in nineteenth-century bourgeois cultural discourse, it should come as little surprise that Said discerned these stereotypes of European cum British and French superiority in his sources. Likewise, it seems no great scholarly achievement to detect—donning the normative glasses of the twenty-first century—traces of racism in the thought of Max Weber or in early German anthropology (Zimmerman 2001, 2006). Andrew Zimmerman's findings are nothing more than a confirmation of this long-established knowledge about the colonialist mindset that permeated European public discourse at the turn of the twentieth century.[18] Problematic, however, is reducing this discursive structure of discrimination to an East/West divide alone. As such, many scholars of postcolonial studies fall short of their own appreciation of the intersectional analytical schemes that they often employ in the analysis of the colonized. The example of Germany reveals the reductive nature in which Said and postcolonial studies have prioritized one of many discriminatory discourses in these bourgeois structures of inequality. When talking about Germany in the late nineteenth century, what kind of country are we discussing?

In the colonial period of Germany, we can observe the inseparable combination of national integration and colonial expansion pushed forward by the cultural, economic, and political elite (Gründer 1991, 21). Yet, this nationalist bourgeoise elite represented only a tiny fraction of the German population. During the period of German colonialism, the country simultaneously experienced a dramatic growth in domestic population. Between 1871 and 1910, the number of Germans increased from 41.06 million to 64.93 million people (Wehler 1995, 494). Together with labor migration from the East to the West, this led to a rapid expansion of the cities combined with rampant social deprivation. At the end of the nineteenth century, 95 percent of the German population belonged to groups of *petit bourgeois* or the large underclass (Preisendörfer 2023, 255). In these milieus, child mortality reached a staggering 40 percent (Wehler 1995, 28). In Berlin, more than 20 percent of residents had no home, only a place to sleep, and slums of the poor were a normal sight (Preisendörfer 2023, 313). Many poor families lived in small attic chambers or in damp rooms in the basements of urban houses (Ring 1872).

In rural areas, the situation was often even worse. In 1852, the famous physician Rudolf Virchow (1821–1902) traveled the south German region of Spessart, then suffering from famine. In his report, Virchow mentions that several generations and often different families usually lived together at one place, with two to three persons sleeping in the same bed (Virchow 1852, 12). In late nineteenth-century Germany, this economic deprivation was accompanied by political discrimination. Until the First World War, most Germans were excluded from political participation. From 1850, the Prussian Parliament was elected by a voting system that translated economic power into voting weight. The three-class franchise system ranked voters according to their tax payments. In this way, less than five percent of the population achieved control over the seat distribution in parliament (Becker and Hornung 2020, 1143). Toward the end of the 1880s, for instance, in the city of Essen only 17 percent had the right to vote. Based on the three-class system, 97 percent of these voters had only one vote each. The sole member of the first class of voters at the time, the industrialist Alfred Krupp (1812–1887), had enough voting weight to elect one third of all representatives of the city council alone (Preisendörfer 2023, 78).

This political and economic discrimination of the poor was expressed in the rise of a sense of social exclusion among Germany's working class. This huge proportion of the country's population increasingly avoided contact with members of other classes and met political and religious authorities with enormous resentment (McLeod 1982, 331). Meeting points of different social classes and political persuasions became rare, and the adoption of "socialism as an alternative way of life" marked the final stage in the alienation of the German working class toward the end of the nineteenth century (1982, 335). In this context, Germany's Social Democrats traditionally "condemned any manifestation of colonial expansion" based on a "host of economic arguments against imperialism" (Ascher 1961, 555). Emblematic of this position was the conclusion drawn by Karl Liebknecht (1871–1919), a representative of the left wing of the Social Democrats, who argued from a Marxist point of view that imperialism was an inevitable concomitant of capitalism (Asher 1961, 563). Until the First World War, the absolute majority of Germany's Social Democrats presented a strong voice against colonialism, attacking German colonial rule—for instance, in the so-called mixed-race marriage debate of 1912—"as a thinly veiled disguise of a race-based and cruel system of economic exploitation" (Guettel 2012, 474). However, in their objection to colonial rule, most Social Democrats nevertheless shared the European colonial mindset in the sense that they, too, were convinced of Europe's higher stage of social development in comparison to the rest of the world (Guettel 2012, 481).

Finally, there was the firmly established discrimination against women and Jews. Hedwig Dohm (1831–1919), an early German feminist, wrote a treatise in 1876 on the situation of women in society. In this book, she advocated for the active and passive franchise of women, which was eventually introduced in November 1918 (Dohm 1876, 58).[19] Even the political program of the Social Democrats had not supported women's franchise prior to the adoption of its revised edition in 1891. In addition, women were denied access to academic education. Despite several steps toward the legal equality of Germany's Jewish population, which was formally granted in 1871, Jewish emancipation did not lead to the disappearance of the fundamental distinction between Jews and Christians. On the contrary, every advancement in the emancipation of the Jews simultaneously meant a fixation on what divided them from the rest of the population (Rürup 1987, 39). Consequently, anti-semitic discrimination remained a characteristic of all walks of life. This was documented in more than 500 writings on the "Jewish Question" between 1870 and 1890 (Preisendörfer 2023, 344).

The very term "*Antisemitismus*" (anti-semitism) is a neologism that appeared for the first time in Germany during the last three decades of the nineteenth century (Rürup 1987, 120). When looking at the book of Hedwig Dohm, the intersectional character of this system of multiple discriminations in the nineteenth century was already clear to her. She ended her book with the question as to what unites black people, Jews, women, and the Hindu Sudra cast, concluding: "They all are suppressed people" (Dohm 1876, 124). Evidently, Dohm anticipated the association of women's discrimination with that of Jews and people of color in a racist epistemology long before Simone de Beauvoir made this case in her *The Second Sex* (Rich 2007, 13). The German example is good evidence in support of the thesis that colonialism was a much more complex system of othering than the simplistic framing of East against West. To a certain extent, the colonized and large parts of Germany's population were knitted together in various orders of suppression.

Conclusions: Eurocentrism and Imperialism

In *Orientalism*, Said described the European colonial mindset as a cultural phenomenon that justified imperial power politics. He did so based on a very selective textual basis well suited to supporting his polemic thesis of the complicity between orientalist scholarship and colonialism. While Said delivered an analysis of the colonial consensus in Europe, he fell short of proving his complicity thesis regarding orientalist scholarship. As John Hobson rightly argued, Said completely fused Eurocentrism with imperialist attitudes (Hobson 2012). However, as the example of the German Social Democrats show, Eurocentrism was easily compatible with an anti-imperialist stance. This critique played a central role in the controversy about his book in which Said was also accused of being utterly selective in his use of sources. Indeed, he did not consult texts by the most relevant European orientalists of the late nineteenth century. Did these scholars really all share a prejudicial view on the East? In what respect did racism permeate their work? What were their connections to imperial politics? Is there any justification for the denial of the academic validity of so-called Western scholarship on Islam? Neither Said nor his postcolonial successors have addressed these questions adequately.

Once put into the world, Said's thesis achieved a hegemonic status in several disciplines of the humanities and the social sciences. *Orientalism* became an authoritative text in its own right. It is the purpose of this book to challenge the hegemony of the Saidian narrative with a complementary counternarrative. In doing so, I put my focus on reconstruction rather than deconstruction. Instead of critically engaging with the assumptions of postcolonial knowledge on Islamic studies, I intend to analyze and reconstruct the emergence of this discipline in the context of nineteenth-century colonialism. Historically, it is a truism that the rise of Islamic studies took place in the period of high imperialism. But what then is meant by the claim that orientalist scholarship was an inherent part of the imperialist tradition? Does this mere historical correlation support Said's thesis?

The following chapters try to give an answer to these questions by addressing essential gaps of *Orientalism*. I will closely examine the life and work of a group of scholars who were crucial in the foundation of modern academic knowledge on Islam. They were all deeply influenced by the scholarly methods of their time, philology, and historical criticism. Protestant revisionist biblical studies impacted strongly on their work.[20] Even more important, they were personally torn between the logics of modern scientific thought and revealed religious knowledge. This group of scholars represents broader national contexts than the Anglo-French-American experience on which Said's thesis completely relied. In fact, orientalist studies were part and parcel of the development of the modern system of science characterized by an intense dialogue of scholars from across Europe (Rabault-Feuerhahn and Trautmann-Waller 2008, 6). Therefore, my study also includes Dutch, German, and Hungarian orientalists and, even more important, it looks in a broader perspective at the role that German scholarship played in the making of Islamic studies. It was German scholars who came to dominate the field in the nineteenth century. Consequently, this book will do what Said promised but never delivered: for the formation of Islamic studies, it is an inquiry into the life and work of authoritative scholars, their canonical texts, and doxological ideas, as well as the organizational features and power structures under which they produced modern knowledge on Islam (Said 1978, 22) The analysis of this complex entanglement of individual biographies with various social processes, however, needs a clear analytical frame of reference. In the next chapter, I briefly sketch out this theoretical framework on which my empirical analysis builds.

Notes

1 In her discussion of "marginality," Spivak refers to the embrace of the term "Third World" to "give a proper name to a generalized margin" (1997, 199).

2 Whether my contribution will be taken up in this debate or not is not in my hands. I deliver it as a complimentary scholarly argument.

3 Postcolonialism as a movement comprises much more than an academic field. It is a set of perspectives with political origins in "Third-Worldism" and manifestations in scholarship, political advocacy, and intellectual movements in the name of the "subaltern" (see Young 2003). In this book, however, I only regard it from the scholarly perspective as an academic discipline.

4 Said certainly knew her work and he briefly met Simone de Beauvoir in Paris. There, he attended a "seminar on peace in the Middle East" at the apartment of Michel Foucault (Said 2000).

5 Farris argues that Said was very much aware of Max Weber's work. However, I do have my doubts about the extent to which this awareness went beyond the ordinary textbook knowledge of the German sociologist prevalent in US academia at that time. In *Orientalism*, he mentions Weber only once, when referring to the usage of "types" by European sociologists and expressing his assumption that Weber considerably influenced the field of the study of Islam (Said 1978, 259). These were assumptions he took from secondary literature, as his endnotes show.

6 I discuss the postcolonial critique of Max Weber's work in more detail in chapter three of this book.

7 For similar arguments regarding this question about academic validity, see also Sivan 1985, 144; Halliday 1993, 159.

8 This homogenizing tendency applies equally to the conceptual dichotomy between the global North and the global South that replaced the hierarchical differentiation between first, second, and third worlds. The binary code between North and South has itself a very old symbolic legacy. According to these historically inherited connotations, the North is the carrier of quite ambivalent sets of values. While the North represents a place of blessing, prosperity, and wealth, it is the seat of evil and the residence of dangerous demons at the same time (see Henningsen 2021, 58). It seems that these symbolic representations often resonate in the contemporary application of the dichotomy between the global North and the global South.

9 Here Said confused purpose with effect. There is no doubt that orientalist scholarship—like scholarship in general—has been used, and normally very selectively, in the justification of political agendas.

10 His information about them apparently comes from a book chapter by Fück (1962) and from Waardenburg's *L'Islam dans le miroir de l'Occident* (1962). The chapter by Fück is an abridged English version of Fück's German book *Die arabischen Studien in Europa* (Fück 1955); see Said 1978, 367, fn. 4–7.

11 A brief overview of the factually shifting European understandings of Islam is provided by Maxime Rodinson's *Europe and the Mystique of Islam* (1988). R. W.

Southern's book *Western Views of Islam in the Middle Ages* is still a valid critique of Said's continuity thesis *avant la lettre* (1962). A classic on the history of imaging Islam through Christian eyes is Norman Daniel's *Islam and the West* (1960).

12 I discussed all these points in more detail in Jung 2011.

13 On the occasion of the 150th anniversary of the University of Göttingen in 1887, Albrecht Ritschl, an eminent Protestant theologian and then pro-rector of the university, expressed this anti-Catholic attitude from a conservative position. Ritschl refuted the Vatican's argument that liberal and social-democratic ideologies resulted from the Reformation by tracing them back to "Catholic internationalism" (Smend 1988, 77). We will come back to Ritschl as a theologian in chapters four and five of this book.

14 Anti-clerical and anti-Catholic positions, however, were also expressed by positive imaginations of Islam. One example is given by the leader of the German Socialist Party, August Bebel (1840–1913). His interest in and positive attitude toward Islam was due to his dislike of the Christian Churches in Germany and czarist Russia (Scheffler 1997).

15 In 1977, Edward Said became an independent member of the Palestinian National Council, the Palestine Liberation Organization's (PLO) parliament in exile, which rejected the Camp David Accords between Israel and Egypt. Said was later also a critic of the Oslo peace process which led to the Oslo Accords between the PLO and Israel in 1993 (Said 2000; Mortimer 2004). Consequently, *Orientalism* is a document of Said's own "critical consciousness," a concept he put at the center of his *The World, the Text and the Critic* (1983, 24). In order to contextualize the deeply personal character of *Orientalism*, compare it also with his memoires (Said 1999).

16 Too often, however, only if they speak the voice of the colonizers. Said's omission of works in Arabic found its continuation in postcolonial studies. Postcolonial literatures have mostly been written in the languages of the colonizers. The discourse on postcoloniality is basically a discourse in English and French. Literary cultural production in Arabic, for instance, has rarely been taken into account (Hassan 2002, 45), as if postcolonial studies and Arabic literary studies did not have much to offer to each other (Hassan 2002, 59; see also Jung and Zemmin 2024).

17 It is necessary to note that at the beginning of his chancellorship, Bismarck did not wholeheartedly embrace territorial policies of colonial expansion. It was only due to internal pressures caused by economic turbulences and challenges to his authoritarian rule, as well as the failure of his foreign policy strategy vis-à-vis Great Britain after the election of Prime minister William Gladstone in 1880, that the German chancellor changed his policies of free-trade expansion to direct colonial rule in the 1880s (Hawes 2017, 128–129; Wehler 1970b).

18 The problem here is not that Zimmerman finds this colonial mindset in Weber's work, but that he claims that it "fundamentally" shaped his scientific work (Zimmerman 2006, 53). This is precisely the reductionist and anachronistic approach of postcolonial theorizing by which the normative position governs analytical insight. I return to this argument in chapter three of the book. On the positive side, Zimmerman is one of those scholars with a postcolonial approach

who clearly addresses German racism against Poles, to which particularly Weber's early writings and lectures give some testimony. See also Boatcă (2016).

19 Hedwig Dohm came from a family that had turned away from Judaism and was the grandmother of Katia Mann, the wife of the German author Thomas Mann (Lahme 2025, 233).

20 As Suzanne Marchand argued, the cultural profile of German orientalism is hardly understandable without taking into consideration the influence of "Higher Criticism" and "liberal forms of Protestantism" (Marchand 2009, 76).

2 Modernity, Religion, and Science: Social Boundary Demarcations and Oriental Studies in Nineteenth-Century Germany

"Different modernities [...] have the promise of emancipation and liberation for all cultures and societies." This seems to be a core assertion of postcolonial scholarship (Mannathukkaren 2015, 299). While *Orientalism* itself is not famous for its conceptual clarity—modernity as a concept does not even appear in its index—this theoretical shortsightedness has changed in postcolonial studies. Postcolonial critique has always been a critique of modernity, or better of "Western modernity" as most of its representatives would put it. But what is modernity more concretely? And what does the attribute "Western" add to it? Here postcolonial writings often remain nebulous, as if these two terms were self-evident. In the beginning, this lack of conceptual precision was perhaps due to the dominance of the humanities in postcolonial theory (Bhambra 2023, vii). Postcolonial critique made a comparatively late and still rather marginal inroad into the mainstream of social theory and sociology.[1] Modernity is a central category in sociology, and postcolonial theorists have accused it and its derivates—modern, modernist, and modernization—of being Eurocentric in nature.

In this chapter, I present my own conceptual stance on modernity. My approach is informed by some essential questions that postcolonial critique has raised concerning the validity of modernity as a core concept in social theory. I suggest addressing these questions using a theoretical combination of Niklas Luhmann's Modern Systems Theory (MST) and theories of social emergence. This combination of theories serves me to define modernity in the singular. As already indicated in the preface to this book, Shmuel N. Eisenstadt's theory of multiple modernities is useful to account for the observation that there are historically different realizations of modernity. The crux of the matter in all this is that modernity simultaneously constitutes an analytical, a historical, and a normative concept. In contradistinction to Gurminder Bhambra, however, I think it is possible to distinguish between these three applications of the concept of modernity (Bhambra 2023, xxx). In the following section I therefore present a distinct analytical theory of modernity. Moreover, I still claim that there is a certain "universal" applicability of this theoretical framework, that is to say, I assign it a global social relevance.

After these theoretical elaborations, I move on to two other essential concepts in sociology which are closely connected with modernity. Both are of central importance in my book: religion and science. These two concepts are highly contested too, in particular that of religion. I define them in accordance with Luhmann's theory as subsystems of modern society. The rise of Islamic studies as a modern academic discipline coincides with the eventual separation of these two social spheres toward the end of the nineteenth century. Therefore, it is more than necessary to include some theoretical reflections on religion and science in the context of a more general theory of modernity. In the final section of this chapter, then, I empirically illustrate my theoretical discussion. I once again will draw from the historical experiences of Germany. This historical excursion describes the rise of oriental and Islamic studies in the context of the making of the modern university in Germany. On both institutional and individual levels, German universities became the core institutions in shaping modern Islamic studies as an academic discipline. Young scholars from Europe and beyond met at German universities, and these became sites of intersection for the various methodological discourses of the emerging humanities and social sciences. These discourses largely contributed to defining the contours of the new discipline of Islamic studies in crucial ways.

Modernity, Modernization, and Multiple Modernities: Conceptual Considerations

In *Rethinking Modernity*, Gurminder Bhramba strongly criticized the conceptual categories of mainstream sociology. In her opinion, these categories depend upon a particular understanding of history that elides colonialism (Bhambra 2023, 179). Sociology has propagated a narrative according to which modernity had its spatial and temporal beginnings in endogenous processes in Europe from where it spread around the globe. Moreover, this Eurocentric modernization theory draws a direct line from a traditional past to a modern future, reflecting the dichotomy between tradition and modernity, a distinction that Bhambra considers as essential in classical sociology (2023, 60).

Like many postcolonial theorists, the judgment of Gurminder Bhambra is apparently predicated on the classical modernization theories that were prevalent in the social sciences from the late 1950s to the 1970s. Under the impact of behavioral sociology and the structural functionalism of Talcott Parsons (1902–1979), these theories assert that the same form of linear social development would be the future of all societies (Robertson 1992, 11). The key conceptual dichotomy in these theories was the juxtaposition of tradition and modernity. This dichotomy was to measure a gradual transformation from religiously organized communities with predetermined identities toward participatory societies with autonomous subjects in which religious norms lose their dominant role in shaping social order (Knöbl 2007, 23–28). Consequently, classical modernization theories predicted a kind of zero-sum game between religion and modernity. The proponents of these theories constructed modernization and secularization as synonymous and universal social processes. In their imagination of modern society, the apparent blueprint was the historical development of the United States (Knöbl 2014, 88).

Presenting this "monochromatic and a-cultural" theory as the dominant concept of modernity in contemporary sociology, however, is an anachronism (Mannathukkaren 2015, 322). In taking this almost outdated theory of modernity as her major point of sociological reference—even in the second edition of her book (2023)—Bhambra's treatment of the sociology of modernity is symptomatic for the mainstream theoretical perspective in postcolonial studies. What postcolonial scholarship still considers to be the hegemonic idea of modernity in "Western" social theory meanwhile only finds a relatively peripheral place in the field. This marginalization of classical modernization theories is basically due to two theoretical developments.

On the one hand, the cultural turn in the social sciences and humanities has clearly reached discussions about modernity in social theory. Instead of a specific arrangement of social institutions, modernity is often thematized as a particular culture of representation. Modern culture is defined as the ambivalent experience of a constantly changing world in daily life (Jervis 2004, 5). Central to this discussion is the understanding of modernity as characterized by social contingency (Wagner 2001). In modern culture, nothing is impossible and ultimately nothing is necessary (Luhmann 1992, 96). Modern society generates a surplus of possibilities and therewith choices (Holzer 2011, 154). Due to this pervasive experience of social contingency, the modern subject feels homeless in the present and haunted by the past (Collins and Jervis 2008, 2). According to Zygmunt Baumann, the certainties of classical modernization theories have been replaced by a kind of liquid modernity in which the feeling of uncertainty has become endemic (Baumann 2007).

On the other hand, the sociological debate about the rise of "post-secular society" decouples secularization from modernization (Barbieri 2015, 43). Consequently, in many works of contemporary sociology, modern orders are no longer seen as necessarily secular in nature. Key in this strand of literature is the theory of multiple modernities as developed by the Israeli sociologist Shmuel N. Eisenstadt (1923–2010). Eisenstadt claimed that a "cultural program of modernity" had spread from Europe around the world, but without leading to a linear convergence of historical societies. Quite the opposite. The reception of this program of modernity in different "civilizational complexes" resulted in a diversity of modern projects. These historical modern projects reflect culturally path-dependent realizations of modernity. Inspired by Karl Jaspers' philosophical speculation in *Vom Ursprung und Ziel der Geschichte* (*The Origin and Goal of History*) (Jaspers 1949), Eisenstadt defined these civilizational complexes as the cultures of the "Axial Age" (Buddhism, Hellenism, Hinduism, Judaism, Confucianism) and their latecomers: Christianity and Islam. For Eisenstadt, it was religious traditions in particular that shaped the diversity of modernity. He thus broke radically with the dichotomy between tradition and modernity that was fundamental in classical modernization theory. The theory of multiple modernities brought religious traditions back in as a potential force in shaping modern projects (Eisenstadt 2000a, 2000b, 2001).[2]

These two theoretical alterations break with three fundamental assumptions of classical modernization theories. First, they refute the idea of modernization as a linear history of social progress toward one institutional model. Second, this theoretical development has disentangled secularization and modernization as related but not synonymous historical processes. Finally, modernization is no longer perceived as a process of the convergence of societies leading to cultural homogenization (Knöbel 2007, 59). When it comes to Eisenstadt's theory of multiple modernities, however, his approach remains Eurocentric in the sense that Eisenstadt maintains the European origin of his so-called cultural program of modernity in both time and space. Moreover, I agree with Gurminder Bhambra that he largely "sidesteps the issue of global interconnections" (Bhambra 2011, 655). As Peter Wagner stressed,

Eisenstadt deals with "civilizational complexes" in terms of coherent and bounded "cultural containers" (Wagner 2008, 12). While classical modernization theories expected the development of cultural homogeneity across civilizations, Eisenstadt's theory tends to build on the idea of cultural homogeneity within them. Both sets of social theory do not articulate the existence of historical entanglements in the rise of modernity. Furthermore, it often remains very vague about what modernity represents in the singular, that is to say, in terms of a generic concept. Theories of multiple and alternative modernities share this conceptual weakness. Yet how can we observe the historical diversity of modernity without, at least implicitly, assuming a form of unity? What is the shared conceptual point of reference of this plurality of modernities? In the rest of this section, I answer this question by drawing from Niklas Luhmann's MST combined with a few thoughts I take from theories of social emergence.

The voluminous work of Niklas Luhmann provides a rich collection of theoretical building blocks with the help of which we can address postcolonial critique against the sociology of modernity. Though deeply rooted in the European sociological tradition, MST offers a non-Eurocentric reading of this tradition. Luhmann's macro-sociological theory is not informed "by the notion of European uniqueness and superiority" (Alatas 2002, 761). In his theoretical edifice, modernity is the non-intended outcome of sociocultural evolution. Modernization emerges not as the project of European Enlightenment, but as an increase in social complexity through an evolutionary change in divergent forms of differentiation. Luhmann identifies four major forms of differentiation: *segmentation*, *stratification*, *center-periphery relations*, and *functional differentiation*. Segmentation is often associated with the highly contested concept of "tribes," but can also refer to the international system, which is internally characterized by so-called like units, that is to say, by territorially demarcated nation states. The term stratification applies to premodern societies, in the historical setting of Europe differentiated into aristocratic, ecclesiastical, and ordinary strata of people. Center–periphery relations reflect in particular the power structure of the colonial system. Finally, modern society Luhmann defined as the relative dominance of functional differentiation among these four major forms of differentiation, yet without merely replacing the other ones, as the previous example of the international system shows. In an evolutionary process, function systems develop by separating themselves from their environment through the construction of communicative boundaries. They maintain these boundaries based on specific codes of operation. The economic system, for example, operates with the binary code of possessing/not possessing and to pay/not to pay, while the specific communication of the legal system is based on the code legal/illegal (Luhmann 1986).

Luhmann's concept of modern society does not require the conventional and deeply entrenched juxtaposition of tradition and modernity, which as we have seen is one of the main targets of critique by postcolonial scholars. In defining modernity as the social dominance of functional differentiation, Luhmann does not understand functions as the result of the decomposition of a social whole. While the sociological tradition from Émile Durkheim to Talcott Parsons understood differentiation with reference to the assumed functional needs of a social whole (Mahner and Bunge 2001, 89), Luhmann considered functions as the "constructions of an observer." Posing the question of function offers observers a possibility of dealing with social contingency (Luhmann 2002, 118). Knowledge of social reality is a form of "self-production" (Rash 2012, 86). In Luhmann's theory, function systems emerge as self-producing social systems by means of communication. From this sociological perspective, the concept of functional differentiation is therefore first and foremost of heuristic value (Luhmann 1986, 11).

In MST, modern society represents an all-encompassing global system of communication, subdivided by self-referential function systems such as arts, economics, education, law, politics, religion, and science. Society, therefore, does not have any purpose or moral quality but arises through the emergent fusion of information, communication, and understanding as a global unity (Luhmann 2017, 250). Functional differentiation as a form of social structure "is planetary and no longer associated with regional differences" (Rash 2012, 85). Modern society is thus world society (Luhmann 1990, 178).

Modern function systems serve at the level of collective and individual action as an abstract horizon of meaning. Social actors recognize the specific communicational codes of the functional subsystems of modern society as situation-defined fictions in their everyday lives (Schimank 2005, 48). They identify specifically economic, legal, political, religious, or scientific discourses. This is where modernity as a generic concept and multiple modernities as its historical realizations meet. The conceptualization of modernity as world society offers a theoretical means for observing global entanglements in the demarcation of boundaries among various social subsystems. In contemporary projects of Islamic modernities, for instance, the communicative codes of modern economic and legal systems are clearly visible. They provide a frame of reference for the reinterpretation of Islamic traditions in current debates about Islamic economics or shariʿa-compliant legal systems.[3]

Combining MST with theories of social emergence contributes further to liberating social theory from some of its Eurocentric assumptions. When defining modernization in terms of social emergence, modernity has no origin in time and space. The concept of emergence relates to the formation of complex and adaptive systems such as ant colonies, global financial markets, the immune system, or neural networks (Holland 1998, 2). It describes different levels of reality with different properties that cannot be reduced to one another (El-Hani and Philström 2002, 5). In modern society, we can roughly differentiate between the macro, meso, and micro levels of social reality. Function systems represent the macro, whereas institutions, organizations, and social movements represent the meso level of society. Finally, there are interaction systems, which are at the micro level of society. Understanding modernization in the meta-theoretical context of social emergence, therefore, liberates differentiation theory from its Eurocentric claim that modernity is a specifically European project. Through the lenses of MST, we can observe emerging forms of functional communication in both premodern and non-European settings. This is precisely the approach I took in an article on social boundary negotiations in the Abbasid Empire. Taking Abu Hamid al-Ghazali's (1058–1111) book *Deliverance from Error* as an example, the article discerns in the philosophical discussion of this Islamic thinker premodern boundary negotiations between emerging realms of religious and scientific communication. These boundary negotiations took place—and that is decisive—in times when the impact of Europe on Muslim regions did not yet play a role (Jung 2024). In his prioritization of religion over science, al-Ghazali was not very different to those European philosophers of the "scientific revolution" (1500–1800) who were devout believers but recognized God as the first cause (Henry 2010, 41–42).

Postcolonial scholars still direct their normatively underpinned critique of so-called Western concepts of modernity against core features of classical modernization theories. There is no doubt about the Eurocentric character of these theories in conceptualizing modernity according to a unique model of social norms and institutions of European (or better North American) origin that ostensibly offers the blueprint for the development of human societies as such. Moreover, classical modernization theories raised the expectation of cultural convergence to the role of a homogenous culture of modernity. A host of historical developments turned these expectations into palpable lies. Consequently, the cultural turn in the social sciences and humanities has also arrived in the sociology of modernity, and modern culture is meanwhile discussed under key terms such as hybridity or diversity. Postcolonial critique, therefore, is directed toward a conceptual ghost of the past. Yet the question remains whether there is still something we should consider to be genuinely modern. What is the conceptual reference point for this multiplicity of modern cultures?

My suggestion in this section was to answer these questions using a combination of conceptual elements from MST with meta-theoretical assumptions from theories of social emergence. Still rooted in the sociological tradition of differentiation theories, the above-described concept of modernity offers a social macrostructure which, as a language of observation, is able to accommodate both global interconnectedness and cultural diversity in the framework of a nonnormative concept of modern world society. From this perspective, modernity is not the property of Europe but of humankind as such. To be sure, this theoretical perspective does not deny the role of colonial power relations in shaping the historical expressions in which concrete realizations of modernity have appeared. The entangled formation of multiple modernities has been dominated by European models over some centuries. However, the historical outcome of this domination should not be confused with modernity as such. As the brief example of al-Ghazali shows, functionally differentiated forms of communication were not alien to non-European cultural settings. Modern boundary negotiations are observable in various cultures, and as the following chapters show, drawing the boundary between religion and science has been a crucial social process in the modernizing world in general. The next section, therefore, will present further clarifications regarding my concepts of religion and science.

Religion and Science as Social Systems

Parallel with the decline of classical secularization theories, religion also increasingly became a highly contested concept. This applies not least to the very discipline of the study of religion itself. This discipline is far from reaching a consensus on the concept of religion itself. Leading figures in the field even refuse outright to define an object of religion. Russell McCutcheon, for instance, denies the research subject of religion any ontological quality (McCutcheon 1997). Timothy Fitzgerald does not assign any conceptual value to religion. For him, religion as a distinct domain of human action is nothing more than a myth (Fitzgerald 2007, 9). The critique formulated by anthropologist Talal Asad consequently has a more visible postcolonial touch. Due to the historical origin of the term "religion" in Christian thought, Asad rejects any claim of it being universally applicable. In his scholarly engagement with questions about Islam and secularism, Asad strongly expresses his dissatisfaction with this universal category of religion. For him the clear-cut distinction between religion and the secular was a Western invention (Asad 1993; Scott 2006, 284). Asad's position clearly resonates further in postcolonial argumentations such as those articulated by Dipesh Chakrabarty and Seyd Farid Alatas. Chakrabarty considered the separation of religion and politics in non-Western contexts to be unsustainable (Mannathukkaren 2015, 304), whereas for Alatas, the use of the concept of religion in non-Christian contexts leads to an "elision of reality" (Alatas 2002, 763). Generally speaking, these critics of the concept of religion share the normative concern regarding the colonial legacy that has shaped both anthropology and religious studies.

I agree with this criticism insofar as I also consider religion to be a modern conceptual construction. Religion is not a transhistorical anthropological constant but has a historically specific and constructed nature. Consequently, the very meaning of religion varies across time and place (Beckford 2003, 7). As a scholarly concept, religion is fundamentally open to interpretation and therefore heavily contested in its meaning. In social practices, however, it is difficult to avoid defining religion. This becomes apparent in the juridical field. In court decisions about the wearing of the Muslim headscarf or the form of religious teachings in public schools, for example, the legal system cannot circumvent defining religion. Lawyers must implement rules according to which claims for religious recognition can be made and possibly enforced. Legal decision-making provides ample evidence for the constant societal struggle over the symbolic, social, and legal boundaries through which religion is demarcated in social practice (Reuter 2014). Legal institutions are among the social sites where boundary negotiations between function systems take place. They provide cases for the observation of the ways in which social actors translate the abstract discourses of social systems into the meaningful semantics of everyday life. In contrast to the above scholarly debate, in everyday life, social actors seemingly find common reference points that help them define religion as a field of social action.

In my own theoretical framework, religion is a specifically modern concept linked to the larger process of functional differentiation. As a generic concept, religion is an innovation of the nineteenth century. Peter Beyer has shown the ways in which intellectuals in China, Europe, India, and in Muslim regions of the world reconstructed their own traditions with reference to this generic concept of religion (Beyer 2006). In the second part of this book, I discuss the ways in which Julius Wellhausen, William Robertson Smith, and Ernest Renan participated in this historical process. This reconstruction of cultural traditions was part of what was called "the invention of world religions," the conventional ordering of some ten corpuses of traditions as mutually acknowledged religions that appeared at the turn of the twentieth century (Masuzawa 2005). This invention of world religions represents a process of colonial entanglements among intellectuals of different cultural backgrounds, shaping the internal differentiation of modern religious system into various "religious programs" such as Buddhism, Christianity, Hinduism, Islam, and Judaism (Beyer 2006). In Luhmann's terminology, this constitutes the segmentation of the global system of religion into different religions. While the global system of religion is the result of the operational closure of a modern function system, the internal differentiation of this system took place in the reorganization of cultural traditions as segmented religious programs. That the discursive reconstruction of Christian traditions by Protestant theologians played a significant role in this construction of the modern concept of religion is without doubt. However, it is the contemporary global recognition of this concept rather than its historically specific origin that counts (Bergunder 2020, 61–67).

In MST, religion represents one specific subsystem of modern society that has gained its relative autonomy through a specific communicative code. Luhmann therefore rejects functionalist claims, for instance that religion is a provider of moral integration (Durkheim 1995) or a mechanism of conflict regulation (Girard 1972). According to Luhmann, religious communication follows a code of immanence versus transcendence, whereby religious observers consider the immanent world from the position of transcendence (Luhmann 2002, 77). Taking his inspiration from Luhmann's approach, Peter Beyer defines religious communication in terms of three binary codes—transcendent/immanent, sacred/profane, and blessed/cursed—that ensure the operational closure of religion as a social system (Beyer 2006, 85). This self-referential operation of the religious system, however, does not lead to the disappearance of religion in modernity. On the contrary. Through this communicative limitation, religion achieves its own specific operational identity within an increasingly differentiating social environment. Luhmann thus opposes the assumption of classical secularization theories that modernization is accompanied by a loss of the functional relevance of religion in modern society. The term "secularization," in his theory, describes a complex process of social boundary negotiations from the point of religion as an observer (Luhmann 2002, 282). From the perspective of the religious system, the world becomes secularized (2002, 289). Secularization, therefore, does not cause the decline of religion but turns it into a clearly identifiable and circumscribed communicative sector of modern society. In this process of social differentiation, boundary negotiations between religion and science have been of crucial relevance.

In Luhmann's theoretical design, the major catalyst in the emergence of the scientific system was the binary code between true and untrue (Luhmann 1992, 273). Pure knowledge as science is thus the evolutionary result of a differentiation between true and untrue knowledge (Luhmann 1992, 170). The operational closure of the social subsystem of science appears in a continuing communication about truth and untruth (Luhmann 1992, 285). In this process, the code of science becomes applicable to all possible observations. Even more important, this code does not imply any selection in a normative sense. Instead, scientific processes are characterized by the dissolution and recombination of experiences by means of analysis and synthesis (Luhmann 1992, 170). This permanent de- and reconstruction of knowledge generates a never-ending state of uncertainty, a form of the contingency of truth that in scientific knowledge production is tackled with the help of varying and changing theories and methods. Scientific approaches aim at reducing complexity and producing meaning. The results of this modern scientific knowledge production are typically communicated in academic publications (Luhmann 1992, 428). As a means of specialized communication, academic journals are crucial in the constitution of scientific disciplines which differentiate the system of science in a horizontal way (Luhmann 1992, 451; Stichweh 1984, 421). In 1912, for instance, the German orientalist Carl Heinrich Becker mentioned the publication of five new journals on Islam as a proof for the firm establishment of the new discipline of Islamic studies (Becker 1912c, 531).

Internal differentiation into disciplines is the mechanism of the systemic self-organization of science, historically taking place in the course of the nineteenth century (Stichweh 1984, 13). Thomas Kuhn once defined the formation of a discipline as the emergence of a scientific community (Kuhn 1970). In an academic discipline, a group of scholars deals with a scientific specialty. They pursue similar educational paths and share a body of literature that represents the discursive context for their research. An academic discipline builds on a common research tradition with its specific conceptual tools, heuristic frameworks, scientific methods, and particular research questions. A scientific community is organized around a common problem. The German orientalist Carl Heinrich Becker expressed this logic of a disciplinary scientific community in an exemplary way in his pilot article "Der Islam als Problem" (Islam as a Problem) (Becker 1910a). This article defining the core questions and methods of the new discipline of Islamic studies opened the first issue of the journal *Der Islam*, which is still published to this day. Becker's "Der Islam als Problem," therefore, should be read as a manifestation of this construction of a scientific community for the study of Islam.

In addition to academic journals, scientific communities discuss their studies at international congresses. In 1873, the First International Congress of Orientalists marked the beginning of a series of academic gatherings predominantly held in Europe. From 1873 to 1976, 29 International Congresses of Orientalists took place, of which three were organized outside "the West" in Algiers (1905), Istanbul (1952), and New Delhi (1964). Yet already at the first congresses in Paris and London (1874), some individual participants and institutional delegations came from non-European countries such as Algeria, Burma, Ceylon, China, Egypt, India, Japan, and Turkey (Jung 2011, 86–87). In his diary, Ignaz Goldziher tells us about his engagement with Muslim participants—jurists, scholars, and sheiks from Algeria, Egypt, and Turkey—at the congress in Stockholm in 1889 (Goldziher 1978, 118). The Ottoman intellectual Ahmed Mithat Efendi (1844–1912), for instance, represented the Ottoman Empire in Stockholm as an official delegate of Sultan Abdülhamid II (1876–1909) (Findley 1998, 27). In his book *Avrupa'da Bir Cevelan* (a round trip in Europe) Ahmet Mithat described his journey to Stockholm and the World Exhibition in Paris. The book can be read as the defense of an Ottoman intellectual against "orientalist" representations of his own culture, while considering Paris as the center of social progress at the same time (Findley 1998). According to Mithat's account, the congress in Stockholm was both an academic gathering and a public event.[4] It was also at these international congresses that specific topics of Islamic studies increasingly marked the evolution of the new discipline.

Historically, Luhmann traces the emergence of the modern system of science back to its separation from religious and moral forms of communication (Luhmann 1986, 153–158). We can observe the differentiation between religious and scientific communication in intense boundary negotiations between faith and truth, between revealed knowledge and scientific knowledge. Historically, the "scientification of religion" was an inherent part of this process. The nineteenth century saw an academic professionalization and with it a major transformation in knowledge about religion. The interpretation of religious texts became subject to the new methods of philology and historical criticism (von Stuckrad 2014). As we will see in the second part of this book, the understanding of religion was embedded in the then-prevalent theories of historicism and evolutionism. We must understand both the construction of the modern concept of religion and the formation of the discipline of Islamic studies as integral parts of these boundary negotiations between religion and science in the nineteenth century. The biographies of all my historical interlocutors in this book show the impact of these boundary negotiations at the micro level. It is one of the core arguments of my own narrative that it was not the colonial context but rather the emergence of the modern systems of science and religion that conditioned the construction of modern knowledge on Islam.

In the late nineteenth century, modern science developed parallel to the self-referential modern system of religion. Science became a "generalized cognitive model" based on globally acknowledged ways of communication with their concomitant forms of scientific categories, institutional models, and academic standards (Drori et al. 2003, 6). Organized in faculties and departments with their specific research areas and educational paths, these academic disciplines constitute the institutionalized content of the modern university. Today a global model, the blueprint for the modern university first emerged in nineteenth-century Germany. This was the century of the undisputed global recognition of German-speaking science (Schnädelbach 1984, 21; Thadden 1988, 46). The role model for the modern university was Friedrich-Wilhelm University in Berlin, founded in 1809 and opened in 1810.[5] In the course of Prussia's educational reforms, the German diplomat and philologist Wilhelm von Humboldt (1767–1835) designed this new form of modern university. In his reform efforts, Humboldt was following his ideal of a close combination of education and research. "The fundamental principles of the Humboldt-University were academic freedom and the unity of research and teaching" (Schnädelbach 1984, 22). Humboldt established this modern form of university against both the traditional university, characterized by its scholasticism, and the Napoleonian model of schools of applied studies, which were directly in the service of the state (Nipperdey 1990, 174). In this way, Wilhelm von Humboldt created an institutional blueprint for the core institution of the rising scientific system that was spreading gradually over the entire globe (Osterhammel 2011, 1133–1135). It was within the confines of this modern university that orientalist studies took place. Again, the German historical experience is crucial for the understanding of orientalist teaching and research as a part of the institutionalization of modern science. The path from Christian theology via orientalism to Islamic studies can be traced along the lines of the development of the modern systems of science.

Orientalism and Islamic Studies at German Universities in the Nineteenth Century

At the beginning of the nineteenth century, the still politically fragmented Germany already hosted about 50 universities whose institutional structures came close to universities in the modern sense. In comparison with the United Kingdom, only Oxford and Cambridge could be considered as fully established modern universities. Taking the German states as a whole, Germany was the European center where modern science emerged (Wulf 2022, 33). While Prussia played a pioneering role in the establishment of the modern university, the other German states soon entered into competition with Prussia in science and higher education. Ironically, the modern German university was actually established in a preindustrial setting by state functionaries and scholars, reflecting to a certain extent the socio-economic weaknesses of Germany's bourgeoisie (Nipperdey 1990, 187). In the second part of the nineteenth century, students from North America, Great Britain, France, and Russia traveled to Berlin, Bonn, Leipzig, or Heidelberg in order to see what a research university was like (Kaube 2020, 22). The rise of the modern scientific system with its various disciplines was both a national and a global phenomenon. German orientalists thus represented a national scientific community and a transnationally connected disciplinary group of scholars at the same time.

The foundation of the *Deutsche Morgenländische Gesellschaft* (DMG), with its academic journal *Zeitschrift der Deutschen Morgenländischen Gesellschaft* (ZDMG), is a good example for this connection of national and international scholarship. Founded in October 1845 in Darmstadt, this association of orientalist scholars included members from Germany's various states and universities, while its 22 corresponding members came from different European countries. In professional terms, they were not only orientalists and theologians, but also librarians, teachers, and diplomats (Preissler 1995, 292–293). First published in 1847, the ZDMG combined essays from the very different subdisciplines of orientalist scholarship, and their authors also represented different European nations and linguistic communities (Brockelmann 1922, 12). The same applies to the *Encyclopaedia of Islam* (EI), which later became the prime reference work for Islamic studies. The first entries in the EI were written by scholars of different national backgrounds in the second half of the nineteenth century (Goldziher 1897), and the first edition was published from 1913 to 1938. While the ZDMG marked the emancipation of oriental studies from theology, publishing articles from subdisciplines such as Assyriology, East Asian studies, Indology, Islamic studies, and Semitic languages, the EI represents the establishment of Islamic studies proper. The reference articles in the EI clearly distinguish research on Islam from the broader field of academic orientalism that was visible in the thematically quite diverging essays of the ZDMG.

With the establishment of the DMG as the professional association of German orientalists, oriental studies as an academic discipline made a major step toward its full emancipation from theology. In the first part of the nineteenth century, Semitic philology was an auxiliary means applied in the exegesis of the Old Testament. The profile of an orientalist was that of a theologian who used Hebrew and Arabic to conduct his exegesis of the Old Testament (Mangold 2004, 48). In the second part of the century, then, Semitic philology took over a leading role in the formation of oriental and later Islamic studies as independent academic disciplines. To be sure, in its foundational phase the DMG was still visibly characterized by this close link to Protestant theology. Among its early members, theologically trained Protestant scholars constituted a clear majority. Even more significant, the members of the first board of the DMG were all born and bred Protestants, with no Catholic members. In this sense, the foundation of the organization itself reminds us of the close connection between oriental studies and Protestant theology. In its early days, "Biblical studies had a fairly firm place in oriental studies" (Preissler 1995, 261).

The case studies in this book demonstrate this connection in the individual biographies of scholars moving from theology via philology to Islamic studies. In this historical context, German scholarship and

German universities gradually assumed a leading role. In the second part of the nineteenth century, they became melting pots for international students and scholars, a role previously played by Paris. In March 1795, the French National Assembly established the "École speciale des langues orientales vivantes". The École represented a "secular" academic institution in the spirit of the French Revolution and also served the colonial interests of France. A key figure among the scholars there was Silvestre de Sacy (1758–1838), who held the chair in Arabic. In the first part of the nineteenth century, his work on Arabic grammar and his edition of texts in Arabic constituted the main source for the evolution of Semitic studies in Europe (Fück 1955). With his pure philology, Silvestre de Sacy attracted scholars and students from the whole of Europe, among them at least twenty from Germany (Mangold 2004, 66). This group of Germans in Paris included Heinrich Leberecht Fleischer (1801–1888), who later became the German doyen of Arabic at the University of Leipzig (1835). The young Fleischer began studying Arabic as an autodidact before enrolling in Semitic studies at the University of Leipzig in 1819. In 1824, he went for three years to Paris, where he was among the most famous students of Sacy. Moreover, there he studied Persian, Turkish, and colloquial Arabic (Stefani 2021, 20). With his intrinsic interest in Arabic, Fleischer fully identified with Sacy's teachings of pure philology.[6]

In a collection of letters that Fleischer wrote to his father and friends, we have a valuable source about the character of oriental studies and French–German scholarly relationships of his time (Preißler 2008). Taking up his chair in Leipzig, Fleischer continued Sacy's approach and became a key figure in the philological education of many important scholars in oriental and Islamic studies (Paret 1968). At Leipzig University, Fleischer introduced disciplinary questions and methods clearly distinct from theology and classical philology. Moreover, he was the driving force behind the establishment of both the DMG and the ZDMG. In this way, he strongly contributed to the construction of oriental studies and its scientific infrastructure as an independent academic discipline. The new generation of orientalist philologists adopted a number of major attributes from classical philology. The new discipline was characterized by a romanticist nostalgia for ancient cultures, deeming them more important than their contemporary expressions. Consequently, the identification and restoration of the texts from a cultural past moved to the center of orientalist scholarship. As in classical philology, "identifying fragments, editing texts, and writing historical commentary" became the core practices in oriental studies (Gumbrecht 2003, 3). In particular scholars like Nöldeke, Wellhausen, and Goldziher dedicated themselves to the task of reconstructing the culture of a remote past, in their case the culture of early Islam.

Sacy is one of the few orientalists with whom Edward Said engaged more deeply in *Orientalism*. He rightly mentioned the key role that Sacy played in the education of European orientalists in the first part of the nineteenth century (Said 1978, 83, 129). Heinrich Leberecht Fleischer, who took over this role from Sacy, however, does not appear in Said's book. It was Fleischer and not Renan, as Said suggested, who systematized Semitic studies and elevated Sacy's formal philology to the scientific standard of the nineteenth century. While Fleischer endorsed Sacy's method, Renan rejected it from a positivist angle as non-scientific (Noronha-DiVanna 2010, 69–70). Many European orientalists of the later nineteenth century received their philological education from Fleischer. At the time when Goldziher joined his seminar in Leipzig (1869), Fleischer's group consisted of twelve students who came from six different nations (Fück 1955, 171). Both Sacy and Fleischer represent the classical type of philological armchair orientalists who never traveled in the Middle East. However, Fleischer was very much known for his contact and exchange with Arab intellectuals by mail. While in Paris, Fleischer met with Rifaʿa al-Tahtawi (1801–1873), who at that time was the Imam of an Egyptian delegation sent to Paris by Egypt's de facto ruler Muhammad Ali (1805–1848) in 1826 (Preissler 1995, 250).[7] Goldziher reported in his Oriental Diary about the excellent reputation Fleischer had among Christian-Arab scholars close to Butrus al-Bustani (1819–1883), one of the leading intellectuals in the movement of the Arab cultural renaissance *al-nahda* (Goldziher 1904, 198; Patai 1987, 109).

Heinrich Leberecht Fleischer did not see any clear-cut and fundamental dichotomy between East and West, and he never supported imperialist political agendas. Yet his thought nevertheless contained traces of the colonial mindset of Europe and the romanticist attitudes of nineteenth-century philology. Fleischer too was convinced that Europe spearheaded modern civilization and, consequently, he expressed ideas such as the widespread assumption that Europe's mission was to awaken oriental culture from its fossilized traditional nature (Karachouli 1994, 178 ff.). However, we can also hear different voices among Germany's orientalists. In his speech at the foundational meeting of the DMG, Andreas Schleiermacher (1787–1858), for instance, outlined the purpose of the new academic association. In Schleiermacher's understanding the DMG was an association for the comprehensive exploration of the Orient.

This purpose, according to him, excluded the fields of European politics and those of missionary work. Schleiermacher argued that German orientalists should not look down on the followers of other religions or the adherents of other forms of government. Furthermore, the members of the DMG should not consider their homeland the standard by which to judge all what is foreign" (Preissler 1995, 283). Apparently, the thinking of orientalist scholars was much more diverse than *Orientalism* insinuated.

The DMG, therefore, is a good example for the polymorphous and multivalent character of the Eurocentric discourse that characterized orientalist scholars and thinkers of Western international theory alike. In his study in *The Eurocentric Conception of World Politics*, John Hobson criticized Said for the conflation of both Eurocentrism with scientific racism and orientalism with imperialist politics. Indeed, the discursive complexities of oriental scholarship should not be submerged by Saidian truisms. In Hobson's terms Fleischer and many other orientalists, but not all of them, were "Eurocentric institutionalists." As I will show in the coming chapters in more detail, most of them firmly believed in universal reason as a property of humanity as such, the evolutionary belief "that *all* are capable of progressing from savagery/barbarism into civilization" (Hobson 2012, 5). Concerning the ways in which Europeans should promote this process, however, they differed in many ways. Among orientalists too, there were scholars with imperialist and anti-imperialist views.[8]

In addition, the philological tradition represented by Sacy and Fleischer increasingly found the critique of interpretative philological scholarship. In Fleischer's teaching, oriental studies was still a field of pure non-European philology, comprising a broad variety of cultures, geographies, histories, and languages (Brockelmann 1922, 3). Yet under the impact of Germany's biblical criticism, historicist methods—and therewith interpretative approaches—increasingly made inroads into oriental studies. At the University of Göttingen, for instance, the theologian and orientalist Heinrich Ewald (1803–1875) challenged Fleischer's role. Ewald made Göttingen a center of critical oriental studies where historicist methods replaced Fleischer's focus on grammar and pure linguistics. Against Fleischer, Ewald strongly promoted philological knowledge as a means for the historical interpretation of texts (Mangold 2004, 99). Again, Theodor Nöldeke, a student of Ewald, was a pioneer in the combination of philology with interpretative approaches. While Nöldeke insisted on focusing on the correct handling of primary sources, he encouraged his students to read them with a historically critical mind (Mangold 2004, 90). In this way, Nöldeke made the newly founded *Reichsuniversität* in Strasbourg a third hub of oriental studies in Germany.[9] He played a crucial role in the transformation of pure Semitic philology into an academic means for sound historical interpretation. In this move, Snouck Hurgronje argued, all later orientalists and the founding fathers of Islamic studies became followers of Nöldeke (Hurgronje 1931, 277).[10] Whether they were studying with Nöldeke or not, the early generation of scholars in Islamic studies took from him an interest in studying the driving forces in early Islamic history based on holy texts and the elaboration of Islamic jurisprudence (*fiqh*).

This brief excursion into the history of oriental and Islamic studies shows the usefulness of the conceptual apparatus regarding modernity, religion, and science based on Luhmann's MST. The rise and further diversification of these two academic disciplines are paradigmatic examples for the establishment of functionally separated discourses on religion and science and their institutionalization in modern society. The philological and critical studies of holy scriptures such as the Bible, the Qur'an, and the Talmud followed a kind of positivist rationalism typical for the establishment of the self-reference of the social subsystem of science. As I show in the coming chapters, the scientific engagement of European orientalists led to very different individual positions vis-á-vis religion and science. While the Catholic Ernest Renan and the Protestant Theodor Nöldeke turned toward rationalist agnosticism, the Protestant William Robertson Smith and the Jew Ignaz Goldziher remained sincere believers despite their deep implication in studies based on historical criticism.

Through the lenses of a macro-sociological perspective, the development of Islamic studies from theology via oriental studies to an independent discipline is an example for the internal discursive differentiation of the system of science. This differentiation became manifest in distinct disciplines, their associated institutionalization, and the publication of disciplinary journals. While the foundation of the *Zeitschrift der Deutschen Morgenländischen Gesellschaft* in 1847 marks the independent scientific communication of philology of non-European languages in the name of the discipline of oriental studies, the importance of the ZDMG for the study of Islam was soon to decline. In 1906, the French *Revue du Monde Musulman* opened the discursive trajectory of the new discipline around a number of new academic journals with an exclusive or relative focus on Islamic issues: *Der Islam* (1910), *Orientalisches Archiv* (1910), *The Muslim World* (1911), *International Review of Missions* (1912), and *Die*

Welt des Islams (1913) (Becker 1912c, 531–533). The publication of journals in English, French, and German is an indication of both the establishment of national scientific communities and the emergence of specific scientific questions concerning Islam that transnational communities of scholars shared. At the micro level, this discursive interconnection of national and international scholarship was accompanied by interactive networks of scholars that evolved from hubs of study such as Paris under Sacy, Leipzig under Fleischer, Ewald in Göttingen, or Nöldeke at the *Reichsuniversität* in Strasbourg.

Conclusions: Islamic Studies and German Imperialism

This chapter argued that an adequate understanding of the rise of Islamic studies and its connection to the imperialist politics of Europe needs a well-defined conceptual apparatus regarding the three categories of modernity, religion, and science.[11] While Said's *Orientalism* (1978) does not offer any conceptual clarification of these three essential categories of the social sciences and humanities, postcolonial critique still addresses features of the sociology of modernity that are meanwhile rather outmoded. Furthermore, postcolonialists have in mind the common textbook-temporalization of modernity "as an era that was ushered in via the Renaissance, rationalist philosophy and the Enlightenment" (Lash 1987, 355). In terms of the concept of modernity, many of the postcolonial critics are still working on the assumptions of classical modernization theories, which only play a marginal role in social science research today. In the first section, therefore, I introduced some basic theoretical elements of Luhmann's MST which my study builds on in macro-structural terms. I argue that the selective application of Luhmann's theory of modern society as world society from the meta-theoretical perspective of social emergence can avoid Eurocentric normativity in the sociology of modernity. Moreover, considering modernity as an emerging macro structure theoretically refutes the assumption that modernity originated in Europe in time and space.

When it comes to postcolonial critique concerning the European/Christian origins of the modern concept of religion, this has rightfully been qualified as nothing more than a "deconstructivist banality" (Dipper 2014, 267). Many ideas about a normative modernity have now shed their (often only partial) origins in Christianity and became part of a mutually acknowledged vocabulary in global debates. This is not only the case when it comes to the concept of religion. The German sociologist Hans Joas, for example, argued that in the making of human rights a multiplicity of cultural and intellectual traditions came together. The complex entanglement of these traditions, according to Joas, is impossible to grasp by simplistic dichotomies such as those between Western and non-Western or European and non-European ideas (Joas 2015, 275). The scientification of religion, that is to say, the nineteenth-century scholarly modeling of a concept of religion under the strong impact of revisionist Protestant theology, was a process of global entanglements and not an intrinsically Christian affair (von Stuckrad 2014).[12] Even more important, Catholic authorities and orthodox Protestants themselves did not easily endorse this concept of religion, as we will see in the chapters to come. Therefore, it is misleading to speak of a Christian concept of religion as such. The origin of the modern concept of religion is very much associated with a specifically nineteenth-century Protestant interpretation of the Christian tradition.

A similarly short-sighted view of European history underlies the argument that the separation of religion and politics only works in Christian Europe. The structural separation of the functional realms of religion and politics did not even find its mirror image on the institutional level in all European states. The radical separation of "church and state" as it appeared at the end of the Third Republic in France was only one path of European state formation. Radically different was the situation in Ireland and Poland, both victims of Europe's "internal colonialism," where religious authorities and political identity markers became core attributes of nation building. Talking about the "secular West" is a crude reductionist interpretation of modern European history.

Against the background of these discussions, my conclusion is that we can apply concepts and categories of "Western social theory" to non-Western histories if we only do it in a reflected and nonnormative way. However, this argument does not deny the role of colonialism and European imperialism in the formation of the global scientific system and Islamic studies as an inherent part of it. In chapter one, I briefly described some of the late colonial endeavors of the newly formed German *Reich*. Germany's imperialist aspirations made an impact on the formation of Islamic studies. This political influence is evident in the foundation of two academic institutions in the German Empire. As in Great Britain and in France, in the light of imperialist aspiration, specific studies on Muslim regions and on Islam became politically relevant and facilitated the implementation of research agendas such as those of Carl Heinrich Becker and Martin Hartmann. The initially successful promotion of contemporary Islamic studies by these two German scholars is something that we can understand in the context of Germany's colonial aspirations. Hartmann was teaching at the Seminar for Oriental Languages in Berlin. Founded in 1887, this institution was the result of a joint initiative of Chancellor Bismarck and the government of Prussia. Hartmann explained the rationale of the Seminar as being that of an institute of "applied sciences" where the curriculum was driven by the economic and political interests of the German state (Hartmann 1912, 614). Therefore, the students were not only taught in oriental languages, but they were also introduced to the cultural, economic, legal, and political affairs of non-European regions (Mangold 2004, 226–236). The primary purpose of the Seminar was not the education of scholars, but that of diplomatic staff and students reflecting the business aspirations of Germany's entrepreneurial class.[13]

By contrast, Becker became a professor at the Colonial Institute in Hamburg (*Kolonialinstitut*). To a certain extent an institution competing with the Seminar in Berlin, the Colonial Institute, founded in 1908, combined teaching and research on non-European regions in a more scholarly direction. The institute served as a kind of forerunner for the University of Hamburg, which was established as late as 1919. The institute's opening ceremony took place on 20 October 1908, in the auditorium of the Wilhelm-Gymnasium in Hamburg. In his opening speech, Werner von Melle (1853–1937) pointed out that it was a "Hamburg institute." Financially it was supported by the city state of Hamburg in agreement with the Imperial Colonial Office in Berlin.[14] The new Colonial Institute would fit into the existing structure of Hamburg's higher education institutions and strengthen their focus on colonial, international, and global economic conditions (von Melle 1923, 486).[15] The Colonial Institute started as an institute of applied sciences. At its Seminar for History and Culture of the Orient, Carl Heinrich Becker taught "Islamic studies." According to Becker, the curriculum included the religion, history, and culture of Muslim peoples in Europe, Asia, and Africa from the seventh century to the present. The emphasis was on the so-called *Realien* (realities) of Islamic regions and not on languages, which should only serve as a means of study (von Melle 1923, 630–631). The purpose of its studies, similar to the Seminar in Berlin, was to teach officials employed in the German administration and to strengthen the economic colonial aspirations of the country (von Melle 1923, 471).

The establishment of both institutions and their specific educational profiles are closely connected to, but not only explicable by, the late colonial ambitions of the German Empire. Likewise, the International Congresses of Orientalists combined academic, economic, and political interests. In 1902, six years before the foundation of the Colonial Institute, Hamburg was the host of the 13th International Congress of Orientalists. The congress was an important step on the road toward the establishment of a university in the city. A further argument for Hamburg was the potential of such an event to benefit the city's role as one of Germany's leading trading towns. The German shipping magnate, Alfred Ballin (1857–1918), offered travel on board his ships from Great Britain and the United States at reduced prices, and local traders supported the conference financially (Theilhaber 2020, 266). The congress hosted about 700 participants, comprising not only scholars but also "publishers, priests, rabbis, judges, doctors and teachers" (2020, 272). At the turn of the twentieth century, oriental studies and philological methods were at the center of academic interest and a means of promoting the international reputation of both a city and its nation. The 15th International Congress of Orientalists in Copenhagen, for instance, was opened by Crown Prince Christian personally. The later King of Denmark (1912–1947) expressed his great appreciation for the engagement of Danish scholars with the Orient. At that time, the University of Copenhagen had already established a number of chairs in the field (Skovgaard-Petersen 2010). At both the Hamburg and Copenhagen congresses, German oriental scholarship dominated the scene. The presentations, however, overwhelmingly concerned academic and not political content. In particular, scholars focused on the "enlightenment" the Orient could offer to mankind as such (Theilhaber 2020, 339).

Finally, the simplistic differentiation between colonialists and colonized often overlooks the fact that the international asymmetrical power relations of imperialism were reflected in class relations within European nation states. In the long nineteenth century, the working and living conditions of most Europeans corresponded to a certain extent with the colonial misery in other parts of the world. Charles Dickens (1812–1870; *Oliver Twist* 1837/38) and Hans Fallada (1893–1947; *Little Man, What Now?* 1933) described this misery in novels for Victorian England and the Weimar Republic. With *Peasants into Frenchmen*, Eugen Weber (1925–2007) wrote a classic about the enforced nationalization of people in the Third Republic of France (Weber 1976). For the Prussian aristocracy and political elite, as I discuss in the next chapter, the East Elbian farm laborers in Max Weber's lecture hardly differed from the suppressed people in the German colonies in Africa. In conclusion, against the backdrop of the controversy on *Orientalism*, both Said and his critics were wrong in perceiving Germany as a kind of exception in comparison to the book's focus on British, French, and American orientalism. Germany was certainly different, a colonial latecomer, but well represented the more general attitudes of Eurocentric imperialism with its great power ambitions. Rather than the political, it was the scientific and religious contexts of German orientalism that should have informed a study such as *Orientalism*. It is these aspects that we examine in the following chapters.

Notes

1 In his article "Indien gibt es nicht" ("India Does not Exist"), Klaus Schlichte argued that European and North American mainstream sociology is still predominantly preoccupied with studies within national confines. Histories of peoples beyond their own national context seldom appear (Schlichte 2023).

2 In this way, Eisenstadt deviated from his previous works, which were clearly written in the context of American modernization theories. In his early career, Eisenstadt was a "disciple" of Talcott Parsons at Harvard. For the relationship between Eisenstadt and Parsons, see Robertson (2011).

3 For a detailed discussion of this, see chapter seven in Jung (2023).

4 Findley quotes Ahmet Mithat's observations at the official reception, where—in a perfect "orientalist" way—the "waiters were dressed in Egyptian costume" (Findley 1998, 35). For an account of such "orientalist" representations at international congresses in Europe, see Mitchell (1989).

5 Later renamed Humboldt University.

6 In the years from 1840 to 1860, an intense debate about Semitic languages, myths, and racial differentiations took place between French and German orientalists (Trautmann-Waller 2008). I briefly come back to this debate in the chapter on Ernest Renan.

7 Rifaʿa al-Tahtawi spent five years in Paris and suggested in his report that Egypt could learn from some French models as long as it makes them compatible with the country's own traditions and cultural heritage (al-Tahtawi 2011). In particular in the first part of the nineteenth century, for Arab travelers Europe was almost synonymous with Paris/France (Abu-Lughod 1963, 87).

8 One of the German scholars of the nineteenth century who did not share this European colonial mindset was Alexander von Humboldt (1769–1859). The brother of Wilhelm von Humboldt did not consider the indigenous people he met during his travels in Latin America to be "barbaric" or backward in civilization. On the contrary, he was captivated by their cultures and spoke of the

"barbarism of civilized man" (Wulf 2015, 71). Moreover, he was a staunch critic of European colonialism and considered the very idea of colonial rule as completely immoral (2015, 118). As early as the turn of the nineteenth century, Alexander von Humboldt based his knowledge on extensive fieldwork abroad. In his work, we can detect the idea of a multipolar notion of modernity very different the Eurocentric perceptions so prevalent in the Europe of his time (see Ette 2009).

9 The *Reichsuniversität* was founded as a modern "model university" by the imperial government of Germany after the Franco-Prussian War in 1870. With the German annexation of the French department of Alsace-Lorraine, Strasbourg was incorporated into the German Reich. The university, with its focus on humanities and cultural studies, was intended to play a core role in the imperial strategy to strengthen the cohesion between Alsace and Germany (Hanisch 2003, 5). Before taking up the chair in Semitic studies at the Reichsuniversität (1872–1906), Theodor Nöldeke was a professor at Kiel University (1864–1872).

10 See the extensive exchange of letters between Snouck Hurgronje and Nöldeke, which lasted from 1884 to 1929 (van Koningsveld 1985a).

11 When it comes to science, the search for alternative scientific modernities is by far less prominent. In the historical discourse on science, also among postcolonial authors, the contributions of different Asian cultures and Islam to the so-called scientific revolution in Europe is part of their narrative of global entanglements. Arguments such as those presented in Sanjay Seth's *Beyond Reason* are more the position of a minority in contemporary scholarship. Seth argues that modern knowledge first had its origin in Europe (Seth 2021, 10), ironically again an argument based on European exceptionalism. I argue against this position in chapter six of my *Islamic Modernities in World Society*, where I more closely examine the so-called golden age of Islamic/Arabic science (Jung 2023).

12 The first chair for the history of religion was established at the theological faculty in Geneva in 1873 (Hjelde 2000, xiv).

13 For a brief history of the Seminar, see Mittwoch (1926).

14 Von Melle came from a prominent Hamburg trading family. He was a senator and chairman of the Hamburg Higher Education Authority and later also served as the first mayor of Hamburg (1919).

15 Among those institutes were, for instance, the Institute of Tropical Medicine, the Bernhard Nocht Institute, still one of the most important German research institutions on tropical diseases.

3 Max Weber: German Imperialism and the Scientific Study of Religion

"Max Weber was an imperialist, a racist, and a Social Darwinistic nationalist"—thus the verdict of Andrew Zimmerman on the German sociologist. For the US scholar, "these political positions fundamentally shaped Weber's social scientific work" (Zimmerman 2006, 53). Zimmerman's essay *Decolonizing Weber* portrays Max Weber as an essentially imperialist and "neoracist" thinker.[1] To be sure, the discussion about Weber and racism is anything but new. Already in the year 1947, Ernst Moritz Manasse (1908–1997) pointed to the linguistically defined race divisions which Max Weber, in his early works, made responsible for national differences between Germans and Poles (Manasse 1947, 194).[2] Manasse examined Weber's view on race subsequently throughout his writings. Starting with the inaugural lecture at Freiburg University in 1885, he analyzed Weber's encounter with race segregation in the United States, his studies on the religion of the Indian caste system, and the assessment of post-exilic Judaism (1947, 192). In Weber's continuing concern for the social implications of race, however, the assumption of the existence of biological races was never the starting point of analysis. Weber's scholarly interest was driven by an empirical observation: the mere existence of forms of race consciousness in different cultures (Manassee 1947, 215).[3] Important in this context is that Weber repeatedly articulated a fundamental critique of "a number of modern race myths" (1947, 210).[4] Following Weber's work chronologically, we can actually read his pathway from national economics into sociology as a gradual distancing from some undeniable elements of racist thought in his youth (Kaube 2020, 211).[5]

Zimmerman and other scholars of postcolonial provenience are the most recent participants in a controversary about the nationalist political leanings of Max Weber. It was once Wolfgang Mommsen (1930–2004) who launched this controversary with the publication of his *Max Weber und die deutsche Politik* (*Max Weber and German Politics*).[6] In this book, Mommsen wanted to present an alternative view on Weber's life and work. According to Mommsen, the mainstream of research on Weber took his scholarly work as the undisputed starting point for their studies. Against this bias toward Max Weber the scholar, Mommsen directed his focus on Weber's attitude toward the political questions of his times. In Mommsen's eyes, politics occupied the central position in Weber's life and work (Mommsen 1959, 7). Since then, Weber has been discussed as a "political controversialist" (Nelson 1976, 114). At the center of this discussion was the dispute about Weber's nationalistic convictions. In a review article on the English translation of Mommsen's book, Gianfranco Poggi accused the author of ignoring "all other contingencies of Weber's tormented life story" for the sake of his political argument (Poggi 1975, 246). In my opinion, it is precisely this mistake that Zimmerman repeats in his essay. Yet contrary to Zimmerman, Mommsen did not fall prey to the hubris of claiming to deliver an explanation of Weber's monumental and diverse work from the perspective of his political positions alone. Moreover, Mommsen admitted that Weber was also a prisoner of his times (Mommsen 1959).

Given the ambiguities and "explosive contradictions" in Max Weber's personality and work (Dahrendorf 2006, 576), any conclusive judgment of this classical figure of sociology is difficult to make. To Bryan Turner, Weber's sociology is a complex, elusive, and polychrome body of work (Turner 1974, 1). Wilhelm Hennis, who studied Max Weber for decades, concluded that, in the end, Weber's science remains to a certain degree incomprehensible (Hennis 1996, 111). Historically, Weber's work was deeply interwoven into the public discourse of Germany. In the late nineteenth century, this discourse shifted from the salience of the "social question" to heated debates about a "cultural crisis." Public intellectuals and scholars identified this crisis in the relationship between religion and modern culture (vom Bruch et al. 1989, 11–13). With this in mind, the degree of self-confidence in Zimmerman's judgment is astonishing. Does he really prove that Weber's complex scholarly work was ultimately fundamentally (!) shaped by his imperialist and racist leanings? Zimmerman construes an image of Weber's complex personality as a neoracist that is in no way inferior to the homogenization of European orientalists by Edward Said. Of course, Zimmerman's reading of Weber is legitimate. Why not add a postcolonial perspective to the many interpretations of this puzzling scholar and his thematically rich work? However, to reduce the man and his scholarship to racism is myopic. The life and work of Weber remains open to many interpretations.[7]

In this chapter, I situate Weber's work in the scientific and public discourses of his time. The argumentation follows my general question about the relationship among religion, science, and imperialist/colonialist politics. Moreover, I contend that a brief analysis of the life and work of Max Weber can enhance our understanding of European oriental and Islamic studies. In his *Ein Leben zwischen den Epochen* (*A Life Between Epochs*), Jürgen Kaube describes Max Weber as a man between two worlds: "At the end of his life, nothing was left of the world into which he had been born" (Kaube 2020, 12). Kaube explains the sociological work of Weber as an attempt to understand this epochal shift with its tension between belief and knowledge, teleology and materialism, and religion and enlightened rationalism (2020, 68). The same observation applies, by and large, to the biographies of the orientalists that I discuss in the chapters to come. Islamic studies evolved within this very same context of epochal tension. Yet Weber was not merely a contemporary of these orientalists who shaped modern knowledge of Islam. The major figures of the newly established academic discipline of sociology and Islamic studies were also in a kind of reciprocal conversation. On the one hand, Max Weber relied in his comparative study of religions on the then available literature of European orientalists. The founding fathers of Islamic studies, on the other hand, reconstructed Islamic history by applying—most often implicitly—some of those concepts and theoretical narratives that formed the toolkits of early sociologists such as Max Weber. Looking first at Max Weber's sociological reasoning, therefore, will help us to better understand the theoretical background of the foundational figures of Islamic studies.

The first section of this chapter begins with some essential biographical remarks on Weber and reflects briefly upon the racist and imperialist tendencies in his early writings. I then move on to Weber's sociological work. Starting with some of his methodological premises, the main part of my examination of Weber's social theory addresses issues of his concept of "religion" and its relationship to modernity.[8] Max Weber's sociology of religion has remained enormously significant for the understanding of the modern world (Chalcraft and Harrington 2001, 1). It is in particular his theses about religion and modernity that relate directly to the intellectual horizon against which orientalist scholars reconstructed Islam as a modern religion. The argument here is that we must understand Weberian sociology as embedded in the abovementioned sense of cultural crisis rather than being the result of the racist and imperialist attitudes he showed in his youth. I conclude this chapter by returning to the reciprocal conversation in which Weber and some orientalists were engaged.

Biographical Remarks and the Freiburg Inaugural Lecture

Weber was born on 21 April 1864, in Erfurt, a provincial town in Prussia. The modern German nation state was yet to be founded. He was the first son of eight children, two of which, his sisters Anna and Helen, died very early in their lives (Kaube 2020, 42). His father, Doctor of Law Max Weber Sr., was the son of a wealthy merchant family from Bielefeld. He became an active member of the National-Liberal Party of Prussia and a salaried member of the municipal council of Erfurt in 1862. Max Weber's mother, Helene Fallenstein, came from a cosmopolitan German-English trading family. She grew up in the family's residence "Villa Fallenstein" in Heidelberg on the river Neckar. Heidelberg and his mother's villa later became the center of Max Weber's life (cf. Treiber 2020). Max Weber Sr. was a religiously indifferent professional politician who supported Bismarck in his *Kulturkampf* against the Catholic Church.[9] Helene Weber, by contrast, was a rather sincere Protestant believer. Going to church on Sundays, reading the Bible, and having conversations about religion at home were a matter of course for her (Kaube 2020, 44). When it comes to the religious background of Weber, the influence on him by his uncle Adolph Hausrath (1837–1909) and his cousin Otto Baumgarten (1858–1934) was even more significant. Both were liberal Protestant theologians, and Baumgarten also represented the *Verein zur Abwehr des Antisemitismus* (German Society for Defense against Anti-Semitism). The young Weber often discussed religious matters with Hausrath and Baumgarten (Honigsheim 2000, 100).[10]

Weber was born into an extended family network that represented both the economic and educational bourgeoisie of Germany. Prussia's upper middle class provided the cultural and socioeconomic contexts in which the young man grew up.[11] Historically, the rise and fall of Prussia became the ambivalent signature of Weber's political writings. In terms of politics, the international role of imperial Germany, the powerful position of the Prussian aristocracy, the relative dominance of military ethics in society, and the myth of Prussia's efficient bureaucracy left imprints on his academic work (Kaesler 2014, 20–21).[12] Finding traits of German imperialism in the young Weber's thought should therefore come as no surprise.

In 1869, Max Weber Sr. took up a position in the municipal administration of Berlin, where he had already represented his party in the Prussian Assembly since 1868. Three years later, in 1872, he also became a member of the newly founded German Parliament, the *Reichstag*.

The family moved from Erfurt to Charlottenburg in Berlin, where Max Weber gained his secondary education at the local grammar school. While at school, he developed his interest in the history of Greek and Roman antiquity, which appears again later in his early scholarly work. The young Weber complemented his study of European antiquity with readings of philosophical literature and the German classics. Moreover, he gained intellectually from the circle of famous guests that his parents received at home. In terms of scholarship, among those guests were well-known personalities such as the historians Heinrich von Sybel (1817–1895) and Heinrich von Treitschke (1834–1896) and the philosopher Wilhelm Dilthey (1833–1911) (Mommsen 1959, 1). Dilthey is known for his fundamental distinction between the natural and the human sciences (*Geisteswissenschaften*) based on the hermeneutical concept of human understanding. This concept appears later in Weber's methodological writings. After finishing school in 1882, Max Weber first studied law in Heidelberg. He then continued his academic education by including fields such as agrarian history, national economy, philosophy, and theology at the universities in Berlin and Göttingen. In 1889, Weber received his doctorate in jurisprudence from the University of Berlin. His thesis dealt with commercial law in Italian cities. Then, in 1892, he submitted his habilitation on Roman agricultural history. This "second doctorate," a necessary post-doctoral requirement for achieving the status of a professor in Germany, was from Berlin University too. In Berlin, he also took the first step of his professorial career, assuming the position of an extraordinary professor in German law and trade law.

In July 1893, Weber was appointed to the chair of national economics at the University of Freiburg. With this shift from law to economics, his academic career really took off. An important aspect of this was his inaugural lecture at Freiburg University in May 1895, which attracted attention far beyond the academic world. In this speech, Weber proclaimed his scientific and political ideas in radical and aggressive terms. He directed a fundamental critique against both the different schools of national economics and the political weakness of the German bourgeoisie (Käsler 1995, 21–22). In Weber's eyes, the German bourgeoisie did not yet have "the maturity today to be the leading political class of the nation" (Weber 1895, 23). It is this speech at Freiburg University that serves as a central source for the postcolonial image of Max Weber as an imperialist and racist thinker. To be sure, we can indeed see Weber's inaugural lecture as a "defense of German imperialism" (Steinmetz 2016, 167). Weber delivered a speech in which he propagated German great-power politics. He emphasized that Germany, as a powerful state at the center of Europe, had to play an important role in world politics (*Weltmachtpolitik*). In Weber's opinion, this role would necessarily include overseas expansion (Weber 1895, 25). Given this emphasis on the country's imperialist ambitions, Wolfgang Mommsen described the inaugural lecture as "the initial spark for the emergence of liberal imperialism in Wilhelmine Germany" (Mommsen 1959, 80). As a bourgeois son of his times, Max Weber saw no alternative to Germany pursuing world politics as a powerful nation state (Vierhaus 1963, 274–275). Indeed, at the end of the nineteenth century, Weber's call for German world politics only could mean joining the club of Europe's imperial great powers.

The imperialist connotations of the talk were accompanied by elements of social Darwinist and racist terminology (Boatcă 2016, 64).[13] This is already obvious in the opening phrase of the speech. Weber mentioned his intention "to make clear the role played by physical and psychological racial differences between nationalities in the economic struggle for existence" (Weber 1895, 2). In his analysis of the socioeconomic situation of the Prussian agricultural economy, which makes up the first part of the lecture, Weber repeatedly employs this kind of terminology. This part of his talk is reminiscent of the spirit of Bismarck's policy of "inner colonization," with its anti-Polish connotations, briefly discussed in the first chapter of this book. A good example is Weber's description of the situation of the German agricultural workers in Prussia. He stated that they are involved in an unfolding "process of selection," an "economic struggle," in which the German peasants leave their homelands "in competition with an inferior race" (Weber 1895, 14). In portraying the Polish agricultural workers as being on a lower civilizational level, the Freiburg address definitely conveyed elements of what can be described as "anti-Polish racism" (Steinmetz 2006, 9). We can put this talk in the discursive context of the European colonial mindset. The young Weber shared basic traits of this Eurocentric worldview that permeated a large part of Europe's academic, economic, and political elite. Based on his inaugural lecture alone, it is not difficult to reconstruct Weber as a scholar influenced by imperialist, racist, and social Darwinist thought.[14]

Weber himself later confessed that he "aroused horror" in the audience in Freiburg with "the brutality of his views" (see Marianne Weber 1975, 216). In the years before the First World War, he described the speech several times as a juvenile expression with which he could no longer identify in many points (Kaesler 2014, 412–413). At the lectern in Freiburg stood a young man who fully identified with Germany's bourgeoise class, whose historically specific views and ideals he largely shared (Weber 1895, 23). In the political part of his speech, Weber demanded from this class that it take over the political responsibility in the newly established German nation state. Weber considered the "broad strata of the German bourgeoisie," to be "political[ly] immature" due to its "unpolitical past" (1895, 25). He saw the bourgeoisie in a weak position, squeezed in between the poles of the Prussian aristocracy and the emerging working class. We can also understand the aggressive voice of his talk, therefore, as a wake-up call directed against this political immaturity of the German upper middle class.

In Weber's analysis, the aristocratic elite of Prussia was not willing to surrender power. The economic means of this aristocracy was largely based on an agricultural production system that meanwhile heavily relied on the exploitation of a seasonal Polish workforce, a form of economic reproduction that Weber considered to be an anachronism in the context of the rising modern capitalist economy.[15] Significant here, already in his inaugural lecture his overarching analytical frame of reference was the rise of modern capitalism. Against the aristocracy's entrenched political and economic interests, Weber advocated the development of the German Empire into an export-oriented, industrialized nation state. In this endeavor of transforming Germany into a powerful capitalist nation state under the leadership of its national bourgeoisie, he considered both the coalition of Germany's imperial dynasty with the Prussian aristocracy and the leadership of the country's working class as politically incompetent and in the end harmful for Germany's national interests.[16] The anti-Polish slurs and the imperialist attitude in this lecture, therefore, were not least also directed against the landholding Prussian aristocracy and their still dominant role in German politics (Kaesler 2014, 407; Mann 1992, 413–414; Weber 1895, 21).

The attempt to judge the scholar Max Weber based on the imperialist and in part racist terminology of this speech alone, however, is extremely reductive. The inaugural lecture of a German professor was both a public event and a scholarly positioning. In reducing the Freiburg address to its political statements, postcolonial approaches miss its important scholarly side. Rita Aldenhoff-Hübinger, for instance, directs our attention to Weber's "critique of the German Historical School of political economy and its ideal of a social policy based on supposedly objective scientific research" (2004, 155). For her, the speech was also a starting point in Weber's methodological reasoning. Aldenhoff-Hübinger stresses Weber's insistence on the standpoint that "there is no specific value inherent in the facts themselves" (2004, 149). She argues that the inaugural lecture already contained Weber's epistemological distinctions between reality and values that later became so important in the German debate about value judgments—value neutrality (*Wertfreiheit*)—in the social and economic sciences (see Hennis et al. 1994).[17]

From the perspective of political theory, Wilhelm Hennis suggests reading the lecture in the thought tradition of the German Historical School too. Hennis, however, points to the emphasis of this school on the analysis of meaning in human action (Hennis 2003, 65). For Hennis, this perspective is clearly at the heart of Weber's *Wissenschaft vom Menschen* (*Science of Humanity*). Hennis points to the methodological fact that, for Weber, the status of the individual human being was the essential point of departure for social analysis. In a similar vein, Victor Strazzeri argues that Weber's early studies on the agrarian working class played a significant role in discovering the central role of culture in social action (Strazzeri 2022). Arnold Bergsträsser, to mention a last example, stresses the specific combination of political passion, historically guided comparative research, and conceptual systematics in Weber's approach to the social sciences. In Bergsträsser's view, this combination characterized Weber's work in general and was already apparent in his inaugural lecture (Bergsträsser 1957, 210). More significantly, Bergsträsser discerns the three major subjects of Weber's lifelong scholarly interests in the Freiburg address: social economics, the process of rationalization, and the sociology of religion (Bergsträsser 1957, 211).

There is no doubt that today Weber's inaugural lecture sounds like the speech of a "nationalistically blinded Max Weber" (Kaesler 2014, 412). However, the imperialist, nationalist, and, in parts, racist elements of Weber's inaugural lecture, discursive signatures of his time, cannot explain his becoming a classical figure in sociology. The "German imperialist Weber" does not explain his lasting and eminent role in the social sciences. Bergsträsser, therefore, suggests looking at the man and his writings as historical in a double sense. Weber's political texts passed away and are only of historiographic relevance today. His scientific work, in contradistinction, has raised ongoing discussions in various fields of the humanities and social sciences (Bergsträsser 1957, 218). This scientific significance of Weber cannot be dismissed because of the meanwhile anachronistic jargon in which he phrased some of his political statements in his inaugural lecture.

Religion and Modern Culture in Max Weber's Thought

Weber's university career was short-lived. In January 1897, he left Freiburg and took over the chair in national economy and finance previously held by Karl Knies (1821–1898) at the University of Heidelberg. Toward the end of the year, however, he began to show the first signs of nervous exhaustion. In March 1898, he received the diagnosis of "neurasthenia."[18] Max Weber suffered from massive insomnia, migraines, and an increasing inhibition to speak in public. In the same year, he applied for a sick leave from the university, as he could barely teach. Weber's health deteriorated further, and for some time he avoided social contact with anyone apart from a handful of people he was very close to (Kaube 2020, 128–129). Despite resuming his scholarly work in 1902, Weber resigned from his teaching position at the University of Heidelberg in 1903, only retaining the formal position of an honorary professor. Until the end of the First World War, Weber lived the life of a private scholar on the economic basis of a substantial inheritance. During these years, he produced most of his academic work, though in public it was rather his wife Marianne (1870–1954) who was known. Moreover, without her editorial work on her husband's unsystematically organized writings, the rise of Max Weber to the status of a founding father of sociology hardly would have been possible (Derman 2012, 31–33). The sociologist career of Weber, thereby, started with the publication of a number of methodological essays and the famous series of articles *Die Protestantische Ethik und der Geist des Kapitalismus* in 1904 (*The Protestant Ethic and the Spirit of Capitalism*). In 1918, Weber returned to university life, initially giving some lectures at the University of Vienna before accepting the call to the chair previously held by economist Lujo Brentano (1844–1931) at the University of Munich in March 1919. Only a year later, Weber died of pneumonia on 14 June 1920 in Munich.

Weber's death came toward the end of a prolonged nineteenth century extending beyond the First World War into the early 1920s. In Herbert Schnädelbach's analysis, the end of this epoch went along with an identity crisis of philosophy and with a severe crisis in the traditional European concept of the human being. At the same time, the modern scientific system became firmly institutionalized, with the human sciences and their idea of historical culture playing a central role (Schnädelbach 1984, 66). The work of Weber was deeply molded by both processes. Moreover, the philosophies of Nietzsche and Schopenhauer and the revisionist works of Protestant theology left traces in his studies (Kippenberg 1993; Treiber

1999; Tyrell 1990). Weber's thought oscillated between the contradictory facets of modernity expressed in romanticist and rationalist philosophies (Breuer 2006, 272). Against this background, Wilhelm Hennis was right to talk about "Max Weber's science of men" (Hennis 1996). According to the German political scientist, the confrontation of the individual with an utterly impersonal—"rationalized"—modern way of life was at the thematical heart of Max Weber's scholarship (Hennis 1996).[19] In pursuing this theme, Weber addressed some of the core questions of disciplines such as history, jurisprudence, national economy, political science, and sociology. In his conceptual and empirical studies, these questions converged with critical discussions about various streams of thought: empiricism, historicism, hermeneutics, neo-Kantianism, liberal Protestant theology, and a new concept of life. It is this complex intellectual context with its intellectual preoccupation with "modern culture" that the founding fathers of Islamic studies also conducted their academic work. Through the study of classical texts, they aimed to discover the specific cultural traits of "oriental civilizations" by comparing them with the contemporary world. Employing philology as the means, they conducted a historically oriented form of cultural studies. However, they did so without reaching the level of reflective and conceptual thought that characterized the work of Max Weber.

Max Weber never presented a systematic description of his scientific theory. His methodological considerations were of a rather fragmentary character. We are talking about a number of scattered essays, often written as casual or commissioned works for different journals. His wife, Marianne, compiled these essays in one volume after Weber's death (Kaesler 2014, 545). Central among those essays is his "Die Objektivität sozialwissenschaftlicher und sozialpolitischer Erkenntnis" ("Objectivity in Social Science and Social Policy"), which was published in 1904. This article appeared in the first volume of the *renewed Archiv für Sozialwissenschaften und Sozialpolitik*. In my own understanding, Weber's article poses four fundamental questions with which we still struggle in the social sciences and humanities today. The first question concerns the very object of our social inquiries. The second asks about "truth" in the social sciences. The third addresses the function and nature of the concepts with which we work. Finally, his essay elaborates on what the specific methodological task is in the study of the humanities. While Weber's answers to these questions are embedded in the discursive environment of his time, they are still of contemporary relevance in a variety of ways. I will briefly sketch out the major arguments of this seminal essay.

The article aims to present the mutually agreed position of the new editorial board of the *Archiv*. This relates in particular to two issues, the construction of precise concepts and the "rigorous distinction between empirical knowledge and value judgments" (Weber 1904, 49). Both play a central role in establishing "objective truths" in a science that is confronted with the "self-evident truths" of everyday life (1904, 50–51). For Weber, the social sciences are cultural sciences (1904, 67). In cultural analysis, however, no absolute scientific objectivity exists. The aim is to understand "the cultural significance of individual events in their contemporary manifestation" (1904, 72). This search for the significance of individual historical phenomena expresses the philosophies of both historicism and hermeneutics, which aim at the idiographic understanding of single events instead of at the nomological construction of causal laws and regularities. His historicist approach becomes clear when Weber argues that the individual social phenomena of our analyses are always a selection from a constantly shifting historical reality (1904, 84). In this process, the significance of social phenomena results from the equally historically determined value orientations of the observer (1904, 76).

Weber defined historically specific value judgments as the principle of the selection of scientific objects. In order to reach "objective" results, however, the methodological task is to conduct a value-free analysis of these value-related research interests (1904, 98). This methodological challenge was at the center of the aforementioned *Werturteilsstreit* in the German methodological debate of the early twentieth century. Given the historical relativity of both observer and observed, Weber demanded the construction of concepts in a strict logical and nonnormative sense (1904, 92).[20] This concept he found in the so-called ideal type. Using this nonnormative ideal type, researchers have transformed empirical observations into a purely analytical construct that serves them as an instrument for the comparison and measurement of reality (1904, 97).[21] In sum, the significance of individual cultural phenomena is the object of the social sciences. It is in understanding them in their own historical meaning that we try to establish something like scientific truth. In methodological terms, we start from the historically changing structures of meaning that social actors apply in their actions guided by the heuristic instruments of merely analytical ideal types.

These epistemological assumptions found their empirical realization in the series of essays titled *The Protestant Ethic*. Written between 1904 and 1906, these essays mark the beginning of Weber's work on the sociology of religion. They have received an outstanding resonance in international scholarship. *The Protestant Ethic* is "arguably the most famous and widely read [text] in the classical canon of sociological writing" (Chalcraft 2001, 1). It is still a foundational text for the study of religion worldwide. In addition, these essays triggered an academic debate about the "Weber thesis" on the relationship between the rise of modern capitalism and ascetic Protestantism.[22] Weber asked how certain religious ideas may have contributed to the rise of the economic spirit that animated the practices of modern capitalist economics. As in the inaugural lecture, modern capitalism as a social reality is at the center of his interest. Weber tries to hermeneutically understand the meaning of this economic spirit with the help of an ideal type that he constructed with reference to the example of Benjamin Franklin (1706–1790). It is in Calvinist ethics that he discerns the empirical reality which comes closest to his ideal type. This particular ethical feature of Calvinism, having been stripped of the historically specific and accidental social practice of its religious roots, developed into an essential aspect of modern culture and the rationalized conduct of everyday life in the context of modern capitalism (Breuer 2006, 35). Weber did not intend to prove that capitalism emerged from Protestantism. He aimed at developing an understanding of the evolution of an extremely rationalized form of life that, in his opinion, increasingly dominated the structures of meaning of modern social actors.

The broader social context of these essays is certainly linked to the abovementioned German public debate about a cultural crisis that accompanied the social boundary demarcations between religion and science. Significant in this regard was Weber's engagement in the so-called *Eranos* circle, founded in 1904 in Heidelberg. This group comprised leading intellectuals from the emerging school of comparative religion and from the *Religionsgeschichtliche Schule* (The History of Religions School), the latter consisting of Protestant theologians such as Weber's friend Ernst Troeltsch (1865–1923). These theologians studied the historical development of Christianity using historical critical methods. In particular Ernst Troeltsch advocated the comparative study of the history of religions within Protestant theology (Chapman 2001, 24). The theologian Troeltsch was key in acquainting Weber with the contemporary literature of revisionist Protestants, and Weber largely adopted Troeltsch's critical position vis-á-vis the Lutheran church. The theologian Friedrich Wilhelm Graf even argued that we could read Weber's *The Protestant Ethic* and other works of his sociology of religion as a kind of indirect conversation with the Protestant theologians of his time (Graf

1987, 145). Indeed, it seems that Weber's comparative study of religions was inspired by the *Religionsgeschichtliche Schule*.

From *Eranos*, we can also trace links to Weber's orientalist contemporaries. Ignaz Goldziher, for instance, mentions his personal acquaintance with one of the founders of the circle, the philologist Albrecht Dieterich (1866–1908), whom he met in Heidelberg in March 1906 (Goldziher 1978, 249). In chapter nine, we will discuss Carl Heinrich Becker's relationship to the scholars of this intellectual circle. Generally speaking, the members of *Eranos* were intellectuals we could label as "Cultural Protestants." The term basically refers to the value background of Germany's educated middle class of Protestant origin, whether they were religiously minded or not. They juxtaposed the normative ideal of an autonomous individual with the increasing bureaucratization and industrialization of society, and their liberal credo combined ideas such as national reform, civic engagement, and bourgeois emancipation. Through a scientifically guided form of education, they aimed at a reconciliation of Christian religious experiences with modern culture (Hübinger 1994, 307–310).[23] In the thinking of Germany's Cultural Protestants too we can discern a more broadly spread concern about social and cultural decline (Ringer 1992, 249). What was, however, Weber's scientific concept of religion?

Max Weber starts his chapter on religious types of "consociation" (*Vergemeinschaftung*) in *Wirtschaft und Gesellschaft* (Economy and Society) with the claim that it is not possible to define religion at the beginning of such an elaboration. In accordance with his methodological position, he declares the experiences, ideas, and purposes of individual actors as his starting point in understanding what religion is (Weber 1978, 399). Consequently, in Weber's sociology, religion is a field of social action. Throughout the chapter we can find many elements that allow us to define the purpose of this kind of action. Religious action aims at mastering suffering, injustice, and the multiple contingencies of life (Weber 1978, 519). It can provide salvation and redemption, as well as moral guidance (1978, 490–492, 430). From the perspective of the sociology of knowledge, Weber describes religion as a central source for particular world views and different ways of life (1978, 451). In these quotes, Weber seems to be thinking in terms of social functions (Kaube 2020, 331), for which the sociology of Émile Durkheim is well known. In Durkheim's functionalist approach, religions, moral orders, world views, and the sciences are specific reflections of social realities.[24] He took up Auguste Comte's (1798–1857) evolutionary idea which states that humanity has developed from theology via metaphysics to science (Lukes 1985, 445). In

Durkheim's thought, religions express the self-awareness of society in a hypostatic and transfigured form (Durkheim 1995, 495).

While French scholars generally adhered to more positivist worldviews, German intellectuals tended to perceive positivism as a threat to sound scholarship (Ringer 2000, 6). Weber, therefore, did not buy Durkheim's idea that religions are only reflections of particular social circumstances, representing a means of integration in premodern societies (Weber 1915a, 269–270).[25] Furthermore, he did not define the distinctiveness of religious action in terms of its ends. Weber defined religious action by its means, by the specific kind of actors with which we interact. These religious actors are supernatural forces, and religions order the relationships between human actors and these forces (Sharot 2001, 22–23). Yet in his sociology of religion, Weber also confronts us with certain ideas of religious evolution not so far from Durkheim's assumptions. Weber talks, for instance, about evolutionary moves from naturalism to symbolism or from orgies to sacraments (Weber 1978, 403; 1915a, 278). While he formally rejected the widespread evolutionist theories of his times, describing the historical transformation of religions from rituals to ethical systems makes them an inherent part of his theory of a general evolution of human rationality at the same time (Küenzlen 1980, 220, 226). This already becomes clear in *The Protestant Ethic*, in which he describes Protestantism as a stage prior to "the development of a purely rationalistic philosophy" (Weber 2001, 37). We will later see that orientalists such as Julius Wellhausen, William Robertson Smith, Snouck Hurgronje, and Carl Heinrich Becker were working with similar evolutionary assumptions in their reconstruction of the Old Testament and Islamic history.

In his methodological writings, Weber insists on a kind of "methodological individualism." Reading his empirical studies, however, we nevertheless often come across texts describing social macro structures (Breuer 2006, 358). His sociology is actually characterized by a double perspective. This is visible when he discusses macro-sociological phenomena such as modern capitalism, the nation state, or religious belief systems. In my eyes, this double perspective found in Weber's approach makes his work on religion and modernity compatible with Luhmann's Modern Systems Theory, which we discussed in chapter two. This is particularly apparent in his short essay "Zwischenbetrachtungen," published in English under the title "Religious Rejections of the World and Their Directions" (Weber 1915b). In the first part of this essay, Weber evaluates different levels of religious rationalization. From an evolutionary perspective, the direction of religious development went from ritualism to ethical absolutism and from social embeddedness to individualization. In the second part, Weber then compares religious ethics with other (nonreligious) ethics in the modern world. These modern spheres of life comprise economics, politics, the arts, and the intellectual sphere of science. When it comes to drawing the boundary between religion and science, he argues that modern forms of empirical rational knowledge pushed revealed knowledge into the "irrational realm." The human search for salvation increasingly developed its own logic and became distinct from other spheres of life (Weber 1915b, 353–357). Translated into Luhmann's language of functional differentiation, Weber talks in this context about ways in which religion acquires its own self-referential form of a specific kind of religious communication.

Elsewhere, I argue that Weber combined his methodological individualism with a deep insight into the structural conditions of modernity (Jung 2023, 138). In his lecture "Wissenschaft als Beruf" (Science as Vocation), Weber articulated the challenges of modernity in metaphorical words. A small group of students, the so-called *Freistudentenschaft* (Free Student Body), invited Weber to give this lecture in Munich in November 1917. Weber gave the talk without a manuscript, and the text, first published in 1919, is based on stenographic notes made on that evening (Löwith 1989, 16).[26] In the lecture, he describes the above nonreligious ethics of modern life as the disenchanted gods of a new polytheistic world in which individuals have to struggle against them as impersonal forces. These impersonal forces, the modern social subsystems of world society in Luhmann's theoretical language, "strive to gain power over our lives" (Weber 1919, 149). While functional differentiation at the macro level represents rationally demarcated realms of specific forms of communication, at the micro level they appear to the individual as competing social forces. In this competition, religion has lost its dominant role in modern society. However, it has not disappeared. In both Luhmann's MST and Max Weber's theory of social action, religion is a part of modernity, though reduced to its own specific form of communication. Religious social action is, from the perspective of the individual, the engagement of social actors with those forces associated with this form of religious communication.

Several streams of thought converge in Weber's conceptual and methodological work. With his focus on meaning, he was in line with the Historical School of National Economics, to which he adhered in the times of his inaugural lecture. In general, his writings are permeated by a historicist worldview. For Weber, history was a guiding principle in the study of social life. As such, he understood this principle in a historicist way. Herbert Schnädelbach described this historicism as a philosophical position according to which all cultural phenomena are historically conditioned and therefore variable in their nature. This position is also visible in Weber's advocacy for a "value-free" social science that rejects all claims to absolute validity in scientific or normative ways (Schnädelbach 1984, 35). Therefore, according to Weber, humanistic research does not look for universal laws, but for an adequate understanding of historically particular social phenomena. The heuristic instruments for this kind of research are given by ideal types. In his methodological combination of the value problematic with the construction of ideal types, Weber was influenced by the "South West German" School of neo-Kantianism, in particular by the work of the philosopher Heinrich Rickert (1863–1936). Similar to Weber in his "Objektivitätsaufsatz," Rickert claimed that social phenomena first become objects of cultural studies subject to their value relevance for the researchers (Schnädelbach 1984, 58). Against this background, Weber's work reflects essential paradigms of thought that characterized the humanities in their emergence as a modern academic field in the late nineteenth century.

Conclusions: Max Weber, the Scientification of Religion, and Islam

The Protestant Ethic and Weber's comparative sociology of world religions are an integral part of what Kocku von Stuckrad once called the "scientification of religion" (von Stuckrad 2014). The modern concept of religion emerged from a process of the entanglement of theological, historical, philosophical, and philological discourses on religious traditions. In this process, Weber's main interest was in variations of the forms of religious rationalization and the peculiarities of the rise of European capitalist modernity. Using non-Christian religions as a means of comparison, Weber wanted to prove that modern capitalism and the process of formal rationalization that he had observed in European history had a uniquely European nature. This process of formal rationalization also characterized his concept of religion and was largely shared by the orientalists with whom we engage later in this book. Similar to other forms of social action, the search for salvation and the communication with transcendental forces increasingly took on a more rationalized form. Together with the disempowerment of magic, this consequent rationalization of religious beliefs was behind Weber's diagnosis of the disenchantment of the modern world (Breuer 2006, 13–23). Disenchantment for Weber means that all kinds of mysterious and incalculable forces have been replaced by a purely instrumental ethic based on rational calculation and technical means (Weber 1919, 139). The modernization theories of the 1950s and 1960s transformed Weber's thesis into a linear process of the disappearance of religion in the modern world. Against Weber's principal historicist point of view, sociologists turned some of his conceptional elements into social laws. This tendency to rather radically juxtapose religion and modernity and understand this as a quasi-historical law of religious evolution already characterized the work of a number of European orientalists. However, in Weber's work disenchantment is not synonymous with secularization understood in terms of a general and linear disappearance of religion. Religion becomes a specific realm of social action, a clearly demarcated social realm, yet with only a relatively marginal role under the reign of modern rationalism (Jung 2011, 73).

The Eurocentric interest of Weber's sociology of religion—proving the unique role of European history in shaping the modern world—has found its criticism not only in postcolonial studies. In particular, a number of publications about "Max Weber and Islam" criticized the Eurocentric nature of Weber's question (Huff and Schluchter 1999; Paul 2003; Rodinson 1966; Turner 1974). Some scholars of Islamic studies, therefore, tend to doubt the applicability of Weberian concepts to Islamic history. They consider Weber's approach to be inadequate for the study of Islam, which should not be guided by concepts based on European particularities. Jürgen Paul, for instance, suggested studying Islamic history based on concepts derived from the specific traits of Islamic societies (Paul 2003, 113–114). However, in my opinion this position underestimates the actual global entanglement of this sociological concept-building and therefore the heuristic value of Weber's concepts. As discussed in chapter two of this book, the modern scientification of religion did not only involve European academia. Groups of intellectuals in China, India, and the Islamic regions of the world were deeply involved in this process of shaping the modern concept of religion (see Aydin 2007; Beyer 2006; Jung 2023, 98–127).[27] With regard to Islam, the problem in Weber's work is instead the sources and the assumptions on which he built his few and fragmented reflections on Muslim history. Weber almost exclusively placed his focus on Sunni orthodoxy and did not take into account the various different religious traditions that have characterized Islamic history. Furthermore, I agree with Bryan Turner that his studies on Islam did not live up to "the standards of his own criterion of value neutrality"; they were partly judgmental (Turner 2016, 216).

This critique of Weber's image of Islam leads us almost directly to the works of the orientalists of his times and the reciprocal relationship they had with the German sociologist. As we will see in the following chapters, the first generation of scholars of Islamic studies rationalized the historical development of Islam by dividing the life of the Prophet Muhammad into a Meccan and a Medinan period, leading from the ethical prophecy of his early revelation to his role as a religio-political leader of the community in Medina. Weber clearly took over this thesis in arguing that Muhammad transitioned from tending to withdraw from the world in contemplation to being a powerful leader in Medina (Weber 1978, 473–474). The history of the Prophet at Medina provided Weber proof for his argument concerning European exceptionalism. This period of early Islam opened a historical development according to which "spoils of war" and "political aggrandizement" played a very different role compared to the that of wealth in Protestant puritanism (1978, 624). In contrast to the outer worldly asceticism of Protestant ethics, Weber argued, Islamic ethics called for an inner worldly activism of an essentially political nature (1978, 635). Echoing the political history writing of Julius Wellhausen, to whom we come in the next chapter, Weber portrayed Islamic history as driven by a form of national-religious Arab awakening. In sharp contrast to Protestant piety, Weber described Islam as the "religion of world-conquering warriors" (Weber 1915a, 269).[28]

Another example for Weber's "religious bias" in the historical analysis of Islam is the specific role he assigned European cities in the emergence of modern capitalism. With reference to Christiaan Snouck Hurgronje, Weber took the example of Mecca as the representative case to compare with his European ideal type (Hurgronje 1888, 1889). Weber juxtaposed the "irrational character" of what he considered to be a typically Islamic city with the increasing rationalization of European cities. By taking Mecca as the basis of his comparison, Weber certainly chose a highly exceptional example to prove his case (Paul 2003, 103).[29] Why not compare European cities with Baghdad or Istanbul? Baghdad, the capital of the Abbasid Caliphate (750–1258), was already a bustling city with a host of economic and scientific activities in the eighth century. In the ninth century, it was a "city of superlatives" as a marketplace and consumption hub (Toral 2025, 98). In terms of trade and science, Baghdad was certainly no less important than Italian city states, and its population presumably exceeded one million inhabitants (Lombard 1992, 129). As for Istanbul, in the 1830s, the Prussian General and later First Chief of the German General Staff (1871–1888), Helmuth von Moltke (1800–1891), spent several years as a military adviser in the Ottoman Empire. In his letters, he showed himself deeply impressed by the cosmopolitan nature of Istanbul. The urbanity of the Ottoman capital went far beyond what von Moltke knew from Prussia (von Moltke 1987). Islamic cities such as Baghdad, Cairo, Cordoba, Damascus, or Istanbul would have offered a better source of comparison as opposed to the provincial town of Mecca. The only qualification, which Weber presumably had in mind, was that it was the site of the Islamic revelation.[30] The problem here is not Weber's ideal type of the city in its heuristic quality, but the empirical case he had chosen to mark the difference between Islamic and European urban developments. If he had applied his ideal type to Baghdad or Istanbul, he would have come to a very different judgment than in the case of Mecca.[31]

This chapter set out to address questions about the relationship between religion, science, and imperialism in Weber's work. This was done in light of Dirk Käsler's suggestion that we take the so-called "Vorbemerkungen" to *The Protestant Ethic* as our departure point for answering these questions and for understanding Weber's academic interest. Talcott Parsons placed the "Vorbemerkungen" at the beginning of his translation of *The Protestant Ethic* essays under the title "Author's Introduction." According to Käsler, this short piece "brings together the results of his decades of research" (Kaesler 2014, 833).[32] Written in 1920, more than fifteen years after the first essay in *The Protestant Ethic*, this text encapsulates Weber's universal historical interest in understanding the modern world. It represents an introduction to the whole of his sociology of religion, rather than to *The Protestant Ethic* alone (Chalcraft and Harrington 2001, 5). While this essay underpins the Eurocentric approach of Weber's work, it is free from any racist, imperialist, or social Darwinist elements. In the first sentence, Weber emphasizes that he is interested in cultural phenomena with universal significance, which in their specific forms could only have appeared in "Western civilization" (Weber 2001, 1). The text is written in the discursive environment of the late nineteenth and early twentieth centuries. Consequently, Weber geographically and culturally located the rise of modernity in Europe, from where it spread to the rest of the world. As in the "Zwischenbetrachtungen," Weber describes this modern world with reference to differentiated social realms such as the arts, capitalist economy, science, and the political institution of the state. Modernity is characterized by these subsystems with their own inner logic that distinguishes them from each other and from religion. One could say that Weber anticipates Luhmann's theory of modern society as based on operationally closed, functional systems.[33] What were the causes and effects of this specific form of occidental rationalism? How does it mold the modern conduct of life?

These were the core questions in Weber's work, which can hardly be traced back to the racist, nationalist, and imperialist utterances of the inaugural speech in Freiburg. That these utterances exist, nobody would deny. Yet, Weber defended Germany's colonial expansion as a means of power politics rather than in terms of a civilizing mission or an expression of cultural superiority. He considered his imperialist propositions as a necessary contingent of Germany's political status as a great power in Europe (Wehler 1970b, 277). German imperialism was not the driving force behind his work. One of Weber's core concerns was to understand modern culture and its relationship to religion from the perspective of the modern individual. In this concern, Weber was convinced of the European origin of modernity, but he did not connect this origin to any kind of European cultural superiority. On the contrary. His evaluation of modern European culture was at least ambivalent. The funeral service for Weber did not begin with a reading from the Christian Gospel, but with a text by the Indian poet Rabindranath Tagore (1861–1941) (Kaesler 2014, 17). With reference to modern culture, *The Protestant Ethic* ends with the verdict: "Specialists without spirit, sensualists without heart; this nullity imagines that it has attained a level of civilization never before achieved." Are these the words of a neoracist thinker? In my opinion not. The coming chapters show how leading European orientalists developed their thought in a similar intellectual environment to Weber's. However, not all of them came to the same negative judgment on modernity as Weber.

Notes

1 With the term neoracist, Zimmerman's is referring to Etienne Balibar's definition of somebody who "denies the importance of biological race while working out a system of cultural differences that functions as effectively as race as a means of underwriting political and economic inequality" (Zimmerman 2006, 53).

2 Manasse was a Jewish German-American philosopher who was born in Prussia and left Germany in 1935.

3 It is not surprising that Weber observed this kind of race consciousness. Howard Winant rightly pointed to the fact that classical sociology arose in a period characterized by racist thought. Therefore, we should not expect that early sociologists such as Herbert Spencer, Karl Marx, Max Weber, or Émile Durkheim could have been "totally immune from the racial ideology of their times" (Winant 2000, 174).

4 Max Weber never shared the widespread anti-Semitic sentiments of his time. The German-Jewish philosopher Karl Löwith (1897–1983), who met Weber as a young student in Munich, described him as a humanist. He mentioned in his memoirs that Weber would not have tolerated the defamation of his Jewish colleagues that Löwith himself experienced after 1933 (Löwith 1989, 17). Even more important, Weber strongly supported colleagues such as Georg Simmel (1858–1918) and Franz Eulenburg (1867–1943) who faced severe problems in their academic careers due to their Jewish background (Ringer 2002, 381). Löwith himself was a student of Martin Heidegger (1889–1976). In sharp contrast to Weber, Löwith described Heidegger as a personality who lacked Weber's integrity. When visiting Löwith in Rom in 1936, Heidegger walked through town, wearing the NSDAP party emblem on his jacket (Löwith 1989, 557). The tone of the letters exchanged between Weber and the Black American sociologist W. E. B. Du Bois casts further doubt on the supposed "fundamental racism" of Weber (see Chandler 2006).

5 A similar development in Weber's thought appears when it comes to his nationalist position in the inaugural lecture. Jakob Lehne argued that at least in his academic writings on nation Weber abandoned the essentialist view of his youth for an "almost constructivist interpretation of the nation in the texts which were published in *Wirtschaft und Gesellschaft*" (*Economy and Society*) (Lehne 2010). For the changing usage of the terms "nation," "national," and "nationalism" in Weber's work, see also Palonen (2001).

6 For an even older book on Weber and German politics, see J. P. Mayer (1944). According to Mayer, Weber's personality and work reflects most perfectly the political life of Germany in the decades between 1880 and 1920.

7 Not unusual a situation for a classical figure in social theory, the postcolonial reading of Weber's works competes with a multitude of other interpretations such as those of a decisionist, functionalist, methodologist, idealist, instrumentalist, or neo-evolutionist provenience. Moreover, the interpretation of Weber's work in the United States, particularly associated with the names of Talcott Parsons and Reinhard Bendix, was always contrasted with a fundamentally different continental reading of Weber (Hennis 2003, 113). This diversity of interpretation is precisely what makes a classical figure so classic.

8 Weber does not use the concept of modernity as such, so this is my transformation of his concepts into a "sociology of modernity."

9 Regarding the German *Kulturkampf*, see my brief description in chapter one of this book.

10 The influence of Germany's liberal Protestants on Weber's thought, however, went far beyond these family connections. Besides his friend Ernst Troeltsch, we should also mention scholars who he met at the *Evangelisch-Sozialer Kongress* (Protestant Social Congress) such as Rudolf Sohm (1841–1917) and Adolf von Harnack (1851–1930) (Swatos and Kivisto 1991, 353), Protestant theologians who were all influenced by Albrecht Ritschl (1822–1889), whom we will meet in chapters four and five of this book.

11 We should be aware that we are talking here of a tiny minority of less than five percent of the German population at this time (Kaube 2020, 25).

12 Regarding the details of Max Weber's life, I rely on the biographies by Kaesler 2014 and Kaube 2020. I only specifically cite them as sources when I directly quote their ideas or words.

13 In his application of Social-Darwinist vocabulary, Weber was following an intellectual current prevalent among German liberals of his time. In applying individualist and collectivist notions of Darwinism, Weber expressed the "twin ideals of German liberalism," combining individual liberty with German national unity (Weikart 1993, 471). Furthermore, Darwinist rhetoric underpinned his bourgeois struggle against the landed aristocracy of Prussia. In a footnote to the lecture, Weber himself points out that concepts such as "breeding" and "selection" are "today common ground" (Weber 1895, 448). But at the same time, he expresses his skepticism about whether the application of these "natural science terms" makes sense in the long run in "the field of economic investigation" (Weber 1895, 448).

14 However, it is important to mention that this vocabulary was not applied by Europeans alone. Arab and Turkish contemporaries of Weber used similar terms in the self-description of their societies. They also bought into the civilizational narrative of catching up with Europe, as expressed in both the Ottoman reform process and the Arab Renaissance movement (*al-nahda*). See, for example, Findley (1998) and Makdisi (2002).

15 In this position, Weber clearly represented the industrialist bourgeoisie of the Western parts of Germany. They advocated the import of cheap agrarian products against the interest of the landed aristocracy of Prussia, the "Junkers," aiming at countering the rise of the socialist movement by providing cheaper foodstuffs for the low-paid working class (Hawes 2017, 135–137).

16 For a study on Weber and the Social Democratic movement in Germany, see Strazzeri (2022).

17 Weber later included this methodological part in the published version of his talk. In the original lecture, the political dimension therefore appeared to have greater weight than in the printed version, which is the one we refer to today (Aldenhoff-Hübinger 2004).

18 Neurasthenia was a fashionable diagnosis in the early nineteenth century that encompassed many maladies, ranging from today's ADHD and myalgic encephalomyelitis (chronic fatigue syndrome) to so-called burnout. With this diagnosis, Weber was in company with famous contemporary artists and writers such as Franz Kafka (1883–1924), Robert Musil (1880–1942), Rainer Maria Rilke (1875–1926), and Egon Schiele (1890–1918) (Illies 2018, 67).

19 Hennis's argument finds its proof in Weber's replies to the critics of *The Protestant Ethic* (Weber 1910). In these texts, Weber once again emphasized that it is the methodical conduct of life, the development of a specific ethical life-style, and the historically specific habitus he called "capitalist spirit" that he was attempting to understand (Chalcraft and Harrington 2001).

20 This relativity between observer and observed we find in Luhmann's work as the problem of double hermeneutics.

21 I personally share this methodological position held by Weber and consider my own conceptual apparatus to be made up of ideal types.

22 This is not the place to take up this still ongoing debate that started with the first review of Weber's essays in 1907. Reading Max Weber's responses, it is indeed surprising how many critics of the "Weber thesis" implied that he wanted to attribute the rise of modern capitalism to Protestantism. In his reply to Felix Rachfahl, Weber wrote in 1910: "Not only did I *myself* call it 'foolish' to imply that it would be possible to derive the capitalist *economic system* from religious motives in general or from the work ethic of what I called 'ascetic' Protestantism." Weber continues that he considered the ideas of ascetic Protestantism as one among others that constituted the "spirit of capitalism" (Weber 1910, 71). My own take on the Protestant Ethic can be found in Jung 2011: 139–156. The paragraph here is also based on this research.

23 The representatives of German cultural Protestantism only began to use this term as a self-designation in the 1920s (Graf 1990, 234).

24 This idea we will encounter again in the work of William Robertson Smith in chapter five of this book.

25 Weber and Émile Durkheim did not engage with each other in their writings. In a short essay, Edward Tiryakian discussed this mutual ignorance between the two founding fathers of sociology. Their methodological antagonism—Weber as the sociologist of social action and Durkheim as the functionalist interpreter of religion and modern society—Tiryakian attributed to the national differences between the two scholars (Tiryakian 1966).

26 Löwith wrote in his memoirs that Weber gave the lecture in the winter semester of 1918/19. I follow the dating of Käsler, who mentions the publication date of the lecture as summer 1919 (Kaesler 2014, 754).

27 In *Islamic Modernities in World Society* (2023), I briefly analyze the conceptual vocabulary of the Muslim reformer Muhammad Abduh (1849–1905) based on his *risālat al-tawḥīd* (The Theology of Unity). I consider this to be a prime example of this global entanglement in constructing a modern concept of religion (Jung 2023, 110–114).

28 The only direct reference to the work of Julius Wellhausen on Islam is in Weber's discussion about political communities in Economy and Society. Here, Weber refers to Arab tribal organization in pre-Islamic times as mentioned by Wellhausen (Weber 1972, 519). At the beginning of his work on ancient Judaism, however, Weber praises Wellhausen's "magnificent work" on the Old Testament in a long footnote (Weber 1921, 2). Weber most probably also knew Wellhausen's work through the discussions of the *Eranos* in Heidelberg. One of its founders,

Albrecht Dieterich (1866–1908), was a disciple of Hermann Usener (1834–1905), with whom Wellhausen exchanged letters. In addition, there was long-term correspondence between Julius Wellhausen and Adolf Harnack (1851–1930), the latter together with Ernst Troeltsch a Protestant theologian who impacted Weber's thought (cf. Smend 2013). Thus, I assume that he was familiar with Wellhausen's work on Islam. An alternative view on Islamic history was presented by Weber's contemporary Thomas Walker Arnold (1864–1930). In his *Preaching Islam*, the British orientalist, who once worked as a teacher in colonial British South Asia, argued that the global spread of Islam was mainly due to its "missionary spirit" and was peacefully carried out by traders and preachers (Arnold 1896). Weber apparently did not consult Arnold's work. The image of Islam as a "religion of warriors," however, also has historical roots. Albert Hourani once argued that European perspectives on Islam, in contradistinction to other religions, were conditioned by the historical experience of the factual military challenge that Islamic empires posed to Europe (Hourani 1966, 207).

29 In a lecture to the "Gesellschaft für Erdkunde zu Berlin" ("Berlin Geographical Society"), Snouck Hurgronje himself described Mecca as a very special kind of city whose approximately 50,000 to 60,000 inhabitants almost exclusively make a living from their sanctuaries. Moreover, despite the period of the pilgrimage, specifically controlled by Ottoman security forces, Mecca even in the late nineteenth century was difficult and dangerous to reach (Hurgronje 1887a).

30 For a more detailed account on Weber's representation of Islam, see Jung 2011, 149–153.

31 Weber only had to consult one of the travel reports on the Arabian Peninsula which were written in his times in order to recognize the peripheral nature of Mecca as an "Islamic city." In William Robertson Smith's account of his trip from Jeddah to Taif, which he undertook in the winter of 1880, the relative remoteness of Mecca becomes very clear. The road to Taif passes Mecca and was highly insecure and very difficult to travel despite being one of the major communication lines between Jeddah and the interior of the Arab Peninsula (Robertson Smith 1881b). I come back to Smith's journey in chapter five.

32 In his 2014 biography of Weber, Käsler apparently decided to write his name Kaesler which I apply in the references.

33 This is, of course, my own reading of the text, which may raise harsh criticism from colleagues who do not share this view.

Part II

Religion and Science in Modern Europe: Three Distinct National Frames

4 Julius Wellhausen: Theology and Orientalism in Germany

"The Koran is Mohammed's weakest performance. The weight of his historical importance lies in his work at Medina" (Wellhausen 1883a, 561). This was the assessment of the Prophet Muhammad by the German historian Julius Wellhausen. Wellhausen was a leading figure in the critical study of the Old Testament before turning his research interests toward Islam. In the second part of this book, I look more closely at the relationship between biblical or "higher" criticism and the discipline of oriental studies. Edward Said admitted to not having paid any attention to this relationship. The following three chapters will show that due to this omission, *Orientalism* suffers from a fundamental void. I would claim that the impact of biblical criticism on oriental scholarship was much more important than that of colonialism. The histories of biblical criticism and oriental scholarship in Europe are inseparably intertwined with each other. This applies in particular to the historical critical study of the Old Testament. Biblical criticism not only provided methods and approaches to academic inquiry for Europe's orientalist scholars but also served to inform the major interest of their studies, the history of Christianity.

In chapter two, I already alluded to the institutional connections between Protestant theology and oriental studies in the formation of the German university. However, the significance of biblical criticism goes far beyond these institutional connections. The historicist critique of the Bible decisively impacted the individual lives of orientalists and their personal attitudes about religion. Their biographies and works must be analyzed in the theoretical frame of ongoing boundary negotiations between the religious and the scientific realms of modern society. It was in the context of these boundary negotiations that the modern concept of religion emerged concomitant with the formation of academic disciplines such as anthropology, ethnology, history of religions, Islamic studies, and sociology.

I will support the above argument with case studies on Julius Wellhausen, William Robertson Smith, and Ernest Renan. All three made their way from theology to oriental studies deeply influenced by the leading German schools of liberal Protestantism and biblical criticism. Furthermore, their works impacted the academic studies of anthropology, the comparative study of religion, Islamic studies, and the sociology of religion. Equally important, the contact of these three scholars with biblical criticism was not only an academic matter but also caused individual crises of belief and severe tensions between them and ecclesiastical institutions. Their image of the Orient was deeply molded by these scientific, institutional, and personal contexts. While acting within three different national environments—Germany, Great Britain, France—they were nevertheless in contact with each other and belonged to one scholarly discourse.[1] The relation between Wellhausen and Robertson Smith even developed into a close friendship, as was documented in numerous letters and their joint work on the *Encyclopedia Britannica.* How did these complex contexts shape their concepts of religion and Islam? In what ways did colonialist, Eurocentric, and racist ideologies impact their studies? I will start with Julius Wellhausen, who was an influential scholar in both the study of the Old Testament and the study of early Islam. The next chapter moves on to his friend, William Robertson Smith, before concluding the second part of this book with Ernest Renan.

The Intellectual Background of Julius Wellhausen

Julius Wellhausen was born in 1844 in the provincial town of Hameln in Lower Saxony. His father was a strongly orthodox Protestant minister with renowned liturgical skills. Wellhausen grew up in a rural environment. Rather than immersing himself in literature, the young Wellhausen enjoyed being out in nature. He left the local school with a comment on his graduation certificate that he apparently lacked any imagination. At the age of fifteen, he moved from Hameln to the lyceum in Hanover, where he was, according to his own words, rather unproductive. Being the son of a minister, it was almost a given that Wellhausen would take up studies of Protestant theology after finishing grammar school. For this reason, he moved to the city of Göttingen in 1862 (Schwartz 1938, 329–331). It was in the scholarly atmosphere of the University of Göttingen that he transformed from a provincial non-bookish young man into a scholar of international renown. Through his studies in Göttingen, he became one of the leading scholars of Europe in the application of historical critical methods to the Old Testament, the holy scriptures of Islam, and Arab chronicles. In an obituary to Wellhausen, his friend and colleague Enno Littmann (1875–1958) called him a scholarly pioneer and a "prince of science" (Littmann 1918, 18). In this first section, I describe the intellectual background against which we have to read Wellhausen's work.[2] Then, I discuss his work on the Old Testament. The third section deals with his studies on Arab poetry, the Prophet Muhammad, and the foundational phase of Islamic history.

The scholarly work of Julius Wellhausen was embedded in the academic culture of Germany's biblical criticism. In particular, the so-called Tübingen School of Protestant Theology around Ferdinand Christian Baur (1792–1860), the prominent theologian Albrecht Ritschl (1822–1889), and his Göttingen teacher Heinrich Ewald (1803–1875) left strong imprints on Wellhausen's thought. Baur was the leading figure in the Tübingen School (Schwartz 1938, 332), which Horton Harris once characterized as being led by its desire to conduct a "purely historical, scientific investigation of the New Testament." In this way, the Tübingen School became a key source for nineteenth century criticism of both the New and the Old Testament (Harris 1975, 1). Over the course of his career, Baur transitioned from orthodox Lutheranism through Hegelian philosophy to an ethical standpoint, ultimately developing a historical-critical method that approached the Bible like any other historical source, underpinned by a carefully considered philosophical foundation (Harris 1975, chapter eleven; Jung 2000, 59–60).[3] Initially interested in hymns and medieval preachers, Wellhausen was immediately captured by the historical criticism of Ferdinand Christian Baur when he came into contact with it through a fellow student who had just returned from the University of Tübingen (Schwartz 1938, 332).

More important than Baur's work, however, was the publication of the first volume of David Friedrich Strauss's (1808–1874) *Das Leben Jesu* (*The Life of Jesus*) in 1835. For Wellhausen, Strauss's book was an important source throughout his career. As late as 1908, he wrote in a letter to the then prominent Protestant theologian Adolf Harnack that he was profiting once again from reading "old literatures": Among them were the works of David Friedrich Strauss (Smend 2013, 534). Strauss, a disciple of Baur, became the most well-known representative of the Tübingen School. In his book, he applied the critical method to the New Testament, and its publication stirred outrage among both scholars and the broader public with an orthodox Christian worldview.[4] *Das Leben Jesu* made Strauss the best-known German theologian in Europe and beyond. The publication of the book transformed Tübingen from a center of Protestant orthodoxy into a center of heresy (Harris 1975, 2). A strong dose of speculative philosophy characterized Strauss's lectures, which he gave in front of "packed auditoriums" (1975, 26). Moreover, his book marked the beginning of a much broader life-of-Jesus debate, which lasted until at least the 1870s (Schweitzer 1913). The numerous and different critics of Strauss unanimously shared the position of considering his book as an attempt to destroy the Christian faith by means of scientific criticism (Graf 1982, 82–83). To a certain extent, Strauss' book contributed intellectually to the "de-Christianization" of Europe. Toward the end of his life, Strauss propagated a materialist Darwinist worldview, answering the question of whether we could still be Christians with an outright "No" (Jung 2000, 61).

In Göttingen, Wellhausen met Albrecht Ritschl, a theologian who also once started as a disciple of Baur. Born in March 1822 in Berlin, Ritschl became one of the preeminent German Protestant theologians of the second half of the nineteenth century. His formative influence impacted a "whole generation of German liberal theologians working in the years before 1914" (Chapman 2001, 14). His father was a bishop in the Lutheran Church of Pomerania. In 1839, Albrecht Ritschl took up theological studies in Bonn, moving via Halle and Heidelberg to Baur in Tübingen. In his years in Tübingen (1845–1846) Ritschl first adopted the positions of Baur before developing his own theological standpoint (Jung 2002, 48–51). In particular, Ritschl began rejecting the historical perspective of Baur on the early Christian church and returned to a more conservative position regarding early Christianity (Harris 1975, 112). In general, however, his own theological theory was strongly indebted to Baur's historical method (Zachhuber 2011, 54).[5] In developing a "theology for the present age that still represents the essence of Christianity" (Rogerson 1995, 81), Ritschl became the most influential Protestant dogmatist since Schleiermacher (1768–1834) (Jung 2002, 49). In sharp contradistinction to traditional Protestant exegesis, however, he maintained the historical-critical perspective. Ritschl demanded an interpretation of the Bible against the orthodox view that the holy scripture "interprets itself" (Lessing 2000, 33).

Wellhausen did not find much interest in Ritschl's systematic theological work and its philosophical underpinnings.[6] The young Wellhausen once confessed that he was not interested in theological and philosophical speculations (Schwartz 1938, 332). Although Ritschl had high expectations regarding Wellhausen (Ritschl 1896, 121), the latter simply stated that he did not understand Ritschl's dogmatics (Schwartz 1938, 333). Yet, in acquainting Wellhausen with the Grafian thesis on the Pentateuch in summer 1867, Ritschl became a switchman in Wellhausen's academic career.[7] In his "Documentary Thesis," Karl Heinrich Graf (1815–1869) dealt with the Pentateuch as a literary corpus employing critical methods. He discerned different sources for and authors of the texts. Thus, Graf focused his analysis on the historicity of the authors and the documents of the Old Testament. He argued that their origins were not only different in style and religious outlook but also separated by different periods of time. Consequently, Graf concluded that the Pentateuch was the result of various redactors who step-by-step combined the different texts, adding the specific perspectives of their times as they did so (Nicholson 1998, 29). This encounter with Graf's hypothesis defined the direction of Wellhausen's future work.[8] However, the fact that Göttingen became Wellhausen's "intellectual birthplace" was mostly due to his teacher, Heinrich Ewald, whose critical studies influenced many European scholars and were described as a "milestone" in nineteenth-century biblical scholarship (de Vries 1968, 55).

Around Easter in 1863, Wellhausen began to read the seven volumes of Heinrich Ewald's *Geschichte des Volkes Israel* (*History of Israel*). Ewald's study fascinated Wellhausen, so he decided to base his own studies on biblical exegesis, as he knew the Bible very well from home (Boschwitz 1938, 5). Wellhausen started to learn Hebrew and to study the Bible according to Ewald's claim that the religious content of the Bible should be understood as something that has emerged historically (Schwartz 1938, 333, 335). Furthermore, he attended Ewald's two-hour seminars in classical Arabic, which took place daily in the early afternoon (Smend 1981, 173). Ewald spent most of his academic life as a student and scholar at Göttingen University. He studied Protestant theology together with Semitic philology, becoming a professor in oriental languages in 1827. In the year 1837, however, Ewald joined the so-called group of the "Göttingen Seven." This group of seven scholars from Göttingen University, which included the famous brothers Jacob (1775–1863) and Wilhelm Grimm (1786–1859), rose in public protest against the abolition of the constitution of the Kingdom of Hanover by King Ernst August (1771–1851). This political action led to the immediate dismissal of Ewald as a professor at Göttingen University (Jung 2000, 131). Having spent four months in England, Ewald was offered a professorship at the University of Tübingen, where he lectured first in philosophy and then, from 1841, in theology. In Tübingen, Ewald initially enjoyed a friendly relationship with Baur and "was generally regarded as a friend and adherent of the Baurian theological viewpoint"

(Harris 1975, 44). From 1845 onward, however, he developed an increasingly critical if not hateful position toward Baur. At the time of his departure from Tübingen in 1848, Ewald was constantly agitating against the three "enemies of Germany," the Catholics, the neo-Lutheran orthodoxy around Ernst Wilhelm Hengstenberg (1802–1869), and the "abominable Tübingen School of Baur" (Harris 1975, 44).

Back in Göttingen, Ewald once again pursued Old Testament and oriental studies. In his historical critical studies of the Bible, he focused on the authorship of the Pentateuch. Ewald was a supporter of the so-called "Supplementary Theory," which claimed that, despite there originally being a single source of the Pentateuch, the text in the Bible had been later supplemented by other sources (Nicholson 1998, 7). In his eyes, the historical critical analysis of biblical texts provided the scientific means for a reconstruction of the divine direction in human history. In this sense, Ewald was a scholarly apologist of Christianity who wanted to confirm the belief in God through scientific work (Rogerson 1995, 93). This is the very same position we will find again in the next chapter on William Robertson Smith. Following Ewald's example, Wellhausen combined theology with oriental studies, and history with semitic philology.[9] From Ewald, he received the inspiration to describe the development of a historical whole by utilizing combinatory intuition (Kraus 1982, 258). Moreover, he adopted Ewald's negative attitude toward the Lutheran Church. Both Ewald and Wellhausen were at the crossroads of German Protestant biblical studies and orientalism.[10] They strongly influenced oriental studies with their methodological approaches to the Old Testament. In a letter to William Robertson Smith in 1879, Wellhausen expressed his gratitude that the Scottish scholar had described him as a true follower of Ewald. Wellhausen himself labeled Ewald in this letter as "our father" (Smend 2013, 59). Even more significant, Wellhausen expressed this high esteem for Ewald in another letter to Robertson Smith almost ten years after his final falling out with his teacher in 1870. This was the very same year in which Wellhausen received his Ph.D. in theology under Albrecht Ritschl, who at that time was the dean of the theological faculty in Göttingen (Jespen 1956, 48).[11]

Wellhausen and the Critical Study of the Old Testament

In October 1872, Wellhausen moved from Göttingen to Greifswald. Although not the faculty's first choice, he eventually received a professorship in theology at the University of Greifswald. In the ten years of his tenure there, Wellhausen wrote his most important studies on the Old Testament, most prominent among them the *Prolegomena zur Geschichte Israels* (*Prolegomena to the History of Israel*), published in 1882. The *Prolegomena* was a second and revised edition of his two volumes *Geschichte Israels* (*History of Israel*), which had already appeared in 1878. In this book, Wellhausen turned against the idea that the Mosaic Laws constituted the foundation of the Jewish religion. The *Prolegomena* is an inquiry into "the historic position of the Mosaic Law" (Wellhausen 1883b, 1). Wellhausen argued that the five books of Moses, the Pentateuch, do not represent a literary, and as such a historical, unity (Wellhausen 1883b, 6). Even more important, his study stated that "Mosaic legislation was not the starting point of Israel's religious institutions" (Surburg 1979, 82). Wellhausen defined it as the later "product of priestly thinking originating in the Hebrew community after the Exile" (Surburg 1979, 82). According to Wellhausen's analysis, large parts of the prophetical literature should be dated as earlier than the Pentateuch, which he considered as a kind of legalistic ossification of previous religious creativity (Plietzsch 2019, 27).

For the orthodox Christian establishment, this historical re-dating of the priestly laws and Wellhausen's assertion of the primacy of prophecy was simply unacceptable.[12] Reading the Bible like any other book was seen as challenging its revealed nature. Traditional Christians therefore considered Wellhausen's thesis as nothing more than heresy. No book had attracted greater public attention than Wellhausen's *Prolegomena* since the publication of Strauss's *Das Leben Jesu*. While most liberal Protestants received his critical reading of the Old Testament positively, the orthodox camp labeled him a subversive, an enemy of the faith, and a denier of the revelation (Boschwitz 1938, 6; Schwartz 1938, 344). The Jewish Reform Movement, however, largely accepted Wellhausen's thesis.[13] For Jewish reformers, the prophetical literature expressed the core values of Judaism in terms of universally applicable religious and ethical values (Plietzsch 2019, 33). A good example for this position was Abraham Geiger (1810–1874), who was also a pioneer in the comparative study of Judaism and Islam (see Heschel 1998; Lassner 1999). Traditionally observant orthodox Jews, however, considered this revisionist dating of the Hebrew Bible and the priority of the prophets as a threat to Judaism. In particular, claiming that the legal dimension of the Torah was an aberration that challenged their very foundations (Fine 1997, 5). The Vatican finally prohibited the teaching of the Documentary

Thesis long into the mid-twentieth century (Coogan 2012, 47). For orthodox Jews and Christians alike, a historical critical reading of the Bible was a threat to their supernatural beliefs.[14]

Wellhausen eventually refined and popularized the Documentary Thesis that he had developed in the "historicist spirit" of the nineteenth century. This historicism provided the philosophical foundation for hermeneutics as a scientific method for the study of the Bible and the rising humanities more generally (Schnädelbach 1984, 33–65). Wellhausen clearly presents this rootedness in the tradition of the critical historicist study of the Old Testament in the introduction to the *Prolegomena*. Here he refers to the works of Graf, Hupfeld, Kuenen, Nöldeke, Vatke, and de Wette, concluding with the statement that his study is broader than the study of Graf and comes close to the kind of research once conducted by Vatke. From the latter, Wellhausen confessed to "have learnt the most and the best" (Wellhausen 1883b, 14). Wilhelm Martin Leberecht de Wette (1780–1849) and Wilhelm Vatke (1806–1882) were pioneers of higher criticism, whereas Eduard Reuss (1804–1891) and his disciple Karl Heinrich Graf provided the preliminary work in the new dating of the Pentateuch. The Dutch scholar Abraham Kuenen (1828–1891) continued this path of critical research at the University of Leiden, stressing and popularizing the historical character of the Bible as a text (Kraus 1982, chapters 7 and 9). This resulted in Kuenen firmly establishing the older thesis of Graf (Smend 2021, 147). This long-lasting nineteenth-century critical research on the Old Testament ultimately found its climax in Wellhausen's work (Nicholson 1998, 11).[15]

In his methods, Wellhausen combined philological knowledge and textual criticism with the literary and tendency criticism of his times. He tried to discover the historical stages of a text by stripping off "layer after layer, beginning with the latest strata on the surface and digging deeper and deeper" (Kratz 2009, 387). In this way, Wellhausen assigned textual building blocks of the Old Testament to different authors and periods of time, constructing a chronological sequence of its historical development (Kratz 2009, 387). This approach is nicely demonstrated in the "Nachträge" (Supplements) of Wellhausen's *Composition des Hexateuch* (*The Composition of the Hexateuch*; Wellhausen 1889).[16] Here, Wellhausen combined his critical readings with previous assumptions by other authors. For instance, he discusses Nöldeke's dating of Genesis 14, which he rejects based on his own literary critical approach. In his analysis of the Hexateuch, Wellhausen discovers three independent narratives that had not only been "cut and sewn," but also considerably expanded and edited after their unification. This finding, according to Wellhausen, establishes a new understanding of the Supplementary Thesis. In his revision of the thesis, Wellhausen profited from Abraham Kuenen's critique of the composition of the Hexateuch, although he did not agree with Kuenen regarding the extent of the later editing of the text (Wellhausen 1889, 312–314).[17] In his conclusion, Wellhausen refutes the assumption that the Hexateuch represents a kind of mosaic of many single and independent narratives. Instead, he suggests reading the text as a few coherent writings, which have, however, gone through several improved and expanded editions (Wellhausen 1889, 301).

The literature on Wellhausen basically agrees on his deep motivation as a historian rather than those of a Protestant theologian who was in search of religious truths. It was the combination of philological and historical interests that drove his work. In 1905, in a letter to his friend Eduard Schwartz (1858–1940), he wrote that the historian always had to be a philologist and vice versa, the philologist a historian (Smend 2013, 447). His ultimate aim in writing the *Prolegomena* was to write a history of Israel based on the philologically grounded examination of the sources of the Old Testament (Miller 1982, 61).[18] From this self-understanding as a historian, Wellhausen disliked all philosophical speculation. In a letter to Theodor Nöldeke, written in October 1905, he declared any kind of philosophy as sterile (Smend 2013, 464). Despite this disregard of philosophy, however, we can detect in Wellhausen's research on the Pentateuch various philosophical streams of his time, such as elements of "romanticism, German Idealism, and historicism" (Kraus 1982, 391). In aiming at presenting the history of Israel as a "historical totality" (Boschwitz 1938, 7), Wellhausen combined ideas of Germany's Historical School with elements of romanticist and idealist philosophies. He tried to judge a historical individual based on that individual's own terms while putting the person into a meaningful whole at the same time (Gadamer 1960, 203). In this effort, he was influenced by elements of Hegelian thought in looking for a kind of "pantheistic enclosure of all individuality in the absolute, which enables the miracle of understanding" (Gadamer 1960, 347).[19]

Typically for the late nineteenth century, Wellhausen's studies are—at least implicitly—characterized by evolutionary thoughts too.[20] In asserting a development from animism via polytheism to monotheism, his *Prolegomena* displays features of theories of evolution which were later propagated by the school of comparative religion (Surburg 1979, 83). We will also meet them in the coming chapters on William Robertson Smith and Ernest Renan. The evolution of Israel's religion, according to Wellhausen's reasoning, developed from its original beginnings of "simple piety" into a later stage of artificial and dogmatic institutions (Kratz 2006, 383, 385). As Smend put it: "The main purpose of Wellhausen's book was to separate the precious early content from its later deformations" (Smend 2021, 154).[21] Hans-Georg Gadamer perceived this idea of a loss of an "authentic past" to a highly formalized and "inauthentic" present to be a consequence of the historicist worldview that emerged in the eighteenth and nineteenth centuries (Gadamer 1960, 221). In modern historical consciousness, following Gadamer, history has lost its *a priori* and became contingent (1960, 207). Philosophies of history, then, reflect this historical contingency in the construction of historical processes either as progress or as decline. The latter, a kind of "inverted teleology," Gadamer saw, for instance, in Wilhelm von Humboldt's interpretation of the course of European history as a decay and a final loss of the perfect culture of antiquity (1960, 204). A similar pattern of historical reasoning was expressed by Wellhausen in his construction of the history of Israel's religion and his veneration of the oral culture of the early prophets of the Old Testament.[22]

In his studies of the historical development of religious communities, Wellhausen was actually a writer of political history (Becker 1918a, 477). For him, history was the history of state and society (Boschwitz 1938, 76), and he wrote this history in the language of Prussian-German nationalism under Chancellor Bismarck. As we will discuss later, Wellhausen's emphasis on political power as a historical force was most pronounced in his studies on early Islam, in particular in his interest in the "political role" of Muhammad in Medina. Suzanne Marchand, therefore, rightly asserted that "for Wellhausen, Muhammad's chief achievement was his statecraft, his Bismarck-like unification of the Arabs" (Marchand 2009, 188). In Wellhausen's effort at political history writing, his role model was the historian Theodor Mommsen (1817–1903). In his *Römische Geschichte* (*Roman History*), Mommsen wrote an explicit *Staatsgeschichte* (history of the state) that reflected the emerging mid-nineteenth-century Prussian ideal of assimilating the individual into the state (Wucher 1956, 47). For Wellhausen, Mommsen was "worth more than all the historians and philologists of Berlin taken together" (Smend 2013, 380).[23] During the winter months of 1884 to 1885, Wellhausen exchanged a series of letters with Mommsen and read the galleys for the second half of the fifth volume of Mommsen's *Römische Geschichte* published in 1885 (Smend 2013, 682). In addition, he was personally connected to Mommsen through his lifelong friendship with Ulrich von Wilamowitz (1848–1931), who became his colleague in Greifswald in 1875. The classical philologist Wilamowitz was married to Mommsen's eldest daughter. In Greifswald, Wellhausen and Wilamowitz developed a mutually beneficial close personal and professional relationship. Wellhausen especially benefited from the discussions with his friend about the study of antiquity and source-critical methods (Smend 1981, 151).

Equally important, Wellhausen's scholarly career ran parallel with the increasing "dechristianization" of larger parts of Europe's population. This process, an inherent part of the social boundary negotiations between religion, science, and national politics, took various forms: the atheism of socialist activists; openly expressed indifference in religious matters; or strong tendencies toward anticlericalism and alienation from the churches (McLeod 1980). In Germany, in its search for a new synthesis of science, culture, and Christian traditions, the Protestant bourgeoisie typically advocated a kind of individualized religiosity in clear distinction from church-administered religion (Hölscher 1993, 214). Traces of this trend toward the individualization of religion apparently run through the work of Wellhausen and contributed to his anticlerical attitude. In his prioritization of the prophets, we can discern both a "romantic bias," narrating history as moving from free to fixed stages, and his appreciation of individuality in religious matters (Miller 1982, 71, 62). According to Rudolf Smend, religion was for Wellhausen first and foremost a matter of the individual and not the organized community (Smend 1981, 170). Based on this concept of religion, Wellhausen argued that the original religiosity of the prophets developed into an artificial priestly product, the "Mosaic Theocracy." The natural cult of ancient Israel had been turned into an armored shell of legally institutionalized monotheism (Wellhausen 1883b, 420–424). The same amalgam of a philosophy of history, set pieces of an evolutionary theory, and scattered romanticist ideas characterized the work of Wellhausen as an Arabist, a frame of reference which he also passed on to the discipline of Islamic studies at large.

Julius Wellhausen as Arabist

In February 1879, Julius Wellhausen undertook his first attempt at leaving his professorship in Protestant theology at Greifswald. In a letter to the orientalist and historian of the Old Testament Justus Olshausen (1800–1882), he asked for help finding a position teaching semitic languages at a philosophical faculty. Wellhausen emphasized that he did not have any quarrel with his colleagues at Greifswald, but that his request was based on the personal issue he had with teaching in the position of a theologian: "It seems like a lie to me that I should train servants of the Protestant Church, to which I do not belong in my heart" (Smend 2013, 98).[24] At Easter in 1880, Wellhausen sent a similar request to the Minister of Education in Prussia, asking to be transferred from the theological to the philosophical faculty at Greifswald. However, this transfer did not occur. Wellhausen then decided to voluntarily resign from his position as a professor of theology at Greifswald University in fall 1882.[25] A couple of months before, he had already told his friend William Robertson Smith about this decision in rather drastic words: "I do not care about my church, [...]; therefore, I am voluntarily resigning from a state appointment which is linked to the church. I do not believe in the possibility of the resuscitation of the stinking corpse, which is called the orthodox, and even the liberal, German Protestant church" (Smend 1995, 241 and Smend 2013, 95). The eminent scholar of the Old Testament could no longer combine his critical biblical studies with the task of a professor of theology and the related demands of the Protestant church.

In 1882, in response to his letter, the ministry in Berlin finally complied with Wellhausen's request and transferred him from Greifswald to the University of Halle. In Halle, he taught semitic languages as an extraordinary professor for three years. After the years spent in this rather precarious position, he was appointed as an ordinary professor at the philosophical faculty of the University of Marburg in 1885. There, Wellhausen taught Arabic and Aramaic languages. Yet given his reputation as a critical scholar, the authorities there had expressly forbidden him to give lectures on the Old Testament. In 1892, Julius Wellhausen eventually returned to his *alma mater*, the University of Göttingen. The successor of Wellhausen's teacher Heinrich Ewald, Paul de Lagarde (1827–1891), died in Göttingen in December 1891. Wellhausen followed Lagarde in being appointed to the chair for oriental languages and remained at Göttingen University until his retirement in 1913 (Schwarz 1938). In the last years of his career, Wellhausen shifted his focus again, now from Islam to the New Testament, working on the Gospels, the Acts of the Apostles, and the Apocalypse (Wellhausen 1903, 1904). In sharp contrast to his studies on the Old Testament and on Arabia, however, his late work on the New Testament found only very little response (Rudolph 1983, 41). In January 1918, Julius Wellhausen died in Göttingen after years of illness.

The years in Halle, Marburg, and Göttingen mark Wellhausen's period as an orientalist studying pre-Islamic Arabia and the early history of Islam.[26] Yet his fascination with Arab history and the Arabic language went back to his times as a student in Göttingen. As already mentioned, Wellhausen took his first lectures in Arabic there and it was Heinrich Ewald who aroused his lifelong interest in the poetry of pre-Islamic Arabia (Rudolph 1983, 18). In addition to working on the Old Testament, he also read Arabic poetry and the chronicle of al-Tabari in Greifswald. In December 1879, he wrote to Graf's teacher Eduard Reuss, who was a professor in Strasbourg, that he was completely fascinated by the high level of scholarship of al-Tabari's historiography (Smend 2013, 63). In the same month, Wellhausen contacted the Dutch orientalist Michael Jan de Goeje (1836–1909), who was the editor of al-Tabari's *The Annals of the Prophets and Kings*.[27] In his letter to de Goeje, Wellhausen announced a visit to the University of Leiden for April 1880. This stay at Leiden would not only give him the opportunity to study primary sources which were not available in Greifswald, but also to learn from "the two men who are most erudite in Arab history" (Smend 2013, 64).[28] In summer 1880, then, Wellhausen copied parts of the manuscript of the Arab historiographer al-Waqidi (747–823) in the British Museum in London (Wellhausen 1882, 6). After his return, Wellhausen lectured in Greifswald on "The Origin and History of Islam" during the 1881/1882 winter semester (Jepsen 1956, 49). Thus, moving to Halle marked his shift from the Old Testament to Arabia primarily in institutional terms, but the two fields of inquiry actually characterized his work right from the beginning of his academic career.

Wellhausen described his new research agenda to Abraham Kuenen as based on two themes. "Firstly, the state of Arab society before Islam, then the political-religious history of the Islamic theocracy up to the first Abbasids."[29] The life of the Prophet Muhammad and the foundation of Islam formed the linchpin of Wellhausen's work on the history of Arabia. In his eyes, Arabia was only known through Islam. Consequently, in his eyes the historian should begin with Islam in order to understand "what lies before it and what lies behind it" (Wellhausen 1882, 1). This beginning was made by Wellhausen with the publication of his *Vakidi, Muhammad in Medina*. The book is a translation of parts of al-Waqidi's *Kitāb al-Maghazī* based on the manuscripts he copied two years earlier in London (Wellhausen 1882). Regarding the time before Islam, Wellhausen published *Reste Arabischen Heidentums* (*Remains of Arab Paganism*) in 1887, whereas his main book on the time after Muhammad, *Das Arabische Reich und sein Sturz* (*The Arab Kingdom and its Fall*) appeared in 1902. In all these studies, Wellhausen remained true to the approach that he applied to the Old Testament. The Arabian studies are based on a combination of the source critical reading of primary texts with a comparative look at existing secondary literature. In contradistinction to his work on the Pentateuch, however, his primary sources in Arabic comprised not only the Qur'an and the sunna of the Prophet, but also a number of works by Arab chronologists and early historians (Rudolph 1983, 30). Wellhausen's major innovation to Islamic studies was precisely the meticulous source critique on which he based his synthetic historical narratives (Rudolph 1983, 12).

Wellhausen's *Reste Arabischen Heidentums* is a very good example of the working method that he transferred from his biblical scholarship to his Islamic studies.[30] The book paints a broad portrait of the culture of Arabia before Islam. For Wellhausen, this culture formed the breeding ground for Muhammad's message. In ten chapters, he described the deities, places of worship, names of gods, and social customs of the "pagan Arabs." Mecca, with its fairs and the hajj, play a central role in this cultural landscape. Therefore, right from the beginning, the Prophet tried to link the Islamic revelation to some of Mecca's essential symbolic elements such as the Kaaba and its black stone (Wellhausen 1887, 69). Pre-Islamic culture is the fertile ground from which Islam evolved: "The Allah of Muhammad only helps the Allah of the ancient Arabs to the full consequence of his own nature" (Wellhausen 1887, 242).[31] Two sources characterize Wellhausen's study. Regarding his data about Mecca, for example, he draws on Snouck Hurgronje's doctoral thesis *Het Mekaansche Feest* and the two volumes on Mecca that Snouck Hurgronje published later in German. Moreover, he makes reference to the work of Ferdinand Wüstenfeld (1808–1899) and Edward William Lane (1801–1879).[32] These secondary sources, however, play a minor role in comparison to the primary sources on which his descriptions are based. On the one hand, he used the holy scriptures, the Qur'an and the traditions of the Prophet. On the other hand, he refers to the manuscripts of Arab historians, especially those of Ibn al-Kalbi (737–819), Ibn Hisham (d. 834),[33] and the geographical description and index of locations by Yaqut al-Hamawi (1179–1229). In his own writing, Wellhausen is constantly moving between his secondary and primary sources, critically discussing their validity. This kind of source-critical reconstruction of historical processes and events was adopted by scholars of the rising discipline of modern Islamic studies.

In continuation of his work on the Old Testament, Wellhausen as an Arabist remained true to his dedication to writing political history. This focus on the political significance of Islam permeated his work on *Muhammad in Medina*, in which he further stressed the epochal change that took place with the Prophet's flight (*hijra*) to the northern oasis of Yathrib, better known under its name Medina. In his article for the ninth edition of the *Encyclopedia Britannica*, he emphasized Muhammad's "thoroughly practical nature" and concluded that in Medina "the politician in him outgrew the prophet more and more" (Wellhausen 1883a, 552–561). For Wellhausen, the historical process of the conversion of "pagan Arabs" to Islam was already far more a matter of politics than religion (Wellhausen 1887, 220). In *Reste des Arabischen Heidentums*, he puts his whole research agenda on the cultural foundations of Islam into a political framework. The pre-Islamic importance of Mecca was for him always political rather than religious. The distinguished nature of the town in pagan culture was considered by Wellhausen to be due to the superior power of its inhabitants and not to its holiness. This predominance of politics, according to Wellhausen, characterized Arab culture before and in Islam (Wellhausen 1887, 94).

The history of the first Arab-Islamic empire became the topic of his *Das Arabische Reich und sein Sturz*. In this book, Wellhausen describes the historical development after Muhammad's death, the period of the Four Rightly Guided Caliphs, and that of the Umayyad Empire (661–750). This period was characterized by the question of legitimate succession (*khalifa*) of Muhammad as a ruler. Wellhausen starts with a short recapitulation of the Prophet's time in Medina, which was the subject of his previous books on Muhammad in Medina. In pre-Islamic times, such was Wellhausen's argument, the Arabs did not understand themselves politically in terms of a state; it was Muhammad's escape from Mecca to Medina that sparked the path to state formation. However, this does not mean that the original revelation was not closely linked to issues of religious morality and justice. The Meccan verses of the Qur'an are ample proof for the religious nature of Muhammad's early message (Wellhausen 1902, 1–2). It was the circumstances the Prophet found in Medina that led to the power of religion being asserted primarily in political terms (Wellhausen 1902, 5). Due to the social conflicts in Medina, the preacher became a ruler (Wellhausen 1902, 3). As a consequence, in Wellhausen's eyes the Islamic community in Medina increasingly came to represent a "national state" (Wellhausen 1902, 16). This in turn led to the first period after Muhammad's death being characterized by the question of who held the future right to rule this state. For Wellhausen, the history of the Umayyad Empire is the history of an Arab national struggle to rule the Islamic state (Wellhausen 1902, 47). Eventually, the Arabs lost this struggle to those who contested the national claim to power with the ideological help of the revolutionary power of Islam (Wellhausen 1902, 310). The demise of the Umayyad dynasty marked the end of the Arab caliphate. The Abbasid Empire, thus ended the national project once started by the Prophet in Medina (Wellhausen 1902, 352).[34]

In writing the history of early Islam, Wellhausen used a similar model to the one he applied to the history of Israel. The history of the Arabs and of Islam was a history of decline. This implicit model structured all the narratives of his main books. In *Reste Arabischen Heidentums*, we learn that Islam made an end to the diversity and tolerance that, according to Wellhausen, characterized the pre-Islamic culture of Arabia (Wellhausen 1887, 85). Islam transformed "the profane fun of Arab paganism" into religious seriousness with a "touch of pietism and purity" (Wellhausen 1887, 225). It put an end to "wine, hunting, gambling and love," and "religion became a compulsion through Islam" (Wellhausen 1887, 225). The Prophet's move from Mecca to Medina replaced the ethical religion of the early revelation by an increasing submission to the normative rules and laws of Islam. Here, the "ossification" of Islamic law plays the same role as the legalist Torah did in his previous studies. While he was still able to see something positive in this legalization in Medina, Wellhausen interpreted Muhammad's work there as a national awakening of the Arabs. The later succession of Islamic empires he understood in terms of a national decline. While Umayyad power was based on a national community, the rule of the Abbasid dynasty—according to Wellhausen—was built on Caesaropapism, religio-political inquisition, and military power alone (Wellhausen 1902, 352).[35]

Conclusions: Wellhausen, Protestantism, and Anti-Judaism

The purpose of this chapter was three-fold. First, I took the example of Julius Wellhausen in order to show the close entanglement of the fields of biblical studies and oriental studies. In the academic world of the mid-nineteenth century, these two fields became unified. In Germany, most orientalists were also Protestant theologians, or they started their academic careers by studying theology. Only gradually did the two disciplines separate from each other, and in the case of oriental studies, it quickly differentiated further into distinct academic disciplines such as Islamic studies, the topic of the present book. In this process, critical approaches to the Old Testament played a crucial role. Not only did they offer methodological tools for Islamic studies, but their highly contested nature also compelled individual scholars such as Wellhausen to abandon their position as theologians. Some Protestant theologians took up new positions, many of them in the fields of Semitic languages and the study of Islam. In addition, scholars of higher criticism often experienced themselves in crises of belief due to their critical research. In an exchange of letters, Karl Heinrich Graf informed his teacher Eduard Reuss about the "mental distress" that his historical critical research had caused for him (Kraus 1982, 244). In the case of Wellhausen, the critical reading of the Bible underpinned his anticlerical attitude and led him to leave his position as a Protestant theologian at Greifswald University.[36] Our understanding of the formation of modern Islamic studies necessarily has to take into consideration these methodological transfers, changes in academic careers, and personal struggles that characterized the life and work of its founding fathers.

The second aim was to describe more specifically the role of Julius Wellhausen for the formation of Islamic studies. In methodological terms, he contributed to shifting oriental studies from its more speculative character toward a historical-philological discipline based on the critical analysis of primary textual sources. It was with Wellhausen that the German tradition of historicism eventually entered the field of orientalist studies (van Ess 1980, 40). Wellhausen's studies became important models for the way in which the coming generation of scholars in Islamic studies constructed historical narratives of Islamic history by using the holy scriptures, Arab chronicles, and the large literatures of Islamic jurisprudence (*fiqh*) as their primary sources in writing Islamic history (see also Motzki 2000, xii). Many scholars of Islamic studies took a similar approach to Wellhausen in reconstructing Islamic history in terms of its "inner dynamics" based on data from specific "master texts" (Machinist 2009, 519).[37]

In addition, some of the core narratives of Wellhausen's work still resonate in contemporary scholarship on Islam. On the one hand, there is the assertion of the fundamentally political nature of Islam that broke through with Muhammad's flight to Medina. Until today, Wellhausen's judgment of Muhammad in the *Encyclopedia Britannica*, emphasizing the Prophet's role as a kind of politician in Medina, resonates in both scholarly and popular descriptions of Islam. In addition, Wellhausen stressed existing paradigms of Muhammad as a "statesman" and that of the fundamental dichotomy between the Islam of Mecca and that of Medina. This alleged dichotomy and the political role of Muhammed had already been emphasized by the Jewish-German scholars Abraham Geiger and Gustav Weil (1808–1889) in their studies of the prophet (Geiger 1833; Weil 1843). The reception of Wellhausen's Arabian studies certainly further advanced the theme of Islam and politics in European scholarship on the Middle East (see also van Ess 1980, 43). On the other hand, Wellhausen's implicit inverted teleology, his narrative of historical developments as processes of decline, visibly impacted on Islamic history writing. Moreover, it corroborated the existing orientalist tendency to present oriental culture as a culture in stagnation. Thinking of himself as a "pure" historian, however, Wellhausen ironically applied to the histories of Israel and Arabia a non-historical standard. Both the model of progress and that of decay are, according to Gadamer, incompatible with genuine historical thought (Gadamer 1960, 206). The interpretation of Islamic history in terms of this unreflective conceptual device characterized scholarship on Islam throughout the nineteenth and twentieth centuries.[38]

The role of Wellhausen's inverted teleology in guiding his interpretative histories brings me to the third and final question of this chapter. What role was played by colonialism, Eurocentrism, and racism in Wellhausen's work? The life and work of Julius Wellhausen hardly resembles the orientalist stereotype of Said's *Orientalism*. Nothing in his studies on Arabian culture and early Islam provides academic knowledge for the justification of colonial oppression or even the annexation of territory by European powers. Although Wellhausen lived during the height of European and German imperialism, colonial politics played no role in either his work or his letters. Of course, his language reflects the nationalist attitudes of the German bourgeoisie during the foundational phase of German state formation. In chapter three I discussed this issue relating to Max Weber's inaugural lecture at Freiburg University. However, despite his full support for Bismarck's policies, in some of his letters he also expressed his disgust over the wide prevalence of Prussian Chauvinism and over one of its core representatives, the historian Heinrich von Treitschke.[39] Paul Michael Kurtz described the political attitude of Wellhausen as a combination of "mid-century liberalism, Bismarckian nationalism, and cultural Protestantism" (Kurtz 2015, 17), not a surprising combination for a German university professor of his times. In conclusion, Said's definition of a typical "orientalist" does not really fit Wellhausen's profile.

Despite this finding, however, the wave of postcolonial criticism has not stopped at Wellhausen. Stacy Davis—who describes herself as an "African American feminist Hebrew Bible scholar"—took Wellhausen "as an example for the use of the Hebrew Bible in racist ways" (Davis 2021, 12). In her eyes, his work "exemplifies the ways in which white Christianity shaped and misshaped an academic discipline" (Davis 2021, 12). Similar to the postcolonial critics of Max Weber, Davis took up a traditional line of critique of Wellhausen's studies on the Old Testament. Accusations of anti-Judaism and anti-Semitism against Wellhausen have been made since the publication of the *Prolegomena*. A key figure in this critique was the Jewish philologist Solomon Schechter (1847–1915). Schechter was a lecturer in Talmudic law at the University of Cambridge and there, in the years 1890 to 1894, a colleague of Wellhausen's friend William Robertson Smith (Maier 2016). Later, Solomon Schechter became the president of the conservative Jewish Theological Seminar of America, furiously opposing the higher criticism of the Bible (Fine 1997, 3). At the center of the conservative Jewish critique of Wellhausen was his theory of decline and the related negative judgment of Talmudic law. As a scholar, Solomon Schechter was not against the new methods of biblical criticism, but he fiercely rejected Wellhausen's conclusions. For him, the law was "not stifling but the highest form of religion" (Fine 1997, 5). It was not so much the critical analysis of the Old Testament by Wellhausen, but the historical narrative that he based on it that, for his Jewish critics, made it "a work of anti-Judaism" (Silberman 1982, 75).

It is not difficult to find some traces of the then widespread German anti-Judaism in Wellhausen's letters and works. In the end, he was a representative of nineteenth-century Protestant theology, which held a predominantly negative view of both the theology and the past and present of Judaism (Jung 2008, 207). Even more important, German Protestant exegesis of the Bible had a formative role beyond the country's boundaries, which therefore justifies posing the question of what the "roots of theological anti-Semitism" are in the tradition of German biblical interpretation (Gerdmar 2009). This applies in particular to the history of Protestantism in the German Reich (1871–1918), the period of time in which Wellhausen's career took place. The publication of his research went side by side with the rise of politically motivated anti-Semitism, increasingly underpinned by racist ideology.[40] I briefly elaborated on that in chapter one of this book. But was Wellhausen therefore an anti-Semite?

After having studied his life and work intensively, I agree with Rudolf Smend that it is not justified to call him an anti-Semite (Smend 1982).[41] Taking him as an examplar of the racist character of nineteenth-century biblical criticism overshoots the mark.[42] In his letters, Wellhausen provides us with ambivalent statements about some of his Jewish contemporaries, but he also clearly expresses his contempt for German anti-Semites such as Paul de Lagarde, Heinrich von Treitschke, or the notorious Christian anti-Semite Adolf Stöcker (1835–1909). In Wellhausen's academic work, the negative image of Judaism was strongly conditioned by his implicit application of what Gadamer termed inverted teleology. However, this speculative philosophical device guided Wellhausen in his judgment on all three monotheist religions in a similar way. His negative attitude regarding Catholicism and the Lutheran Church, therefore, paralleled his pejorative judgments on Rabbinical Judaism and Islam. Finally, despite his contempt for ecclesiastical Christian institutions and often secularist societal positions, Wellhausen considered himself a Christian throughout his life (Smend 1982, 266). Thus, it does not come as a surprise that for him "the true history of Israel found its goal in the Gospel of Jesus Christ" (Jepsen 1956, 53). This "Christological" bias in the judgement of Judaism and Islam played an additional but not central part in Wellhausen's work. Yet it was much more visible in the life and work of his friend William Robertson Smith to whom we now turn.

Notes

1 The differences in national contexts went hand in hand with variations in their Christian denominations. Wellhausen and Robertson Smith were Protestants of Lutheran and British-Victorian backgrounds, while Ernest Renan was raised in the Catholic faith.

2 To a large extent, this intellectual background plays a significant role in the works of Robertson Smith and Renan too. This will become evident in the following chapters.

3 In Baur's emancipation from traditional orthodox theology, he took his inspiration from Schelling, Schleiermacher, and Hegel (Harris 1975, chapter ten).

4 The enormous public resonance in response to Strauss's book was due not only to its Christological dimension, but also to the fact that his Hegelian approach of speculative rationalism was also understood as a fundamental critique of monarchical rule in the political climate of his times (Graf 1993, 161).

5 In his discussion of the Tübingen and the Ritschl Schools, Johannes Zachhuber argued: "Baur's original project of theology as Wissenschaft under the conditions of nineteenth-century German historicism and philosophical Idealism remained in many ways the guiding framework for the work of Ritschl and his school as well" (Zachhuber 2013, 19).

6 It was in particular the philosophies of Immanuel Kant (1724–1804) and Hermann Lotze (1817–1881) that influenced the theology of Albrecht Ritschl (Wrzecionko 1964).

7 In his *Prolegomena zur Geschichte Israels*, Wellhausen described this "revelation" by his encounter with Ritschl as follows: "Then, in the summer of 1867, I learned that Karl Heinrich Graf had assigned the law its place behind the prophets, and almost without knowing the basis of his hypothesis, I had won for it: I was able to admit to myself that Hebrew antiquity could be understood without the book of the Torah" (Wellhausen 1883b, 3–4).

8 The work of Graf became increasingly popular during Wellhausen's studies in Göttingen. In a letter to his Dutch colleague Abraham Kuenen in 1879, he wrote that the "heresy" of Graf had made rapid progress in the previous decade and was meanwhile even accepted among some orthodox Lutheran theologists (Smend 2013, 62).

9 Despite Ewald's extremely negative attitude toward the Tübingen School, Wellhausen nevertheless adopted the methodological tools previously used by Baur and Strauss for application in his investigation of the Old Testament (Harris 1975, 250).

10 Regarding Ewald as an orientalist, see the brief description in chapter two of this book.

11 Biographical works attribute the separation between Wellhausen and Ewald to political differences. Apparently, Ewald demanded that his student should declare Bismarck and the King of Prussia to be evildoers and villains. Given the high esteem of Bismarck for the nationalist Wellhausen, he was not willing in this case to follow his "academic father," who never forgave him his unconditioned support of Prussia's leadership (Schwartz 1938, 37).

12 The first five books of the Bible, the Torah in Jewish tradition, consist of Genesis, Exodus, Leviticus, Numbers, and Deuteronomy. The second part, then, is divided into the former and latter prophets, whose histories continue the history of Israel where the Torah ended (Coogan 2008, 20).

13 The Jewish Reform Movement took part in the efforts of nineteenth-century historical critical and philological scholarship, advocating critical approaches to sacred Jewish texts. The movment found its scientific institutionalization in the *Verein für Cultur und Wissenschaft der Juden* (Society for Jewish Culture and Science), established in Berlin in 1819, and later in the *Hochschule für die Wissenschaft des Judentums* (Higher Institute for Jewish Studies), a kind of Reformist Rabbinical Seminar that existed in Berlin between 1872 and 1942 (Feldt 2019).

14 The historical-critical analysis of the Bible is particularly problematic for orthodox Protestants. The Protestant Reformation's doctrine of *sola scriptura*

(by the scripture alone) asserted that the Bible alone is authoritative regarding Christian teachings and belief. The Bible "interprets itself" and is not interpreted by the traditions of the church, the Pope in Rome, or the decisions of clerical councils (Kraus 1982, 6). The scientific critique of the holy scripture, therefore, has a tendency to undermine the authoritative nature of the Bible.

15 For a comprehensive description of the history of critical studies of the Old Testament since the Reformation, see Kraus 1982. In this book, I put my focus on historical criticism in Germany and will therefore not present the work of Abraham Kuenen in more detail. For a collection of articles on Kuenen, see the anthology edited by Dirksen and van der Kooij (1993).

16 The Hexateuch (six books) adds the Book of Joshua to the Pentateuch. Recent research, however, considers the book of Joshua to be independent and rejects the existence of a Hexateuch in the times of the emergence of Joshua (Rösel 2009).

17 Wellhausen was in regular correspondence with Abraham Kuenen from 1874 until the Dutch theologian's death in 1891 (Smend 2013, 843).

18 Apparently, this exclusive reliance on the biblical text was one of the major problems of Wellhausen's work. Therefore, it was argued that "many of the assumptions and conclusion of the Graf-Wellhausen Hypothesis have been discredited by archaeology" (Surburg 1979, 91). This argument has been extended by schools that claim that biblical accounts should be discounted if not corroborated by archaeological or extra-biblical data (Kallai 2009, 455).

19 Wellhausen admired Goethe, and therefore the body of thought of the German poet certainly impacted on his work. However, it seems somehow exaggerated to draw a direct line between Wellhausen's dichotomy of "oral and written prophecy"—the prophets and the Torah—to Goethe's "orientalist fantasies" (Raz 2023, 24). It also seems to be similarly deterministic to derive Wellhausen's approach directly from Herder (Lessing 2000, 152). Wellhausen's studies integrate various streams of philosophical thought, although he himself did not explicitly engage with or reflect upon them. In this context, Gadamer's hermeneutic concepts seem much more appropriate for making sense of the multiple influences on Wellhausen's work.

20 According to Trüper, Wellhausen admired the "evolutionist social anthropology" in Robertson Smith's work on kinship in Arabia (Trüper 2020, 163–164).

21 We will see later that precisely this was also the credo of Ignaz Goldziher in his studies on Islam.

22 It is important to note that this inverted teleology was not limited to shaping European historical thought alone. The Islamic Reform Movement of the nineteenth century applied this model in a similar fashion, legitimizing its reformist agenda with references to an authentic past, the golden age of the Prophet and his companions. I elaborated more on this argument in Jung 2021.

23 He wrote these lines in a letter to Helene Justi, the wife of the orientalist Ferdinand Justi, in March 1900 (Smend 2013, 380).

24 Justus Olshausen was a theologian and orientalist who studied with Silvestre de Sacy and later specialized on Iranian literature and history. At the time

of Wellhausen's request, he was a professor at the University of Königsberg (today's Kaliningrad) and a counselor at the Prussian ministry of education, with responsibilities regarding all Prussian universities (Schmitt 2014). Given his academic background and position at the ministry, he was certainly the ideal contact for Wellhausen when seeking an appointment in Semitic languages at the philosophical faculty of a Prussian university.

25 Wellhausen informed the Prussian Minister of Education about this decision in April 1882 (Smend 2013, 98).

26 It is impossible to give a comprehensive overview of Wellhausen's studies as an Arabist in this chapter. Therefore, I only describe what I consider necessary for the general argument in my book. For a brief, but rather comprehensive description of Wellhausen as an Arabist, see Kurt Rudolph's article in a special issue of the journal *Semeia* (Rudolph 1982).

27 I briefly mentioned de Goeje's role as editor-in-chief of the complete works of al-Tabari in chapter one of this book.

28 Most likely these two men were de Goeje himself and his colleague Reinhart Dozy (1820–1883). At Leiden, Wellhausen also met Christiaan Snouck Hurgronje, who was a student of de Goeje and who received his PhD degree from the university in 1880. Furthermore, it was the university at which Wellhausen's colleague Abraham Kuenen held a professorship in theology.

29 Wellhausen wrote this in his last letter to Kuenen on 6 December 1891. Kuenen died only four days later (Smend 2013, 273).

30 The only new dimension Wellhausen introduces to his Arabian studies is a comparative view on Hebrew culture, based on his previous studies. He even claims to discern a kind of family resemblance between Arab and Hebrew cultures (Wellhausen 1887, 141).

31 While his whole book emphasizes and displays this relationship between Arab culture and Islam, Wellhausen nevertheless claims that the monotheist nature of Islam essentially originates from Christianity, with which Arab paganism was closely familiar, particularly in its ascetic form (Wellhausen 1887, 240–242).

32 Wüstenfeld published a number of edited texts in Arabic. Among those was the biography of the Prophet by Ibn Hisham and Yaqut al-Hamawi's works, which served Wellhausen as primary sources.

33 The biography of Prophet Muhammad by Ibn Hisham basically preserved the earlier compilation of prophetic traditions by Ibn Ishaq (704–767).

34 A year before the publication of *Das Arabische Reich*, Wellhausen had expressed his interest in writing this political history of the Arabs in a letter to Ferdinand Justi in which he told his friend that his interest ends with the fall of the Umayyad period and the beginning of Abbasid rule (Smend 2013, 395).

35 The term Caesaropapism appears again later in Max Weber's work. He probably took it from his reading of Wellhausen.

36 It is necessary to mention that reference to "German Protestant theology" or even "Protestantism" should not give the impression that we are speaking of a homogenous group. In Friedrich Wilhelm Graf's words: "Protestantism does not

exist in Germany" (Graf 1993, 157). Whether in academic or popular terms, we are talking about a highly diverse field of religious beliefs and practices.

37 Machinist emphasized that "Wellhausen generally made very little reference to sources outside of the Bible" (2009, 501). In his studies on Arabia and Islam, he expresses some comparative views, but there, too, he largely adheres to "get[ting] his master texts right" (Machinist 2009, 502).

38 This "inverted teleology" clearly guided the thought of Islamic reformists in the nineteenth century too (see Jung 2021).

39 His support for Bismarck's policies he expressed in a letter to William Robertson Smith in September 1887; he mentions his disgust for Heinrich von Treitschke in a 1905 letter to his colleague Nöldeke (Smend 2013, 209, 464).

40 For a comprehensive overview of the image of Judaism in this period, see Heinrichs 2000.

41 In making a distinction between anti-Judaism and anti-Semitism, I would take the position of David Nirenberg, who assigns a much broader meaning to the former concept than to anti-Semitism, which is conceptually and historically narrower in meaning and specifically racist and politically motivated in sense (cf. Nirenberg 2013).

42 I consider the critical re-reading of scholars such as Wellhausen to be a necessary task of contemporary scholarship. However, Stacy Davis based her article almost exclusively on secondary literature that is affirmative to her position. Moreover, she seems to be unaware of the fact that Jewish and Christian scholars were often competing for the very same positions at European universities (see also Maier 2016). The postcolonial critics of Wellhausen would be more convincing if they also critically engaged with literatures that do not merely endorse their point of view and if they included more primary sources in their evaluation.

5 William Robertson Smith: Theology and Orientalism in Great Britain

England's "most distinguished Orientalist" (Burkitt 1894, 684)—this was the assessment of William Robertson Smith made by the Cambridge theologian Francis Crawford Burkitt (1864–1935). While Julius Wellhausen was not really on Edward Said's radar, Robertson Smith briefly appears in Said's *Orientalism*. Over the course of a couple of pages, Said described him as a prototypical "orientalist." In *Orientalism*, Robertson Smith represents one of those "white European experts" who formulated "general truths" about Arabs and Muslims. These truths he supposedly based on a "coercive framework" which included his own "private mythology and obsessions" (Said 1978, 237)—an accusation which, I have the suspicion, could equally be directed against *Orientalism*. Referring to Robertson Smith's travels in the Hejaz (1881b), Said claimed that Robertson Smith "could speak about Muslims, modern Islam, and primitive Islam without bothering to make distinctions" (Said 1978, 235). He even considered Smith's vocabulary as "devoid of historical grounding" (1978, 235). Said registered Robertson Smith among those Europeans who despised the East thoroughly, with the aim of keeping "the Orient and Islam under the control of the White Man" (1978, 238). This chapter will show how little Said's assessment has in common with the reality of the Scottish scholar's life and work. Indeed, Said seemingly "was completely unaware of the social, historical, and methodological context or complexity of Smith's work" (Bošković 2021). On the following pages, I try to make sense of this complexity. In so doing, I aim to answer the very same questions as in the previous chapter. I am interested in Robertson Smith's concept of religion, his image of Islam, and the ways in which colonialism, Eurocentrism, and racist ideologies may have framed his studies.

In stark contrast to Said's pejorative assessment of Robertson Smith, there is broad scholarly agreement on the significance of several of his works, as evidenced by the initial quote from Burkitt. Robertson Smith played a pivotal role in the development of the comparative study of religion, advancing the thesis that religion has a fundamentally social origin—a perspective that would become a foundational component of the social sciences more broadly (Warburg 1989, 41). From the standpoint of Islamic studies, Ignaz Goldziher considered Robertson Smith's research in the field of pre-Islamic family law in Arabia to be groundbreaking (Goldziher 1886a, 20). Almost legendary is Émile Durkheim's (1858–1917) praise for "Smith and his school" (Pickering 1984, 61). The French sociologist described reading Robertson Smith's *Lectures on the Religion of the Semites* as a "revelation," strongly pushing his interest into the direction of the sociology of knowledge and of religion (Pickering 1984, 61).[1] Sigmund Freud (1856–1939) read the same book in June 1912, "just after embarking upon the writing of *Totem and Taboo*" (Booth 2002, 259). According to Gorden Booth, Freud basically summarized Robertson Smith's thesis expounded in the *Lectures* (Booth 2002, 259, 262). Today, only small, specialized circles still discuss Robertson Smith's theses (Eriksen 2022, 118). His once so famous "theory of sacrifice" is meanwhile fully outdated (Warburg 1989, 51). The relative marginalization of Robertson Smith in contemporary scholarship is thus understandable. Yet, of lasting significance are not his conclusions, but his methodological innovations. He contributed decisively to the introduction of comparative socio-anthropological methods into modern scholarship on religion (Levine 1997, 617). Said was not interested in these methodological achievements. His assessment presumably was built alone on Robertson Smith's combination of Christian apologetics with an evolutionary-minded Victorian British worldview. Yet the historical imprint of Victorian times does not diminish the scientific significance of Robertson Smith (Holloway 2000). In this case, the methodological side rules over the historical context. Both method and context will be at issue in this chapter.

As with Wellhausen, I will begin with some biographical data and the description of the scholarly environment in which the young Robertson Smith developed his body of thought. This environment partly overlaps with the intellectual background that also shaped Wellhausen's academic career. The revisionist Protestant theology of Germany had a decisive influence on Robertson Smith's academic work, and it was him who spread and propagated the higher criticism developed by Abraham Kuenen and Julius Wellhausen in Great Britain (Houtman 2000, 231).[2] Due to this role, his employer, the Free Church of Scottland, accused him of heresy. I discuss the resulting "Robertson Smith heresy affair" in the second section of this chapter in relationship to his work on the Old Testament. I interpret this controversy as a prime example of the boundary negotiations between religion and science in nineteenth-century

Great Britain. I then take up his studies on early Arabia in the third section. These studies clearly mark the shift in Robertson Smith's academic track toward the anthropology of religion. This shift took place after his dismissal from his professorship at the Free Church and characterized the work of his new appointments at the University of Cambridge. At the end of the nineteenth century, Robertson Smith became famous far beyond British academia for his work on Semitic culture and on sacrifice. In historical terms, we must see him therefore as a nodal point in the scholarly network of nineteenth-century studies on religion and Islam.

Biography: Scottish Origins and the Impact of German Theology

William Robertson Smith was born on 8 November 1846 in Keig, a village in Aberdeenshire, in the rural Northeast of Scotland. His father came from a humble social background but had worked his way up to become the headmaster of the West End Academy in Aberdeen. In 1845, his father William Pirie Smith was ordained as a minister of the Free Church of Scotland, and together with his wife, Jane Robertson, and their first daughter, he moved to Keig to take up his post as minister of the Parish of Keig and Tough (Maier 2009, 9, 12). The Free Church was a conservative, evangelical offshoot of the National Church of Scotland which had separated from the latter in May 1843. The separation concluded a more than ten-year conflict with the National Church over the proper limits of state intervention in ecclesiastical affairs. Furthermore, the evangelical founders of the Free Church criticized the "rationalist theology" of the National Church and advocated the "acknowledgement of mankind's absolute dependence upon divine grace" (Wheeler-Barclay 1993, 64). It is significant for the religious dedication of Robertson Smith's father that he gave up his position as a school principal in Aberdeen to move to the countryside and serve as a minister for the newly established parish of the Free Church. In Keig, William Robertson Smith grew up in a deeply religious family in which "the Bible pervaded everybody's lives" (Maier 2008, 30). His younger sister reported that "all the psalms from the Scottish psalter would have to be learnt by heart" (Maier 2016, 65). William was the oldest son of nine children. He and his siblings were brought up in a household in which "religious studies, the sciences, mathematics and languages were fields for daily discussion" (Beidelman 1974, 3). The parents encouraged reading in general, though religious literature played a dominant role. Due to his bad health and economic problems, Robertson Smith never attended a public school. Instead, his father taught him and his brother at home (Maier 2009, 25).

In 1861, William Robertson Smith took up studies at Aberdeen University at the age of fourteen. His performance there was outstanding, in particular with regard to mathematics and the classical languages of theology. At the age of twenty, he enrolled at the New College in Edinburgh to pursue his two major interests, natural science and biblical studies. At New College, his Hebrew teacher, Andrew Bruce Davidson (1831–1902), made a profound impact on him. Davidson was versed in the methods of biblical criticism and perceived the scientific study of the Bible as a necessary foundation for the Christian faith. With this position of "believing criticism," Davidson gave Robertson Smith's peculiar scholarly career its fundamental direction (Black and Chrystal 1912, 77). In 1867, Robertson Smith wrote his first essay in the field of biblical scholarship. This early essay already dealt with the central question of his future works: "Was the history of Israel the history of God or just any history?" (Rogerson 1995, 116). For Robertson Smith, the answer had to be found in the resolution of the contradictory aspects of revealed and unvarying truths and the historical particularity in which divine prophecy had appeared (Beidelman 1974, 6). In one of his first publications, "Prophecy and Personality," he already argued that history and prophecy were always both the product of human personality and the manifestation of the supernatural factor (Robertson Smith 1868, 97).

In his search for knowledge, Robertson Smith visited the continent, in particular Germany, several times. In comparison to the elementary achievements of biblical studies in Britain, German scholarship of the Old Testament was enormous (Rogerson 1995, 138). As early as 1865, he took up lessons in German, and in May 1867, he paid his first visit to Germany. His interest in German scholarship was entirely driven by his religious mission. He learned Hebrew and German in "preparation for his ecclesiastical life" (Black and Chrystal 1912, 84). On his first visit to Germany, Robertson Smith presumably met with Richard Rothe (1799–1867) in Heidelberg, shortly before the Protestant theologian died in 1867. The young scholar was deeply impressed by Rothe and his book *On Dogmatics* (Rogerson 1995, 83–85). Rothe was born in Posen, which today is Posnań in Poland, and studied theology in Heidelberg and Berlin. At the University of Heidelberg, he attended the lectures of the German philosopher Georg Wilhelm Friedrich Hegel (1770–1831) throughout the years 1816 to 1817 (Wagner 1998, 436). Inspired by Hegel's philosophy of the state, Rothe developed a theology of Christianity without church. Rothe promoted a kind of individualized Christianity that should be united with the idea of a universal constitutional state. The church, in Rothe's view, was a dying institution. It was the task of Christians to liberate themselves from this anachronistic institution. While Rothe grounded the legislation of his universal state in Christian morality, this state should not have the task of implementing dogmas of the Bible or the Reformation. Rothe understood the modern state and modernity as such in a civilizational sense as a higher stage of Christianity (Dörfler-Dierken 2001, 60–66). Rothe's theology was molded by the ideas of the Enlightenment and Hegelian thought. For him, the Reformation indicated the transition of Christianity from its traditional ecclesiastical phase to a modern unity of morality, religion, and politics (Wagner 1998, 438). Rothe interpreted the Bible in a historical way, not a normative one. From the perspective of critical biblical studies, he understood the norms of the Bible not as the eternal will of God, but as historically contingent narratives that call for hermeneutical interpretation (Dörfler-Dierken 2001, 52).

Richard Rothe taught Protestant theology in Wittenberg, Bonn, and finally in Heidelberg. Orthodox Protestants, however, looked upon his theology as nothing more than a thinly disguised kind of secularism (Cashdollar 1889, 388). William Robertson Smith, however, was attracted by the way in which Rothe combined the advanced historical critical method with his personal piety and deep commitment to the Reformation.[3] From his own apologetic position, Robertson Smith considered biblical criticism to be a tool to reconcile modern culture with a personal commitment to God through Jesus Christ (Rogerson 1995, 93). Moreover, we can discern Rothe's concept of the uniqueness of Christianity in human civilization in Robertson Smith's thought (Jung 2015, 347). The encounter with Rothe probably gave him a clear example for his own lifelong scholarly mission of "showing how scientific explanation could sustain genuine faith" (Livingstone 2015, 453). While fully endorsing higher criticism as a scientific method, Robertson Smith nevertheless rejected the thought of those German theologians who treated theology as nothing more than an "abstract science" (Black and Chrystal 1912, 84). Consequently, he did not endorse radical rationalist approaches such as those advanced by representatives of the Tübingen School. In a letter written during his second trip to Germany in July 1869, he even went so far as to call David Friedrich Strauss an infidel (Black and Chrystal 1912, 60, 85–88). In the end, in theological terms, Robertson Smith came to perceive the Tübingen School as by far too rationalistic.

William Robertson Smith therefore gave up his initial plan of studying in Tübingen during the summer of 1867 and finally ended up at the University of Bonn. Smith arrived in Bonn in April 1867. There he first met with Carl Schaarschmidt (1822–1908), who was an extraordinary professor in philosophy. George C. Robertson, a philosophy professor at University College in London, provided Robertson Smith with an introduction letter to Schaarschmidt, who received the young scholar cordially (Maier 2009, 87). Robertson Smith and Schaarschmidt remained in a friendly collegial relationship throughout their lives. In Bonn, Robertson Smith experienced a very different religious environment than that he was used from home. Although part of Protestant Prussia, in religious terms Bonn and Western Prussia were characterized by their Catholic majority population. Moreover, religious indifference and doctrinal divergences among Protestants were much more widespread than Robertson Smith had encountered in Great Britain.

The presumably deepest impression on him, however, was made by Albrecht Ritschl.[4] He met the leading German Protestant theologian on his second trip to Germany in 1869 in Göttingen. Robertson Smith described the lectures of Ritschl as the most enlightening experience of this summer in Germany (Black and Chrystal 1912, 111). Ritschl had studied briefly with Rothe in Bonn, and he shared with him and with Wellhausen's teacher Ewald a sincere belief in the vision of the presence of God's will in history. However, in their theological positions, the three scholars differed in various aspects. For Ritschl, the theological reorientation toward the Reformation revolved around the concept of justification and a historicist Christology. From this perspective, he defined Jesus Christ as a role model that manifested the "essence of Christianity." With this proposition, he basically followed the more general trend of the nineteenth-century German subjectivation of the Christian faith. As a divine model, Jesus Christ transcended all ethnic and social boundaries, replacing the particularisms of the Old Testament by a universal moral community. Consequently, from the perspective of a certain idea of religious evolution, Christianity appeared to be the ultimate and perfect version of the three monotheist creeds (Rohls 1997, 773–775). In Ritschl's theology, the divine will is revealed in the vocation of Christ. Those who believe in this divine will find justification in their individual experience of acting in a morally correct way in ordinary life. The contemporary Christian believer, according to Ritschl's interpretation of Christianity, worked for the Kingdom of God through the fulfillment of his or her duties in everyday life (Hübinger 1994, 172). Ritschl's religious ethics of everyday life appealed to Germany's growing middle class and associated Protestant justification closely with lived communities and social practices (Nipperdey 1988, 69). Ritschl's complex combination of community, faith, religious evolution, and daily social practices entered Robertson Smith's later studies on Semitic religions. The Scottish theologian turned Ritschl's practical theological advice into a theoretical concept of the social sciences in claiming that myth is subordinate to ritual practices and therewith the social origin of religion (Jung 2015, 348). Moreover, the theology of Albrecht Ritschl resonated in Robertson Smith's own interpretation of the Christian faith as the participation of the faithful "in a relationship with God through Christ" (Wheeler-Barclay 1993, 65).

Robertson Smith's trips to Germany and his full engagement with its reformist Protestant theology were fundamental encounters in the merger of sincere faith with rationalistic theology based on historicist and philological methods. German critical scholarship consolidated his lessons of "believing criticism" which he had learned from his teacher Davidson in Edinburgh. German Protestant theology contributed essentially to making Robertson Smith a Christian apologist for whom the scientific study of the Bible did not contradict the message of Jesus Christ. Robertson Smith was both a convinced biblical critic and a "fervent evangelical." His personal commitment was to bringing modern scholarship into the "service of theology" (Rogerson 1995, 147–149). For Robertson Smith, following the "honest practice of a higher criticism" was only a dangerous endeavor if "it is begun without faith" (Robertson Smith 1874, 233). Those, however, who have not forgotten that the history of the Bible "is no profane history, but the story of God's saving self-manifestation," biblical criticism is a means of confirming the Christian faith (Robertson Smith 1874, 233).

The Heresy Affair: The Believing Critic on Trial

Returning to Edinburgh in May 1870, Robertson Smith became the elected successor of Professor Sachs, the previous holder of the chair of Hebrew and the Old Testament at the Free Church College in Aberdeen. In November 1870, he was ordained a minister of the Free Church, which was a requirement for taking up this chair (Beidelman 1974, 7; Black and Chrystal 1912, 123). Yet his passion for German higher criticism soon gave his career an unexpected turn. Employed by an evangelical institution, Robertson Smith nevertheless became the most important disseminator of continental biblical criticism in Great Britain: "The view of the Old Testament so ably advocated by Robertson Smith was indeed in all essentials that of Wellhausen" (Burkitt 1894, 684).[5] He first presented this view to a larger audience in his article "Bible" published in the third volume of the ninth edition of the *Encyclopedia Britannica* in 1875. The editor in chief of this edition was Thomas Spencer Baynes (1823–1887), a professor of logic and English literature at the University of St. Andrews. Presumably Baynes had commissioned Robertson Smith to write a number of theological entries due to his pioneering role in transmitting the theory and method of biblical criticism in Scotland. In particular, he asked the young scholar to reflect the international standard of this new scholarly approach to the holy scriptures when writing his entries. Through his contributions to the *Encyclopedia*, Robertson Smith's historical and literary critical approach to the Old Testament found a much broader audience in the anglophone world than the narrow confines of academia would have provided (Beidelman 1974, 13; Maier 2009, 202).[6]

Robertson Smith starts his article under the entry "Bible" by introducing its aim, which was "give a general account of the historical and literary conditions under which the unique literature of the Old and New Testaments sprang up" and "were brought together in a canonical collection" (Robertson Smith 1875, 634). Regarding the book of Deuteronomy, with reference to the thesis of Graf he points to the difficulties in supposing that its "legislative part is as old as Moses" (Robertson Smith 1875, 637). Robertson Smith introduced his readership to the Graf-Kuenen-Wellhausen thesis according to which the Pentateuch consists of a number of texts written by different authors who actually lived in different ages. He continues that these various textual elements were fused into one narrative only at a later point in time (Robertson Smith 1875, 638). The essay delivered a well-informed description of the way in which the new school of historical criticism interpreted the Old Testament. This is to say, Robertson Smith explained the critical thesis of the "composite authorship of the Pentateuch" (Houtman 2000, 223). Yet at no point did he call the divine nature of the text into question. For the evangelical hardliners in the Free Church and in Scotland more generally, this article nonetheless fully transgressed the boundaries of the acceptable. For them, the Bible was an "unimpugnable authority" that supplied "an infallible divine guidance" to its readers (Cheyne 1995, 33). The idea that the holy scriptures of Christianity may be interpreted like any other book was unacceptable for the influential conservative wing of the Free Church: "The inerrancy of the Bible was so intimate a part of their religious thought and life that a denial of it seemed to threaten the destruction of faith itself" (Glover 1954, 16).

The publication of Robertson Smith's articles in the *Encyclopedia* became a public affair. Rumors about his "heresy" circulated, leading to public agitation against him and his views. Opponents and supporters of Smith engaged in a public controversy lasting for several years. Initiated by an anonymous pamphlet—"Infidelity in the Aberdeen Free Church College"—this controversy about Robertson Smith's heresy was "fully reported in the Scottish press" (McCleery 2007, 301). In an anonymous review in 1876, the author argued that Robertson Smith does not go as far as the Tübingen School, but that his article clearly proposes that the scriptures of the Old Testament would not stand the critical test of modern scholarship (Maier 2009, 151). In January 1877, to quote another example, an article in *The Glasgow News* accused him of paraphrasing "Dutch criticism," in this way associating him with Abraham Kuenen. The Protestant theologian at Leiden University "stood in ill repute among the Scottish orthodoxy" (Houtman 2000, 224). Under this rising public outcry, the Church felt compelled to take a serious look at the case of Robertson Smith (Tulloch 1876–1877, 545–547).

Confronted with these accusations of heresy, Robertson Smith strongly reaffirmed his Christian faith. At the same time, he reiterated that the critical method provides a better understanding of the Bible and is therefore in full service of religion. Without a doubt, he remained true to his mission of propagating believing criticism. While conducting historical critical studies, William Robertson Smith nevertheless adhered to almost all traditional Presbyterian doctrines and to the supernatural origin of the Christian faith (Glover 1954, 24). The development of his critical view on the Bible did not affect his sincere Christian convictions. The sermons he held as a preacher between 1871 and 1881 strongly support this conclusion. They "reveal a Smith who believed that Jesus had called him personally to the service of his kingdom" (Rogerson 1995, 145). As a consequence of the controversial public debate, Robertson Smith himself demanded a formal indictment against him by his church. In this way, he aimed to put an end to the charges against him. In 1877, after legal procedures within the Free Church, Smith was eventually suspended from the college at his own request (Beidelman 1974, 19–22). In May 1880, however, the General Assembly of the Free Church rejected his formal condemnation for heresy by a rather narrow margin (Maier 2009, 182).

This decision in favor of Robertson Smith could not really stop his opponents. In June 1880, his "Animal Worship and Animal Tribes among the Arabs and in the Old Testament" appeared in the *Journal of Philosophy*. This publication soon reignited the public agitation against him. The starting point of the article is the hypothesis of his friend John Ferguson McLennan (1827–1881).[7] In his social evolutionist writings, McLennan suggested that all societies pass through a totemic stage in which a tribe is named after an animal or a plant. The appropriate form of religion in the most ancient societies, according to McLennan, was this social institution of "totemism," further linked to matriliny and exogamy (Rivière 1995, 297). Robertson Smith was the first scholar to apply this speculative hypothesis to the Old Testament (Kuper 2016, 7). In his article, Robertson Smith combined McLennan's evolutionary thesis of "primitive societies" with the discussion of German orientalists on ancient Arab culture. In the text and references there frequently appear the names of German scholars such as Baudissin, Nöldeke, Osiander, and Sprenger. With regard to Hebraic literature more specifically, he quotes *De Gentibus et Familiis Judaeis*, the dissertation that Wellhausen had submitted in Göttingen in 1870 (Robertson Smith 1880, 471). The article offers a comparative view on data from Arabia and the Bible, a perfect match of his academic interests. In focusing on family, kinship, and marriage in the ancient Arab context, Robertson Smith delivered a sort of pilot article for his future work. Even more important, the text represents an interesting combination of German orientalism with Victorian religious evolutionism, tracing a historical path from so-called primitive religions to monotheism. Similar to the comparative studies of Julius Wellhausen, Robertson Smith tried to identify the religious ideas of ancient Israel by aiming to trace "their progressive enlightenment" toward monotheism (Kuper 2016, 7). Smith argued that Arabia had moved through a stage of totemism also visible among the tribes in "the land of Canaan" (Robertson Smith 1880, 475). The kinship practices condemned by the Hebrew prophets, according to him, were therefore "remnants of old usage, of an ancient system of kinship through women" (Robertson Smith 1880, 477). The article concludes that "the second commandment, the cardinal precept of spiritual worship, is explicitly directed against the very worship of the denizens of air, earth, and water which we have been able to trace out" (Robertson Smith 1880, 483). Consequently, Robertson Smith ends with the proposition that "it does not appear that Israel was, by its own wisdom, more fit than any other nation to rise above the lowest level of heathenism" (Robertson Smith 1880, 483).

Less than one month after the publication of Robertson Smith's essay in the *Journal of Philosophy*, a minister of the Free Church in Edinburgh directed a fierce attack against him in the Scottish press. The Rev. Georg Macaulay called upon the church authorities to prohibit Robertson Smith from exercising his functions as a minister and professor of the Free Church. For Robertson Smith's opponents, this article was further proof of his continuous undermining of "the morality, authority and integrity of the scripture" (Livingstone 2004, 2–3). Even worse, Macaulay accused him of "pollut[ing] the moral sentiments of the community" with his views (Livingstone 2004, 2–3). A year after the publication of "Animal Worship," on 24 May 1881, a clear majority vote of the General Assembly of the Free Church finally removed Robertson Smith from his chair of Hebrew and Old Testament studies at its college. The verdict did not deprive him of his status as a minister and would have allowed him to continue receiving his salary from the Free Church. However, while he remained a passive minister of the Church, Robertson Smith refused to continue receiving his salary (Maier 2009, 182–184).

In the summer of 1881, Robertson Smith accepted the co-editorship of the *Encyclopedia Britannica*, after having unsuccessfully applied for a chair in mathematics in Glasgow. He moved to Edinburgh, where he published his work on the Old Testament in two volumes: *The Old Testament in the Jewish Church* (1881a) and *The Prophets of Israel* (1882). The first book is a collection of thirteen lectures given during the first three months of the year 1881 in Edinburgh and Glasgow. In the preface to the first edition, Smith tells us that the "sustained interest" in critical biblical studies found its proof in the average attendance of these lectures being about eighteen hundred people (Robertson Smith 1892, ix).[8] In his first lecture, "Criticism and the Theology of the Reformation," he laid out his understanding of biblical criticism as "a branch of historical science" (1892, 1). This lecture nicely sums up his position as both a historicist scholar and a sincere Protestant believer. Smith declares his scientific approach as "the truly Protestant study of Scripture" and anchors its method in the Reformation (1892, 16). He explains to his audience the difference between an ordinary reading of the Bible and its scientific analysis. While an ordinary reading is, according to Robertson Smith, eclectic and devotional, the scholarly examination of the holy scriptures differentiates between the divine book and the human understanding of it. Robertson Smith's stress on the active role of human recipients already played a part in the theological work of Richard Rothe (Schaper 2008, 16). According to Robertson Smith, contemporary scholars address the historical nature of the Bible in the same way as scientific approaches explain the historical character of any other ancient book (Robertson

Smith 1892, 2–3). In this sense, the method of historical criticism does not need any special reference to the Bible, which also "bears the stamp of time" (Robertson Smith 1892, 16). In Robertson Smith's conclusion, therefore, the believing criticist does not know any "discordance between the religious and the scholarly methods of study" (Robertson Smith 1892, 18).

William Robertson Smith in Cambridge: Studies on Ancient Arabia

In the last phase of his career, William Robertson Smith held different positions at Cambridge University. On 1 January 1883, he was appointed as a reader to the Lord Almoner's Chair of Arabic at Cambridge. The appointment process was not a straightforward affair, but Robertson Smith's application was bolstered by the recommendations of a number of important European scholars such as de Goeje, Kuenen, de Lagarde, Nöldeke, and Wellhausen. In their testimonials, all these theologians and orientalists emphasized Smith's excellent knowledge of Arabic (Black and Chrystal 1912, 464–466). From the autumn of 1883, Robertson Smith was first a member of Trinity College and then an elected fellow of Christ's College in 1885. At Trinity College he met Sir James George Frazer (1854–1941), which marked the beginning of a very close friendly relationship between them (Philsooph 1995, 331). Drawing on the ideas of Edward Burnett Tylor (1832–1917), Frazer developed an evolutionary model according to which human history went through stages from magic via religion to science (Kohl 1997, 57). The contact with Frazer strengthened Robertson Smith's evolutionary historical approach. In February 1886, Robertson Smith applied for the vacant position of university librarian at Cambridge, which was much better paid than his professorship. However, alongside the continuing task of editing the *Encyclopedia Britannica*, managing a major university library certainly created a "double strain" for him (Maier 2009, 244).[9] Not surprisingly, these busy years went hand in hand with the gradual decline of his already fragile health. Therefore, it came as a relief when he finally assumed the position of the Sir Thomas Adam Chair of Arabic in 1889. William Robertson Smith died of spinal tuberculosis only five years later in Cambridge, on 31 March 1894, at the age of 47.

While at Cambridge University, Robertson Smith worked as an orientalist who remained a Protestant theologian and a Christian apologist at heart. His studies of Semitic languages and the cults of pagan Arabia were driven by the very same motivation as his work on the Bible. He employed the comparative study of Semitic religions as a tool to prove the divine nature of the holy scriptures. For Robertson Smith, the study of pre-Islamic Arabia became a comparative necessity in understanding God's plan of salvation through a hermeneutical process. With this motivation in mind, he had already begun taking lessons in Arabic from Paul de Lagarde in Göttingen in 1872. His Arabic language skills served as a means of proving wrong the more radical forms of criticism such as those espoused by scholars of the Tübingen and Leiden Schools. In sharp contrast to them, Robertson Smith wanted to show the special character of the revelation of the Old Testament through comparison with other Semitic texts. For him, perceiving Christianity as just another form of Semitic religion was an anathema (Rogerson 1995, 85).[10]

Robertson Smith described the purpose of his inquiry into the Old Testament as an attempt to show "the changing form and the permanent substance of prophecy" (Robertson Smith 1871, 266). In so doing, his history of religion was deeply shaped by the nineteenth-century Victorian notion of evolutionary progress (Whitelam 1995, 181). According to this philosophical trope, progress meant the historical evolution of religion from "primitive" to increasingly rationalized forms. From a profoundly Christian apologetic perspective, Robertson Smith addressed the history of mankind in terms of a possible scholarly reconstruction of the "objective process in which God was at work" (Rogerson 1995, 152). The Old Testament, as well as the ancient Semitic religions before it, were thus "preparations for Christ." Through the historical analysis of religious developments, he wanted to prove "God's plan of revelation and redemption" (Robertson Smith 1876, 347). In this effort, he embarked on Semitic studies primarily in his search for the spiritual foundations of Christianity. In Robertson Smith's understanding, Judaism, Christianity, and Islam were all "positive religions" (1903, 1). They were advanced monotheist religions consciously taught by "great religious innovators" (Robertson Smith 1903, 1). Anyone who seeks to discover the origins of these positive religions, according to Robertson Smith, must search for traces among older unconsciously transmitted religious traditions. Thus, the study of ancient Arabia was a mere necessity.

In 1885, Robertson Smith published *Kinship and Marriage in Early Arabia*. He again employed McLennan's general thesis of totemism. In the preface, Robertson Smith tells us that he wants to collect and discuss the available evidence for the existence of "the system which McLennan has expounded under the name of totemism" (Robertson Smith 1903, xiii). His hypothesis was that the Semites passed through a stage of totemism before they became separated into a southern and a northern branch. While the "primitive organization" of the northern Semites, for Robertson Smith in particular the Canaanites and the Arameans, changed early, the Arab tribes maintained totemism until the coming of Islam. Therefore, he concluded, research on totemism among the Semites must "always start from Arabia," where elements of "primitive religions" have survived (1903, 252–253).[11] This reconstruction of kinship in Arabia was an inherent part of Robertson Smith's comparative studies for the anthropological understanding of the Old Testament and the evolution of the Christian faith. The anthropological approach, in this endeavor, was a direct consequence of his friendship with McLennan and the adoption of the theory of totemism.

Robertson Smith invited several internationally known colleagues to contribute their knowledge to *Kinship and Marriage*. The book's purpose was to construct a hypothetical picture of the Arab social system "consistent with all the Arabian facts" (Robertson Smith 1903, xiii). The orientalists Goldziher, Nöldeke, and Wellhausen assisted him and contributed extra references to important texts (Black and Chrystal 1912, 483). Ignaz Goldziher participated in the first and second editions (1903) of the book.[12] In the new edition, he not only did the proof-reading but also added numerous notes to it. In his diary, Goldziher regretted that William Robertson Smith had preceded him in publishing about Arab family law before he himself was able to do so. Therefore, Goldziher wrote, he could not show that his studies comprised more subjects than Islamic jurisprudence (Goldziher 1978, 113). This support of leading orientalists, however, did not mean that they all shared Robertson Smith's theses.[13] The publication of *Kinship and Marriage* was "the most important result of his interaction with McLennan's work" (Schaper 2008, 18). The scientific evolutionism of the Scottish lawyer and ethnographer enabled Robertson Smith to fuse his Christian apologetic theological interests in a "progressive revelation" with some of the then contemporary scientific advances of the later nineteenth century (Schaper 2008, 18).

By far the most influential book by Robertson Smith, however, became his *Lectures on the Religion of the Semites*. First published in 1889, it comprised eleven lectures of which he delivered nine at the invitation of the Burnett Fund between October 1888 and October 1891 (Robertson Smith 1927, xiii). These lectures are a classic in the comparative study of religion, impacting strongly not only on Émile Durkheim, but on a far wider range of European anthropologists, psychologists, sociologists, and theologians. In this book, Robertson Smith continued his previous research on the pre-Islamic culture of Arabia, aiming at a reconstruction of the evolution of Judaism and Christianity from more ancient Semitic religious traditions (Warburg 1989, 44). According to Robertson Smith, we only can comprehend a system of positive religion if we "know the traditional religion that preceded it" (Robertson Smith 1927, 2). For him, the Semites built an ancient unity of nations comprising among others the Hebrews, the Arameans, and the Arabs, based "on the ground of similarity of language" (Robertson Smith 1927, 8). Through the "Semitic nations" runs a "close family likeness," and despite a very temporary "Hellenization," they did not experience a "permanent disturbance" of their original traits (Robertson Smith 1927, 12–13). Defining ancient religions not as systems of belief, but as certain public practices, Robertson Smith identified in the ritual of sacrifice the fundamental institution of ancient religion (Robertson Smith 1927, 27).

Building again on theories and methods from McLennan, Kuenen, and Wellhausen, Smith framed an evolutionary religious history in a sociological form, making him one of the founders of the modern sociology of religion (Beidelman 1974, 31–35, 68). Implicitly applying the conceptual dichotomy between tradition and modernity, Smith defined ancient religion as a holistic but unconscious social order, based on the mythological understanding of fundamental ritual practices. This definition later appears in a similar way in Émile Durkheim's (1922) description of "mechanical solidarity."[14] In this "rude form," according to Robertson Smith, primitive religion was a collectively binding moral force (Robertson Smith 1903, 53). After his dismissal from the chair at the Free Church College, Robertson Smith did not change his academic direction. He remained a theologian and continued unswervingly in his mission to reconcile Christian faith with modern scholarship. At Cambridge, however, he did so by excelling in oriental studies, once the "auxiliary field" of Christian theology (Rogerson 1995, 13). In so doing, Robertson Smith combined his philological studies with a strong anthropological interest, which is documented by his several journeys to the Middle East. From the time of his first trip to Cairo in 1878 to his last trip to Egypt in 1890, he traveled to Palestine, Syria, and the Arab Peninsula, as well as Algeria and Tunisia (Shiel 1995, 85).

In his analysis of tribal Arabia, Robertson Smith claimed that the "influence of religion over conduct was of no little use in the slow and difficult process of the consolidation of an orderly society out of barbarism" (Robertson Smith 1903, 64). In his account of pre-Islamic Arabia, Robertson Smith combined his theological reasoning with a "scientific" evolutionary approach, declaring Semitic rites to be the rudest and most visibly primitive in character (1903, 338). It is important to stress, however, that in his evolutionary approach he did not share the agnostic or even atheist attitudes of most Victorian sociocultural evolutionists such as Edward Burnett Tylor or Herbert Spencer (1820–1903). They propagated positivist science as a means of undermining the authority of the church. It was their common judgment "that institutional religion is by its very nature corrupt, inferior and inimical to personal religion" (Wheeler-Barcley 1993, 73), an attitude we previously observed in Julius Wellhausen's understanding of Christian religiosity and his staunch opposition to the Lutheran Church. William Robertson Smith, by contrast, continued on his path of scholarly enlightened Christian apologetics and supported Christianity's ecclesiastical institutions (Wheeler-Barcley 1993, 61). With his theory of a kind of gradual religious evolution, William Robertson Smith clearly repudiated Herbert Spencer's transformation of Darwin's naturalistic "survival of the fittest" in a theory of social evolutionism (Livingstone 2004, 15). Ironically, it was precisely Robertson Smith's application of evolutionary theory to the historical development of religious rituals and scriptures that provoked the campaign by the orthodox wing of the Free Church against him. Darwinism as a theory of natural evolution, however, was, after heavy initial criticism, rather quickly domesticated within the world of Scottish theological thought (2004, 9).[15]

Conclusions: Orientalist Studies in the Service of Christ

William Robertson Smith was a "major figure in the intellectual life of late Victorian Britain," and his work contributed in particular to the development of the disciplines of anthropology and the study of religion (Eriksen 2022, 118). Smith transferred the central ideas of three of Germany's most eminent Protestant theologians—Heinrich Ewald, Richard Rothe, and Albrecht Ritschl—to a British audience, once describing them as the "leading influences" on his career (Black and Chrystal 1912, 534–535). More significantly, Smith's work was instrumental in introducing the ideas of Germany's liberal Protestant theology into the conceptual apparatus of the social sciences and the humanities. The dominant theme throughout his life, however, was his Christian faith.

Right from the beginning of his career, he considered higher criticism to be merely a scholarly means that could never take from him his "personal fellowship with God in Christ" (Robertson Smith 1869, 134). William Robertson Smith was convinced that in the Bible "God and man meet" (1881a, 18). Following an apologetic mission, he used critical methods in order to discern in the holy scriptures the distinction between the "accidental and the essential, the human conjectures and the divine truth" (1881a, 5). At the individual level, Robertson Smith was able to reconcile the modern realms of scientific and religious communications. For him personally, reading the Bible as a scholar and as a devout Christian were two sides of the same coin. In doing so, however, Smith gave priority to religion. For him, "every new progress in biblical study must in the end make God's great scheme of grace appear in fuller beauty and glory" (1881a, 29). Nevertheless, his individual reconciliation of science and religion was torn apart at the structural level. The heresy affair and his dismissal by the Free Church may be interpreted in this way. In the discursive environment of Victorian Britain, he became the victim of the public boundary negotiations between scientific and religious claims. In the end, his scholarly career, taking him from being a Protestant theologian to an orientalist, was shaped by these societal negotiations of the nineteenth century.

This imprint of the times in which he lived characterizes Robertson Smith's academic studies too. In his concept of religion, I discern three different perspectives. In assigning religion a social origin, Robertson Smith contributed strongly to the scientific study of religion as a social phenomenon. In this sense, it is true that "...the anthropology of religion was from the first very largely an anthropology of the Bible" (Kuper 2016, 6). While this anthropological contribution has had a lasting effect, his philosophy of religion became increasingly questionable. Molded by Victorian evolutionism Smith applied a theory of religion from primitive (unconscious) to rationalized (conscious) forms. His history of religion, structured by universally applicable consecutive stages, anticipated features later incorporated by classical theories of modernization. To a certain extent these features also characterized Max Weber's thought and that of Ernest Renan, with whom we deal in the next chapter. Moreover, evolutionary ideas also appear among the founding fathers of Islamic studies—as we will see in later chapters of this book. Today, the study of religion considers these theories as flawed, in particular when constructed in a linear and universally applicable way. Finally, there is Robertson Smith, the Protestant believer and his theological concept of religion. His interpretation of religion as a personal fellowship with God in Christ is deeply molded by nineteenth-century Protestant thought. In particular, we can detect the subjectivation of the Christian faith as propagated by those leading German theologians whom Robertson Smith met during his various stays in Germany. It was this complex amalgam of theoretical elements that generated his "academic truths" rather than any "coercive framework," as Edward Said claimed.

Robertson Smith's specific theological concept of religion and his general Christian apologetic mission profoundly impacted his largely negative attitude toward Islam. To be sure, in his scholarly works, Islam plays a rather marginal role. In *Kinship and Marriage*, for instance, Smith only refers to the Prophet's changes to family law on a few pages in order to prove his theses about ancient Semitic rules.[16] Islam only comes into the foreground in his "Journey in the Hejaz" and in some of the short essays that he published in Scottish media. In those publications, Smith described Islam as a form of "organized hypocrisy," undoubtedly applying the perspective of a liberal but evangelical Protestant (Robertson Smith 1881b, 493). From this perspective, he perceived the "Muslim God" as too far from the worshipper and argued that in Islam, devotion degenerated into a formalistic system of "vain repetition" (Robertson Smith 1881b, 511). Based on his observations in the Hejaz, Robertson Smith concluded that Muslims were ignorant about their own faith, only knowing a "few formulas and prayers" (Robertson Smith 1881b, 567). It is obvious that he saw Islamic worship in sharp contrast to the sincere intimacy of his own relationship with Christ. While he assigned Islam a place among the historically advanced positive religions, when he viewed Muslim religiosity through the lens of his Protestant convictions, it nevertheless completely paled against the light of Christianity. Protestant religious individualism was definitely the standard against which Robertson Smith measured Muslim religiosity. When it comes to the Qur'an, we can additionally detect the impact of his dedication to historical criticism. Robertson Smith judged the role of the Qur'an according to his own critical reading of the Bible and the interpretation of the Old Testament, which he shared with Julius Wellhausen. Accordingly, he viewed the Qur'an as the major reason for the lack of "the most needful reformations" that needed to take place among Arabian people. In sharp contrast to the revolutionary content of the Bible, thus Robertson Smith's analysis, the Qur'an is a text that basically suits established Arabian conditions. This is because the Prophet Muhammad himself "largely accommodated his precepts to the natural prejudices of the Arab mind" (1881b, 567). For William Robertson

Smith, therefore, the holy scriptures of Islam were "the bulwark of all prejudices and social backwardness in the East" (1881b, 568).

In Robertson Smith's judgment on Islam, the biblical scholar and the Protestant apologist converged. Not surprisingly, he also perpetuated the conventional truism of the predominance of politics in Islam. This he claimed at least with regard to the Ottoman Islamic officials he met in the Hejaz (Robertson Smith 1881b, 490). Generally speaking, his travel accounts are peppered with stereotypes that match some of those in Said's *Orientalism* (1978). Over several pages, for instance, Robertson Smith very positively describes Ismail, "the confident servant" of his friend Mr. Wylde (1881b, 498). In his conclusion, however, he then admitted that he was "almost tempted to think him no Oriental at all" (Robertson Smith 1881b, 501). Yet, Robertson Smith continues that this would have been a very superficial judgment for somebody who clearly was in "his temperament, his ambitions, his enjoyments, his vanity [...] thoroughly Eastern" (1881b, 501). In the end, he concludes, "Arabs are simple people" who do not know law but only public opinion as is typical for people from "the East" (1881b, 532, 523). In his non-academic writings, "orientalist" dichotomies such as that between the East and the West are discernable; in the "ethnographies" of his Arabian travels, the scholarly minded Robertson Smith almost disappears. This does not mean that he was a racist in the sense of considering these dichotomies as essentialist in nature. He explicitly stated that Arabs and Muslims, in principle, could also make progress and overcome the "backwardness of the East." However, he considered that the way toward reform and a "freer attitude" in reading the Qur'an would only come via achieving "a better knowledge of the ethics and religion of the Western nations" (Robertson Smith 1881b, 568).

This proposition brings me to the last question of this chapter, how colonialism may have framed William Robertson Smith's studies. There is much evidence for his conviction that the civilizing mission of the British Empire was justified. In Ottoman rule Robertson Smith saw nothing more than organized "unprincipled intrigue" (Robertson Smith 881b, 490). His Arab companions in the Hejaz seemingly supported him in this view. According to Robertson Smith, in the eyes of the Arabs, the "hated rule of the Turks [...] is viewed as little better than organised robbery" (1881b, 487). Consequently, he interpreted Arab resistance against the "Ottoman yoke" as an Arab call for British supremacy: "The idea is certainly gaining ground that England is the country whose protectorate would be most acceptable and most fruitful in good results"

(Robertson Smith 1881b, 495). In comparison to the relative indifference of Wellhausen regarding German imperialist efforts, Robertson Smith clearly expressed support for the colonialist claims of the United Kingdom. But can we draw a direct line from this political support for the Empire to the motivation and purpose behind his academic work? Certainly not!

William Robertson Smith considered his scholarship definitely not to be in the service of British colonialism. In his academic work, colonial ambitions are completely absent. In the preface to the first edition of the *Lectures on the Religion of the Semites*, Smith clearly stated the reason behind his research: "A right understanding of the religion of the Old Testament is the only way to a right understanding of the Christian faith" (Robertson Smith 1927, xiv). This motivated his studies of both the Old Testament and Semite religion. If Robertson Smith worked in the service of anybody, then it was in the service of Christ. In any case, in content his scientific work on the Old Testament and on Arabia was completely useless for the justification of British colonialism. The findings of this chapter turn Said's description of Robertson Smith upside-down. Said styled the scattered Eurocentric, or better Christocentric, utterances made by Robertson Smith in the "Journey in the Hejaz" into the purpose of his academic studies, which supposedly only delivered "the cachet of additional authority" (Said 1978, 235). However, neither Robertson Smith nor Wellhausen conducted their scientific studies with an imperialist political purpose. At least my own examination of the life and work of these two scholars did not find any evidence to underpin Said's generalizing allegations. While Robertson Smith was deeply motivated by his theological mission, Wellhausen was driven by the hermeneutical exploration of historical pasts. Whether this conclusion also applies to Ernest Renan, in Said's understanding the most authoritative orientalist of the nineteenth century, the next chapter will show.

Notes

1 According to Pickering, it remains open what ultimately the "flash of insight" was that Durkheim received from his reading of Robertson Smith (Pickering 1984, 67–69) Margit Warburg claimed that Durkheim's *The Elementary Forms of Religious Life* is "permeated by Robertson Smith's principal ideas" (Warburg 1989, 55).

2 On biblical studies and higher criticism in Victorian Britain, see Riesen 1985 and Rogerson 1995.

3 Despite this fascination for Rothe's methods and personal piety, Robertson Smith never adopted the German theologist's anticlerical position regarding the church. For Robertson Smith, faith and church belonged together. The role of the church in Protestantism also divided him and Wellhausen.

4 For Ritschl, see also my comments in the previous chapter on Wellhausen.

5 It should be mentioned that Smith did not spread Wellhausen's theses uncritically. In his review of *Die Geschichte Israels*, he argued that Wellhausen owes most to Kuenen and Vatke, before delivering a brief but critical description of the book (Robertson Smith 1879). Against those who associate Wellhausen's account of the Pentateuch with a "revolutionary novelty," Robertson Smith rightly argued that Wellhausen had many "forerunners" in Germany and Holland, where the critical study of the Pentateuch was conducted by "the master hand of Kuenen" (Robertson Smith 1892, 227, fn. 1). In addition, it is necessary to mention that he was a representative of critical biblical studies in the tradition of the Graf–Kuenen–Wellhausen approach, whereas he clearly differed from them in his theological point of view and rejected their "purely rational explanation" of the development of Israel's religion (Houtman 2000, 233).

6 Toward the end of the nineteenth century, about 50,000 copies were sold in the UK and the USA (McCleery 2007, 301).

7 William Robertson Smith and McLennan were friends from when they met for the first time in the Edinburgh Evening Club in 1869. The Club consisted of artists, bankers, lawyers, physicians, and professors and existed for five years (Maier 2009, 73).

8 His *Prophets of Israel* was also based on a series of eight lectures which Robertson Smith gave in Edinburgh and Glasgow. These two series of lectures give a comprehensive picture of his work on the Old Testament. Their purpose was, according to him, "to expound [...] the problems and methods of modern criticism of the Old Testament, and so to enable the laymen of Scotland to follow with intelligence the controversy then occupying the Courts of the Free Church as to the right of criticism to assert itself within the Churches of Westminster Confession" (Robertson Smith 1882, xxiii).

9 Robertson Smith became the chief editor of the *Encyclopedia Britannica* after the death of Sir Thomas Spencer Baynes in 1887.

10 Robertson Smith did not limit his comparative endeavor only to texts. In his ethnographic account of his "Journey in the Hejaz," he frequently compares his observations with data from the Old Testament. A good example is his comparison between Bedouin warfare and the laws of Deuteronomy: "This [the Bedouins' rules of war] is a modification of the old ferocity of Semitic warfare in the same line as the law of war in Deuteronomy" (Robertson Smith 1880, 520).

11 In this idea we can see the impact of the theory of "survivals" on Robertson Smith, a notion which was fashionable among the early anthropologists in Victorian Britain. The argument here is that some of the social institutions of ancient societies have survived among the Bedouins of the Arab Peninsula and therefore can be observed in the present. Robertson Smith applied this theory to both his studies on the Old Testament and those on Semitic religions (Livingston 2004, 14).

12 Goldziher met Robertson Smith at the 6th International Congress of Orientalists in Leiden (1883) for the first time. While there, he had a dinner with him and Abraham Kuenen, which aptly illustrates the interaction among orientalists, Protestant theologians, and scholars of Islamic studies (Goldziher 1978, 95). In April 1897, Black offered Goldziher the opportunity to revise some of the articles by Robertson Smith for the Biblical Encyclopedia, which Goldziher declined due to overwork. In June 1897, however, Goldziher agreed to revise the new edition of *Kinship and Marriage* in order to pay his "tribute to the holy name of William Robertson Smith" (Goldziher 1978, 214, 217).

13 A good example of this critique is Theodor Nöldeke, who wrote a remarkable review of more than 40 pages on the book. He praised it as "unusually stimulating" and acknowledged significant similarities between his and Robertson Smith's basic views. The bulk of the article, however, is a detailed, source-based critique of Robertson Smith's arguments. In particular he criticized the generalizing application of "totemism" to the Arab tribes and the way in which Robertson Smith described Arab culture in the times of the Prophet Muhammad (Nöldeke 1886, 167, 171). More generally speaking, from the position of a historian, Nöldeke wanted to show that Robertson Smith's findings were not as safe as it might at first seem. In his eyes a historian and philologist should generalize less and not apply such a dogmatic construction as Robertson Smith had done with reference to McLennan's thesis (1886, 149). Ignaz Goldziher struck the same chord in his review of the book. Despite praising his Scottish colleague for his work, Goldziher argued that some of the generalizations and conclusions of the author went beyond what "the data could be used for when viewed in a cool light" (Goldziher 1887, 23).

14 In *De la division du travail social* (The Division of Labor in Society), Émile Durkheim defined modernization as the gradual transformation of mechanical societies to organic forms of solidarity. According to him, while mechanical societies were predominantly characterized by segmentation, organic societies had emerged from the moral validation of the division of labor. The collective consciousness of mechanical societies, thus Durkheim, rests on a rather rigid consensus of moral religious, and cognitive beliefs, whereas organic solidarity is characterized by the ideal of the moral cooperation of abstract individuals (Durkheim 1922).

15 For a brief overview of Darwin's reception within Scottish theology, see the section "Darwin in Scotland" in Livingstone 2004, 6–10.

16 Some of these essays are quoted by his biographers, see Black and Chrystal 1912; Maier 2009. In *Kinship and Marriage*, Robertson Smith's judgment on Islam is also rather negative. He argues, for example, that in spite of the improvement of the status of women by the Prophet Muhammad, their position in society has steadily declined. He acknowledges the efforts of the Prophet, but comes to the conclusion that in pre-Islamic Arabia "women moved more freely and asserted themselves more strongly than in the modern East" (Robertson Smith 1903, 121–122).

6 Ernest Renan: Theology and Orientalism in France

"Semitic was Renan's first creation, a fiction invented by him in the philological laboratory" (Said 1978, 141). There are very few experts on Ernest Renan who would endorse this assertion made by Edward Said. Of course, Renan was well known for his propagation of the "Aryan myth" (Poliakov 1974). This "scholarly" myth suggested that Indo-European culture was of a progressive nature, while the Semitic culture bore the opposite characteristic of being immobile in time and space. Accordingly, he claimed that it was therefore the Aryans who had contributed to the universal progress of human civilization, whereas Semites tended to be dissociated from this historical process (Olender 1992, 12). Renan built on this thesis in his *Histoire générale et système comparé des langues sémitiques* (1858). He argued that despite their invention of religious monotheism, Semites were devoid of any analytical spirit or creative imagination (Priest 2015b, 312). This idea of Indo-European cultural supremacy, however, was by no means the invention of Ernest Renan. The French thinker only made use of what had been shared in one form or another by a good many of the scholars in nineteenth-century Europe.[1] He basically delivered a culturally deterministic synthesis of different contemporary works on Semitic languages (Trautmann-Waller 2008, 175). His *Histoire générale* was also far from being the "chief instance" of the orientalist "scientific project" (Said 1978, 88). In assigning Renan this prime role in orientalist scholarship, Edward Said inflated the French scholar's real position far beyond what it really was in the academic world of the nineteenth century.[2] In fact, many of Renan's biographers do not even mention his contributions to oriental studies (Niewöhner 2000, 7). Of course, Renan took part in the scholarly discourse of European orientalists, but his work in this area did not hold high esteem among many of his peers. Renan's *Histoire général* therefore had very little impact on the development of orientalist scholarship (Tolan 2019, 227). Who then was Ernest Renan?

Frankly speaking, this question is difficult to answer. In the literature about Renan, we are often confronted with an "uncertain or fragmentary image" (Millepierres 1961, 8). The life and work of Renan was ambiguous, complex, and full of contradictions. Over time, his texts and lectures displayed "flagrant ambiguities of a political, religious and methodological character" (Noronha-DiVanna 2010, 70). Renan's biographer Harold Wardman, for instance, described him as a "mixture of prophet, visionary, reformer and spiritual leader" (Wardman 1964, 212). Apart from his reputation as an orientalist, Renan was known as an autobiographer, a historian, a moralist, a novelist, a philologist, a philosopher, and even as a poet (Lee 1996, 19; Peyre 1969, 22). Ernest Renan's eclectic body of thought shows, among other things, traces of Comte's positivism, Cousin's philosophical eclecticism, Franz Bopp's comparative grammar, German biblical criticism, German Idealism, and Spinoza's pantheism, as well as the influence of the works of the historian, poet, and politician Alphonse de Lamartine (1790–1869), the historian Jules Michelet (1798–1874), and the philosopher and mathematician Blaise Pascal (1623–1662) (Blinkenberg 1923). Not surprisingly, Julius Wellhausen once described Renan as somebody who easily could come up with something to say on just about any topic (Smend 2013, 385).[3] Snouck Hurgronje echoed this judgment in a letter to Ignaz Goldziher in 1884, emphasizing Renan's ability to reproduce what others have already said in a "beautiful and original way" (van Koningsveld 1985b, 38). Indeed, Ernest Renan wrote on history, philosophy, politics, and religion in general, and about the culture and social politics of France and Europe in particular. In these writings, he oscillated between positivism and Romanticism, royalism and democracy, scientism and Christian belief, quite ambiguous positions that were reflected in Renan the "republican by association, atheist by implication, Protestant by marriage, and Bonapartist by employment" (Priest 2015a, 61).

As a French public intellectual, Renan reached out to large audiences among educated Europeans. In the second half of the nineteenth century, he became a writing celebrity in France. As a scholar, however, his reputation was often disputed and could hardly be said to match his fame in the public sphere. This applies in particular to the previously mentioned thesis on the stagnant Semitic mind. It is true that scholars such as Kuenen, Robertson Smith, and Wellhausen shared with Renan the idea of the Semites as a single people united by language (Pasto 1998, 468). Yet they criticized or even refuted the application of his determinist theory of the "Semitic mind." We can count Heinrich Ewald, Ignaz Goldziher, Abraham Kuenen, Max Müller, William Robertson Smith, and Heymann Steinthal among the most prominent critics of Renan in this regard (Robertson 1924, 33).[4] In a long review in the *ZDMG*, Steinthal (1823–1899) delivered a devastating critique of Renan's *Histoire générale*. The German philologist and founder of the journal *Zeitschrift für Völkerpsychologie und Sprachwissenschaft* (*Journal for Folk Psychology and Linguistics*) strongly questioned the conceptual, linguistic, methodological, and philosophical qualifications of his French colleague (Steinthal 1857).[5] In his memorial speech on the death of Renan, "Renan as Orientalist," Ignaz Goldziher expressed this criticism in a more benevolent manner (Goldziher 1893). He praised Renan for his synthesis of Semitic philology in *Histoire générale*, while criticizing him for his misguided ideas on Aryan and Semitic cultures. He excused the scholarly shortcomings in Renan's works by pointing to their literary merit. Goldziher presented Renan more as an artist than as a scientist.[6] Elevating Ernest Renan to the role of a leading scientific authority in orientalist and Semitic studies may have suited *Orientalism*'s polemic intentions, but this was far from being a sober description of the realities of nineteenth-century scholarship.

In this chapter, I put my focus on Renan's struggle with the competing imperatives of the religious and scientific spheres of modern life. Furthermore, I look at the role that he played in shaping the modern image of Islam. My own story about Renan will necessarily be of a fragmented nature too. The complexities of Renan's work and his eclectic intellectual positions make it impossible to do him justice in one chapter. In the following, however, I will argue that Said did not get it all wrong. While it is Said's invention that Renan played a foundational role in the field of oriental studies, it is nevertheless true that Renan contributed strongly to the dissemination of "orientalist" stereotypes. This applies in particular to the pejorative image of Islam in Renan's texts, which impacted European perceptions of the Muslim religion. If we wish to gain a more precise understanding of this impact, it would be wrong to turn to his *Histoire générale* as a source. Instead, we should analyze his bestseller, *Vie de Jésus* (*The Life of Jesus*), and the public lecture "L'Islamisme et la science" ('Islam and Science'), which he gave at the Sorbonne in 1883.[7] These two sources provide a clear picture of his pejorative view on Islam. My first step here is to put Renan's biography in its intellectual and historical contexts. I then look at Renan's representation of Christianity, for which I turn to his studies of the Bible and his *Vie de Jésus* as my primary sources. The third section, then, will deal with the image of Islam that he disseminated in the broader public. In the conclusion, I will discuss the findings of this chapter together with those on Wellhausen and Robertson Smith and make some observations to conclude the second part of this book.

From Brittany to Paris: Biblical Criticism and Renan's Crisis of Faith

Ernest Renan came from a modest, rural social background. He was born on 28 February 1823 in the village of Tréguier in Brittany. The family of his father, Philibert Renan, was in fishing and coastal shipping, while his mother, Magdelaine Féger-Lasbleiz was the daughter of a respected trading family of the town of Lannion. After their marriage, the couple took over the grocery store of Alain Renan, the grandfather of Ernest (Millepierres 1961, 14–16). In his early childhood, it was especially his elder sister Henriette who took care of him. Philibert Renan died at sea near Saint-Malo in 1828 under mysterious circumstances, leaving the family in an economically desperate situation (1961, 22–23). The experiences of his childhood, the culture of Brittany, and traditional Catholicism apparently molded the personality of Renan decisively (Lasserre 1926). His educational path took him through several Catholic institutions, where he impressed his teachers enormously and was awarded a number of school prizes. In 1838, the later Bishop of Orléans (1849–1878), Abbé Dupanloup (1802–1878), awarded him a scholarship. The fifteen-year-old Renan left Tréguier to study theology at the Catholic seminaries of Saint-Nicolas-du-Chardonnet, Izzy, and finally Saint-Sulpice in Paris. Ernest Renan clearly was on his way to taking up an ecclesiastical position in the Catholic Church. However, at Saint-Sulpice he experienced a fundamental crisis of faith and decided to leave the seminary and the Catholic Church in 1845 (Millepierres 1961, 39–106).

The literature on Renan unanimously points to this "religious crisis" of his youth when seeking to understand his work on the individual level. Although this crisis eventually occurred at the seminar in Saint-Sulpice, the process leading to it must have started some years before, possibly when he was studying at Izzy. There, he made his first acquaintance with the ecclesiastical physicist Abbot Pinault (1793–1870) and his *Traité élémentaire de physique* (Elementary Treatise of Physics). This work by Pinault represented a turning point for the young Renan, raising in him an essential question concerning the priority of science or faith (Fayolle 2019, 286). Important in his intellectual formation was also his reading of German authors such as Hegel, Herder, Kant, and Mommsen, and of rationalist Protestant theology, including David Friedrich Strauss and the Tübingen school (Noronha-DiVanna 2010, 72–78).

At Saint-Sulpice, Renan's personal negotiations between the different truths of science and religion became more pronounced by the encounter with his teacher of Hebrew and classical languages, Arthur-Marie Le Hir (1811–1868). Renan found in Le Hir his ideal of the combination of being both a "scholar and a saint." Le Hir, like Renan also from Brittany, analyzed the Bible as a historical book by human authors using critical methods, comparing the holy scriptures with the poems of Homer for his students (Millepierres 1961, 83). The young Renan was enthusiastic about this combination of German criticism with Semitic philology. The teachings of Le Hir made Renan a convinced and critical philologist (Renan 1936, 210). While the *Traité élementaire* had furnished him with a first model of scientific thought, now philology replaced physics and the natural sciences (Fayolle 2019, 287–288). At Saint-Sulpice he fully engaged in studying Hebrew as the necessary means for a sound historical understanding of the Bible. Moreover, Renan began to learn German in order to directly access the most sophisticated critical exegesis of the Bible that was available at that time. In stark contrast to Le Hir, however, he was no longer able to reconcile the scholarly study of Christianity with the dogmas of the Catholic Church. His philological approach to the Bible increasingly came at odds with the traditional Catholic dogmas about the Christian revelation (Lee 1996, 68). In his critical reading of the holy scripture, Renan came to the conclusion that the text was full of contradictions, historical inaccuracies, and factual mistakes. His studies at Saint-Sulpice consequently undermined his belief in the supernatural origins of the doctrines of the Roman Catholic Church. He now found he had to separate from the Catholic Church he had once so loved (1936, 219).

Ernest Renan apparently could not stand the tension between religious belief and scientific truths. The path Robertson Smith chose of living scholarship and orthodox belief in harmony did not work for the French intellectual. Starting with his rationalist doubt of miracles, Renan increasingly began to refute the supernatural claims of Christianity more generally (Millepierres 1961, 81).[8] For him, the solution to this fundamental crisis demanded a choice between modern scholarship and Catholicism. In October 1845, Renan left the seminary of Saint-Sulpice and only some weeks later the Catholic Church. His life-long mission now became the reconciliation of reason and a faith without supernatural beliefs. On this path, Renan developed a philosophy of history in which science took on an almost divine role (Michaelis 1913, 101). After breaking with his ecclesiastical career, Renan initially resided as an independent boarder at M. Crouzet's boarding house for boys. At "Pension Crouzet," he paid 30 francs for board and lodging and was in turn paid for providing an hour and a half of revision lessons in Greek and tuition in mathematics to secondary students in the evening. This left him with plenty of time to pursue his own intellectual interests throughout the rest of the day (Millepierres 1961, 112–113). Finalizing his Bachelor of Arts in 1846, Renan received the Volney prize for an essay on Semitic languages in April 1847. In the same year, he became a member of the Société Asiatique (Asian Society) on the recommendation of the Indologist Eugène Burnouf (1801–1852).[9] Furthermore, he studied comparative religion under Burnouf and Persian under Ètienne Marc Quatremère (1782–1857). Quatremère was a previous student of Silverstre de Sacy and a renowned professor of Persian and Semitic language at the School for Oriental Languages in Paris.[10]

Between autumn 1848 and spring 1849, Renan wrote *L'Avenir de la science* (*The Future of Science*). The book advocates science as a means of establishing order and moral power for humanity (Renan 1890; Robertson 1924, 22–23). Renan's senior mentors, Eugène Burnouf and the historian Augustine Thierry (1795–1856), however, advised him against its publication. Thus, as a full book, Renan's "divination of science" did not appear before the year 1890. This book is an expression of the inherent consistency of Renan's worldview. In the preface to the official publication, he describes the book as confirmation of the continuity of the fundamental idea that had accompanied his career since Saint-Sulpice: his belief in the progress of reason that replaced his Catholic faith (Renan 1890).[11] Renan wrote *L'Avenir de la science* in the positivist spirit of nineteenth-century French scholarship. This form of positivism, however, should not be confused with its narrow technical meaning of today. Positivist scholars such as Auguste Comte (1798–1857) were convinced that rational faith in modern science would gradually replace irrational religious beliefs (Plé 1996, 11, 447). From this perspective, positivism was a kind of innerworldly faith in the power of human welfare, civilizational progress, and science (LeGouis 1997, 28).[12] In October 1849, Renan then went to Italy on a government mission to classify historical manuscripts previously inaccessible to French scholars. After his return to Paris in 1850, he accepted a position at the Department for Oriental Manuscripts of the Bibliothèque National to make a modest living. In addition, he completed his philosophical doctoral thesis on the Islamic philosopher Ibn Rushd (1126–1198)—*Averroès et l'averroïsme*—in August 1852. Written under the supervision of the French philosopher and educational reformer Victor Cousin (1792–1867), Renan's thesis found almost no resonance among his orientalist colleagues (Irwin 2006, 167).[13]

After leaving Saint-Sulpice, it was once again Renan's sister Henriette who supported him financially and in his work. From her position as a "free thinker," she also encouraged him in severing his ties with the Catholic Church. In the 1850s, the siblings lived and worked together on some of Renan's projects for a few years (Priest 2015a, 40). In 1856, Renan married Cornélie Scheffer (1830–1894), the niece of the Dutch-French painter Ary Scheffer (1795–1858). The marriage to this "educated, literate young woman" from a well-off Protestant family gave Renan access to new social circles in Paris. Later, Cornélie took over from Henriette the task of copying and editing his works (Priest 2015a, 41–42). In October 1860, his Parisian social connections led to Renan being entrusted with an archaeological mission to Phoenicia. The Emperor Napoleon III (1852–1870) sponsored this expedition, which brought Renan to Lebanon and Palestine. On this mission to Phoenicia, he collected Semitic inscriptions and bolstered his scholarly profile in order to pursue an application for the position of the chair in Hebrew at the Collège de France (Renan 1862b). The position had remained vacant since the death of Ètienne Quatremère in 1857 (Priest 2015a, 48).[14] Henriette accompanied him on his trip to the Middle East but died of Malaria in Byblos, Lebanon, on 24 September 1861 (2015a, 49).

After his return from Lebanon, Renan reached the pinnacle of his scholarly career with his appointment to the Chair of Hebrew, Chaldean, and Syriac at the prestigious Collège de France. However, due to the uproar around his inaugural lecture in February 1862, he was suspended from his post only four days later. Renan's suspension was instigated by the Catholic establishment, which was scandalized by the following passage on Jesus in his inaugural lecture: "A man so great that, although in this place everything ought to be judged from the standpoint of positive science, I should not wish to contradict those who, impressed by the unique character of his achievement, call him God" (quoted in Robertson 1924, 38). The highly critical response of conservative circles and the Catholic establishment to his forthcoming publication of *Vie de Jésus* (1863) subsequently made his reinstatement impossible. In June 1864, his position as chair at the Collège de France was finally canceled by ministerial decree (Wardman 1964, 84). Before regaining his professorship after the collapse of the Second Empire in November 1870, Renan was living by his pen. From December 1864 to June 1865, he and his wife traveled throughout Egypt, Syria, Asia Minor, and Istanbul (Wardman 1964, 94–96). Consequently, it would be wrong to portray him as a stereotypical Saidian "orientalist" whose knowledge was a "shimmering fantasy" that "depended on absence."[15] As we will see, his travel experiences in the Middle East had an impact on his work. In 1878, Renan was elected to the Académie française, and in June 1883, he was appointed administrator of the Collège de France. Although Pope Pius IX called him "the European blasphemer" (Robertson 1924, 81), Renan enjoyed high prestige and strong influence in the intellectual life of France and beyond (Wardman 1964, 169). Ernest Renan died on 2 October 1892 at the age of 69, and received a state funeral in Paris (Euchner 1996, 46–49; Lee 1996, 277–79; Robertson 1924, 1–39).

Vie de Jésus: Spiritual Scandal and Literary Success

When defining the grand academic project of Renan the scholar, we must look at the seven volumes of his *Histoire des origines du Christianisme* (History of the Origins of Christianity).[16] Beginning with *Vie de Jésus* in 1863, Renan published seven volumes plus an index, the last appearing in 1883. In addition, under the title *Histoire du peuple d'Israël* (The History of the People of Israel), he wrote five books based on his studies of the Old Testament. It was for this work on the Bible, Christianity, and Judaism that Renan's philological expertise proved to be most instrumental (Peyre 1969, 14). In this respect, he was highly representative of the group of scholars to which Julius Wellhausen and William Robertson Smith also belonged. He was a "classical orientalist" in the sense of being primarily interested in the Bible and Christianity. His reception among his peers, however, was rather cold. In his review of *Histoire du peuple d'Israël*, Robertson Smith, for instance, accused Renan of bending all the available historical facts. While the arguments of the critical historians of Germany and Holland were governed by "laborious analysis and evaluation of the sources," Robertson Smith saw Renan's conclusions as based entirely on his own imaginative view (Robertson Smith 1887, 609, 616). Even Edward Said mentioned this "savage attack" by Smith.[17] Severe criticism of this nature leveled against Renan was even more pronounced in the scholarly responses to *Vie de Jésus*.

In *Vie de Jésus*, we meet Jesus of Nazareth as a figure with contradicting faces. He is a rational *savant* (learned) and a bearer of romantic stereotypes at the same time (Pitt 2000, 93, 100). In Renan's reconstruction of the life of Jesus, he presents us with a man who is embedded in romantic primitivism while at the same time being a man of reason. Paradoxically, the Semitic "noble savage" of Galilee (Manuel 1962, 10) was able to spark a universal process of progress. On the one hand, we encounter Jesus in the form of a naïve peasant: the rustic man from Galilee who lived in perfect harmony with the "gentle and peaceable society" around him. Renan's Jesus was deeply rooted in a natural environment that had escaped the impact of worldly civilization in the Greek sense. This terrestrial paradise, according to Renan, is reflected in the idea of the Kingdom of God (Renan 1863, 83, 92). On the other hand, the rational genius of Jesus made him the founder of an undogmatic religion. In the miracles of Jesus Renan discerned the mere popular conceptions of his social environment. They were an imposition of the peasant culture of Galilee, a kind of "violence done to him by his age" (1863, 144). In order to satisfy the dominant ideas of the community, Jesus let the people believe in the revealed character of his power and his resulting superiority over them (1863, 97). In Jesus' pronounced rejection of any kind of dogmatism, however, Renan saw the dream of a comprehensive social revolution (1863, 84).[18] In his construction of the ambiguous character of Christ, Renan built his narrative on an evolutionary history of universal progress intertwined with his understanding of Christianity as a "pure religion." To purge the Christian faith of its supernatural pretensions, Renan propagated a "secularized" form of radical Christian rationalism (Olender 1992, 77).

Ernest Renan's book became the most popular biography of Jesus ever written. Published in 1863, more than 66,000 copies had been printed within the first six months (Baird 1992, 376). The book was both "a massive commercial success and a spiritual scandal" (Hanna 2015, 23). With the publication of *Vie de Jésus*, Renan left the restricted world of academic scholarship and moved into the much broader realm of the general reader. The book appeared in fifteen editions within thirteen years. A more scholarly first edition was followed by a series of popular reprints in various languages. By 1947, *Vie de Jésus* had been published in 84 translations across twelve languages (Perrine 2007, 65). Due to its poetic style, Renan's book achieved the status of a classic in French literature (Robertson 1924, 40). In fact, it ranked second on the list of most popular books directly behind *Les Misérables* by Victor Hugo (1802–1885) (Perrine 2007, 65).

In his biography of Christ, Renan built on a reversed evolutionary perspective of the philosophy of history that characterizes his *L'Avenir de la science*. In *Vie de Jésus*, he replaced the deification of science by the secularization of Christ. Similar to *Das Leben Jesu* by David Friedrich Strauss, published three decades earlier, Renan's book presented Jesus as a mere historical being.[19] Not surprisingly, this humanization of Christ triggered a massive controversy in Catholic France as well. The Catholic clergy heavily condemned the book, instructing their congregations "not to read, own, or borrow it" (Hanna 2015, 24). Pope Pius IX (1846–1878) placed it on the Index of Prohibited Books within a month after its first publication.[20] The Catholic establishment in France simply accused Renan of blasphemy (Perrine 2007, 66). Against this vociferous reaction of the Catholic clergy, the French liberal press "consistently proclaimed Renan an Icon of free expression," and the sheer number of pamphlets and overwhelming variety of responses to the book were themselves "a testament to the strength of the Renanian challenge" (Priest 2015a, 152). Similar to the response that the article "Bible" caused for Robertson Smith, the publication of *Vie de Jésus* caused a public uproar that ultimately cost Renan his professorship at the Collège de France. The magnitude of this public controversy becomes palpable in the fact that it was the Emperor Napoleon III himself who sent Renan a letter of suspension from his chair, writing: "Indeed, as you will understand, it is impossible for the State to tolerate in a public teaching chair the denial of one of the foundations of the Christian religion."[21]

In stark contrast to the public success of his book, the scholarly reception of *Vie de Jésus* was anything but impressive. The resonance of Renan's book in the German Protestant milieu was extremely weak. Ironically, Renan's image of Jesus unquestionably reflected core arguments of German Protestant biblical criticism. His book presented Jesus in a similar way to the idealized understanding of the prophets of the Old Testament reflected in Wellhausen's studies. In fact, German Protestantism in the nineteenth century was generally receptive to biographies of Jesus Christ.[22] Yet not to this first "Catholic" version. German Protestants tended to see Renan's biography of Jesus as a poetic work laced with undeniable traces of Roman Catholicism (Nowak 1998).[23] German Protestant scholars clearly did not like the "disarming beauty and simplicity" of Renan's narrative (Pitt 2000, 91). A good example for this negative reception in Germany is the brief reference that Friedrich Nietzsche made to Renan. In his *The Antichrist* (1902), Nietzsche referred to his previous enthusiasm regarding the work of David Friedrich Strauss. In his youth, he had been interested in the contradictions of religious traditions, but now he took his scholarship too seriously to engage with that kind of literature. Moving to Renan, Nietzsche described the French scholar as a "psychological buffoon" ("*Hanswurst in psychologicis*"), stating that Renan's portrayal of Jesus as both a genius and a hero was just outrageous (Nietzsche 1902, 397–398).[24] In terms of serious biblical scholarship, however, it was probably Albert Schweitzer (1875–1965) who made the most devastating judgment. In his seminal volume on research on the life of Jesus, he denied *Vie de Jésus* any right to being considered an example of critical biblical research. For Schweitzer, Renan simply wrote a very successful but tasteless piece of "Christian art" (Schweitzer 1913: 182).

The condemnation of *Vie de Jésus* by German scholars did not stop the success of the book. On the contrary, the avalanche of critical responses to Renan apparently enhanced its popularity. According to Robert Priest, it was precisely the hybridity of the story, combining "so many diverse strands in contemporary culture," that made the book so prominent among "such a broad range of audiences" (2015a, 69). Ernest Renan applied the historical perspective of scholars such as the historians Thierry and Burckhardt to the life of Jesus in order "to describe the intellectual and spiritual evolution of Christianity from contemporary Jewish messianic beliefs." In this process, Priest argued, the "world-historical 'great man'" was able to "transcend and transform the context from which he emerged" (Priest 2015a, 79–80). If we wish to gain a better insight into the motivation and aims behind the work of Renan, Edward Said's narrative is not really of any help. It is the author of *Vie de Jésus* on whom we should put our analytical focus. Attempting to understand the "personality of Christ" was a "perpetual fascination" throughout Renan's career (Pitt 2000, 89). We can retrace Renan's preoccupation with the life of Jesus to the young seminarian at Izzy and throughout his integration into the philological academic life of Paris, which "culminat[ed] in his appointment to the Collège de France" (Priest 2015a, 67). But how could the Semite Jesus become a genuine innovator for humanity as such?

The answer to this question Renan gave in the first chapter of *Vie de Jésus*. Indeed, as "the chief scientific sponsor of the Aryan Myth in France" (Poliakov 1974, 206), Renan was forced to explain the paradox of how a Semite could take over such a world-historical role. Theoretically, Renan considered religion to be an anthropological constant. In his eyes religiosity differentiated humanity from all other living species. The universal achievement of Semitic culture in human civilization was to push it toward monotheism. In this way, Semites contributed to the formation of "the religion of humanity" (Renan 1863, 29). This civilizational development, however, was only possible in the move from Semitic Judaism to Indo-European Christianity. In this process, Jesus became the switchman.

The confused mixture of culture that was Judaism was only put on a systematic track by this great man Jesus. It was the interpretation of Hebrew culture by this "incomparable man, to whom the universal conscience has decreed the title of Son of God" (1863, 35). For Renan, the agency of Jesus freed Christianity from its Semitic bonds. Only through the work of this, in Renan's eyes, greatest son of man ever born was Christianity able to emerge from Judaism by becoming fully immersed in the Indo-European culture of the Greek and Roman worlds (1863, 2). In severing monotheism from its oriental cultural bonds, Christ was able to proclaim a "religion of humanity that was established not upon blood but upon the heart" (1863, 124). Only by drawing heavily on the then contemporary theme of the "world-historical 'great man'" (Priest 2015a, 80; Renan 1863, 24) could Renan reconcile his cultural determinism with a history of religious evolution.

The literature on Renan is almost unanimous in its assessment that Ernest Renan partly portrayed himself in his figure of Jesus Christ. According to Harold Wardman, he created an alternative "messianic religion of progress with himself as its God" (Wardman 1964, 212). Robert Priest underlined the role of "current debates about history, religion, and politics" in *Vie de Jésus* (2015a, 69). For him, the personality of Renan's Jesus was "a narcissistic cipher for the author" in the context of these debates (2015a, 106). Alan Pitt argued that Renan perceived his own attachment to the new faith of scientism as synonymous with Christ's turning away from Judaism (Pitt 2000, 89). According to Pitt, Renan embodied the new individualism of his generation in Christ, "placing God inside the individual" (Pitt 2000, 97), a kind of individualism which Renan reclaimed for himself in his romantic, self-conscious aestheticism (Blinkenberg 1923, 203). Blinkenberg ended his study with the conclusion that Renan's perfect human being is himself (1923, 204). Renan proclaimed Jesus Christ to be the unchallenged foundational figure of a religion of humanity that evolved from Christianity. Consequently, in the end his own apostasy remained incomplete. Regarding "Christianity's foundation as the most important event in history and its founder as history's noblest product" (Lee 1996, 269), Renan actually revealed himself to be a Christian apologist at heart.

Ernest Renan on Islam: The "Resurrection of Judaism in its Exclusively Semitic Form"

In his essay "Origines de la Bible" (The Origins of the Bible) Ernest Renan acknowledged the work of Kuenen, Reuss, Graf, and Wellhausen while at the same time subjecting them to a critical assessment. For the French scholar their work was not definitive. In his eyes, the German Protestants "lacked taste, the habit of appreciation of comparative literature, and a complete understanding of the Orient and antiquity" (Renan 1886, 5). The stiffness of their exegesis, according to Renan, reveals the theologians in them who worked in too closed a space without the necessary contact with the learned world outside Protestant theology (Renan 1886, 5). More than twenty years later, Renan was apparently getting even for the negative reception that his *Vie de Jésus* had received at the hands of German Protestant scholarship. Renan's critique, however, cannot hide the indebtedness of his work to German Protestant theology. He also framed the narrative of *Vie de Jésus* along the Graf–Kuenen–Wellhausen thesis. The Galilean great man put an end to the "legalistic degeneration" these scholars detected in the Pentateuch and thus to his religious commitment to Judaism (Pasto 1998, 447; see also Renan 1863, 30–32). In Renan's book, Jesus resolves the alleged contradictions in the religious history of Israel by reconnecting monotheism with the individualistic spirit of the early Hebrew prophets. Moreover, Renan shared some of the core theoretical premises on which also Wellhausen and Robertson Smith grounded their studies. The narrative of *Vie de Jésus* builds on a similar vision of evolutionary progress from paganism to monotheism and its universal realization in Christianity. In his concept of a "pure religion," we can detect elements of apologetic Protestant theologies framing Christianity in terms of a historically particular religion with a universal potentiality.

In addition, Renan's philosophy of history is reminiscent of the ideas of the Protestant French historian and conservative statesman François Guizot (1787–1874). In his *Histoire générale de la civilization en Europe* (General History of Civilization in Europe), Guizot narrated the history of European civilization as a constant process with France at its center. Employing diverse intellectual sources such as Calvinism, French social thought, German Idealism, and Romanticism, Guizot saw a divine plan in the continuous progress of European civilization. Due to the Christian unity of Europe, thus the core argument of his *Histoire générale*, European diversity evolved into a cultural totality. In addition, in Guizot's view, human civilization was realized in Christianity (Guizot 1828).[25] Although Guizot was a fierce opponent of French positivism (Plé 1996, 100 ff.), positivist speculations about civilizational progress in the nineteenth century appear to be compatible with his apologetic theory of a Christian modernity.[26] In Renan's work, too, there was no doubt about the absolute supremacy of Christianity in the history of humanity: "The world will be eternally religious, and Christianity, in a broad sense, is the last word in religion (Renan 1860, 27).[27] It was this Christocentric conviction of the meanwhile agnostic Renan on which he based his judgment on Islam and on Muslims more generally.

Vie de Jésus played an important role in disseminating Renan's pejorative image of Islam. Although the story of the book takes place long before the foundation of Islam, Renan refers to the Muslim religion in some places. In his inaugural lecture at the Collège de France, he had already declared Islam to be the contemporary expression of the original *ésprit sémitique* (the Semitic spirit). In his lecture he stated that it was this spirit that makes Muslims the "other" of Europeans. Renan characterizes Islam through its "religious fanaticism, its disdain for science, and its suppression of civil society," claiming that Islam simply represents the complete negation of Europe (Renan 1862a, 198). In their ways of thinking and feeling, according to Renan, Europeans and Muslims have nothing in common (1862a, 188). In his speech, Renan admits that the Jews and the Arabs were the dominant trading powers in the Middle Ages (1862a, 192). He even points to the military superiority of the Muslim empires (1862a, 197). Yet, the Europeans were able to change this power relation and they do not owe anything to the Semites, despite their religion (1862a, 193). While the origin of Christianity is in Judaic monotheism, the Christian religion became "less and less Jewish" over time. The progress of Indo-European people is the result of their moving further and further away from the Semitic spirit. Therefore, the future belongs only to Europe and it will conquer the whole world (1862a, 198).

The biography of Jesus by Renan was predicated on these axioms. In his bestseller, he used Islam in terms of "the other" of Christianity. Renan presented Islam as the fundamental opposite to Christianity in perpetuating the Semitic mind in its purest form. In explaining the anti-Christian character of Jerusalem, for instance, Renan refers to Islam as "a form of resurrection of Judaism in its exclusively Semitic form" (1863, 121). In his interpretation, Jerusalem fundamentally differed from the idyllic character of the Galilee countryside with its "energetic, brave, and hardworking people" (Renan 1863, 56). He described Jerusalem and its environment as the presumably "saddest country in the world," completely dominated by the religious fanaticism and pedantry of the Pharisees (1863, 56). In following the "purely barbarous, un-mitigatedly [sic] absurd" science of the Jewish doctors—"denuded of all moral elements"—the Pharisees were the predecessors of the "empty science" that, according to Renan, the Muslims had learned from their Jewish predecessors. He accused both Jewish and Muslim scholars of a shared "contempt for Greek culture" and therewith "European civilization" (1863, 118). In Renan's conceptual world the distinction between Christianity and Islam, between Galilea and Jerusalem, between Europe and Muslims was determined by the organizing power of the Aryan myth.

The French biographer of Jesus simply declared that Muslims and Jews had never understood Christ's "delightful theology of love." For them, the "God of humanity" remained unknown (Renan 1863, 62). They were prisoners of the stagnant nature of the Semitic mind. In the foundation of Christianity only Jesus was able to escape the stifling confines of Semitic culture, preparing the civilizing path toward a universal religion of humanity. In comparing Jesus with other religious figures, Renan invigorated the classical Christian stereotype by describing Muhammad's prophecy as some kind of morbid epilepsy (1863, 143).[28] Consequently, for Renan, Islam everywhere bears something "sordid and repulsive about it" (1863, 27). *Vie de Jésus* contains an utterly negative picture of Islam in which Renan draws on his theory of cultural determinism together with established stereotypes about Muslims, Islam, and the Prophet Muhammad. Significantly, he underpins these stereotypes with the authority of the eyewitness. Due to his travels in the Eastern Mediterranean, Renan was able to establish authority through the argument of "having been there." Already in the introduction to *Vie de Jésus* he emphasizes that his knowledge not only relies on the philological analysis of documents alone, but also on his having personally "seen the places where the events occurred" (Renan 1863, 23). He informs his readers that he has "traversed, in all directions, the land of the Gospels." As he did so, he observed the "striking agreement of the texts with the places" (Renan 1863, 23). On his scientific mission to Phoenicia, he had before his eyes "a fifth Gospel" (1863, 23). The eyewitness Renan, therefore, could claim that beautiful Galilea had meanwhile become a sad country "through the ever-impoverishing influence of Islamism" (1863, 56).

These examples may suffice to show that *Vie de Jésus* contained a parallel narrative on Islam too. This extremely pejorative narrative Renan disseminated broadly through the enormous success of his book. This image of Islam was by no means the result of erudite oriental studies. Most of his knowledge on Islam Renan did not gain from the philological study of primary sources in Arabic. Instead, he drew largely from the then available travel literature or from secondary sources such as the Muhammad biography of Gustav Weil or the *History of the Arabs* by Caussin de Perceval (1795–1871).[29] This assessment is further confirmed by Renan himself, who admitted that he remained mediocre in Arabic throughout his life (Renan 1936, 210). In addition, this image was the result of observations during his "Phoenician mission," which took place immediately after the civil war in Lebanon and the massacre of Christians in Damascus in 1860. In this war between the Druze and Maronite Christians more than 15,000 Christians were killed in less than four weeks and about 100,000 were forced into migration (Schölch 1987, 412). These violent events and the concomitant devastation of many parts of the regions he was traveling certainly left a strong impression on Renan's perception. Yet, these events were triggered by economic disruptions and the imperial interventions of both the Ottoman authorities and European powers in the precarious ethno-religious balance of Greater Syria rather than by "the impoverishing influence of Islamism." According to the available sources, on his two oriental travels Renan had very little direct contact with Muslims (Schäbeler 2016, 56–57). In sharp distinction to his German colleague Heinrich Leberecht Fleischer, Ernest Renan also never really engaged with Arab and Muslim intellectuals through correspondence.[30]

On 29 March 1883, Ernest Renan gave his lecture "L'Islamisme et la science" (Islam and Science) at the Sorbonne. This lecture is a document of the continuities in the otherwise often puzzling nature of Renan's eclectic thought. It clearly continues to propagate his pejorative image of Islam. Renan attempts to sort out "one of the strongest confusions of ideas" that appears in the usage of terms such as *Arab science*, *Arab philosophy*, *Arab arts*, *Muslim science*, and *Muslim civilization*. To anticipate his conclusion, for Renan none of this exists. In his eyes, everybody who ever traveled the Orient or Africa knows how "fatally limited [...] the mind of the true Muslim believer" is (Renan 1883, 2). A kind of a foolish pride characterizes Muslims who have "the deepest contempt for education, for science, for everything that constitutes the European spirit" (Renan 1883, 3). Through conversion to Islam, all differences between races and nationalities disappear and only the blindly believing Muslim remains. Renan's single exception are the Iranians. According to him, they were able to escape this fate, but they are in principle "more Shiite than

Muslim" (1883, 3).[31] The core argument of Renan's lecture is the essential incompatibility of Islam with modern science. In this way, he basically repeats what he had already said in his inaugural lecture at the Collège de France in 1862. In that speech, Renan rejected the existence of an age of Arab science and philosophy which, according to him, was nothing more than a pathetic translation of Greek science and philosophy (1862a, 191). Consequently, his conclusion is that the so-called golden age of Islamic science under Abbasid rule (ca. 800–1200) never existed. What was considered as a period of Islamic enlightenment, following Renan, was the result of forces which Islam—at this period of time—was not able to suppress.

At the Sorbonne, Renan reiterated that Greece was the only original source of true knowledge (1883, 11). What we came to call Arab science was in reality only science written in Arabic (1883, 16). And it is much less Islamic. In Renan's interpretation of Islamic history, Islam always had persecuted but not supported science and philosophy. In this persecutory attitude, he admitted, that similar to Islam, the theology of the Occident was no less vigilant regarding the sciences. However, in Renan's reasoning, in Europe religion has not succeeded in erasing the modern spirit of science as had happened in Islam (1883, 18). Regarding the few Muslim philosophers that Renan even acknowledged, he concluded: "To honor the Islam of Avicenna, Avenzoar, Averroes, is as if one were honoring the Catholicism of Galileo" (1883, 19).[32] These remarks regarding Catholicism show that "L'Islamisme et la science" was to some extent directed against religion in general. In his personal negotiation between the modern systems of religion and science, Renan undoubtedly opted for the primacy of science. The denigrating tone of his talk, therefore, was not directed at Islam alone.

The public castigation of Islam by the famous French *homme de lettres* did not go unchallenged. Renan received a series of responses from Muslim intellectuals of whom the most famous were by the Islamic reformer Jamal al-Din al-Afghani (1838–1897), the Ottoman writer Namık Kemal (1840–1888), and the Russian Imam Ataullah Bajazitov (1846–1911).[33] These responses reflected very different positions and addressed different audiences. Al-Afghani's reply, which was not published in Arabic, emphasized Islam's fundamental adaptivity to historical change. While he agreed with Renan regarding the harm which orthodox religious figures can do to science, he fiercely rejected his denigrating description of the Arabs as culturally inferior (al-Afghani 1883). From a much more religiously apologetic perspective, Namık Kemal emphasized the civilizing potential of the Muslim religion for shaping an Islamic kind of modernity. Kemal denied Renan had any knowledge of Islam and refuted his arguments step by step (Kemal 1962). In a similar way Ataullah Bajazitov disproved Renan's theses in nine steps. Arguing for a reconciliation between modern science and religion, the Russian Imam accused Renan for basing his argumentation on the superficial observation of some contemporary phenomena among Muslims (Biazitov 1883).[34]

Conclusions: German Scholars as Pioneers of Classical Orientalism

In Renan's work we can see an attempt to reconcile the different ethics of arts, morality, religion, and science (Wanning 1999, 9). He basically became known in three fields. First, Renan contributed to the discussion of French politics, in particular after the Franco-Prussian war in 1870. In this field, his article on nationalism, "Qu'est-ce qu'une nation?" ("What is a Nation?"; Renan 1882), has remained a scholarly reference until today.[35] Second, Renan the classical orientalist wrote extensively on the history of Israel and the origins of Christianity, work that reflected his expertise as a philologist and his knowledge of Hebrew. However, even during his lifetime, his orientalist peers received his studies with considerable criticism, and his scholarship in this area did not outlast its historical moment. Finally, there is Renan's role in the foundation of the *Corpus Inscriptionum Semiticarum*, the collection of ancient inscriptions in Semitic languages that originated in his Phoenician expedition. This collection is arguably Renan's most enduring scholarly legacy (Robin 2011, 125).

When it comes to the development of Islamic studies proper, Renan was only a marginal figure. In contrast to Julius Wellhausen, he never really engaged in the study of Islamic history. Apart from his academically insignificant dissertation on Ibn Rushd, he only published two pieces on Islam (Renan 1851, 1883). Both are mere impressionistic reflections of the author rather than the result of philological or historical research efforts. They are based on secondary sources alone. Renan never really engaged with Muslim intellectuals or, as a philologist, with primary sources in Arabic. Therefore, the Ottoman reformer Namık Kemal was right in his conclusion that Renan had no real knowledge of Islam (Kemal 2016, 169). Kemal saw Renan's "L'Islamisme et la science" essentially as an expression of Renan's deep hostility toward religion as such (Kemal 2016, 202). There is no historical evidence for the veracity of Said's claim that Renan occupied a "hegemonic position" in oriental studies (see also Wokoeck 2009, 8). In mere scholarly terms, Renan's orientalist scholarship is almost negligible for our understanding of the rise of Islamic and Middle Eastern studies.

This does not apply, however, to his role in spreading "orientalist" and racist stereotypes as a famous public intellectual in France. Through the lens of his key theoretical device, the opposition between Semitic and Aryan "races," Renan assigned Islam an unfavorable place in human civilization, as the previous section of this chapter has shown. For Renan both Semites and Indo-Europeans represented the two "noble" cultural units of humanity, by far superior to other cultures. China, Renan argued in "L'Avenir religieux" always has remained inferior to Europe (1860, 761). According to him, "China, [...] is not dying of old age, but of an indefinitely prolonged childhood" (1860, 762). All he could wish for the "wild races" of Africa was a "gentle death" (1860, 773). The worldview of Renan was clearly organized by a hierarchy of races according to which the Indo-European is superior to the Semitic and those two—due to their monotheism—to all other human races. In the literature on Renan, however, the precise nature of his racism is disputed. For Zeev Sternhell, for instance, Renan belonged to the "second wave of the deconstruction of the thought of the Enlightenment" (2010, 15). He saw Renan's conviction of the fundamental inequality of humanity based on "biological determinism" (2010, 248). Against this position, Robert Priest argued that Renan "was an enemy of biological racism and a celebrant of the Jewish contribution to humanity" (Priest 2015b, 315). Given the many inconsistencies in Renan's work, we may well find some evidence for each position. In my analysis, Renan comes closest to the type of "neo-racist thinker," to which Andrew Zimmerman—wrongly in my opinion—ascribed Max Weber. Renan applied a system of cultural differences that he also used to justify French colonialism and a complex, multilayered system of national and international inequalities.[36] In Renan's writings we can frequently find justifications for Europe's civilizing mission, in particular with regard to the colonization of Africa. He deemed colonialism to be a political necessity. Renan did not see anything "offensive in the conquest of countries of an inferior race" (1872, 92–93).[37]

The decisive organizing concept in Renan's system of cultural racism was religion. Europeans have achieved absolute, racial superiority through Christianity, with Jesus Christ transferring the Semitic concept of monotheism into Indo-European culture. Stripping Christianity of its supernatural pretentions—thus Renan's agnostic conclusion—consequently opens the path toward a universal and secular "religion of humanity." In his explicit racism, Renan clearly differs from Wellhausen and Robertson Smith. The concept of fundamentally different races does not play an organizing role in their oriental studies. Evidently, racist theories were not necessarily a general conceptual foundation of nineteenth-century oriental scholarship. However, we can find different versions of a Christian kind of Eurocentrism in the works of all three scholars. That is why third parties were certainly able to make use of aspects of their writings in the name of colonialism and anti-Semitism. Not least because their lives unfolded in systems of multiple discriminations—imperial power relations, national social questions, oppression of women, and rising anti-Semitism—which from an intersectional perspective also impacted on their works.

The thought systems of Renan, Smith, and Wellhausen were to a large extent part of the same discursive universe that was grounded in Germany's revisionist Protestant theology and its application of the historical critical method to the Bible. In Renan's reconstruction of the origins and development of Christianity we can find traces of the theological perspectives of Albrecht Ritschl and Richard Rothe. Like Ritschl, Renan saw Jesus as the essence of Christianity. He linked Jesus' role in establishing the idea of a universal moral community with Rothe's view of modernity as a higher, though secular, stage of Christianity. Renan's philosophy of religion follows the models of nineteenth-century German Protestant theology but strips it of its supernatural religious content.[38]

Edward Said believed that Great Britain and France "were the pioneer nations" in oriental studies, lifting them above the work done in Germany, Italy, Russia, and elsewhere (Said 1978, 17). The second part of my book suggests that it was instead the other way round. When it comes to classical orientalism in the nineteenth century—that is to say, when it comes to historical criticism and the application of critical hermeneutic methods to religious sources—it was German scholars who were the pioneers in the field. More precisely, it was a specific group of Protestant theologians and Semitists at universities in places such as Bonn, Göttingen, Leipzig, Strasbourg, and Tübingen, and at the Dutch University of Leiden. These universities were the discursive nodal points for European orientalists and the foundational figures of Islamic studies. I suggested analyzing this discursive network through the lenses of social boundary negotiations between the realms of science and religion in nineteenth-century Europe. Julius Wellhausen, William Robertson

Smith, and Ernest Renan were all—in Max Weber's terms—wrestling with the apparently incompatible ethical demands of "the gods of science and religion."

When it comes to the individual level, the outcome of this struggle ended differently for each of the three. While Robertson Smith's Christian faith was unshakable, Renan turned from Catholicism to agnosticism under the impact of his historical critical reading of the Bible. Julius Wellhausen remained somehow between the two, apparently combining a pronounced anticlericalism with his adherence to a very individualized form of the Christian faith. In institutional terms, Robertson Smith and Wellhausen lost their chairs in Protestant theology and took up positions in Arabic and Semitic studies. Initially, Renan also lost his chair at the Collège de France, but was eventually able to regain it after the fall of the Second Empire and the subsequent establishment of the secularist Third French Republic. In addition, all three cases show ways in which the critical study of the Bible contributed to the internal differentiation of the system of science. Institutionally, in these three cases we can observe not only the gradual separation of oriental studies from theology but also the establishment of new academic disciplines such as anthropology, comparative religion, and Islamic studies.

In conclusion, all three scholars entered oriental studies via theology, based on their desire to understand the origin of their own Christian faith. The scholarly puzzle that faced them was the relationship between revealed eternal truth and the historical and textual inconsistencies they found in the Bible. The historicist, philological critique of the holy scriptures was the way in which they tried to gain knowledge. This they shared, whether working in a British, French, or German national context. In this sense, their studies were European. Regarding the origin of their approaches and their major philosophical assumptions, however, German Protestant theology had a strong impact on Renan, Robertson Smith, and Wellhausen.

Socially, this discourse was embedded in the broader historical process of a "dechristianization" of Europe. Together, academic reasoning and social transformations were shaping a new understanding of religion. Max Weber conceptualized this process in his thesis of religious rationalization. In formulating his concept, he was also informed by the work of some of the orientalists and Protestant theologians we have discussed so far.[39] The evolutionary tendencies in orientalist scholarship, the individualization of faith promoted by Protestant revisionists, and the Eurocentric convictions of European scholarship in the nineteenth century somehow converged in Weber's sociology of religion. This historical process took place in the political context of colonialism. Yet it was not shaped by colonial interests. Considering the three case studies in this part of the book, there is no evidence for the frequently reiterated Saidian assertion "that Western studies of the East were tied to colonial rule itself and actually created colonialism" (Quinn 2017, 22). This accusation does not even realistically apply to Renan's work, although he strongly supported French colonial ambitions in his lectures and writings. Whether the case is any different regarding the founding fathers of Islamic studies I will discuss in the following three chapters, which make up the third part of this book.

Notes

1 Suzanne Marchand, for instance, traces it back to the German philosopher Friedrich Schlegel (Marchand 2009, 328). See also the study by Poliakov 1974.

2 See also the book chapter "Islam, the Philological Vocation, and French Culture: Renan and Massignon" (Said 1980). Here Said underpins his choice of Renan because in France "Islam played a far more central role for its own sake than anywhere else in Europe" (1980, 59). He does not further substantiate this questionable assertion.

3 Wellhausen did so by comparing Renan with the theologian Adolph Harnack.

4 However, it should be mentioned here that Friedrich Max Müller (1823–1900) was one of the major propagandists of "Aryanism" in the British Empire. Motivated by his romantic enthusiasm for India, he studied philology in Leipzig. In 1848, he moved to Oxford, where he obtained a post as a professor in 1868 (Klimkeit 1997, 29–30). Müller was convinced that Indians and Europeans shared an "Aryan past," for which the Rig Veda provided the oldest source. Yet, while Indian culture fell into stagnation, Europe developed further. For Müller, this degeneration of Indian culture was due to historical processes and not of an essential nature. Therefore he considered it to be reversible (Ballantyne 2002, 41–43). This is where his difference to Renan comes into play, whose cultural determinism Müller rejected.

5 Steinthal's concept of "folk psychology" could be considered a predecessor of cultural anthropology, which deals with the construction of symbolic systems (Kalmar 1987). I will return to Steinthal in the chapter on Ignaz Goldziher.

6 Goldziher delivered this speech to the Hungarian Academy of Sciences on 27 November 1893. I will return to this in chapter seven.

7 It is worth noting that neither of these two books play any role in *Orientalism* (Said 1978).

8 According to Robert Priest, Renan was much more confrontational regarding miracles than his Protestant forbears. Priest argued that this was linked

to the "heavy emphasis on the miraculous and supernatural dimensions of Christianity" and the mid-nineteenth-century ultramontane piety of French Roman Catholicism (Priest 2015a, 77).

9 From 1847, Renan was a lifelong member of the Society and its president from 1884 until his death.

10 Unless otherwise indicated, I am following the biographical data provided by the Société des Études renaniennes (see: https://ernest-renan.fr/biographie/).

11 In 1890, his scientific enthusiasm had eroded due to the relatively weak progress he had experienced in political and social affairs. However, he continued to see science as the only means left that in principle could better the lot of humanity (Renan 1890, xix–xx).

12 Pitt argues that the French positivism of the 1840s to the 1860s was less characterized by Comte's thought than by a pantheism "that accentuated self-development as a means of realizing God within oneself" (Pitt 2000, 81).

13 Ignaz Goldziher, for instance, described Renan's book on Ibn Rushd as a study completely devoid of detail and consistently superficial in its generalizing voice (Simon 1986, 354).

14 This compilation of Phoenician inscriptions remains one of the more lasting scholarly achievements of Ernest Renan. First published in his *Mission de Phénicie* (Phoenician Expedition) through Renan's initiative, they later found their way into the renowned *Corpus Inscriptionum Semiticarum* (Corpus of Semitic Inscriptions), which was published by the Académie des Inscriptions et Belles-Lettres (Dussaud 1951, 9).

15 Wendy Shaw, for instance, claimed this in her book on museums in the late Ottoman Empire. Taking secondary literature as her references (Jenkyns and Morris) she was placing Renan among scholars who conducted their scholarship "without setting eyes on the regions they studied" (Shaw 2003, 64–65).

16 In the introduction to *Vie de Jésus*, Renan briefly lays out his lifelong project of seeking the "Origin of Christianity" (Renan 1863, 1–2).

17 Said referred to this review in *Orientalism* without, however, discussing it in relation to his claim that Renan held a leading role in orientalist scholarship (Said 1978, 235). It is worth mentioning that in Robertson Smith's own work, publications by Renan do not play any significant role. The same applies to Wellhausen's studies of the Old Testament.

18 Robert Priest emphasized the importance of the concept of revolution for Renan, counting over forty instances of permutations of the word "revolution" throughout his book (2015a, 89).

19 Renan referred to Strauss's "excellent" book as one of the major inspirations for his own work (Renan 1863, 223). Moreover, he mentioned its French translation as a suggested reading that "leaves little to be desired" (1863, 3). See also the exchange of letters between Renan and Strauss on the occasion of the Franco-Prussian War in 1870 (Renan 1992).

20 A good part of the orthodox criticism was apparently due less to his "positivist" attacks on Catholic dogmas such as miracles than to his portrayal of Jesus as a rustic, "ignorant" peasant (Pitt 2000, 93).

21 This part of the letter by Napoleon III is quoted by Simon-Nahum Perrine (2007, 65).

22 See my discussion of Albrecht Ritschl's theology in chapter four.

23 Apart from a negative response to Renan's Catholic background, the attitude of German Protestants also reflects nationalist tensions between Germany and France.

24 Nietzsche was essentially inspired by the writings of Julius Wellhausen in his religious-philosophical reflections. In contradistinction to Wellhausen, however, Nietzsche employed Wellhausen's thesis of the degeneration of the Hebrew religion not in order to rehabilitate pre-exile prophecy, but rather to discredit Christianity (Sommer 2008, 52–53).

25 For an analysis of Guizot's thought, see Weintraub 1966.

26 We can find similar ideas about an individualistic religion of humanity in the work of Émile Durkheim. Although an agnostic with a Jewish upbringing, Durkheim also located the origin of a secular, individualistic morality in the individualist spirit of Christianity (Durkheim 1898).

27 "Le monde sera éternellement religieux, et le christianisme, dans un sens large, est le dernier mot de la religion" (Renan 1860, 790).

28 Renan's descriptions of the Prophet Muhammad also are evidence of his often-confusing positions. Ten years earlier, in his essay of 1851, Renan presented Muhammad as an utterly worldly and historical figure who followed his political interests (1851, 1079). In this essay, Renan denies Muhammad the "title of a Prophet": "His whole life reveals a reflection, a combination, a policy, which hardly fit into the character of an enthusiast obsessed with his divine visions" (1851, 1080). Apparently, in Renan's view, the Prophet Muhammad was both an epileptic and a rational politician.

29 See Dussaud (1951, 197) and Renan (1851, 1065). Gustav Weil was a professor of oriental languages at the University of Heidelberg. Aside from his biography on Muhammad, he became famous for his translation of *One Thousand and One Nights*. Caussin de Perceval was a professor of Arabic at the Collège de France. His *Essai sur l'histoire des Arabes avant l'islamisme, pendant l'époque de Mahomet et jusqu'à la réduction de toutes les tribus sous la loi musulmane* (An Essay about the History of the Arabs before Islam, during the Epoch of Muhammad and until all the Tribes were subjected under Muslim Law) was published in 1847 in Paris: Librairie de Firmin Didot Frères.

30 Regarding Fleischer, see chapter two in this book.

31 This special position of the Iranians is of course based on Renan's thesis of the cultural superiority of the Indo-European race. Only from this perspective can one deny that Shiites belong to the Muslim community.

32 Renan used here, as always, the Latin names of these Muslim polymaths: Avicenna (Ibn Sina, 980–1037), Avenzoar (Ibn Zuhr, 1094–1162), Averroes (Ibn Rushd, 1126–1198).

33 Birgit Schäbler published the texts of all three responses in German translations (2016).

34 As there is not enough space to go into more detail about this debate here, see Jung (2011) and Schäbler (2016).

35 During my political science studies at Hamburg University in the 1980s and 1990s, this lecture by Renan was still part of our curriculum on nationalism. Renan delivered it on 11 March 1882 at the Sorbonne. He argued against the habit of confusing the concept of the race, defined ethnographically or linguistically, with the nation. According to Renan, a nation is not defined by dynasties, interests, linguistic groups, races, or religions. The nation is a historically constructed spiritual and moral community, a solidarity based on past and future sacrifices (Renan 1882).

36 In this context I apply the term "neoracist" most certainly *avant le letter*, as Renan's linguistically underpinned theory of racial differences was shaped before biological racism became the dominant theory.

37 For a more comprehensive discussion of Renan's concept of race, see Weinberg (1958).

38 The affinity Renan had with German scholarship before the 1870 war is also documented in his becoming a corresponding member of the Prussian Science Academy in 1859 and an external member of the Bavarian Academy in 1860 (Gertzen 2020, 170). Moreover, in *L'Avenir de la science* he wrote: "Germany [...] had been my mistress for several years" (1890, iii). On Ritschl and Rothe, see also chapters four and five.

39 Weber provided very few references in his work, but he did mention Snouck Hurgronje, Albrecht Ritschl, and Julius Wellhausen as sources in his religious studies.

Part III

Founding Fathers of Islamic Studies: The Formation of a Modern Academic Discipline

7 Ignaz Goldziher: Islamic Studies and Jewish Reform

"Oh, don't make our Islam look so bad!" This was Ignaz Goldziher's response to a letter from Martin Hartmann (1851–1918) in October 1906. The German Arabist had informed his Hungarian colleague about the progress he had made in writing the handbook *Der Islam: Geschichte—Glaube—Recht* (*Islam: History—Belief—Law*). In his letter, Hartmann had admitted that he was writing this book in a general mood of discontent toward Islam (Hanisch 2000, 266–267). First published in 1909, *Der Islam* addressed the broader public and appeared in numerous editions. In this book, Hartmann described Islam as a culture in a state of stagnation. He presented the Qur'an as a text full of slogans and military campaigns rather than a moral codex outlining a system of religious beliefs. He described the Prophet Muhammad first as a poet and later as a social organizer who received his revelation in a state of "mental illness" (Hartmann 1909).[1] It was a reaction to this kind of stereotyping that prompted Goldziher's response. Goldziher saw Islam as having many facets characterized by a broad spectrum of Muslim social practices in which Islamic traditions found diverse historical expressions. Eighty years before the anthropologist Talal Asad described "Islam as a discursive tradition" (Asad 1986), Ignaz Goldziher already understood Muslim religious practices in a similar way. He argued against the stereotypical image of Islam construed by his German colleague Hartmann from a historicist perspective. In Goldziher's understanding, Islam was not a holistic structure based on holy scriptures alone. Instead, he suggested that Muslim understandings of the Qur'an and hadith depended on the specific historical and social conditions in which Muslims live.[2]

Edward Said's claim that Goldziher was among those "orientalists" who thought that Islam could be "studied apart from the economics, sociology, and politics of Islamic peoples" is simply wrong (Said 1978, 105). Even worse, he totally disregarded the fact that Goldziher belonged to the scholarly group of "pro-Islamic Jews" (Lewis 1968). The Hungarian scholar was part of a tradition of Jewish scholarship on Islam that coincided historically with the period of Jewish emancipation in Europe.[3]

Starting around 1830 with the work of Abraham Geiger (1810–1874), many Jewish scholars reconstructed Islam as a "rationalist religion free of mysticism and apocalypticism" (Heschel 2019, 62). They focused on the theological traditions and legal interpretations that Islam and Judaism shared. In his book *Was hat Mohammed aus dem Judenthume aufgenommen*, Geiger analyzed "those stories in Muslim scripture that are loosely based on the Hebrew Bible" (Lassner 1999, 129).[4] For some of these Jewish scholars, "the study of Islam became a template for the ongoing Jewish de-orientalization of Judaism" (Heschel 2019, 63–65). A form of Jewish tradition of Islamic studies emerged in Germany that spread from the rabbinical seminaries to the German university landscape (Hartwig 2009). In part following this tradition, Goldziher pointed to parallels between Judaism and Islam (Libson 1998, 168). In the academic milieu of the Jewish Reform Movement, he combined his scholarship with being a liberal Jewish pietist and—in his youth—a "crypto-Muslim" whose Islamophilia almost brought him close to conversion (Turán 2023, 15). Even more significantly, as a Hungarian Jew, he belonged to the "internal Orient" of Europe (Rohde, 2005). In one way or another, Goldziher was repeatedly confronted with prejudices against his Jewishness, and his minority status as a Jew clearly influenced his academic career (Turán 2023, 8). Therefore, the Hungarian scholar of Islam "started out as a reformer of Judaism" (Goitein 1979, 323). Consequently, Said's judgment on Goldziher makes no sense.

Together with Christiaan Snouck Hurgronje and Carl Heinrich Becker, Goldziher belongs to a group of scholars who were the founding fathers of Islamic studies as a modern academic discipline. They charted out various research areas for the discipline and made contemporary Islam a subject of their studies. For the Danish scholar Johannes Pedersen (1883–1977), for instance, the encounter with Snouck Hurgronje and Goldziher had a decisive impact on his academic career. Starting out in the footsteps of Julius Wellhausen as a scholar of the Old Testament, Pedersen fully turned to Islamic studies after having studied with Snouck Hurgronje and Goldziher in the years between 1909 and 1912. He even followed Goldziher in spending three months at the al-Azhar, and Snouck Hurgronje's approach to study contemporary Islam inspired his future research (Simonsen 2016). In his article commemorating Goldziher after his death in 1921, Richard Gottheil (1862–1936)—also a disciple of Fleischer in Leipzig and later a professor at Columbia University in New York—praised Goldziher for leveling entirely new paths for the study of Islam (Gottheil 1922, 191). For his Italian colleague

Carlo Alfonso Nallino (1872–1938), Goldziher was simply the most notable scholar in the "science of Islam," whose vast, profound, and innovative work wrote history in Islamic studies at the turn of the nineteenth century (Nallino 1922, 236).

We will see that Goldziher's writings comprise a wide range of vastly different topics regarding matters of Muslim law, theology, and social practices in historical critical analysis. Moreover, he was a nodal point in the network of the emerging scientific community of Islamic studies, aptly documented in his estate, which contained more than 13,500 letters with around 1,650 correspondents (Varsányi 2024, 100). Among them were Snouck Hurgronje and Becker, who were not only colleagues, but also friends of Goldziher. In the third part of my book, I focus on these three scholars who finally shaped the contours of Islamic studies in the twentieth century.[5] In so doing, I am again guided by the central question about the relationship among colonialism, religion, and science in their life and work. The chapter on Carl Heinrich Becker will end with a conclusion to this part of the book.

In the first section of this chapter, I present Goldziher's biography with a focus on the ways in which traditional Jewish education, academic studies, and personal religious sentiments converged in his life. In this convergence we can see—albeit from a Jewish angle—some parallels to the biography of William Robertson Smith and his attempt to reconcile faith with science. The second section, then, analyses the relationship between Jewish reform and Islamic studies in Goldziher's career. In particular the reason he withdrew from the study of Judaism and turned his attention to Islam is the central theme of this section. This change in direction was accompanied by his development of a strictly individualized practice of Judaism which—in my eyes—resembles the religious attitude of Julius Wellhausen. Finally, I shift my focus to Goldziher's multiple contributions to Islamic studies and his lasting impact on the development of the discipline. What kind of image of Islam did Goldziher convey to his audiences?

Biography: Academic Aspirations and Hungarian Realities

Ignaz Goldziher was born on 22 June 1850 in Székesfehérvár (Stuhlweissenburg), a provincial town situated about 50 km from today's Hungarian capital Budapest. He had two siblings, one of whom died young, at the age of four. His father, Adolf Goldziher (1811–1874), followed in the family's economic tradition of trading in leather. The family had a Sephardic background, and Goldziher's ancestors had moved from the north-German city of Hamburg to Hungary in 1735. With the help of private teachers, Adolf Goldziher provided his son with an early education that combined a high appreciation of scientific knowledge with Jewish traditions and humanist values. From an early age on he taught his son in Hebrew and theological matters. Between 1860 and 1865, Ignaz Goldziher attended the local Catholic high school (Turán 2023, 1–2). In the religiously and ethnically mixed population of Székesfehérvár, the young Goldziher was in close contact with Christian children and sometimes even attended church services with them. By the age of five, Goldziher claims, he had already read the Bible and the Talmud (Goldziher 1978, 18). According to his biographer Raphael Patai, a daily routine of intensive studies characterized Goldziher's childhood, leaving him only five hours of rest at night (Patai 1987, 15). There is no doubt regarding the significant role that religion, and in particular Judaism, played in his childhood. In his diary, Goldziher thus described his religious Jewish identity as "the pulse of his life" (Goldziher 1978, 33).

In 1865, the family moved from Székesfehérvár to Pest, the town on the eastern bank of the Danube which merged with Buda and Óbuda in 1872 to become Budapest. This move was triggered by the economic problems his father's business was facing (Haber 2004, 75). Given the family's often fragile economic situation, Adolf Goldziher strongly promoted a scholarly path for his son. He essentially wanted to "save his son through scholarship" (Turán 2023, 242). In the winter semester of 1865/1866, Goldziher enrolled at the University of Budapest, studying linguistics, philosophy, and orientalist philology (Goldziher 1978, 24–25). Through his study of oriental languages—Arabic, Hebrew, Persian, and Turkish—he made the acquaintance of Ármin Vámbéry (1832–1913). Vámbéry was an internationally renowned expert in the Turkish language who had traveled in Central Asia, Iran, and the Ottoman Empire. The context of his academic success in Hungary was the nationalist dimension of Hungarian orientalism, which emphasized the "Turkish connection" in search of the "ethnic, linguistic, geographic, and historical origins of the Magyars" (Turán 2023, 48).[6] Vámbéry introduced Goldziher to Baron József Eötvös (1813–1871), who was the Hungarian Minister of Religion and Education between 1867 and 1871. As part of his educational reforms, Eötvös, a liberal Catholic politician, supported young scholars with grants intended to later lead them to university positions. Eötvös was already a supporter of Vámbéry's academic career, and the Turcologist convinced him to provide his very talented student with a scholarship, facilitating Goldziher's subsequent studies in Berlin, Leipzig, Leiden, and Vienna (Haber 2006b, Turán 2023, 41–43).[7]

In 1868, Ignaz Goldziher arrived in Berlin at the "Hochschule für die Wissenschaft des Judentums" (Higher Institute for Jewish Studies). In Berlin, he studied with Abraham Geiger, Moritz Steinschneider (1816–1907), and Heymann Steinthal.[8] In scholarly terms, they made Goldziher more familiar with the biblical criticism of the Tübingen school, the Jewish tradition of Islamic studies, and the methods of comparative religion.[9] Even more important, at the Hochschule he encountered the ideas of Germany's Jewish Reform Movement. After his stay in Berlin, Goldziher acquired his sound knowledge of oriental philology during a fourteen-month sojourn in Leipzig (1869–1870). At Leipzig University, he became a member of the scholarly circle around Heinrich Leberecht Fleischer with its international group of students. With great enthusiasm Goldziher attended Fleischer's seminars on literature and linguistics in Arabic, Persian, and Turkish. Moreover, he studied Sanskrit grammar under Hermann Brockhaus (1806–1877), one of Germany's leading Indologists and the brother-in-law of the composer Richard Wagner (1813–1883). In his seminars and private conversations, Fleischer also increased Goldziher's interest in Islamic studies, especially in the area of Islamic law (Goldziher 1978, 41). In Leipzig, Goldziher had the opportunity to immerse himself in the study of the available secondary literatures in English, French, and German, and he made excerpts from the Leipzig manuscripts in Arabic (1978, 44). Soon, Goldziher mastered Arabic to such a degree that Fleischer assigned him with the teaching of his basic courses, making him known among the students as the "little sheikh" (Skovgaard-Petersen 2010).

Ignaz Goldziher completed his doctorate under Fleischer on 22 July 1870. Upon his departure from Budapest, he had made the commitment to minister Eötvös of submitting his thesis during the winter semester of 1869/1870. He had brought most of the text of his dissertation *Studien über Tanchum Jerushalmi* (Studies on Tanchum Jerushalmi) with him from Berlin. In this study, Goldziher examined the life and works of Tanchum Jerushalmi (1220–1291), a Jewish exegete of the Bible who wrote his commentaries in Arabic (Preissler 1995, 299–300). Goldziher had already passed his oral exam in December 1869, giving him more time for his studies. This meanwhile also included core works associated with the Grafian thesis of the Pentateuch. Goldziher discussed the studies of Graf, Kuenen, and Vatke with his Hungarian friend Moritz Kleinmann

(1843–1915), thus making contemporary biblical criticism a firm part of his academic knowledge (Goldziher 1978, 43). Moreover, he engaged with a number of Protestant theologists at Leipzig, among them, for instance, Frank Delitzsch (1813–1890), with whom he had intense discussions on the Talmud and Jewish philosophies (1978, 45). In a letter to Theodor Nöldeke more than thirty years later, Goldziher pointed to the importance of critical biblical studies for his own work. Becoming familiar with the Grafian thesis decisively molded his philological approach. He began to read Jewish and Islamic traditions through the same methodological lenses as Abraham Kuenen and Julius Wellhausen did with regard to the Old Testament.[10]

In March 1871, Goldziher left Leipzig, and moved on to the University of Leiden, where he met Reinhard Dozy (1820–1883) and Michael Jan de Goeje (1836–1909).[11] Fleischer secured him the positive reception of these two leading Dutch orientalists with his introduction letters (Schorsch 2016, 128). Furthermore, during the six months in Leiden, Goldziher made use of the large collection of manuscripts in Arabic of which de Goeje was in charge (Goldziher 1978, 48). The scholarly atmosphere of Leiden encouraged him further in his decision not to follow the strict linguistic path of his teacher Fleischer, but to place the study of Islam at the center of his scientific endeavor. For Goldziher, the philological perfection that his teacher Fleischer in Leipzig had preached thus turned from an aim into a means. According to the notes in Goldziher's diary, the critical approach to Islamic traditions of the scholars in Leiden was fundamental to this development in his academic career (Goldziher 1978, 50). In his future studies of Islam, Goldziher was further inspired by the idea of universal history writing which he encountered in reading *Geschichte der herrschenden Ideen des Islams* (History of the prevailing ideas in Islam) by Alfred von Kremer (1828–1889). In the introduction to his book, the Austrian orientalist and diplomat sketched out a comparative approach to a universal history of humankind. According to von Kremer, in writing this kind of history we must compare the history of European culture with that of the Orient (von Kremer 1868, XIV). Alfred von Kremer developed this understanding of history through the participant observations he made as a diplomat in Alexandria, Beirut, and Cairo, which decisively molded his orientalist scholarship. Goldziher adopted Kremer's point of view in analyzing Islamic history from a universalist perspective as a history of ideas (Simon 1986, 31–33). Moreover, Goldziher complemented this scholarly approach with his own participant observations during his "Muhammadan year" (Goldziher 1978, 24), that is to say, the "oriental study tour" he undertook from 1873 to 1874. His encounter with prominent figures in the Islamic Reform Movement probably enhanced his conviction that there is no fundamental contradiction between Islam and modernity.

While on his travels to the various European universities, Goldziher's strong supporter Baron Eötvös died in February 1871. When Goldziher was leaving the Hungarian capital, Eötvös had promised him a chair at Budapest University upon his return. Eötvös's successor, however, did not feel obliged to keep this promise. Instead, he granted Goldziher another scholarship, which facilitated his oriental study tour to the Middle East. The new minister provided him with a grant for collecting manuscripts and for the study of regional dialects (Conrad 1993, 112). In retrospect, Goldziher himself emphatically asserted that the purpose of his journey was to immerse himself fully in Islam and its sciences. He described his sojourn in the Middle East "as a part of his Muslim learning" (Goldziher 1978, 56). More precisely, Goldziher aimed to find out more about the forces that motivated the transformation of the "Judaic cult at Mecca into the colossal world religion of Islam" (Goldziher 1978, 56).[12] In this way reflecting the previously mentioned tradition of nineteenth-century Jewish scholarship on Islam, Goldziher wanted to understand the impact of Islam on the ideas and morals of Muslim society. Therefore, his goal was not only to collect manuscripts, but also to meet with scholars and ordinary people of the region. Some of the contacts with Arab scholars were facilitated through introduction letters by Heinrich Leberecht Fleischer. They also provided him with access to the intellectual circles around the famous representative of the Arab Renaissance movement Butrus al-Bustani (1819–1880), whom he met in Beirut in 1873 (1978, 55–57).

Goldziher's journey to the Middle East began on 15 September 1873. He embarked on a steamer on the river Danube that brought him to Istanbul. There, he initially had to stay in quarantine. This "torturous" experience of quarantine apparently intensified the feeling of despair and homesickness that characterized the beginning of his oriental study tour (Conrad 1990; Patai 1987, 91). In Goldziher's travel diary, the Ottoman capital is depicted in rather negative terms. He described Istanbul as a depressing site, characterizing it as corrupt, with "bakshish hunting" people (Patai 1987, 97). This image may have been caused by the loneliness he felt under quarantine, but it was apparently also an expression of the generally chauvinist attitudes with which Hungarian nationalists typically perceived the people of the Balkans and Ottoman

Turks. Generally speaking, Goldziher's travel records present us with some largely denigrating descriptions of most of the Christians, Jews, and Turks he met in Istanbul and later in Beirut, Cairo, Damascus, and Jerusalem. Christian missionaries he even considered to be "religious swindlers," whereas he saw in Protestant Arabs a degeneration of the "original Arab race" (Patai 1987, 110).[13]

In sharp contradistinction to these judgments, Goldziher sketched the Muslim Arabs mostly as cultivated and enormously rationally minded friends. In Goldziher's diary, his engagement with the Arab Muslims of the region is transformed into a "pure fairy tale" (Goitein 1979, 324). In Cairo, the Hungarian Jew even donned Muslim garb in order to attend Islamic prayer services at a mosque. Moreover, he participated in lectures at the famous al-Azhar University and became a member of a group of students who regularly met with the eminent Islamic reformer Jamal al-Din al-Afghani (1823–1899) in a coffee shop in the Abedin quarter.[14] Goldziher tells us about their discussions on Islamic and European philosophy with al-Afghani, whom he described as a freethinker with a rather heretical mind. As we will see later, the reformist attitude of this group of young Muslim students matched Goldziher's own desire for religious reform. The Islamic Reform Movement represented a kind of religious rationalism that became a standard for him to measure Jewish reform attempts. The impact of these encounters with reformist Muslim intellectuals on Goldziher hardly can be underestimated. During his stay in Cairo, Goldziher wrote that his thought became fully committed to Islam. He even began to believe in the prophecy of Muhammad, going so far as to call Islam "his monotheism" at this time (Goldziher 1978, 71). In his travel diary, Goldziher expressed ambivalent judgments of Christians and Jews on the one hand, and more positive views of Muslims on the other. Bringing him close to conversion, these conflicting views may be interpreted as a "classic example of the crisis of faith," which many young scholars experienced who were under the impact of historical critical scholarship (Schorsch 2016, 139).

In his diary, Goldziher described his journey as the happiest period of his life. However, this year of "honor, glory and light" abruptly ended after six months (Goldziher 1978, 50). In Cairo, he received the bad news that his father was dying in Budapest. Goldziher's return to Hungary in April 1874 marks a decisive break in his life. It put an abrupt end to the joyful years of European and Middle East travels. Back in Budapest, he discovered that the promised professorship in Semitic languages had been handed to Péter Hatala (1832–1918), a Catholic theologian. Hatala's qualifications were limited to three years of experience in Palestine that he had had as a Christian missionary. Apparently, he had been moved from theology to the faculty of arts due to his critique of the Vatican's claim of the infallibility of the Pope. It is difficult to gauge whether it was Hatala's problems with the Catholic Church or rather anti-Semitic sentiment directed toward the young Jewish scholar were behind this story, most probably both.[15] For Goldziher, however, a "martyrdom" began, lasting for thirty years until he finally became a salaried full professor in Semitic languages at the University of Budapest in 1905 (Simon 1986, 49–51). As a private lecturer and later an unpaid professor at the University of Budapest, Goldziher was compelled to find an income from alternative sources. Therefore, he accepted the position as chief secretary of the reformist Neolog Jewish community of Pest in January 1876.[16] It was Goldziher's task to organize the community's secretariat and its educational institutions (Goldziher 1978, 81–82). This non-academic position was a source of deep chagrin for Goldziher, and his diary is a document of the grief, insult, and misfortune he felt during those three decades. In his notes, Goldziher described his daily work as a form of slavery and constant humiliation (1978, 139–140). According to him, he only had his free time, nights, and vacations for his scientific work (1978, 92–93).[17] In 1879, he married Laura Mittler (1854–1925), and the couple had two sons. The elder son, Miksa Adolf, committed suicide in 1900, thus saddening Goldziher's life further.[18]

During the very same period of time, however, Goldziher earned a reputation as an internationally renowned scholar of Islam. The secretary of the Neolog congregation was a member of several world-leading scientific association and of the Academies of Science in Amsterdam, Bavaria, Budapest, and Prussia. Under the applause of his colleagues, he was awarded with a gold medal at the Congress of Orientalists in Stockholm (1889) by King Oscar II of Sweden. While he was apparently suffering under the daily routine of his job, Goldziher was nevertheless able to publish constantly on the highest international level and to maintain a huge network of international scholars. Even more significant, while waiting for a professorship in Budapest, he rejected all the frequently offered professorships from leading universities such as Cambridge, Heidelberg, Königsberg, Lahore, Prague, and Strasbourg. To a certain extent, Goldziher's tremendous scholarly career contradicts the impression we get from reading his diary. How was it possible for him to forge such an academic career based on work he was only able to do at night and during his scarce leisure time? Edward Ullendorff (1920–2011) was presumably right in his judgment "that the much-maligned leaders of the Jewish community did show very reasonable consideration to their internationally famous secretary" (Ullendorff 1979, 554). How can one explain Ignaz Goldziher's fierce loathing of the representatives of Budapest's Jewry in his diary? The answer to this question lies in the peculiar mixture of Goldziher's personality and the specific historical context in which the life of the Jewish reformer and scholar of Islam unfolded. To sketch out both his personality and the context of his life is the task of the following section.

From Jewish Reform to Islamic Studies: The Making of an International Scholar

The pursuit of religious reform, the autonomization of modern science, and the formation of the Hungarian nation state converged in the life of Goldziher. His particular pathway to Islamic studies is knit into the context of the religious and political particularities of the Hungarian Jewry. The scholar Goldziher was a Hungarian nationalist "who advocated religious reform as a means for the national integration of Hungarian Jewry" (Jung 2014, 108). Around 1880 in Hungary, only about 47 percent of the population were Magyars, and in many parts of the country the colloquial language was German (Haber 2006a, 74). Among the major different ethnic groups—Croats, Germans, Magyars, Rumanians, and Slovaks—Jews amounted to approximately 900,000 people at the end of the nineteenth century. The Jewish population had resulted from several subsequent waves of immigration from both Western Europe and Galicia. In this way, the Hungarian Jewry represented a blending of the Eastern European culture of the *shtetl* with progressive, reform-minded Jews from the West. In particular Jews from Germany played an important role among reformist Hungarian Jews. They brought the culture of the Jewish Enlightenment to Hungary, and German rabbis spread the ideas of the German Jewish Reform Movement in the country. Literature in German found a widespread readership among those Hungarian Jews who were linguistically not separated from their German co-religionists (Pietsch 1999, 55). The Orthodox Jews, however, strongly rejected the attempts of the reformist camp to establish a nationwide inclusive religious organization. The emerging rift between the two religious camps was further exacerbated by the support of the Jewish Reform Movement for Hungarian quests for national independence from the Habsburg

Empire during the bourgeois revolutions from 1848 to 1849. In this context, the schism in the Hungarian Jewry became a political connotation as the Orthodoxy was rejecting this form of Jewish assimilation into the Hungarian nation. Orthodox Jews considered a nationwide organization of Hungarian Jews as turning Judaism into nothing more than a religion (Katz 1998).

In 1867, Hungarian Jews achieved the status of legally equal citizens. Shortly afterwards, minister Eötvös convoked a national Jewish congress in Budapest between 1868 and 1869 which discussed educational and institutional reforms as a means for Jewish national integration. However, the orthodox wing heavily opposed this kind of institutional re-organization. In particular educational reforms, which included the replacement of traditional Talmud schools by modern academic teaching seminars for rabbis, found their fierce objection. As a result, they left the congress under protest, thus deepening the already existing rift among the Hungarian Jewry. The reformist camp, the Neolog movement of which Goldziher would later become secretary, now rallied further behind Hungarian nationalists and advocated complete assimilation into the Hungarian nation (Pietsch 1999, 14–15). The effects of these national developments also left deep traces at the local level. In his dairy, Goldziher mentions an episode in his hometown that is closely linked to this schism in the Hungarian Jewry. In 1853, the local rabbi, Meir Zisper, apparently did not deal adequately with a case of divorce. This at least was the opinion of the orthodox camp in Székesfehérvár. His rival Gottlieb Fischer raised a controversy by calling him a heretic who was not qualified to be an authority in Rabbinical Law. After three years of quarreling, Zisper resigned from his position, although a majority of the Jewish constituency in the town kept following his reformist path. Consequently, Székesfehérvár's Orthodoxy turned to the government in Budapest to ask for permission to establish their own official congregation (Katz 1998, 52–55). In retrospect, Goldziher positioned himself between the two sides, but emphasized that his father strongly supported his personal friend Zisper, whose brother, Marcus Zisper, had taught Goldziher his first lessons in the Talmud at the age of eight (Goldziher 1978, 19).

However, Goldziher received his first systematic education in the philosophy and traditions of Judaism from his private teacher Moses Wolf Freudenberg between 1861 and 1865. Teaching the young Goldziher in Judaism for five to six hours daily, Freudenberg, an expert in the Bible and in Hebrew grammar, left a lasting impression on Goldziher. While he belonged to the conservative minority in Székesfehérvár, Freudenberg was also a close friend of Goldziher's father. He conveyed to the young boy a peculiar blending of rationalism, orthodox belief, and ethical rigor. Goldziher's religious attitudes were strongly molded by Freudenberg's worldview. In Goldziher's own words, the "old teacher" gave his thought the "highest aims and his soul the noblest intentions" (Goldziher 1978, 20). Under the impact of Freudenberg's teachings Goldziher began to perceive both the Orthodox and the Reformists with disdain, a position that later placed him between all chairs with regard to Hungarian Judaism (Goldziher 1978, 19–23). Already at the beginning of his time with Freudenberg, Goldziher wrote his first publication, *Sichat Jiczchak: Abhandlung über Ursprung, Eintheilung und Zeit der Gebete* (*Sichat Jiczchak: A Treatise on the Origin, Division and Time of Prayers*). Published in 1862, this book by the 12-year-old Goldziher was a critique of the Jewish Orthodoxy, which, according to Goldziher, did not live up to its own standards of abiding by the law (Haber 2004, 2006a, 63). In retrospect, Goldziher considered this book to be the foundation for his later reputation as a religious freethinker (Goldziher 1978, 22). At the same time, it indicates his interest in Jewish studies, which he confirmed less than ten years later with the submission of his aforementioned doctoral thesis. The thesis was the first study in which Goldziher applied the newly acquired philological knowledge and tools of comparative religious studies (Schorsch 2016, 122). Even more important, both texts are predecessors of sorts to his first major book, *Der Mythos bei den Hebräern und seine geschichtliche Entwicklung* (*Mythology Among the Hebrews and Its Historical Development*), in which he certainly presented himself as Jewish reformer and a scholar of Judaism (Goldziher 1876).

The mindset of both the religious reformer and the scholar Goldziher was eventually molded by the body of thought of Abraham Geiger, whom he personally met when studying in Berlin. Born in 1810 in Frankfurt am Main, Geiger grew up in a rather traditional Jewish family. Studying in Heidelberg and Bonn, Geiger came to the conclusion that only the application of the historical critical method to Jewish traditions would liberate German Judaism from its cultural stagnation. Like many of his contemporary Christian reformists, Geiger aimed to reconcile religion and science, making the scholarly analysis of holy scriptures a prerequisite for religious reform. A critical reading of the Jewish Bible, according to Geiger, would reveal its inherent universal message and therewith the unquestionable compatibility of Judaism with modernity. From an apologetic point of view, he criticized Christian theological convictions that framed Judaism as being fundamentally incompatible with modernity. In this way, Abraham Geiger merged historical criticism with faith in a way that strongly impacted Goldziher's worldview. In 1833, in this historical context of scholarship and religious reform, Geiger published his study on Muhammad and the Qur'an at almost the same time as David Friedrich Strauss's biography of Jesus. Since the publication of *Das Leben Jesu* by Strauss in 1835/36, Geiger repeatedly expressed his admiration for the book (Fraisse 2016, 207). Geiger's own "epoch-making" book "plac[ed] Qur'anic texts into the context of rabbinic texts," combining Jewish with Islamic studies. Drawing on his excellent knowledge of Arabic, which he acquired at the University of Bonn, and his masterful knowledge of Jewish literatures, Geiger set a standard for a generation of Jewish scholars to come (Heschel 2019, 68–69).

Without any doubt, Goldziher belonged to this generation. Goldziher described the encounter with Geiger and his work in his diary as a real revelation (Goldziher 1978, 33, 123). In particular Goldziher clearly linked his own revolutionary approach to studying Islamic hadith literature to the source-critical methods that he had learned through Geiger (Goldziher 1978, 122–123). In his Islamic studies, Goldziher fully adopted Geiger's credo that "true criticism of dogma is its history" (Fraisse 2016, 209).[19] In his engagement with Geiger, Goldziher absorbed important nineteenth-century scientific ideas such as evolutionism, historicism, and religious rationalization. Moreover, the religious reform agenda of Geiger and the reformist circles around him in Berlin became something like a blue-print for his own reform attempts. Not least, Goldziher's constantly expressed disgust for religious orthodoxies are reminiscent of the harsh and polemic critique to which Abraham Geiger subjected Jewish and Christian orthodoxies throughout his life. Placing himself in the Hungarian context between orthodox rejectionism and reformist assimilationism, Goldziher reflected this intellectual climate of the German Jewish Reform Movement, however, in a completely different political and social context. This different context contributed decisively to the failure of Goldziher's reform aspirations at home (Jung 2014, 112).

The endpoint of his engagement in Jewish studies came very early in his career with the publication of *Der Mythos bei den Hebräern*. Published in 1876, Goldziher wrote most parts of the book during his oriental study tour. The book was a critical "manifesto" against Ernest Renan's racist thesis of the "Semitic mind" and its lack of mythology that the French scholar put forward in his *Histoire générale* in 1855 (Turán 2023, 104). Goldziher based his study on the comparative theories of both the

Anglo-German scholar Max Müller and Heymann Steinthal's mythology of early ethnic groups (Schorsch 2016, 139). Goldziher mentions Steinthal's treatise on Hebrew mythodology as the first inspiration for writing his own book (Goldziher 1876, XXIII). In his critique of Renan's thesis, Goldziher built on an evolutionary theory of the history of religion. According to this theoretical perspective, myths are a distinct and universal stage of human development. Goldziher claimed that "as a necessary form of human spiritual life, there can be no unmythological races" (1876, XV). Based on his ethnological theory of races, Renan successfully spread his axiom on cultural race differences among a broad audience that not only included scholars (1876, 4). Therefore, Goldziher also directed his own book not only to colleagues, aiming to reach a "wider circle of educated readers" (1876, IX). According to Goldziher, Renan's thesis was completely unhistorical. Referring to Steinthal's "psychological" critique and Müller's historical arguments, Goldziher argues that the claims advanced in *Histoire générale* had already been disproven by contemporary mythodological scholarship (1876, 8–11). As a precursor to religion, in the course of human cultural evolution "myth becomes either history or religion" (1876, 17). Twenty years after the publication of his book, Goldziher reiterated his critique of Renan in a letter to Martin Hartmann, writing that "the spiritual life of a people is not based on its race, but on its historical destinies" (Hanisch 2000, 62).[20]

Goldziher wrote *Der Mythos* first in Hungarian and then translated it into German in order to reach a broader audience (Goldziher 1876, IX). Thus, his expectations regarding the reception of his study among orientalists, historians, and scholars in comparative religion were extremely high. However, the response to the book in the academic world was rather cold. Although Max Müller himself ensured that *Der Mythos* was published in an English translation in 1877 (Goldziher 1978, 86), Goldziher did not receive the academic acclaim he had expected. While he described its reception in the United Kingdom rather positively, it received an overwhelmingly critical response in Germany. In a letter to his Leipzig mentor Fleischer, he mentioned his disappointment over the critique made by his previous fellow students from Leipzig.[21] In addition, the reception among his co-religionists in Hungary was largely negative too, even including his old Talmud teacher Freudenberg (Schorsch 2016, 142). Apparently, many Jewish readers of Goldziher's book felt deprived of their own history because he had embedded Jewish history within a pan-Semitic history of religions (Niewöhner 2004, 180). He found his main local adversary in David Kaufmann (1852–1899).[22]

Goldziher regarded Kaufmann as the originator of a campaign directed against him, which portrayed the publication of his book as heretical. He accused Kaufmann of inciting public opinion against him. Viewing him as his principal local academic rival in the study of Judaism, Goldziher believed that Kaufmann sought to eliminate him by publicly branding him a heretic. Goldziher accused a group of people close to Kaufmann of collecting signatures among "the Jewish mob" of Budapest in support of his removal from the position as secretary of the Neolog community (Goldziher 1978, 87–88). For Goldziher, therefore, the publication of his first serious book in Jewish studies almost ended in a fiasco.

The predominantly negative reception of *Mythos* by both the scientific community and the Jewish congregation was one among other factors pushing Goldziher toward Islamic studies.[23] In this regard, the critique of his Hungarian home front was presumably the worst. As already mentioned, in Goldziher's worldview, Jewish reform and Hungarian nationalism were inherently woven together. In 1902, Goldziher looked back on his academic career and stated that he had "opened up new perspectives in the field of Arabic literature and the criticism of the sources of Islam" which found universal international acclaim. However, his most important duty had been to devote his energy to Jewishness in his writings in Hungarian language (Goldziher 1978, 231). This entry in his diary is a clear expression of the intersection of scholarship, Jewish reform, and Hungarian nationalism in Goldziher's life. The cold reception of his book was fuel to his almost pathological hatred of many of his fellow Jews, who from then on also included the scientific community of scholars on Judaism. On New Year's Eve in 1893, Goldziher lamented that he had not continued on the path of Jewish studies.[24] However, he did not see himself as fitting into a scientific community consisting of "street urchins, sales agents, moneybags, and liars" (1978, 167). Despite its critical reception, Goldziher's only real book in Jewish studies can tell us a great deal about the scholarly background with which he later addressed Islam. It gives us a summary of the influential forces that framed Goldziher's scholarly work. The names of scholars who we already encountered in the previous chapters—Ewald, Geiger, Graf, von Kremer, Kuenen, Mommsen, Müller, Nöldeke, Schelling, Steinthal, Tylor—appear throughout the book. The same applies to the sources in Arabic which Goldziher frequently employed for comparative reasons. Here we find references to the hadith compilations by Muslim and by al-Bukhari, as well as to the geographer Yaqut al-Hamawi.[25] It is in relationship to this emerging scientific community and their sources that Ignaz Goldziher became a founding father of modern Islamic studies.

Islamic Studies: Pure Religion and Historical Distortions

The enormous frustration with the Jewish community regarding reform and his scholarship on Judaism did not affect the deeply religious nature of Goldziher's personality. Despite all the quarrels with ordinary and academic Jews, he remained a sincere believer throughout his life. Goldziher understood Judaism in terms of a universal and rational ethical message, rejecting all forms of scholasticism and ritualistic worshipping. For Goldziher, Judaism first and foremost had a very deep emotional meaning (Haber 2006a, 55). In the rationalization and individualization of his faith Goldziher closely followed the developments that we have observed in reformist Protestantism. His attitude to Judaism is almost a mirror image to Wellhausen's anti-clericalism and individual spiritualization of Christian belief.[26] As his biographer Robert Simon argued, Goldziher lived a "bourgeois society concept of religion," making Judaism into an intimate and individual religious practice in private life (Simon 1986, 129). Goldziher himself tells us that he developed his own religious system, making his home Jewish in a higher sense. His religious education of his children concerned the prophets and the psalms; "all lies were banished and omitted from their education" (Goldziher 1978, 111). While the "pietistic people from Moravia" did not stop accusing him of heresy, Goldziher "built a temple of truly God-believing messianic Judaism at home" (Goldziher 1978, 111). At the same time when he made this decisive step to an inward-looking practice of his religion, Goldziher also began to divert his scholarly energy from Judaism to the study of Islam.

Ignaz Goldziher did not become famous as a Jewish reformer, but as a foundational figure of the study of Islam. As such, his scholarly work is enormous both in its thematic breadth and in the sheer number of publications. Goldziher's last student, Joseph Desomogyi (1899–1976), compiled and edited a large proportion of his essays, amounting to six volumes of works. Among these we find articles on a multiplicity of topics and in different languages. A few examples of the article titles serve to illustrate the diversity of Goldziher's work: "The Spanish Arabs and Islam" (in Hungarian, 1877); "Jugend- und Strassenpoesie in Kairo" ("Youth and Street Poetry in Cairo," 1879); " Le cult des saints chez les musulmans" ("The Cult of Saints among Muslims," 1880); "Altarabische

Wiegen- und Schlummerlieder" ("Old Arabic Lullabies and Slumber Songs," 1888); "Über Bibelcitate in muhammedanischen Schriften" ("On Bible Quotations in Muhammadan Writings," 1893); "Hebräische Elemente in muhammedanischen Zaubersprüchen" ("Hebrew Elements in Muhammadan Spells," 1894); "Materialien zur Entwicklungsgeschichte des Sufismus" ("Materials on the Historical Development of Sufism," 1899); "Neutestamentliche Elemente in der Traditionslitteratur des Islams" ("Elements of the New Testament in the Literature of Islamic Traditions," 1902); "Zauberelemente im islamischen Gebet" ("Magical Elements in Islamic Prayer," 1906); "Neuplatonische und gnostische Elemente im Hadith" ("Neoplatonic and Gnostic Elements in Hadith," 1908); and "Die Gottesliebe in der islamischen Theologie" ("The Love of God in Islamic Theology," 1919).[27]

These examples clearly illustrate Goldziher's widespread interests in and comprehensive knowledge on Islam. In his major book publications, we can find a chronological line that leads him from Islamic law (*fiqh*) (Goldziher 1884), critical studies of Islamic traditions (*hadith*) (1888a and 1888b), and ancient poetry (1896) to the history of Qur'anic exegesis (*tafsīr*) and its culmination in contemporary thoughts of Islamic reform (1920). Goldziher's studies almost exclusively relied on the historical critical reading of classical and—in the case of Islamic reform—contemporary texts. In the spirit of Abraham Geiger, the analysis of these classical texts served him as the central source for his reconstruction of Islamic history. As in the critical readings of the Bible by Wellhausen or the Tübingen school, Goldziher sought to show the ways in which Islamic religious traditions reflect the social and political conditions of the times of their origins. At the same time, similar to William Robertson Smith, Goldziher attempted to discover pure Islamic revelation by analytically liberating it from these narrative historical distortions. In this way, he built up a program of modern Islamic studies with the critical analysis of Islamic traditions and their interpretations as its methodological core.

In *Die Zahiriten: Ihr Lehrsystem und ihre Geschichte* (*The Ẓāhirīs: Their Doctrine and their History. A Contribution to the History of Islamic Theology*; 2007, first English translation in 1971), Goldziher published his first comprehensive book on an issue of Islamic law. The reference to theology in the English title is somehow misleading. With its chosen topic of the rather special Madhab al-Zahir, the book is not so much about theology (*kalām*) but is focused more on the development and origins of Islamic jurisprudence (*fiqh*). In Goldziher's time, this "fifth madhab" of Sunni Islam was not yet very well known, and he had chosen it for its rather rigid literalism, largely rejecting core methods of legal interpretation such as personal rational judgment (*ra'y*) and analogical reasoning by the jurist (*qiyās*) (1884, 4).[28] In contradistinction to his predecessors, Eduard Sachau (1845–1930) and Alfred von Kremer,[29] Goldziher argued that Islamic jurisprudence (*fiqh*) did not develop so much from the doctrines of the Qur'an and the normative traditions of the Prophet (sunna), but primarily from the reasoning of speculative jurists. In this way, Goldziher radicalized the first critical examination of Prophetic traditions made by von Kremer, who considered them to be "largely created by the generations of the Companions and the Successors" of Muhammad (Motzki 2000, 8). In the preface of his book, Goldziher made the statement that guided his future work. He explained that the work was based on his conviction that the study of the historical development of *fiqh* plays a foundational role in our understanding of Islam. In Islamic studies, he continued, besides research on the Qur'an and the hadith, the historical unfolding of the methods of Islamic jurisprudence (*usūl al-fiqh*) were of prime concern (1884, V–VI). Throughout the twentieth century, the scientific community in Islamic studies largely followed Goldziher in this premise.[30]

In 1888 and 1889, Ignaz Goldziher released the two volumes of his famous *Muhammedanische Studien* (*Muhammedan Studies*). Due to the rather critical reception of *Die Zahiriten*, Goldziher was reluctant to publish the study. Therefore, the overwhelmingly positive response to the first volume of *Muhammedanische Studien* from senior scholars such as Theodor Nöldeke and Alfred von Kremer came as a great relief. This was a confirmation of the innovative character of his work (Goldziher 1978, 112–116). Dedicated to his friend Snouck Hurgronje, the first volume deals with topics such as the relationship between tribalism and Islam, the Shu'ubiyya, the use of language among pagan and Muslim Arabs, and traditions among the Turks (Goldziher 1888a).[31] For the future development of Islamic studies, however, the second volume was groundbreaking. Containing his approach to studying the huge corpus of hadith literature which he had already begun to formulate in *Die Zahiriten*. In the second volume of *Muhammedanische Studien*, Goldziher fully transferred the critical reading of the Pentateuch to the study of Islamic holy scriptures. There, he elaborated in detail his thesis on the origin of Islamic traditions that he had published two years previously in an essay. According to this thesis, the stories of Muhammad and his companions that are presented in the hadith collections are anachronistic projections into the lifetime of the Prophet. Their origin reflects the historical contexts of the second and third centuries after the Prophet's death (Goldziher 1886, 365). This thesis challenged the confidence that some European orientalists had in the authenticity of many of the traditions they had been studying (Goldziher 1888b, 5). Theodor Nöldeke, for instance, expressed in several letters he wrote to Goldziher that he did not share the severity of his critique concerning the authenticity of most hadith. According to Nöldeke, many of them may be relevant descriptions of the life and actions of Muhammad. However, in 1905, Nöldeke finally admitted that Goldziher was right, stating that he was a pioneer in the study of Islamic traditions who discovered the real essence of their meaning (Simon 1986, 281).[32]

Goldziher's approach to the interpretation of Islamic traditions had a lasting impact on the study of Islam in Europe and beyond. However, it was an explicit critique of Islamic religious scholarship too. A hadith is a narrative about statements and actions of the Prophet that was transmitted orally (Goldziher 1888b, 3–11). In Islamic sciences, the existence of falsifications of these narratives was not unknown. Yet, the means of their critique was fundamentally different to Goldziher's approach. This difference Goldziher made clear in his *Muhammedanische Studien*. Muslim scholars developed a system for confirming their authenticity. The method for this investigation is to trace back the hadith to the time of the Prophet via a chain of reliable guarantors. In Arabic, this chain of guarantors is called the *isnād* of a hadith. Scholars proved the personal integrity and religious orthodoxy of all the individuals who make up an *isnād*. Only if all guarantors or narrators of the chain of names are morally and religiously unassailable is a hadith considered to be authentic. In Islamic sciences, this system of hadith critique comprises an elaborated hierarchy of the qualification of the guarantors from "trustworthy" via "harmless" to "no liar" (1888b, 140–142).[33] Not surprisingly, Islamic orthodoxies reacted to Goldziher's historical critical analysis of their religious traditions in the same manner as the Christian and Jewish orthodoxies did to his critical analysis of theirs. They completely rejected this historical critical scientific proof as directed against the revelation itself. Against this critique stood Goldziher's claim that in the Islamic history of ideas we can see a tendency to express diverging religious, social, or political opinions in the form of a hadith (1888b, 131). For instance, Goldziher presents examples of the "innumerable series of hadith" that were intended to underpin the local patriotism of individual regions and cities in Islamic empires (1888b, 128). Moreover, there are numerous pious sayings that were falsely attributed to the Prophet

(1888b, 155). According to Goldziher, due to their focus on the chain of traditionalists, Muslim scholars failed to see the striking anachronism characterizing the majority of the traditions (1888b, 149).

As we have seen, Goldziher did not question the authenticity of the Islamic revelation as such. However, he applied to Islam his own modern concept of religion. Goldziher differentiated between the universalistic internal ethics of a religion and the historically contingent forms in which it appears. Based on this concept, his critical analysis of Islamic sources did not question their original and revealed core content. The diverse historical forms of Islam he explained as the result of contingent developments and not of the unfolding of any specifically Islamic religious core. From this standpoint, in his popular *Vorlesungen über den Islam* (*Lectures on Islam*), Goldziher defined the absolute submission to God as the central idea of the Islamic religion (Goldziher 1910). In this book, which served as a textbook on Islam throughout the twentieth century (Turán 2023, 239),[34] Goldziher emphasized the omnipotence of God as the characteristic feature of Islam. The Muslim believer is convinced of this all-pervading power of God, and the belief in pure monotheism is the nature of the Islamic revelation.[35] However, it would be wrong to understand Islam as a normative and ethical system based on this core alone. On the contrary, the history of Islam is also a history of assimilation and of adjustment to new ideas, political realities, social conditions, and historical circumstances. Already in its foundational phase, Goldziher argued, Muhammad constructed an eclectic religious system due to his close contact with Judaism and Christianity, as well as the pagan religious environment of Mecca (Goldziher 1910, 1–15). In the course of Islamic history, then, Goldziher observed the direction of an increasing deviation from this religious and spiritual core. He blamed "quibbling religious jurists" for submerging Islam's pure monotheism (1910, 45). Originally a purely non-dogmatic and essentially spiritual religious message thus became distorted (Goldziher 1914, 287).[36] In line with European orientalists and contemporaneous Islamic reformers, Goldziher described Islamic history as a history of decline. As such, he appears to have endorsed the point of view of such eminent anti-clerical and anti-orthodox Muslim intellectuals and reformers as Muhammad Abduh (1849–1905) and Rashid Rida (1865–1935). In his final work on Qur'anic exegesis—*Richtungen der Islamischen Koranauslegung* (*Directions of Islamic exegesis of the Qur'an*, 1920)—he frequently referred to their writings in the reformist journal *al-manār* (*The Lighthouse*).

A broad examination of his work shows that Ignaz Goldziher made ambivalent judgments on Islam. According to Shelomo Dov Goitein, Goldziher expressed his increasing resignation with regard to Islam and Muslims in statements such as "the young Muslims of today have neither knowledge and understanding of, nor real interest in their religion" (Gothein 1979, 326). In his later years, Goldziher apparently extended his frustration with Judaism to Islam. To be sure, this frustration never led to Goldziher accepting the image of Islam as a trans-historical and stagnant holistic system in the sense of Said's *Orientalism*. Yet he also located the beginning of Islam's deviation from its anti-dogmatic and spiritual religious essence in Muhammad's move to Medina. Under the social and political conditions of Medina, the ascetic prophet transformed into a "statesman and warrior" (1910, 27). To a certain extent, we can discern in Goldziher's most popular work, *Vorlesungen über den Islam*, the idea of the "political character of Islam" too. In contradistinction to Wellhausen, however, Goldziher stressed the historical nature of this close association between Islam and politics. Consequently, he considered this historical development as reversible. The way toward this revision, according to Goldziher, would be a critical historical reading of the Qur'an. In 1898, in a letter to Martin Hartmann, he wrote about his wish that the historical critical reading of the Qur'an would become a core element of the teachings at the al-Azhar in Cairo. Goldziher imagined Islamic universities at which higher criticism would be a part of the theological studies program as it was in Christian theological faculties in Europe (Hanisch 2000, 115). The application of science to the holy scriptures of Islam would open up for a restoration of their original religious core. In this proposition we can definitely see parallels to William Robertson Smith's conviction that biblical criticism—in the end—could serve to prove the Christian revelation. For Goldziher, Islam and modernity were not incompatible. In adopting the hermeneutics of critical scholarship, Islamic reformers would be able to bring about religious and social change in the Muslim regions of the world.

Conclusions: At the Crossroads of Orient and Occident

In the preface to his textbook on Islam, Duncan Black MacDonald (1863–1943), professor at the Hartford Theological Seminary and one of the leading orientalists of his times in the United States, venerates Goldziher by posing the rhetorical question "What Arabist is not deep in his debt?"

(MacDonald 1902, viii). Indeed, the Hungarian scholar paved the way for generations of academics in Islamic studies to come. He was still on the curriculum when I was studying Islam in the 1980s. The continuing relevance of his work is not only a feature of Western European universities but also visible beyond.[37] The focus of attention thereby is Goldziher's historical critical reading of Islamic traditions. The Protestant theologist and orientalist Richard Hartmann (1881–1965) once described the analysis of the hadith literature in Goldziher's *Muhammedanische Studien* as "the crown" of his Hungarian colleague's academic work (Hartmann 1922).[38] Indeed, until today, Goldziher is known for his revolutionary approach to studying Islamic traditions, in particular the analysis of hadith. Goldziher reconstructed Islamic history with the voluminous hadith literature as his primary source. He based this reconstruction on the observation that "every opinion, every party, every representative of any doctrine" expressed their view in the form of a hadith to gain legitimacy (1910, 42). Consequently, a scholar is able to detect the conflicts and ideas that prevailed at the time of their making. The most important field of study in the history of Islamic ideas, according to Goldziher, was Islamic jurisprudence (*fiqh*). It is in the centuries-long discussions of Islamic jurisprudents that we can analyze the historical development of Islam. Here, we discern the "distortion" of the original religious core of Islam. Following Goldziher, it was Islamic law "which in its casuistic degeneration would soon become fatal for the direction of religious life and religious science" (1910, 48).

In his studies, Goldziher seems to have applied a substantial concept of religion as a kind of anthropological constant of humankind. In doing so, however, he argued that historically religion never appears as detached from the social and historical conditions in which people live. For him, this also applies to Islam. Therefore, Goldziher emphasized that we cannot study Islam detached from its historical periods of development, its geographical spread, and the ethnic characteristics of its believers (1910, 15). Consequently, he considered Islam to be compatible with modern social change. In his last book, *Die Richtungen der islamischen Koranauslegung*, Goldziher rejected the prevailing belief that Islam was incompatible with modern social change, pointing out that it had already been disproven (Goldziher 1920, 310). In his reflections on the Qur'anic exegesis of the Islamic modernists, he considered Muhammad Abduh as the "real creator of Islamic modernism in Egypt" (Goldziher 1920, 323). According to Goldziher, Abduh had adopted Jamal al-Din al-Afghani's ideas and made his journal *al-manār* the center of the "Abduh school," with Rashid Rida as his "translator" (1920, 323–324). In his analysis of Abduh's writings in *al-manār*, he comes to the conclusion that "nothing modern is foreign to him" (1920, 355). Based on his reading of Abduh's and Rida's journal Goldziher understood the Islamic Reform Movement of the nineteenth century as a clearly modernizing force.

In his understanding of Islam as a religion, we can clearly discern Goldziher's own ideas of Jewish reform. As mentioned before, Goldziher's thoughts do not match the stereotypes in Edward Said's *Orientalism* (1978). Considering Goldziher at the individual level, Turán described him as being engaged in an internal conflict between being "a traditionalist oriental Jew of sorts" and "an occidental Reform ideologue" at the same time (Turán 2023, 228). Turán put Goldziher at the crossroads of the Orient and the Occident. Indeed, the life and work of Ignaz Goldziher perfectly embodies the historical entanglements that are in fact so appreciated by many scholars of postcolonial studies. As a Hungarian Jew, he was exposed to the "internal colonialism" of Europe. His thinking on religious reform was molded by the forces of liberal Protestant revisionism, by the Jewish reform ideals of *Wissenschaft des Judentums*, and by the intellectual thought of the Islamic modernists, most profoundly expressed through his encounter with Jamal al-Din al-Afghani in Cairo. Goldziher's biography needs to be understood in terms of the structural unfolding of religion, science, and the Hungarian nation state. Of course, Goldziher was not free of some of the Eurocentric assumptions of his times. This applies especially when it comes to his liberal religious values and the societal role of science. However, in his youth, he showed a very ambivalent and overall critical attitude toward Europe. In his travel diary, for instance, he characterizes European Jews as sharing an "inner hollowness" (Patai 1987, 113). Frequently, Goldziher lamented the European style of architecture in Beirut, Cairo, and Damascus. The young Goldziher expressed a kind of disenchantment with modern European life. In Islam, then, he found the unspoiled authenticity he was missing in Europe (Haber 2006a, 136). It was definitely not the mindset of colonialism that led this founding father of Islamic studies on his scholarly path. Goldziher confirmed his fundamental critique of European colonialism as late as 1911 in a letter to Martin Hartmann. In this letter, Goldziher characterized the Italian occupation of the Ottoman territories in Libya as an immoral period ruled by the law of the jungle (Hanisch 2000, 391). How this relationship to European colonialism differed in the case of his friend and colleague Christiaan Snouck Hurgronje is the topic of the next chapter.

Notes

1 In his obituary on Martin Hartmann, Carl Heinrich Becker subjected *Der Islam* to a devastating critique, stating it would be an "act of piety" if the remaining copies of Hartmann's book were simply destroyed (Becker 1920, 488).

2 In his seminal article, Talal Asad argued that "Islam is neither a distinctive social structure nor a heterogeneous collection of beliefs, artifacts, customs, and morals." It is simply "a tradition of Muslim discourses that addresses itself to conceptions of the Islamic past and future, with reference to a particular Islamic practice in the present" (Asad 1986, 14). In the preface to the *Die Zahiriten*, Ignaz Goldziher described the purpose of his analysis of books on the Islamic legal tradition thus: "In order to judge the spirit of Islam, we must assess the relationship between its development and its sources to recognize to what extent freedom or slavishness, the tendency to progress or cling to the antiquated, active intellectual work or inert thoughtless persistence prevail in this development" (Goldziher 1884, V). In short, Goldziher advocated reading the Islamic scriptures in light of social practices as a discursive tradition which Muslims refer to in their contemporary concerns.

3 Regarding Jewish scholarship on Islam see Heschel (2018), Kramer (1999), and Mangold-Will (2021).

4 Geiger wrote his book in German; an English translation appeared under the title *Judaism and Islam* (Geiger 1970).

5 According to my knowledge, Jean-Jaques Waardenburg was the first person to dedicate a book-length publication to these three orientalists, also including in his book the French scholar Louis Massignon (1883–1962) and the American Duncan Black MacDonald (1863–1943). Apart from my own work (Jung 2011), Lisa Medrow published a book in German on the three scholars (2018).

6 Goldziher did not endorse Vámbéry's studies and described him later as an academic fraud (1978, 27).

7 For a brief article on Eötvös and his liberal thought, see Menczer (1939).

8 The influence of Steinthal on the young Goldziher was also evident in an article on gestures among the Arabs that Goldziher published in Steinthal's journal *Zeitschrift für Völkerpsychologie und Sprachwissenschaft* (*Journal of Folk Psychology and Linguistics*) in 1886 (Goldziher 1886b). This pioneering article was followed by four essays on the habitual, ritual, and magical gestures of the Prophet Muhammad. However, this work by Goldziher did not find much resonance in the academic community (see Holtzmann and Ovadia 2024).

9 It was not the first time that Goldziher came in contact with biblical criticism, but it was in Geiger's environment that he first began to truly understand the Tübingen School (Goldziher 1978, 39).

10 This 1904 letter to Nöldeke is quoted by Simon (1986, 266).

11 In Leiden, he later also made the acquaintance of Christiaan Snouck Hurgronje, who was a student there.

12 As we will see in the next chapter, this quote seems to echo Dozy's theory of the origin of Meccan cults in Judaism.

13 However, he did not extend this judgment to the Christian Arab intellectuals he met later on in Beirut and Damascus.

14 On the al-Azhar, see Goldziher's essay "Universitäts-Moschee el-Azhar" (The University Mosque al-Azhar, 1879).

15 Until 1905, only 35 full professors with a Jewish background were appointed at the three universities in Hungary. Only ten of them remained Jewish, the rest converted to Christianity (Turán 2023, 45). Conversion, however, was a clear anathema for Goldziher. In a later letter to his mentor, Fleischer, Goldziher reported on the anti-Semitism among the government bureaucracy that prevented him from being promoted to a full professorship at Budapest University (Schorsch 2016, 137).

16 According to Peter Haber, the term "neolog" has unofficially been used for "reformist" in the Hungarian language (Haber 2006a, 159).

17 Contrary to the impression one gets from Goldziher's diary, this secretarial position was, in fact, quite powerful. Together with a staff of ten, Goldziher managed the affairs of Europe's largest Jewish congregation and was responsible for its "manifold religious, educational, medical, charitable, cultural, and social activities" (Patai 1987, 30).

18 See the Goldziher memorial website hosted by the Library and Information Centre of the Hungarian Academy of Sciences (MTAK): https://goldziheren.mtak.hu/a-csalad/.

19 Fraisse argues that Goldziher adopted Geiger's approach but modified it in one crucial point. In contrast to Geiger, Goldziher saw the carrier of cultural dynamics in Judaism not as the individual but as the Jewish community as such (Fraisse 2016, 214–215).

20 Despite the fact that Goldziher visited Renan in Paris and held a speech on the occasion of the French scholar's death in Budapest (1893), he apparently disliked Renan's work. Therefore, I agree with Sabine Mangold that Renan's writings caused both an "existential destabilization and a methodological challenge" for the young Goldziher, which he addressed with his innovative scholarly achievements in the field of oriental studies (Mangold 2011, 86–87).

21 This critique may have been partly justified due to the often-speculative character of Goldziher's book and some rather questionable philological arguments (cf. Turán 2023, 104).

22 David Kaufmann was a Jewish scholar from the Habsburg province of Moravia. He studied Jewish theology at the Seminary in Breslau and was ordained as a rabbi in 1877. In the same year, he was appointed as a professor at the Rabbinical Seminary in Budapest, which was an institution run by the Neolog congregation of which Goldziher was the secretary. As a prolific writer on Jewish history, in particular on art history, and as a professor at the Seminary, he was indeed a competitor to Goldziher's aspirations in the field of Jewish studies (Miller 2025). Moreover, Goldziher and Kaufmann had to interact in the educational activities of the Rabbinical Seminary.

23 An important second reason was the resistance Goldziher experienced when attempting to implement his own educational ideas at the Rabbinical Seminary in Budapest (see Turán 2023, 109–118).

24 Goldziher distanced himself from Jewish studies to the extent that he no longer mentioned his book, not even in the obituary lecture he gave on the occasion of Ernest Renan's death in 1893 (Niewöhner 2004, 184).

25 Here Goldziher used similar sources to Wellhausen. The two collections of hadith by Muslim and al-Bukhari are perceived as *ṣaḥīḥ* (true) among Sunni Muslim scholars. Muhammad al-Bukhari (810–870) compiled about 7397 traditions with a full chain of transmitters in 97 books. Abu al-Husain Muslim (817 or 821–875) was one of the first traditionalists, and compiled about 3000 to 4000 hadith (different forms of counting) in his books (see Juynboll 1993 and Robson 1979).

26 In a letter to Martin Hartmann in 1910, Goldziher explained that the privatization of religion would be his ideal solution to questions of religion and politics (Hanisch 2000, 348).

27 These essays can be found in Desmogyi (1967–1970).

28 In Islamic law, there exist four "official schools" (*madhāhib*; sing. *madhhab*): Hanbali, Hanafi, Maliki, and Shaafi Law. The Zahiriyya is another, mediaeval orthodox school of law attributed to one of his early authorities, the Cordovan Ibn Hazm (994–1064). One of the core principles of the Zahiriyya is to eliminate any kind of subjectivity in Islamic law, basing it only on the "evident meaning" of holy texts. In his book, Goldziher almost exclusively draws from the writings of Ibn Hazm (Turki 2002).

29 Eduard Sachau (1845–1930) was a professor in Semitic languages at the University of Vienna and later director of the Seminar for Oriental Languages in Berlin (on the Seminar, see also chapter two of this book and the chapter on Carl Heinrich Becker).

30 Turán suggests seeing Goldziher's emphasis on Islamic law and his way of addressing it as a specifically Jewish angle due to his early exposure to and knowledge of Rabbinic law and Jewish discourses on oral law (Turán 2023, 120).

31 Ignaz Goldziher was the first scholar to study the Shuubiyya more deeply in the two chapters on this topic in his book *Mohammedanische Studien* (1888a, 147–218). The Shuubiyya was a movement in early Islam (800–900) of a predominantly Persian ethnic background, denying Arabs any priviliged position within the Islamic community (Enderwitz 1997, 513). For an article on Goldziher and the Shuubiyya, see Larson (2005).

32 Goldziher's radical thesis about the constructed nature of almost all hadith and his fundamental critique of Islamic sciences became the dominant thesis in twentieth-century Islamic studies. In its radical form, it is no longer tenable (Motzki 2014). For an anthology on the state of the art in contemporary hadith studies, see Motzki et al. (2013).

33 In his *Vorlesungen*, Goldziher stressed that Muslim scholars were aware of the forging of Prophetic traditions and described their critical method as "an incredibly interesting scientific discipline" (Goldziher 1920, 42).

34 The book comprises six chapters in accessible language, a kind of the state of the art from Goldziher's perspective. Originally, he prepared these chapters as presentations for a series of lectures to which he was invited by the "American Committee for Lectures on the History of Religions." In the preface to the book, Goldziher explains that due to health problems he had to cancel his planned lecture tour to the United States and decided to publish the lectures in their original form in German (Goldziher 1910, IX).

35 Nöldeke derived this concept of God directly from Judaism, stating: "Muhammed's concept of God is essentially that of the Old Testament; only he emphasizes the omnipotence and the unbounded arbitrariness of God much more, and his holiness less so" (Nöldeke 1892, 67).

36 In this argumentation, Goldziher comes close to Wellhausen's critique of Deuteronomy or Renan's description of the Jewish jurists of Jerusalem.

37 Several articles about Goldziher have appeared in Turkish scholarship in particular; see, for instance, Yazıcı 2020; Seyhan 2024a, 2024b.

38 A hadith is a kind of report about the Prophet's everyday practice and sayings. In Islamic law hadith serve as a source for legal scholars alongside the Qur'an (Motzki 2014, 3). Goldziher distinguished between hadith and sunna, both of which have the meaning of traditions of the Prophet, as follows: A hadith is an oral report traced back to Muhammad, while sunna refers to accepted religious or legal practices as conducted by the early Islamic community (Goldziher 1888b, 11).

8 Christiaan Snouck Hurgronje: Islamic Studies and Dutch Colonialism

"The experience acquired by adapting myself to the peculiarities of Mohammedans, [...], has impressed me with the firm conviction that between Islam and the modern world an understanding *is* to be attained" (Hurgronje 1916, 177). Thus, the conclusion of Christiaan Snouck Hurgronje in his book *Mohammedanism* (1916). He agreed with his friend and colleague Ignaz Goldziher that the Muslim regions of the world would also find their way into modernity. They disagreed, however, regarding the way in which this would occur.[1] While Goldziher relied on the reformative agency of Islamic modernists, Snouck Hurgronje built his opinion instead on the evolutionary power of modernization as a structural process. In the same book, the Dutch scholar wrote: "[...] the irresistible power of the evolution of human society, [...] is merciless to laws even of divine origin and transfers them, [...], from the treasury of everlasting goods to a museum of antiquities" (Hurgronje 1916, 128). Implicitly, Snouck Hurgronje was applying post-Second World War modernization theory at the beginning of the twentieth century. His scholarship was animated by the assumptions of this theory before it was defined. For him, religion and modernity were a zero-sum game. For him, the compatibility of Islam and modernity went hand in hand with the secularization of Muslim societies.

The above quotes suggest the judgment of an utterly secularist scholar. But on a personal level, did religion only play the role of an object of study for Snouck Hurgronje? The still ongoing controversy of his conversion to Islam raises doubts. In January 1885, Christiaan Snouck Hurgronje was circumcised by a barber in Jeddah, and a few days later he spoke the *shahada*, the confession of the Muslim creed, in front of an Islamic jurist and two representatives of the Ottoman governor of the Hejaz (de Vries 2011; Witkam 2022, 84). These procedures, observed by official witnesses, subsequently allowed Snouck Hurgronje to stay for half a year in the holy city of Mecca. Under his "Muslim name" Abdul Ghaffar, he conducted field studies there which strongly advanced his future career. For Peter van Koningsveld, therefore, Snouck Hurgronje's conversion was a "conversion of convenience," an "insincere form of conversion performed only to obtain certain interests" (van Koningsveld 2016, 89). Van Koningsveld considered the young Dutch scholar to be a "fraudulent convert" who aimed solely at opening for himself the gates to Mecca (van Koningsveld 2016, 89).[2] As a public controversy around Snouck Hurgronje in the 1980s showed, van Koningsveld's opinion has not been unanimously shared.[3] Factually, Muslims and non-Muslims have been completely split in their judgment of the sincerity of Snouck Hurgronje's conversion. Yet, there is no doubt that becoming Abdul Ghaffar decisively facilitated both his scholarly and political careers.

Among Europe's orientalists, Snouck Hurgronje was an exception. Throughout his professional life, he combined the study of Islam with an engagement in colonialist politics. In his orientalist scholarship, Snouck Hurgronje initially devoted himself to the study of Islamic law, just as his friend Ignaz Goldziher did. His teachers at Leiden University did not really support him in this endeavor, as Europe's classical orientalists tended to consider *fiqh* as "nothing but dry-as-dust casuistic" (Drewes 2022, 525). However, Goldziher encouraged Snouck Hurgronje to take the path of studying Islamic law as a form of "cultural history" (Drewes 2022, 525).[4] In this way, these two scholars set a new direction for the study of Islam in Europe (Pedersen 2022, 540–541). Ignaz Goldziher and Snouck Hurgronje followed the same methodological path as Julius Wellhausen did. They conducted Islamic studies as a "philology of the real" (*Realphilologie*) that in opposition to mere linguistical philological methods promoted the expansive exploration of texts as witnesses to past historical realities (Trüper 2014, 186). Their studies on Islamic law were also a means to write the history of Islam.

However, applying philological skills to texts—indexing, correcting, and editing Semitic texts in the fashion of his teacher de Goeje—was not Snouck Hurgronje's passion (Witkam 2021, 350). In his major publications, the two volumes on Mecca and the two on the Sultanate of Aceh in North Sumatra, he integrated ethnographical data through field research into his work. Moreover, these four volumes would never have been written without his embroilment in the colonial policies of the Netherlands. It was Snouck Hurgronje who first formulated a consistent Islam policy for the Dutch colonial administration in East India. Regarding his studies on Aceh, Snouck Hurgronje even dons the role of a "military anthropologist" who conducted field research in the interest of colonial authorities engaged in civil war (McFate 2019, 417). His innovative introduction of ethnographies into Islamic studies, therefore, was not merely an academic affair.

Given his significant role in the colonial politics of the Netherlands, this chapter focuses on the role of Dutch colonialism in the life and work of Snouck Hurgronje. The Dutch orientalist lived a "double life" of sorts in which he drew from two different social networks. On the one hand, he was part of a close-knit network of European orientalists and political representatives of the Netherlands. On the other hand, Abdul Ghaffar maintained life-long contacts with Muslims, both from Arab countries and from the East Indies (van Koningsveld 2016, 90).[5] The first section presents biographical data tracing his path from being a student of theology, via his activities as an orientalist and colonial advisor to his position as a professor at Leiden University. The focal point of this is his engagement with the hajj and his trip to Mecca. Then, I shift to the historical context of Dutch colonialism in the East Indies and analyze Snouck Hurgronje's Islam politics through which he sought to integrate the colonized territories into a form of Dutch Commonwealth (Witkam 2022, 91). Finally, I try to assess his contribution to the field of Islamic studies in connection with his colonial Islam policies. In this section, I also take a closer look at the two volumes that he published on Mecca. To what degree is Snouck Hurgronje a scholar who undertook his academic work in the service of colonialism?

Biography: Orientalist and Colonial Advisor

Christiaan Snouck Hurgronje was born on 8 February 1857 in the village Oosterhout in the Dutch province of Brabant. The Protestant Hurgronje family originally came from Artois in France and migrated to the Netherlands in the seventeenth century. His father, Jacob Julianus Snouck Hurgronje (1812–1870) was a minister of the Dutch Reformed Church, which followed the Calvinist tradition of Protestantism. Christiaan was the son of his second marriage to Anna Marie de Visser (1819–1892). In 1848, his father had started an affair with Anna Marie, the daughter of a colleague of his, and was therefore removed from his priestly position. As divorce was impossible, he left his first wife and their five children and moved with Anna Marie to Great Britain. After Jacob Snouck Hurgronje's first wife died in 1854, the couple married and settled down in Oosterhout in 1856. In 1870, Jacob Snouck Hurgronje passed away, and Christiaan grew up with his mother and his two elder sisters. He attended school in the nearby town of Breda, where he also received an education in classical languages, which was necessary for admission to university. As he came from a family of Protestant theologians, it was not surprising that the young Snouck Hurgronje initially chose this pathway. In 1874, the whole family moved to Leiden, where Christiaan Snouck Hurgronje joined the Protestant theological faculty.[6]

As alluded to in previous chapters, Leiden University was a European center for both the critical study of the Bible and for oriental studies. The towering figure in Protestant theology at Leiden was Abraham Kuenen. Most certainly, the young Snouck Hurgronje was introduced there to the Grafian theory of the Pentateuch in the Kuenen–Wellhausen version. According to a letter he wrote to the German orientalist Enno Littmann, Snouck Hurgronje also studied the writings of the Tübingen school with great enthusiasm (Littmann 1936). It was from the teachings of Protestant theologians that he derived his critical understanding of religion as a historical and cultural phenomenon (Buskens and Kommers 2022, 248). In the area of oriental studies, Leiden was known through the work of the Arabists Reinhard Dozy and M. J. de Goeje. Taking his exams in theology in April 1878, Snouck Hurgronje quickly renounced his priestly career and continued his academic education with the study of Semitic languages under Dozy and de Goeje. Inspired by the methods of biblical criticism, he could not see any academic future in studying Protestant theology. In his view, therefore, turning to the study of Arabic and Islam was a much more attractive path to follow (Littmann 1936, 446). Just two and a half years later, in November 1880, Snouck Hurgronje submitted his PhD thesis—*Het Mekaansche Feest* (The Mecca Festival)—which he wrote under the supervision of de Goeje (Hurgronje 1880). He chose this topic in response to de Goeje's suggestion that he "write a follow-up to Dozy's study of Jewish influences on the genesis of Islam" (Buskens and Kommers 2022, 174). In *De Israëliten te Mekka van Davids tijd tot in de vijfde eeuw onzer tijdrekening* (*The Israelites at Mecca from the Time of David to the Fifth Century of Our Era*), Dozy argued that the foundational time of the Meccan sanctuary goes back to the time of David (Dozy 1864).[7]

In his dissertation, the 23-year-old Snouck Hurgronje rejected Dozy's thesis that the Meccan cults had Jewish origins. Instead, he argued that the hajj, the pilgrimage to Mecca, basically belonged to a set of pre-Islamic Arab customs appropriated by the Prophet for pragmatic reasons. This claim already appears in the introduction to his study. Snouck Hurgronje underlines that the survival of Arab paganism in Islam was due to the ingrained conservatism of the Arabs to which Muhammad had to pay tribute (Hurgronje 1880, 4). The topic of Snouck Hurgronje's doctoral thesis, however, was not a mere academic affair. On the contrary, the hajj was also a highly political matter. In 1873, the Honorary Advisor for Native Affairs, K. F. Holle (1829–1896), presented an investigative report on the social consequences of the hajj among pilgrims from the East Indies. In his conclusion, Holle stipulated that some of those returning from Mecca were "instigators of fanaticism and zealotry" (Steenbrink 1993, 79). Consequently, he argued that these returnees were not qualified for administrative positions in the colonial government (Steenbrink 1993, 76–79).[8]

In the eyes of the colonial government, the hajj was a complicated affair. On the one hand, colonial rule increased security on the islands and, among other factors, helped facilitate the hajj (Kaptein 2014, 123; Laffan 2003, 357). Colonial rule, thus, increased the number of Indonesians coming to Mecca. On the other hand, the Dutch authorities considered visits by Indonesian pilgrims and religious scholars to Mecca as posing a threat. Due to the lack of a scholarly center for religious education in the East Indies, Mecca adopted this role for Muslims from the region. In 1901, estimations put the size of the community of Indonesian residents in Mecca at about 1,000 people (Krieken 2022, 268). This raised concerns on the part of the colonial government that some members of this community might return to the East Indies as agents of pan-Islamism and try to undermine Dutch rule (Kaptein 2014, 5). Consequently, studying the Muslim pilgrimage was in part also a work of "applied scholarship," as it was relevant to policymakers in the government at The Hague. This circumstance strongly contributed to paving the way for Snouck Hurgronje's later studies in Mecca (Hurgronje 1888, 1889).

Between 1880 and 1887, Snouck Hurgronje pursued his academic career initially in Strasbourg and then in Leiden. Shortly after the defense of his doctoral thesis, he began studying Semitic languages under Theodor Nöldeke at the Reichsuniversität in Strasbourg. The young Dutch scholar and the doyen of German orientalism developed a life-long friendship, documented in their lasting and extensive exchange of letters (van Koningsveld 1985a). In October 1881, he became a lecturer at the Municipal Institute for the education of colonial civil servants in Leiden and at the Higher War School in The Hague (Witkam 2022, 74). Snouck Hurgronje held only a low-paid position at the Municipal Institute until 1887, and it was in this period that he published the bulk of his studies on Islamic jurisprudence (Fück 1955, 232). In addition, his stay in Jeddah and Mecca (1884–1885) also fell during this period. Through his philological study of the hajj, Snouck Hurgronje became convinced that research based on textual sources alone will not suffice to understand the Muslim pilgrimage and the nature of the Indonesian community in Mecca. Therefore, he wanted to gain insights into the daily life of Mecca (Buskens and Kommers 2022, 193). In August 1884, Snouck Hurgronje arrived at the Dutch consulate in the Red Sea port of Jeddah.

In Jeddah, the Dutch consul, Johannes Adrianus Kruyt (1841–1927), was soon to leave for Penang, and his position therefore had to be refilled. One of the tasks of the consul there was to organize the pilgrimage of East Indian Muslims to Mecca.[9] Kruyt considered orientalist knowledge to be an advantage for the position in Jeddah, and indicated that Snouck Hurgronje should try to apply.[10] Looking for employment and oscillating between his scholarly and political interests, he seriously took this suggestion into consideration, as his correspondence with de Goeje shows. To his disappointment, however, the government appointed Joan Adriaan de Vicq (1857–1899) as the new consul. Missing this opportunity for a departure from the academic path, Snouck Hurgronje continued to pursue his research interests in Mecca. In February 1885, after his conversion to Islam, he went from Jeddah to Mecca, where he spent almost six months until August 1885. His access to the city and its people was facilitated by Raden Aboe Bakar Dajajadiningrat (1859–1914), a West Javanese resident in Jeddah and Mecca. Snouck Hurgronje and Raden Aboe Bakar became close friends, and the Dutch scholar convinced consul De Vicq to hire his Javanese friend as a translator and informant for the consulate. Raden Aboe Baker served for the Dutch consulate in Jeddah until his retirement in 1911 and continued to furnish Snouck Hurgronje with all kinds of information from Mecca after he had left the holy city (Witkam 2021, 360–361).

In Mecca, Snouck Hurgronje became acquainted not only with the Indonesian community living there, but also with local Islamic scholars, among others Ahmad Zayni Dahlan (1817–1886), the then highest mufti of the Shaafi school of law and the head of Islamic scholars in Mecca.[11] These positions made Dahlan a nodal point in a large international network of Muslim religious scholars. Snouck Hurgronje became a member of his circle of students and met with Dahlan on an almost daily basis. The teachings and writings of the Meccan Sheikh contributed a great deal to Snouck Hurgronje's work on Mecca and to his article "Der Mahdi" (The Mahdi), in which he presented the evolution of the Mahdi expectations in Islam and the contemporary historical relevance of this evolution

(Hurgronje 1885a, 147).[12] Shortly before the beginning of the hajj, however, Snouck Hurgronje had to leave Mecca hastily by official order of the Ottoman authorities. In an article in the German newspaper *Münchner Allgemeine Zeitung*, he explained that he was the victim of an intrigue launched by the French consul in Jeddah. An article in the French journal *Temps* had apparently presented him as a person collecting antiquities while disguised as a converted Dutch scholar studying Islam in Mecca. When it reached the Ottoman authorities, this article triggered his eviction from the Arab peninsula (Hurgronje 1885b).[13] Back in Leiden, Snouck Hurgronje resumed his teaching position at the Municipal Institute and worked on articles and the two books that were based on the data he collected from Mecca.

However, his expulsion from Arabia did not subdue his thirst for adventure and further research abroad. In March 1889, Snouck Hurgronje left Leiden for the Dutch East Indies, where he arrived as an "unattached official" in Batavia. The position was funded by a two-year allowance from the government to study Islam in Java (Hamburger 2022, 550). In 1891, he declined de Goeje's offer of a professorship at the University of Leiden, and later he also declined an offer to take up the chair previously held by William Robertson Smith at Cambridge (1904). Instead, Snouck Hurgronje remained in the East Indies, where he accepted a permanent position as "Adviser for Eastern Languages and Muhammedan Law" to the colonial government (Littman 1936, 448; Wertheim 1972, 322). He remained in this position under different titles until his return to Leiden in 1906.

In the East Indies, Snouck Hurgronje made use of his already large Muslim network and "went native" again, as he had done in Mecca previously. He continued to present himself as Abdul Gaffar and was married twice, although almost in secrecy, to women from the Indonesian aristocracy, together with whom he had five children.[14] In the East Indies, Snouck Hurgronje pursued two major intertwined aims. On the one hand, he undertook ethnographic studies, first in Java and then in Aceh, where he settled from July 1891 to February 1892 to collect data on the culture, religion language, politics, and economy of the Achenes (Hurgronje 1906a, 1906b).[15] The political importance of this study was given by the fact that the Dutch colonial army fought a long-lasting counter-insurgency war against anti-colonial resistance groups in this sultanate in northern Sumatra. On the other hand, Snouck Hurgronje designed a specific kind of Islam policy for the colonial administration based on his orientalist knowledge and the fieldwork in Aceh. Moreover, in the years 1898 to 1899, he was even directly engaged in the counter-insurgency operations of the Dutch military in Aceh (Hamburger 2022, 557).

After seventeen years in the East Indies, Snouck Hurgronje returned to Leiden in 1906, leaving his wife and five children behind. In Leiden, his teacher de Goeje had just resigned from his university chair in Semitic languages and Snouck Hurgronje succeeded him. In 1910, he married Ida Maria Orth, who was a teacher at a secondary school for girls in Leiden. The couple had one daughter, who was born in 1914 (Carvalho 2010, 77–78). While teaching at Leiden University until 1927, he continued to be an often very critical advisor to the government on colonial politics. He wrote a number of scholarly and policy articles and published his *Lectures on Islam* (1915), which were based on a series of presentations he had given in the United States. The majority of his academic work, however, had already been published before he became a professor at Leiden University. On 26 June 1936, Snouck Hurgronje died at the age of 79 in Leiden. According to his own stipulations, only his medical doctor and friend Professor van Calcar accompanied him to the grave, making his funeral a rather quiet affair (Littman 1936, 458).

Colonialism: Snouck Hurgronje and Dutch Islam Politics in the East Indies

Snouck Hurgronje took up his position in the East Indies at a time in which the Dutch government was decisively revising its colonial policies. Until the beginning of the nineteenth century, the colonial territories of the Netherlands in East India had tended to resemble a set of scattered trade outposts rather than an integrated colonial state (Tagliacozzo 2000, 90). In the context of the Aceh war (1873–1903), liberal forces in The Hague increasingly pressured the government to employ new policies of deliberate state-building in the East Indies. Adopting the narrative of a Dutch civilizing mission, these policies became known under the term of "new ethical politics." This label was coined after the publication of the booklet *De ethische koers in de koloniale politiek* (*The Ethical Course in Colonial Politics*) by the journalist Pieter Brooshooft (1845–1921). It was a quite large umbrella of policy suggestions for the East Indies that was officially inaugurated with a speech by Queen Wilhelmina (1880–1962) in 1901 (Kaptein 2014, 4; Steenbrink 1993, 92). The thirty years of war in Aceh, "one of the cruelest chapters of Dutch colonial history" (Missbach 2010, 39), clearly shows the violent side of this civilizing mission of the

Netherlands.[16] Disguising the reality of colonial suppression as a moral obligation was first and foremost a means of defending colonial interests against the protests of Liberals and Socialists at home. The ideology of ethical politics was a means of presenting the fact of colonial suppression as a task of modernizing East India's backward society (Locher-Scholten 1994, 111). In this situation, Snouck Hurgronje was a crucial strategic figure whose advice to the colonial government "helped to split the resistance movement" in Aceh, leading eventually to an end of the war (Missbach 2010, 39).

The new "civilizing rhetoric" of the Dutch government depicted colonialism as a means of elevating the people of the East Indies to the level of Dutch civilization. Ultimately, however, the so-called ethical politics also served the long-term aim of binding "as many parts of the archipelago to the mother country as possible," as well as administering and exploiting them (Missbach 2010, 42). Snouck Hurgronje fully shared this aim of strengthening the ties between the colonies and the Netherlands against internal and external threats (Vlekke 1945, 179).[17] Not surprisingly, however, these state-building policies of the colonial government regularly triggered incidents of local resistance against Dutch rule. The government in The Hague tended to identify this resistance to colonial rule with Islam more generally. The proselytizing influence of Islamic political ideas caused anxiety in Batavia and The Hague. The Muslim religion became a central challenge to their colonizing project (Tagliacozzo 2000, 87). Considering Islam as the major political force undermining its colonial state-building process, the Dutch government saw the orientalist Snouck Hurgronje as the perfect, readily available expert (Waardenburg 1988, 572). There is no doubt that the colonial situation was a crucial factor in Christiaan Snouck Hurgronje's career.

The Dutch obsession with the challenges of pan-Islamism was the pivotal point in Snouck Hurgronje's professional life as an orientalist and a colonial advisor. The political establishment in The Hague perceived pan-Islamism as a major threat to Dutch rule in the East Indies, a force that could rally Muslim people under the banner of the Ottoman sultan against the colonial government (Kaptein 2014, 5). The roots of the pan-Islamist ideology in the nineteenth century were at least partly in response to European colonialism. With religious sentiment as its ideological source, pan-Islamist ideologies were a potentially unifying force for Muslim people. Both Islamic reformers and Ottoman politicians employed pan-Islamic rhetoric for their aims (Landau 1990). In particular, the Hague regarded Arab immigrants to the East Indies as "religious fanatics."

These Arab residents had the civil status of *Vreemde Oosterlingen* (Foreign Orientals), and the colonial government perceived them as "potential adherents of the Pan-Islamist ideology" (Kaptein 2014, 5). In 1890, these Arabs numbered around 20,000 people, with the largest communities living in Batavia, Surabaya, and Palembang (Krieken 2022, 269). In their threat-perception, Dutch politicians therefore fused pan-Islamism with a degree of "Arabophobia" (Kaptein 2014, 6).

The war in Aceh ran parallel to the long reign of the Ottoman Sultan Abdülhamit II (1876–1908), who increasingly relied on the ideological force of pan-Islamism to fight the "double legitimacy crisis" that the Ottoman Empire faced. Abdülhamit II integrated religious dignitaries and Islamic jurists into the state elite and began to lay claim to the title of caliph. Selim Deringil argued that the Ottoman Sultan was trying, on the one hand, to defend the political integrity of the Empire against European powers. On the other hand, through his recourse to Islam, he was attempting to bolster his autocratic rule against the domestic opposition (Deringil 1998). Perceiving the Sultan-Caliph in Istanbul as some sort of political and spiritual leader for the Muslims of Dutch East India, the colonial administration was—wrongly—afraid the Ottoman Empire could support the anti-colonial resistance in Aceh (Krieken 2022, 260–261).[18] In addition, they were aware of the fiercely anti-British agitation by the Islamic modernists Jamal al-Din al-Afghani and Muhammad Abduh. In 1884, they published eighteen issues of the reformist journal *al-ʿurwah al-wuthqā* (The Firm Bond) from their exile in Paris, which also had reached the East Indies. In this journal, the reformists called for a necessary fusion of the anti-colonial struggle with measures of Islamic religious and social reforms. Employing religious concepts as a means of political unity, the Islamic Reform Movement was propagating national self-determination for Muslim peoples (Lutfi al-Sayyid 1968, 88).

Against this background, Christiaan Snouck Hurgronje with his erudition in Islamic law, his linguistic skills, and the personal experience from Mecca was a perfect fit for designing the Islam politics of the Netherlands.[19] However, he was an extremely critical advisor who by no means just spoke the language of the colonial administration. This is documented in the introduction to the English translations of his two volumes on Aceh. Instead of introducing the reader to the rich ethnographic observations of the study, Snouck Hurgronje justifies Dutch policies concerning the subjugation of the Acehnese. He emphasized that this aim was only achieved after Governor van Heutsz took over in 1898 and methodically pursued putting an end to the insurrection (Hurgronje

1906a, XIV). Moreover, Snouck Hurgronje stressed that this was only possible due to the accuracy of his own analysis that pointed to the significance of the religious factor in this war (1906a, XVI). In these two books on the Acehnese, the readers are addressed not only by the ethnographer Snouck Hurgronje, but also by the man in his position as an advisor to the colonial government who both strongly endorses and sharply criticizes Dutch colonial policies.

In the judgment of Snouck Hurgronje, the ignorant political majority in the Netherlands had followed a misguided strategic policy in the East Indies. Only under the pressure of the various insurgencies did the government gradually recognize that the long-term policy goal of making the Acehnese part of the "community of civilized nations" could only be achieved by using military force (Hurgronje 1906a, VII–XVII). In propagating this civilizing mission, Snouck Hurgronje was a central figure in the Netherland's colonial reform policies. In the Office of Native Affairs, he "left a whole school of followers" who all adhered to the idea of ethical politics (Steenbrinck 1993, 91). Snouck Hurgronje advocated the development of a conscious Islam policy that was intended to guide the population of the East Indies in this modernization process. Eventually, the colonial territories were expected to become an integral part of the Dutch realm. The ultimate goal of Snouck Hurgronje's Islam policies was to win over the loyalty of the population of the East Indies to the Netherlands.

The core problem in this process, according to Snouck Hurgronje's analysis, was the religious learned (*'ulama'*), who mobilized resistance against the colonial administration by invoking a jihad. This, in Snouck Hurgronje's eyes, was a completely outmoded "mediaeval doctrine" that the Muslims had to get rid of. Otherwise, they would not be able to join the community of developed nations. In the second volume of *The Achehnese* he concluded: "The passion for religious war which is so deeply rooted in the teaching of Islam is more marked among the Achehnese than with the majority of their fellow-believers in other lands, who have come by experience to regard it as a relic of a bygone age" (Hurgronje 1906b, 337). Consequently, he considered winning the war in Aceh as the first and most necessary step in the Netherlands civilizing mission. The development of closer ties between the local population and the Dutch government only could happen through a victory over this form of politicized Islam that he perceived at the heart of the problems in Aceh (Hurgronje 1906b, 351). Military victory in Aceh came first, and then the "underdeveloped" inhabitants of the Durch colony could be elevated to the level of European civilization (see also Steenbrinck 1993, 76).

The above quotes are evidence of the three almost axiomatic assumptions on which Snouck Hurgronje relied in his Islam politics. Firstly, he unconsciously applied a theory of modernization *avant la lettre*. As already mentioned in the introduction to this chapter, he was convinced that the history of modernity was the history of a universal and inevitable development of social progress toward a secular society. Second, for Snouck Hurgronje, Islam was both a religion and a political ideology. Future policies had to promote the separation of religion and politics, leaving Islam as a matter for the individual religious believer. Finally, he distinguished between law and practice in Islam, promoting a "constructivist" perception of Islam which understood the practice of its religious traditions as historically and socially contingent (Bowen 2012). Consequently, for Snouck Hurgronje, a modern Islam was not impossible. Against the background of these three general assumptions, we can understand his colonial policies concerning Islam in the way that Jan Just Witkam defined them. The Leiden professor in Islamic codicology summarized them under five themes. The religious practices of Muslims should not be restricted by the government, including conducting the hajj. The authorities should consciously monitor the circulation of ideas among Muslims. Islam policies must attempt to exclude religion from secular domains. The real enemy is the anti-colonial ideology of pan-Islamism, against which the Dutch authorities must work by means of association and emancipation (Witkam 2022, 91–92). In what ways did Snouck Hurgronje address these themes in concrete political actions?

A first answer to this question we can find in his studies on Aceh. For the implementation of his colonial political vision, Snouck Hurgronje utilized the multiplicity of research data that he had discovered through his analysis of the political, religious, and social realities of Acehnese society. In particular, he identified two local social institutions as means for limiting the influence of politicized Islam on the archipelago's population: The authoritative status of the region's traditional aristocracy and the great variety of local manifestations of customary law. He believed that the loyalty of the indigenous people for these two non-religious traditional institutions should be utilized in curbing the power of the local *ʿulamaʾ*. According to his observations, these local Muslim leaders were only partially and temporarily able to establish the normative authority of Islamic law (Hurgronje 1906a, 15). According to Snouck Hurgronje's observations, the traditional aristocrats of the East Indies factually administered justice in accordance with customary norms. While these norms were often presented as a corpus of almost sacred traditions, they were in fact rather flexible institutions alongside Islamic law and easily adjustable to new historical conditions (1906a, 10). Regarding Islamic law, however, the local aristocratic leaders only showed a sort of superficial compliance (1906a, 15). In Snouck Hurgronje's reasoning, the traditional political elite in Aceh and other parts of the islands perceived the various Islamically inspired insurgencies and the political agitation of the *'ulama'* as a threat to their own privileges and right to local rule. Therefore, he considered the Indonesian aristocracy to be a natural ally of the colonial administration (1906a, 160).

Based on his study of the Acehnese, Snouck Hurgronje drew the conclusion that the colonial administration should utilize the power of the archipelago's traditional non-religious political elite. This suggestion was not entirely new, but it began to spread from the middle of the nineteenth century among some colonial bureaucrats (Lapidus 2002, 660). What was new was the "scientific" authority of the scholar with which Snouck Hurgronje now underpinned this political strategy. In an article in 1911, he later explained his strategic view on the Islam politics of the Netherlands. This view basically rested on two pillars. First, the colonial legislators should make use of the legitimate institutions of customary law in fighting the normative power of Islam. In "purely religious matters," however, he called on the Dutch authorities to remain neutral and guarantee religious freedom of worship (Hurgronje 1911, 288).[20] Snouck Hurgronje clearly advocated for a strict differentiation between religion and politics when dealing with the East Indian population. The guarantees of religious freedom, however, should be accompanied by the full use of military force against any kind of propagation of political Islam (see also Benda 1972, 88). Second, Snouck Hurgronje suggested building a modern system of education based on the Dutch model (Hurgronje 1911, 288). In these educational institutions, the younger generation of local aristocrats could be educated according to European scientific principles. He perceived this generation as the natural allies of the Dutch government, based on the assumption that they would lose their ties to Islam and join the colonial state-building project (Steenbrink 1993, 89).

The Islam politics of Snouck Hurgronje were not only a result of his academic studies. As he had previously done in Mecca, in the East Indies the Dutch scholar also combined his orientalist knowledge with information from his extended Muslim network. Snouck Hurgronje's Islam politics definitely show traces of his contact with Muslim thinkers. In the

East Indies, prime among them was the Islamic scholar Sayyid Uthman b. Abd Allah al-Alawi. Sayyid Uthman was the descendent of a famous scholarly family from Hadramout, today's Yemen. Immigrants from Yemen played an important role among the Arab population of the East Indies. In the 1840s, Uthman studied in Mecca, with Ahmad Zayni Dahlan being among his teachers. Having spent almost two decades in the Arab region, he returned to Batavia in 1862 and made a remarkable career "as a scholar, publishing pioneer, and colonial advisor" (Bruckmayr 2024, 105). Indeed, Sayyid Uthman became a colonial advisor on Snouck Hurgronje's advice. During Sayyid Uthman's long collaboration with Snouck Hurgronje (1889–1906), the Dutch administration appointed him as Honorary Advisor for Arab Affairs in 1891 (Kaptein 2014, 103). One of Snouck Hurgronje's orientalist colleagues, L. W. C. van den Berg (1875–1927), met Sayyid Uthman in the 1880s. Then advisor to the government in the East Indies, van den Berg described Uthman as "the most important authority on Islamic theology and law in the archipelago," stressing his loyalty toward the Dutch colonial administration (2014, 109).[21]

In his publications, Sayyid Uthman used both Arabic and Malay, the latter to reach the ordinary Muslims in the region (Bruckmayr 2024, 105). Sayyid Uthman played the role of mediator between local Muslims and the colonial government, thereby directing his religious authority toward both constituencies (2024, 107). Sayyid Uthman's critique of both mystical Islamic movements and the kind of reformist Islamic modernism embodied by Jamal al-Din al-Afghani, Muhammad Abduh, and Rashid Rida aligned with Snouck Hurgronje's opinion of these groups.[22] Uthman was already in his sixties when he first contacted the young Snouck Hurgronie in a series of letters starting in August 1886. Thus, the Dutch scholar already knew him when he arrived in the East Indies and was convinced of his usefulness regarding his Islam policies (Kaptein 2014, 120). Reading and commenting on Uthman's books, Snouck Hurgronje was very familiar with the Sayyid's interpretation of "true Islam" (2014, 111). In 1894, he described Sayyid Uthman in a letter to Goldziher as his best Arab friend who combines a very orthodox point of view with tolerance. According to Snouck Hurgronje, Uthman's writings in Malay exerted a very positive influence over the Muslims of the region (van Koningsveld 1985b, 80).

In his popular writings, Sayyid Uthman described the positive side of Dutch rule: The colonial government guaranteed the freedom of religious practice, assisted in the building of mosques, and facilitated the implementation of modern technologies such as steam ships, the telegraph, public street-lighting, and clean drinking water. In Sayyid Uthman's judgment, even the security situation of the archipelago had been ameliorated under colonial rule (Kaptein 2014, 116). Even more important, when it came to the administration of Islamic law, he "was very supportive in introducing and promoting Dutch policies" (2014, 137). Together with Sayyid Uthman, Snouck Hurgronje could design an informed policy "relevant to controlling the Muslim population in the Netherlands East Indies" (2014, 139). Similar to Snouck Hurgronje's relationship with Ahmad Dahlan in Mecca, we see here another example of the collaboration between an Islamic scholar and a European orientalist that mutually benefited their individual interests (Freitag 2003, 60). Without any doubt, Sayyid Uthman's position as an Islamic scholar also profited from his close relationship to Snouck Hurgronje and the colonial government (Kaptein 2014, 264). These examples clearly prove wrong Edward Said's thesis concerning a passive and silent Orient. The nineteenth-century image of the Orient resulted from the entanglement of orientalists and "Orientals" through "exchange, dialogue, re-appropriation, contestation and confrontation" in a context of certainly asymmetric power relations (Buskens and Kommers 2022, 173).

Studies on Islam: Law, Mecca, and the Acehnese

The remarkable acceptance Snouck Hurgronje found among Muslim scholars and laymen brings us back to Snouck Hurgronje the orientalist scholar. There is no doubt that *The Achehnese* is "a classic study of colonial ethnography" (Missbach 2010, 56).[23] As mentioned before, the author did not hide the colonial purpose of his study, referring in the first sentence of his introduction to the instructions he had from the colonial government to investigate the political implications of religion in Aceh (1906, V). Moreover, the writing style of Snouck Hurgronje represents the Acehnese as "speechless objects" instead of presenting them as what they were, indispensable informants and sometimes even partners in his search for knowledge (Kołodziejczyk and Charbrowski 2023, 58).[24] His scholarly authority in matters of Islam, however, also made him a "European mufti" in the eyes of many of his Muslim collaborators.[25] Snouck Hurgronje's influential position of a governmental advisor would have been impossible without his orientalist erudition. More significantly, his profound knowledge of Islam, especially when it comes to Islamic jurisprudence, was an indispensable part of the reputation which he enjoyed among his Muslim interlocutors. The learned orientalist and the colonial advisor in Islamic and Arab affairs were inseparably interconnected.

Although one of Snouck Hurgronje's motivations for choosing the topic of his doctoral thesis was due to the political interest in the hajj, the core arguments of his *Het Mekaansche Feest* were clearly directed toward a scholarly audience. The "revolutionary ideas" of *Het Mekaansche Feest*, the two propositions on the pagan origin of the hajj and the Prophet's construction of the Abrahamic legend, were of a purely academic nature. In the scientific community of orientalist scholarship, Snouck Hurgronje caused a stir by extending the foundational role of the patriarch of the Old Testament to Islam (Witkam 2022, 76). Even more significant, he rejected the divine origin of the pilgrimage to Mecca, one of the five pillars of Islam, and described it as an "instance of strategy and power politics" paying tribute to the cultural environment in which Muhammad had to act (Witkam 2022, 77).[26] In applying the critical methods acquired in his studies in Protestant theology to his study of Islam, Snouck Hurgronje revised certain assumptions on Islamic history in a similar way to Wellhausen in his work on the history of the Old Testament. He and his friend Ignaz Goldziher made the critical reading of the prophetical traditions an inherent part of modern Islamic studies. They strengthened the thesis on the fabrication of the hadith to justify ideas and actions that occurred in much later periods of Islamic history. Snouck Hurgronje's orientalist peers largely emphasized the scholarly innovation of Snouck Hurgronje's doctoral thesis. Johannes Pedersen, a leading Danish orientalist and a student of Snouck Hurgronje, for instance, emphasized the perspicacity and maturity of the book by the young scholar. According to Pedersen, he clearly showed his philological ability to utilize a broad range of primary sources after having studied Semitic languages for only two years (Pedersen 2022, 538–539).

Regarding orientalist scholarship, *Het Mekaansche Feest* significantly advanced the knowledge of early Islam. Thereby, Snouck Hurgronje's innovative argumentation nevertheless reflected upon an existing scholarly context. Regarding secondary sources, for instance, Snouck Hurgronje mentions the two Muhammad biographies by William Muir and Alois Sprenger—despite them being, in his opinion, often "incorrect and incomplete"—and cites Sprenger fifteen times. Moreover, he expresses his gratitude to Nöldeke's *Geschichte des Qorâns* (The History of the Qur'ān), from which he "drew a lot of information" when writing the first chapter about the hajj in Islam (Hurgronje 1880, 10).[27]

Even more important, Snouck Hurgronje dissertation was further confirmation of the already established European scholarly discourse on the political character of Islam, similar to Wellhausen's article in the *Encyclopedia Britannica* (1883). As mentioned in chapter four, Wellhausen also heavily consulted Snouck Hurgronje's thesis when writing his *Reste Arabischen Heidentums*, thus further corroborating the assumptions of *Het Mekaansche Feest*. The thesis that the "real history" of Islam began with the Prophet's exile in Medina and that Islam therefore represents both a religion and a political ideology was one of the core themes that Snouck Hurgronje also transferred into the discipline of modern Islamic studies (Pedersen 2022, 536).

The other area where Snouck Hurgronje had a strong impact on the foundation of modern Islamic studies was in his work on Islamic law. Interestingly, he never published a concise work at full book length on *fiqh*. Predominantly written in Dutch, his work on Islamic law remained of a rather "casual character" represented by occasional essays and papers often on the publications of other scholars (Pedersen 2022, 540). In 1884, for instance, his critique on the third edition of L. W. C. van den Berg's *Beginselen van het Mohammedaansche recht* (*The Principles of Islamic Law*) appeared in *De Indische Gids* (Snouck Hurgronje 1884). This extended article of 164 pages is a relentless critique of van den Berg's handbook. While Snouck Hurgronje based his article on a multiplicity of primary sources in Arabic, he accused his "predecessor" in Batavia of using only translated sources, a lack of acquaintance with his subject matter, and a lack of historical sense.[28] Snouck Hurgronje's devastating review was something like a public "sensation," as van den Berg's book represented the standard "manual of Islamic law for future civil servants in the East Indies" (Drewes 2022, 526).

From his posting in Aceh, he wrote another lengthy book review, this time on the German orientalist Eduard Sachau's (1845–1930) *Muhammedanisches Recht nach schaafitischer Lehre* (Muhammadan law according to Shaafi teachings). In this book, Sachau, the director of the Berlin seminary for oriental languages, aimed to provide an introduction to Islamic law for German colonial administrators. Sachau's manual was also unable to escape Snouck Hurgronje's harsh criticism, although this attack on his German colleague was less fierce than that on van der Berg. In Snouck Hurgronje's judgment, Sachau's choice, understanding, and presentation of his sources were often wrong. Yet despite all the mistakes, he concluded that he appreciated "Sachau's textbook as a most welcome sign of awakening interest in the study of Islam among German

Orientalists" (Hurgronje 1898, 167). This conclusion points specifically to the study of Islamic law. In the first pages of his review, Snouck Hurgronje describes his core understandings of *fiqh*. He argues that Islamic law aimed for the comprehensive control of the religious, political, and social life of humanity. This ideal, however, has never been able to be achieved by Islamic jurists. On the contrary, historically the gap between ideal and social reality continuously increased, leading to a certain differentiation between religious and worldly powers. Consequently, Islamic law has developed into a cultural body of knowledge independent from state authorities that represents an Islamic utopia (Hurgronje 1888, 125–129). Throughout his life, Snouck Hurgronje retained this image of Islamic law. As late as in 1922, he wrote in the *Revue du Monde Musulman* that Islamic law "wanted to subject the details of life, even the most minute, to immutable rules" (Hurgronje 1922, 426). Against this image of Islam as an ideal systematic structure of a holistic culture, Muslim practices have always appeared to be deficient. It is this image of Islam, with its emphasis on Islamic jurisprudence, that gradually became a "matter of course" to scholars of Islamic studies in the course of the twentieth century (Pedersen 2022, 541).[29]

Snouck Hurgronje's studies on Islamic law contributed to promoting his scholarly career. Yet it was his works on Mecca, especially the second volume about daily life in the holy city, that "established the reputation of the young orientalist as an outstanding scholar" (Buskens and Kommers 2022, 168). Snouck Hurgronje published the two books in German, then the most important language in international scholarly circles. In the preface to the first volume, Snouck Hurgronje thanked Theodor Nöldeke for revising his manuscript for style and doing a final proof-reading of the German language (Hurgronje 1888, XXIII). It was the first volume—*Die Stadt und ihre Herren* (*The Town and its Rulers*)—which evidently served Max Weber for his discussion of the typical Islamic town. In *Economy and Society*, Weber argued, with direct reference to Snouck Hurgronje's "graphical description," that Mecca and thus Islamic towns as such display the typical characteristics of "clan towns" until the present day (Weber 1972, 739). *Die Stadt und ihre Herren* comprises four chapters, a short description of the town and then its history from the times of the Prophet in three steps, ending with a critique of Ottoman rule not being able to properly organize the Hejaz due to a lack of money (Hurgronje 1888, 188). Weber drew from these chapters for his very brief assessment in *Economy and Society*. Much more important, however, became the second volume of Mecca, which was translated into English.

The English version of *Mekka—Aus dem heutigen Leben* was published as late as in the year 2006 under the title *Mekka in the Latter Part of the 19th Century: Daily Life, Customs and Learning. The Moslims of the East-Indian Archipelago* (Hurgronje 2006).

The title of the English translation follows the chapters of Snouck Hurgronje's *Mekka II*. The book starts with observational descriptions of life in town (Hurgronie 1889, 1–101). These are about trade, social conflicts, different ethnicities, slaves, sheikhs, houses, festivals, etc. In the second chapter, we read about family life (1889, 102–199) in all his various facets, before moving on to "science" in Mecca (1889, 200–294). In the chapter on science, Snouck Hurgronje refers several times to his teacher Dahlan and his role as the highest sheikh among the religious learned in the town. Finally, he describes the life of the *Djāwah* in Mecca, a collective term for the Malayan people in Arab regions (1889, 295–296). This part of the book is the only section with relevance for Dutch colonial policies in the East Indies. It was among returnees from the *Djāwah* that the Dutch government suspected there were propagators of pan-Islamist ideologies. Studying Indonesian Muslims in Mecca gave Snouck Hurgronje first insights into the "social, political, and religious situation in Aceh," making him convinced he was the right person to develop a counter-insurgency strategy based on further fieldwork in the East Indies (van Dijk 2022, 336–337). Going back to the scholarly perspective, in all the chapters of his books on Mecca, Snouck Hurgronje combines his observations with more historical knowledge. The two volumes are thus an excellent example of the way in which he combined his classical knowledge as a philologically and historically trained orientalist with the eye of the ethnographer. Regarding the study of religion, he even anticipated fashionable approaches of today such as the practical turn in religious studies, with its focus on the "everyday" and "lived religion."[30]

Conclusions: Orientalist *and* "Master Spy"

Peter Hamburger gave his essay on Snouck Hurgronje's career the title "Orientalist or Master Spy?" (Hamburger 2022). At the end of this chapter, I am not comfortable answering this question either way. Instead, Snouck Hurgronje appears to me to be both an orientalist scholar and a person deeply engaged in the policies of Dutch colonialism. Looking at his shifting career as a whole, it is difficult to differentiate between the two. His pathway from Protestant theology to Semitic studies and his earlier works were—if at all—only loosely connected to the colonial situation of the Netherlands. In terms of his ethnographic interests, Snouck Hurgronje initially clearly approached them from a scholarly angle. He criticized European orientalists' incomplete knowledge of "the intellectual and social life of the Orientals" due to their almost complete reliance on books. Therefore, he defined the major purpose of his stay in Mecca as being to observe Islamic life as the necessary complement to textual studies, enabling him to meaningfully study Islam in the future (Hurgronje 1888, XIX–XX).[31] In his books about Mecca, questions of Dutch colonial rule still played a subordinated role.

The role of colonial policies in Snouck Hurgronje's scholarship, however, clearly changed with his move to the East Indies. In particular, in his ethnographic work on Java and for *The Achenese*, designing Dutch Islam politics based on collected scholarly data was a clear purpose.[32] It seems that in the course of his career, colonial interests increasingly overrode mere scholarly purposes. Yet in Snouck Hurgronje's colonial ambitions the key concept was not exploitation. On the contrary, strongly criticizing colonial politics of exploitation he wholeheartedly advocated education as the central task for Dutch colonialism. From an explicitly Eurocentric perspective, he was an ardent devotee of the Netherland's ethical politics. Snouck Hurgronje pursued this Dutch civilizing mission until the end of his life. He was convinced that in Indonesia "a compromise between Islam and humanism was possible" and that education was the means to achieve this goal (Otterspeer 2022, 503). He maintained this strong belief in the normative and moral justifications of the Netherlands' ethical politics even toward the end of his life, when these policies had become an utterly "outdated ambition" (2022, 515).

When it comes to the relationship between religion and science, Snouck Hurgronje evidently did not enter an inner conflict between scholarly knowledge and faith. In contrast to the protagonists of our previous case studies, he easily quit his studies in Protestant theology without experiencing any personal crisis. Snouck Hurgronje's conversion to Islam also remained to some extent a superficial process. In a letter to Ignaz Goldziher, he described Islam as a religion focusing on practical matters that could easily be adopted. In the ongoing dispute about Snouck Hurgronje's Muslimness, therefore, I would agree with those who do not consider his Muslim belief sincere. This does not mean that his conversion was purely a means of expediency. It was part and parcel of his fully embracing local life and becoming a nodal point within a Muslim social network. However, when I analyze his work, Snouck

Hurgronje appears to me to be a typical agnostic. How else should we otherwise understand his statement that "the treasuries of Islam are excessively full of rubbish that has become entirely useless" (Hurgronje 1916, 139)? Keeping the elements of evolutionary modernization theories that are evident in his thought in mind, we can identify the idea of the replacement of religion by science in Snouck Hurgronje's worldview and scholarly reasoning.

From a Saidian and postcolonial point of view, Snouck Hurgronje was certainly in the service of colonialism. However, not in the stereotypical way that *Orientalism* suggests. Snouck Hurgronje was not an armchair scholar who constructed the other of Europe based on classical texts. On the contrary. His ethnographic work in Mecca and Aceh to a certain extent anticipated the "anthropology of Islam" of today. For Snouck Hurgronje, Islam did not represent an essentialist cultural unity that he studied separately from the historical conditions under which Muslims lived. In stark contrast to the stereotypical image presented in *Orientalism*, his work was based on a very intimate knowledge of Muslim everyday life in its social complexity. Snouck Hurgronje "ventured far beyond the library" (Hamburger 2022, 567). This knowledge he was only able to acquire through his "being there" and his non-racist approach to non-European people. In this regard, for instance, he did not distinguish between "natives" and Europeans when it came to appointments in the colonial administration. Those who did so, he accused of applying "a fictitious racial distinction" (van den Doel 2022, 288). In his ethnographic studies, Snouck Hurgronje expressed a non-essentialist understanding of the cultures observed (Bowen 2022, 315).[33] The non-applicability of the above "orientalist" stereotype to Snouck Hurgronje does not say that he was not involved in facilitating Dutch colonial rule in the East Indies. To a certain extent, his life and work were part of European imperialism. This imperial participation also plays a role in the career of his German colleague Carl Heinrich Becker, to whom I now turn in the last case study of this book.

Notes

1 Snouck Hurgronje made his first contact with Goldziher by letter in 1880 and then met him in person at the International Congress of Orientalists in Leiden in 1883 (Hurgronje 1921, 457–458).

2 Dick van der Meij, however, indicated that van Koningsveld "heartly disliked Snouck" and therefore might have been biased in his judgment (2022, 19).

3 The controversy started with a lecture by van Koningsveld in November 1979. The debate about the scholarly credentials, political implications, and moral questions around Christiaan Snouck Hurgronje's position in Dutch academia was taken up by the media and therefore even became a public affair (see Carvalho 2010, 92–115). In contemporary Indonesia, a clear majority seems to regard Snouck Hurgronje today as somebody who infiltrated Islamic circles in the interest of the Netherlands' colonial administration (Hamburger 2022, 546).

4 In a letter to his colleague Nöldeke, Snouck Hurgronje's teacher de Goeje criticized his student's interest in Islamic law as follows: "He is full of Fikh and I do not believe that he would change front again" (quoted in van der Zande 2022, 123; fn. 31). On Goldziher's impact regarding Snouck Hurgronje's studies on Islamic law, see Hurgronje (1921).

5 See also the introduction of Buskens and van Sandwijk (2022).

6 In the biographical details, I followed Carvalho (2010, 23–26).

7 Reinhart Dozy was well known for the four volumes of his standard work *Histoire des Musulmans d'Espagne*, published in 1861 and later translated into English under the title *Spanish Islam: A History of the Moslems in Spain* (1913). In his *De Israëliten te Mekka*, Dozy argued that the "ancient ceremonies of the Meccan festival" were adopted from Jewish legends and incorporated into Islam by Muhammad (Dozy 1864, 112).

8 Snouck Hurgronje did not endorse this assumption and emphasized that most of the pilgrims had never played any political role (Hurgronje 1911, 272).

9 The consulate in Jeddah supervised the pilgrimage of about 4,000 to 7,000 Muslims from East Asia per year (Snouck Hurgronje in a letter to Goldziher in July 1884; van Koningsveld 1885b, 37).

10 It was actually J. A. van Kruyt who asked the Netherlands' Minister of Foreign Affairs for an allowance for Snouck Hurgronje, whom he had personally met in Holland in 1884 (Carvalho 2010, 41).

11 This paragraph is based on the article by Ulrike Freitag (2003), which gives an excellent overview and analysis of Snouck Hurgronje's stay in Mecca and his relationship with Dahlan. Snouck Hurgronje himself wrote in the article "Een Rector der Mekkaansche Universiteit" ("The Rector of the University of Mecca") about his encounter with Dahlan (Hurgronje 1887b).

12 The meaning of al-Mahdi is the "divinely guided" one (Gibb and Kramers 2001, 310). His exceptional position is that of an absolutely guided person of the past or of an expected future. In his article Snouck Hurgronje reconstructs the historical evolution of this kind of an eschatological Mahdi in Islamic history with reference to the then contemporary Sudanese Muhammad Ahmed al-Mahdi (1844–1885) who declared himself Mahdi and headed the Sudanese insurrection against Egyptian and British rule (Gibb and Kramers 2001, 310–313).

13 Before describing the affair leading to his expulsion from Arabia, Snouck Hurgronje briefly introduces the readers to the purpose of his stay in Mecca. His intention was to study the "domestic, social and political life of contemporary Muslims," which for the student of Islam was only possible by "seeing Mecca itself" (Hurgronje 1885b, 3).

14 Snouck Hurgronje was first married to Sangkana in 1890 and had four children with her. After Sangkana's death, he married the then only 13-year-old Siti Sadijah and had one son with her (Rohmana 2018). When he moved to Leiden in 1906, Snouck Hurgronje left Siti Sadijah and his five children back in the East Indies. However, he maintained contact with his "Indonesian family" through his friend Hasan Mustapa. The denial and secrecy around these marriages stemmed from that fact that it was forbidden for the staff of the colonial government to marry indigenous people (Rohmana 2018).

15 I refer in this chapter to the two volumes of the English translation—*The Achehnese*—of Snouck Hurgronje's books, which were first published in Dutch as *De Atjehers* by Brill in Leiden in 1893 and 1894.

16 Snouck Hurgronje assisted the Dutch governor-general Johannes Benedictus van Heutsz (1851–1924) in the violent suppression of the insurgencies in Aceh. According to official Dutch accounts, 21,685 Acehnese were killed between 1899 and 1909 (McFate 2019, 435). Freriks talks about an estimated 100,000 lives and half a million wounded (Freriks, 2021, 708). Snouck Hurgronje apparently protested against the brutal treatment of the population and eventually broke his ties with van Heutsz in 1903 (McFate 2019, 435).

17 As late as in 1915, Snouck Hurgronje confirmed this position in his dispute with the German orientalist Carl Heinrich Becker. The dispute occurred after Becker defended the Ottoman-German call for a jihad against the Entente powers in November 1914 (see the following chapter).

18 Van Krieken mentions an Acehnese delegation that arrived in Istanbul in April 1873. They asked Sultan Abdulaziz (1861–1876) for support against the Dutch troops in Aceh. The arrival of this delegation resonated in the Ottoman press. However, the debate about a possible military intervention soon faded and so did the public attention regarding the Aceh war (Krieken 2022, 260–262).

19 According to different accounts in the literature, Snouck Hurgronje apparently spoke 12–16 languages.

20 Unfortunately, Snouck Hurgronje did not really define what "pure religion" was. Yet his understanding was presumably heavily predicated on Protestant understandings of religion as the private affair of the individual. This was also quite similar to Ignaz Goldziher's practice of "pure Judaism" at home.

21 Van den Berg was an advisor for oriental languages to the colonial administration before Snouck Hurgronje. The two scholars had a rather tense relationship (Kaptein 2014, 104), and Snouck Hurgronje subjected him to his biting criticism (see the following section of this chapter).

22 The different opinions of Goldziher and Snouck Hurgronje on the Islamic Reform Movement may also have been a result of the close relationship between the Dutch scholar and Sayyid Uthman.

23 It should be mentioned that Snouck Hurgronje's study was not the only book on Aceh in his times. In the years between 1888 and 1900 alone, more than 25 publications on Aceh appeared. Parallel to Snouck Hurgronje, General van Heutsz also published a small book outlining his view on the war in Aceh: *De onderneminging van Atjeh* (*The Acehnese Enterprise*). Yet, all these publications were to

some extent political writings that did not address the topic of the population of Aceh. In this sense, in presenting an ethnography of the Acehnese people, Snouck Hurgronje had a completely different objective (Kuitert 2023, 150–151).

24 The fact that Edward Said took the colonial and paternalistic writing style of his sources as the reality on the ground is a clear indicator of the problem with his thesis of the silent Orient.

25 Wertheim called Snouck Hurgronje "the mufti of Dutch Imperialism" (Wertheim 1972, 321).

26 This thesis on the pagan origin of the hajj, however, has never been well received among Muslim scholars (see for example: Armayanto et al. 2023, 277–278).

27 William Muir (1819–1905) published his book *The Life of Mahomed* in 1858 and Alois Sprenger *Das Leben und die Lehre des Mohammad* in 1861. Nöldeke's book on the Qur'an appeared in 1860.

28 Snouck Hurgronje also referred to Ignaz Goldziher's work very positively several times, for instance to his book *Die Zahiriten* (1884, 74).

29 Snouck Hurgronje and Ignaz Goldziher essentially presented Islam as some sort of "law religion." Jacques Waardenburg once argued that Snouck Hurgronje's emphasis on Islam as a normative order reflects his own Calvinist religious background. Snouck Hurgronje, whose religious socialization took place under the dogmatic structures of Dutch Calvinism, was presumably guided by a quite familiar concept of religion as a systematic normative order of belief (Waardenburg 1962, 273). One could add here that the young Goldziher was also molded by his legalist Talmud studies and therefore equally predisposed to being drawn to legal studies in Islam.

30 See, for instance, the paradigmatic books for this trend by Nancy Ammerman (2007) and Meredith McGuire (2008).

31 This desire to observe "authentic Muslim life" was also expressed by Snouck Hurgronje in his last letter to Ignaz Goldziher from Jeddah in January 1885. In this letter, he told his Hungarian friend under the veil of secrecy that it was his plan to settle for some time in Mecca. This, Snouck Hurgronje continued, would certainly not work without any visible outward expression of the Islamic faith (*ithhār al-islām*). However, he stated that he had found a rather easy way to achieve this (van Koningsveld 1985b, 44).

32 This was much less the case in his ethnographic work in Jeddah and Mecca. In assessing the photographs of Snouck Hurgronje taken in the two cities, Ulrike Freitag argued that they demonstrate Snouck Hurgronje's genuine anthropological interest (Freitag 2022).

33 This is also confirmed in many of his letters. In June 1903, for instance, he wrote to Goldziher that a rather limited spirit prevailed in orthodox and pietistic circles. On Java, however, he encountered many believing Muslims who were also willing to transgress established boundaries of their creed. He further wrote about the high intellectual potential of some of the students of medicine being taught by European teachers (van Koningsveld 1985b, 140–141).

9 Carl Heinrich Becker: Islamic Studies and German Imperialism

The discipline of Islamic studies "is and remains the creation of the two friends Goldziher and Snouck" (Becker 1922, 214). Born in 1873, Carl Heinrich Becker was two decades younger than Ignaz Goldziher and Christiaan Snouck Hurgronje. He belonged to a later generation of scholars and, not surprisingly, he saw the two orientalists as his teachers.[1] In Becker's writings, we find a host of references to the work of these two scholars. Nevertheless, it makes sense to consider Becker, along with Goldziher and Snouck Hurgronje, as one of the founding fathers of modern Islamic studies. It was Carl Heinrich Becker who held the world's first chair in Islamic studies that was established at the Colonial Institute in Hamburg in 1908 (Franke 2010, 169). In 1910, Becker founded *Der Islam*, a journal for the culture and history of the Middle East that has been an important outlet of the discipline until today. Through the journal and his own work, Becker "helped to demarcate the newly emerging field's content and basic assumptions" (Hirschler 2006, 321). Regarding the German national environment, Becker marked the turning point in the disciplinary development of oriental studies in his establishment of the study of Islam as an independent discipline (Haarmann 1974, 57).

Like Snouck Hurgronje, Carl Heinrich Becker combined an academic career with a political one. In Becker's case, however, it was Prussian educational politics in which he was actively engaged. Only later did he emerge as a commentator on Germany's imperial politics. Between 1901 and 1916, Becker pursued his career as an orientalist in Heidelberg, Hamburg, and Bonn. Then, he accepted the offer of an appointment at the Prussian ministry of culture, where he was employed at the department for higher education. There, his task was to develop the field of international studies at Prussia's universities. In the context of the First World War, this field enjoyed highest priority for the imperial government in Berlin. Later, in 1921 and between 1925 and 1930, Becker served as minister for culture and education in Prussia (Trüper 2014, 181). His move from academia to politics was motivated by both ambition and dissatisfaction with the academic world. In a letter to Theodor Nöldeke,

Becker described himself as a scholar who was not made for quiet work sequestered in his study. Rather, he was driven by a personal interest in social engagement and a desire to work for a large and powerful institution. Furthermore, he considered it important that someone socialized within academia should take over the position at the ministry.[2] His personal profile as a German orientalist and the first professor of Islamic studies, as well as his role as an active politician in the field of higher education, makes Carl Heinrich Becker a perfect case study for the purpose of this book.

Regarding religion, Becker came from the milieu of Germany's cultural Protestants that I briefly discussed in chapter three on Max Weber. In his personal life, however, the boundary negotiations between religion and science hardly played any role. For Becker, these boundaries seemingly had been drawn in both institutional and personal terms. He had lost his faith in church doctrines at a young age, but he seems to have retained a rather diffuse and individualized religious sentiment throughout his life (Wende 1959, 47). When it comes to modern social boundary negotiations, it was ongoing questions about the relationship between science and politics that shaped his career, both as a scholar and as a minister. Carl Heinrich Becker increasingly pursued Islamic studies as a kind of applied science in the context of the imperial ambitions of the German Empire. "Islam politics" for Becker was "world politics." In this respect, there is a parallel with Snouck Hurgronje's approach to Islamic studies, although Becker did not engage directly in Prussia's colonial enterprises and conducted his research from his study rooms in Hamburg and Bonn respectively. In his conceptualization, Islamic studies was a field of both cultural studies and colonial politics. Becker defined the new discipline in sharp distinction to the orientalist obsession with philology, the activities of Christian missionaries, and what he considered to be the dilettantism of journalists and colonial administrators in writing on Islam (Medrow 2018, 139–140).

Against this background, I place the focus in this chapter on Becker's concept of Islamic studies as a new discipline and the nature of his commentary on German imperial politics. Beginning with the usual biographical remarks in the first section, the second step of this chapter is to analyze his framing of modern Islamic studies. My point of departure is Becker's paradigmatic article "Der Islam als Problem" ("Islam as a Problem") from 1910, the "foundational document" of Islamic studies in Germany (Paul 2018, 43). The third section, then, takes a closer look at his imaging of Islam and the role of Muslims in the context of European and German colonial politics. In this part, I refer especially to his publications on Christian missionaries, East Africa, and Turkey. Becker's activities in the field of higher education and as a minister of culture will only play a marginal role in this chapter.[3]

Biography: From Orientalist Scholarship to Cultural Politics

Carl Heinrich Becker was born on 11 April 1876 in Amsterdam as the fourth of six siblings. In contrast to the rather modest socio-economic background of his "teachers," Goldziher and Snouck Hurgronje, Becker came from an affluent bourgeois family. His father, Carl Becker (1821–1897), was a leading manager of the Dutch branch of the Rotschild banking house. In 1870, he retired from this position. For the rest of his life, Becker's father devoted himself primarily to his art collection and held a number of honorary positions such as the president of the Frankfurt Arts and Crafts Association and a member of the board of a music academy there (Müller 1991, 20–21). Julie Schöffer (1839–1917), Becker's mother, was also born in Amsterdam and came from a rich German trading family. In 1882, the Becker family decided to move back to Germany, and Carl Heinrich Becker grew up in Frankfurt. In Frankfurt, Becker attended the Goethe-Gymnasium (Goethe High School) from 1886 to 1895. Immediately after graduating from high school, he began his university studies. Becker first went to Lausanne for a semester, then he studied in Heidelberg (1895–1897 and 1898–1899) and Berlin (1897–1898). In Lausanne, he followed courses in Protestant theology for one semester. He took up studies of Hebrew during high school, and in Lausanne he attended lectures on critical readings of the Old Testament. Yet studying theology was not really his calling. For his second semester, he moved to Heidelberg and took up oriental studies under Carl Bezold (1859–1922), who was an expert in Accadian and Semitic languages. In Heidelberg, Becker also became familiar with the intellectual circles around Max Weber. Under the supervision of Bezold, Becker defended his doctoral thesis on the biography of the Umayyad caliph Umar ibn Abd al-Aziz (682–720) in 1899. Then, he returned to Berlin, where he studied Arabic and Persian under Martin Hartmann and Islamic law under Eduard Sachau (Müller 1991, 22).

In August 1900, Carl Heinrich Becker embarked on a journey to the Middle East. He first attended the World's Fair in Paris before traveling on to Spain. There, he spent three months at the Royal Library of San

Lorenzo de El Escorial studying the works of Arab historians. Then, he went via Tanger and Naples to Cairo. In Egypt, he took lessons in colloquial Arabic and made further studies of manuscripts in Arabic. In addition, he traveled several times to Upper Egypt and once to Khartoum in Sudan. In Khartoum, Becker was particularly interested in the Mahdi movement and the colonial policies of Great Britain. In April 1901, Becker returned via Istanbul, Greece, and Italy to Germany, before once again making a journey to Egypt and Syria between December 1901 and spring 1902. On this last trip, Becker met with the Islamic reformer and then Great Mufti of Egypt, Muhammad Abduh (1849–1905) in Cairo and attended lectures at al-Azhar University (Ritter 1937, 177; Wende 1959, 19–20). Becker concluded his formal academic education with a habilitation in Semitic philology on "Die Frau im Islam" ("Women in Islam") on 3 May 1902. From that time on, he was qualified to teach university courses, and he began to give philological lectures in Syriac, Ethiopian, and Arabic languages (Wende 1959, 21). In 1905, Becker married Hedwig Schmid, the daughter of a banker from Augsburg, with whom he later had three children. In 1906, he was initially appointed as an extraordinary professor at Heidelberg University, becoming a full professor in 1908 (Medrow 2018, 136; fn. 275). Presumably, this quick career was facilitated by the fact that the Indian Muslim Reform University in Aligarh, established by the famous Indian Muslim reformer Sayyid Ahmad Khan (1817–1898), offered him a chair in Arabic at the same time. Becker rejected the offer from Aligarh and remained in Heidelberg (Jung 2011, 201).

Two scientific communities converged in the scholarly formation of Becker. On the one hand, there is the international community of orientalists and the early founding fathers of modern Islamic studies. Becker dedicated the first volume of his collected academic essays, *Islamstudien. Vom Werden und Wesen der Islamischen Welt* (*Studies of Islam: On the Development and Nature of the Islamic World*), to Julius Wellhausen, Ignaz Goldziher, Theodor Nöldeke, and Christian Snouck Hurgronje. Through this dedication he wished to express his "gratitude and veneration to his masters" (Becker 1924, VI).[4] In his obituary on Wellhausen, Becker emphasized the importance of his older colleague in his own career. Having read Wellhausen's *Prolegomena* during high school helped Becker shape his future career choice. The real ingenuity of Wellhausen's individual scholarly achievements, however, Becker saw in the field of Arab studies, especially in his *Das Arabische Reich und sein Sturz* (Becker 1918a, 474–475). On the other hand, as a student in Heidelberg, Becker came into contact with Germany's *Religionsgeschichtliche Schule*, which I already mentioned in chapter three. He attended lectures held by the philologist and scholar of religion Albrecht Dieterich (1866–1908), one of the founders of the *Eranos* circle and from 1904 to 1908 editor of the *Archiv für Religionswissensschaft* (*Archive for the Science of Religion*).[5] On Saturdays, Becker participated in the *jour fix* at the house of Marianne and Max Weber, joining intellectuals and scholars such as Ernst Bloch, Albrecht Dieterich, Stefan George, Eberhard Gothein, Karl Jaspers, Georg Jellinek, Georg Lucács, Georg Simmel, Werner Sombart, and Ernst Troeltsch (Haridi 2005, 113, fn. 88; Müller 1991, 37–59; and Ritter 1937, 176). There is no doubt that Becker's conceptual approach to study Islam was deeply molded by the philosophical and historical thoughts of these networks of German scholars.[6]

During his time at Heidelberg University, Becker taught regular courses in Semitic languages and Islamic history. In the winter semester of 1906, he began with a series of public lectures on modern Islam. These apparently well-attended lectures were directed toward a broader audience and served to promote Islamic studies as a modern discipline liberated from the traditional confines of philology (Wende 1959, 21). Moreover, most of his early publications were related to the political and economic history of medieval Egypt and included some studies of Papyrus manuscripts. Most important in his early writings were the two volumes of *Beiträge zur Geschichte Ägyptens unter dem Islam* (*Contributions to the History of Egypt in Islam*), which were published in 1902 and 1903 respectively. In the first volume, Becker wrote about history writing in the Fatimid empire and edited fragments of manuscripts of the Fatimid chronist, historian, and government official al-Musabbihi (977–1030). These were texts he had copied in the months he had spent at El Escorial in Spain. For the revision of the book manuscript, he thanked his teacher Carl Bezold, who took over this task while Becker was traveling in Syria (Becker 1902). In the second volume (Becker 1903), Becker described the economic development of Egypt in the first centuries after the Prophet, the system of taxation, the Arabization and Islamization of the country, and the rule of the Tulunid dynasty (868–905).[7]

These more classical orientalist studies based on primary sources, however, only featured in the early period of Becker's academic career. In autumn 1908, he moved from Heidelberg to Hamburg, where he was appointed as professor for the history and culture of the Orient at the newly established Colonial Institute.[8] Becker's time in Hamburg (1908–1913) was the most important period in his scholarly life. It was in

Hamburg that Becker replaced the profile of a classical orientalist with that of a scholar of modern Islamic studies. The professorship at the Colonial Institute enabled him to articulate problems on contemporary Islam related to questions such as the history of the Ottoman Empire, the "Oriental Question," or the Islam politics in Dutch East India (Müller 1991, 64–65). In his letters to Karl Rathgen (1856–1921), a well-known economist and professor at the Colonial Institute, Becker expressed his delight at the profile of his new chair. Rathgen strongly supported Becker's appointment, knowing of his interest in the economics and politics of Muslim regions. He pointed out to Werner von Melle (1853–1937), chairman of the Hamburg Higher Education Authority, that Becker knew the Orient from a long stay and was not only a philologist. Even more important, Rathgen explained, he gave very successful lectures on modern Islam and was versed in the political and economic development of the Middle East. Given von Melle's keenness not to appoint a classical orientalist to the position, Rathgen's proposal of offering Becker the chair at the Colonial Institute received his enthusiastic reception (von Melle, 1923, 480–481).

In his scholarly work, Becker began to engage in working on Islamic law and culture more broadly, in particular regarding the role of Islam in the context of colonial politics. The Institute represented for him a role model for the study of world politics. The study of contemporary Islam came to dominate his teaching and research, while the study of regional languages served merely as a means to an end (von Melle 1923, 631). Given its task to educate Germany's colonial administrators, Becker developed an idea of Islamic colonial studies that combined an academic discipline with the demands of an applied form of science. Paradigmatic in this respect was Becker's lecture "*Ist der Islam eine Gefahr für unsere Kolonien?*" first published in *Koloniale Rundschau* (The Colonial Review) in 1909. Referring to the German colonies in West and East Africa, Becker questioned the potential threats that Islam could pose to the German colonial administration, the Christianization of the region, and the spread of European civilization in Africa more general. Like his Dutch colleague Snouck Hurgronje, Becker emphasized the need for in-depth knowledge on Islam among colonial administrative staff. Only with this knowledge would they be able to facilitate the integration of the Muslim population into the state-building processes in the German colonies in Africa. According to Becker, the Colonial Institute should provide this academic in-depth study of Islam to its students (Becker 1909, 157, 186).

During his time at the Colonial Institute, Carl Heinrich Becker increasingly involved himself in the university policies of Hamburg. Teaching about twenty students sent by the foreign ministry in Berlin for only two semesters was not what he considered to be higher education.[9] The aim of Becker and his colleagues was to educate a future generation of scholars. However, under the prevailing conditions, it was impossible to provide a real academic education. After five years in Hamburg, his attempt to transform the Colonial Institute into a new model university had reached a complete stalemate (Wende 1959, 30–33). Therefore, in summer 1913, Becker accepted a chair in the history and languages of the Orient at Bonn University. In Bonn, then a rather provincial town compared to Hamburg, he nevertheless saw a better opportunity for continuing his scholarly and administrative struggle for the establishment of the modern discipline of Islamic studies. From the time of his arrival, Becker argued that Islamic studies should be organized in a separate unit, while teaching his initial lectures on Islam to about fifty students from all faculties. With the beginning of the First World War, Becker embedded his lectures more and more in the context of world politics (Wende 1959, 36–38). On the occasion of the 57th birthday of Emperor Wilhelm II (1859–1941) in January 1916, Becker gave the lecture *Das türkische Bildungsproblem* (*The Issue of Education in Turkey*) at the Friedrich-Wilhelm-University in Bonn. In this lecture, Becker spoke not merely as an orientalist, but already as a policymaker in higher education. With regard to the alliance between Germany and the Ottoman Empire, Becker argued that "Turkey" was suffering from a problem in its education system. Beyond issues of its politics and economics, the solution to this problem would determine the country's future (Becker 1916a, 363).[10] Half a year later, the university professor Carl Heinrich Becker left academia and took up a new position in the Prussian ministry of culture.

In 1919, Carl Heinrich Becker became a permanent secretary in the ministry. In this position, he was confronted with three basic problems of post-First World War Germany: the relationship of Prussia to the rest of German regional states regarding cultural policies; the reform of German universities; and the reform of the country's general system of education (Wende 1959, 82). For a short period of time in 1921, Becker served as a minister himself. His second period as minister of culture and education lasted from 1925 until his resignation in 1930. In his work as a political bureaucrat and minister, Becker consequently defended the foundational features of the Humboldtian university and the autonomy of science (Ritter 1963, 278). Moreover, he considered the school system as a means for the democratization of Germany's youth and tried to push back the ever-increasing anti-Semitic and nationalist radicalization of German students (Wende 1959, 252–268). After his resignation, Becker was appointed as a full professor in Berlin and received an honorary doctorate at the juridical faculty of Kiel University. In August 1930, he went with his son to the United States, where he gave about thirty academic and popular lectures before engaging in international cultural works in the following two years (Wende 1959, 302–304). From September 1931 to April 1932, Becker traveled through Japan, China, Dutch East India, Iran, Iraq, and Syria as a member of an educational mission of the League of Nations. Carl Heinrich Becker died in February 1933 of pneumonia, at the age of only 57 years (Ritter 1937, 179, 184–85).

Becker's Image of Islam: The Hellenist Foundations of the Islamic Civilization

In 1910, while a professor at the Colonial Institute in Hamburg, Becker established the journal *Der Islam*. This new journal, with its focus on the Muslim regions of the world, was one of the first outlets of the new scientific community of Islamic studies.[11] Becker himself opened the first issue of the journal with a paradigmatic essay, *Der Islam als Problem* (*Islam as a Problem*). Mark Batunsky described Becker's article as "an attempt to bid resolute farewell" to many of the core assumption that had characterized the field of oriental studies in the nineteenth century (Batunsky 1981, 288). Given Becker's interest in applied research, his title—"Islam as a problem"—had an ambiguous character. In German, the title refers to Islam as a subject of academic research and to Islam as an issue of European colonial politics. Islam was both a scholarly concept of a new academic discipline and a relevant factor in shaping colonial political practices, such as Snouck Hurgronje's Dutch Islam politics. In Germany in the years before the First World War, Islam politics revolved around questions of German colonialism in East Africa and the country's relationship with Iran and the Ottoman Empire. While Becker's essay can be linked to German imperialism, this connection should not be taken as clear proof of Edward Said's thesis. The intersection of Islamic studies and European colonialism was quite complex, as the thought of Carl Heinrich Becker shows. How did he define the new "Wissenschaft vom Islam" (science of Islam)?

In Becker's eyes, Islamic studies was a historical discipline combined with philological methods pertaining to languages spoken by Muslim people. In terms of meaning, Becker pointed to the conceptual application of Islam to three distinct phenomena: a particular religion, oriental empires, and the cultural whole of a particular civilization. For him, Islam primarily referred to a unitary kind of Islamic civilization. Islam as a religion—at least based on classical scholarship—had supposedly shaped this unity of Islam: "State and society, science and economic life are under the rule of the religious formula" (Becker 1910a, 3). This perception, according to Becker, was the conventional view of Islam in his times. While this assumption reflects "orientalist" stereotypes, Becker suggested that contemporary scholars must question this view of a history of Islam subordinated to religion. In his pilot article, he asked whether religion was indeed the decisive factor in shaping Islam as a unitary civilization (1910a, 3). In the subsequent pages of his essay, Becker looks at different factors, especially at the political and economic dimensions, that according to him played significant roles in the historical construction of Islam as a civilization. For Islamic studies, Becker therefore suggested treating Islam as a scholarly problem by posing the question: "How did the civilizational unity of Islam come into existence and what role does the religious element play in this historical development?" (Becker 1910a, 4). Without any doubt, Becker's concept of an Islamic civilization did not match the Saidian stereotype of Islam as a "cultural synthesis" that could be studied separately from the economics and politics of the East (Said 1978, 105).[12]

Following Becker's analysis, Islam initially built on religious revelation. Historically, however, it developed into an Islamic civilization with a multiplicity of different faces. This complex and multi-facetted Islamic civilization, according to Becker, was not shaped by religion alone. In his historical understanding, the unifying cultural power of Islam as a civilization was due to its absorption of Hellenism (1910, 15). Before coming to Hamburg, Becker published his book *Christianity and Islam* in 1907. Inspired by the latest approaches in the comparative study of religion at the time, he laid out in this book the thesis that Christianity and Islam shared a common background in Hellenism (Morrone 2021, 375). According to this thesis, the medieval cultures of the Orient and the Occident were identical. Becker proposed that, in both regions, we are essentially "confronted with the Christian worldview as it was developed in the Orient of the seventh and eight centuries" (Becker 1907, 416). Due to different religions, languages, and people, Becker argued, this identity in the culture of both civilizations became completely disguised (1907, 388). The Orient, Becker continued, remained in the shared cultural tradition of the Middle Ages.[13] In the Renaissance and the Reformation, Europe—instead—liberated itself from its traditional form of Christian Hellenism (1907, 428). While in Christian Europe a new kind of Greek humanism was born, Islamic history continued within the confines of similar questions to those we know from Christian antiquity.[14] This preoccupation of the Orient with what Becker defined as the passing problems of medieval Europe he saw manifested in the formation of the enormous body of Islamic law (1907, 417). In the Muslim history of ideas, the comprehensive claim of religious law and Islamic mysticism have remained the dominant forces (1916a, 368). Modern "man" was the discovery of Europe, whereas in the Orient Islamic law, the "all-encompassing nature of this legal doctrine of duties," prevented modern developments (1918b, 44). While grounding the origin of Islamic civilization in Hellenism, Becker nevertheless perceived Islamic traditions in a holistic sense based on the idea of religious law.[15]

The first volume of Becker's *Islamstudien* starts with four essays under the rubric "Zur Einleitung" (As an introduction). These essays, written between 1910 and 1921, all underline his thesis of the common cultural foundations of the Orient and the Occident (Becker 1918b, 40). It was the humanism of the Renaissance that eventually differentiated Europe from the Islamic parts of the world: "It created a fundamental difference in the conception of man and humanity" (Becker 1921, 34). In his address to the Annual Conference of German Orientalists in Leipzig on 30 September 1921, the then minister in the government of Adam Stegerwald (1874–1945) emphasized again that for him Islam was not part of Asian but of European cultural developments (1921, 26). Becker's conceptual point of departure was Ernst Troeltsch's *Kulturkreistheorie* (theory of cultural circles). The German theologian considered European and non-European cultures as historically constructed but nevertheless relatively closed cultural wholes. In this conceptualization, European culture clearly differed from other cultures but is, according to Troeltsch, not superior to them. In this sense, Troeltsch's Europeanism was not characterized by Eurocentrism (Schmiedel 2016, 242). Becker largely followed Troeltsch's theory of cultural circles and the historical development of European culture. However, he criticized the German theologian's rigid separation of oriental and occidental culture, according to which Islam is a part of Asian culture (Becker 1921, 26). Expanding Troeltsch's thesis of the historical emergence of European culture to partly include Islam, Becker argued that Islamic civilization is also based on the same three

Urgewalten (primal forces): oriental antiquity, Hellenism, and dogmatic, cultic, and mystical elements of Christianity (1921, 28). Consequently, for Becker Islam as a civilization was not synonymous with Islam as a religion.

Becker published an overview article on the religious dimension of Islam for the general reader under the title "Abriss der islamischen Religion" ("Outline of the Islamic Religion").[16] This handbook article largely referred to the then current secondary sources, in particular the works of Goldziher, Snouck Hurgronje, and Wellhausen. In it he defined Islam as a unique religion which nevertheless drew on Judaism and Christianity in both its form and content (Becker 1912a, 331). In contrast to the prevailing view, however, he rejected the assumption that Islam had been spread through military force: "It was not religion that was spread by the sword, but the worldly rule of the Arabs" (Becker 1914a, 3). Becker claims that those people who came under Arab military rule had converted peacefully to Islam. It was not the spread of Islam but the establishment of Arab-Islamic empires that was the result of military campaigns (1912a, 332–333). Even in his inaugural article in *Der Islam*, Becker strongly underscored differentiating between political expansion and religious conversion in Islamic history (1910, 6). Given the relatively close contact between Becker and Max Weber in Heidelberg, it is telling that in his writings Weber nevertheless propagated the thesis of Islam's spread by military means.[17]

Once Carl Heinrich Becker took up his position in Hamburg, his studies basically built on his broad reading of secondary sources. He rarely went back to the study of primary sources such as in his earlier works. This applies to Becker's description of the life of Prophet Muhammad too. In this case, he drew from the work of Snouck Hurgronje and the Italian scholar Leone Caetani (1869–1935), who was also a strong advocate of the thesis that the hadith literature was of a fabricated nature. Consequently, Becker told his readers that the transmitted practices and sayings of the Prophet only represent to a very small degree the accurate historical details of his lifetime. As such, the Arab biographies of Muhammad were basically biographically arranged hadith material (1913, 520).[18] In his judgment of the historical accuracy of this material, Becker closely followed Goldziher's interpretation of the anachronistic nature of the hadith. He described most of them as fictional stories of later times (1913, 521). Their critical analysis, however, provides insights into the "great battles" of Islamic history and the ways in which the new religion adapted itself to the changing intellectual environment (1912a,

352–353). From this perspective, Becker did not portray Islam in stagnation, but as a living and adaptable cultural entity. Islamic civilization, for him, was a multi-facetted culture open to historical and social change.

Against this background, Carl Heinrich Becker was convinced that Islam as a religion did not represent a general obstacle to Muslims joining the modern world (1918b, 49). If contemporary Muslims would only get rid of their medieval worldview—such was Becker's take—Islam and modernity could meet. Like Ignaz Goldziher, he saw in the Islamic modernists a potential force in the modernization of Muslim people (1918b, 50–52). The rationalist and nationalist intellectual modern movements among Muslims could offer indigenous forces of reform (1916a, 374). Becker identified the problem with contemporary Islam in the confrontation of the traditional Islamic orthodoxy, in particular the jurisprudents, with the modern culture of Europe (1912a, 381). The future of Islam, according to Becker, depended on its adaptability to modern European culture—however, not through complete emulation. The modernization of Muslim regions should be anchored in a new interpretation of their own cultural traditions. Becker identified the major obstacle to this indigenous modernization as being the system of traditional Islamic education. As such, he considered the "helping hand" of Europe to be a necessity. In the context of the war alliance between Germany and the Ottoman Empire, Becker perceived Germany as the ideal "schoolmaster" to best guide Turkey unselfishly toward this critical adaptation of European culture by embedding it in its own traditions (1916a, 378). Becker understood Germany's cultural foreign policy in terms of aiding Turkey in its own development and strengthening of the nation (Mangold-Will 2013, 263).

In this way, Becker advocated a kind of self-conscious modernization of the Orient under European guidance. In his reasoning, however, this process would not necessarily end in an atheist worldview. On the contrary. Islam as a religion, Becker argued, contains many ethical and religious elements with the help of which Islamic modernists could build a modern religion (1912a, 383). Clearly, Becker rejected some of the core "orientalist" stereotypes that Edward Said and postcolonial scholars have generally associated with European scholarship on Islam. Even more significant, in proposing his thesis of the shared cultural fundaments of Islam and Christianity, Becker did not construct Islam as the ultimate other of Europe. As already discussed above in this section, the differences between European and Muslim cultures Becker perceived as being not of an essential but of a historical nature. Becker identified the major cause of these differences—this should be stressed again—in the historically evolved prescriptions of Islamic law. While considering *fiqh* as one of the most original cultural features of Islam on the one hand (1912a, 354), he blamed the orthodoxy of Islamic jurisprudence for the "backwardness" of the Muslim regions of the world on the other. Islamic law, according to Becker, represented the stifling ideals of Muslim traditionalism (1904, 238). Following Waardenburg, Becker perceived Islamic law as substantial to Islam in the sense of a comprehensive normative ideal that was in a permanent status of protest against historical reality (Waardenburg 1962, 249). Becker clearly adopted Snouck Hurgronje's position of the wide gap between the ideal and practice in Islamic law. In the end, he shared the diagnosis of many orientalists that it was the power of this normative ideal of this "all-encompassing nature of this legal doctrine of duties" that prevented the modern development of Islam (1918b, 44).

Ignaz Goldziher and Christiaan Snouck Hurgronje did not apply explicit theoretical frameworks in their studies. They barely reflected upon the evolutionary and historicist assumptions in their works, instead taking them for granted. In this respect Becker was different. He developed his thought on Islam in explicit though rather eclectic and unsystematic reference to various set pieces of the conceptual apparatus of early sociology and the discipline of comparative religion. Germany's *Religionswissenschaftliche Schule* and Max Weber made a strong impact on his academic work. While acknowledging the philological roots of Islamic studies, in "Der Islam als Problem" he suggested informing the study of Islam by concepts and methods from the rising academic disciplines of the social sciences and humanities (Becker 1910a). Becker frequently referred to essays by Max Weber, such as The Protestant Ethic (Becker 1921, 33; 1918b, 52), the sociology of medieval towns (Becker 1921, 36), "oriental despotism" (Becker 1916a, 383), and Weber's sociology of religion (Becker 1916b, 54).[19] Alexander Haridi pointed to the concept of universal history shared by Becker, Troeltsch, and Weber. According to his analysis, all three German scholars struggled with the question of the European origins of modernity (Haridi 2005, 109–110).[20] Furthermore, Becker adopted the critical attitude toward the instrumental rationalization in European modernity that characterized Weber's philosophical position. In Becker's later writings we can even detect a similar "antipathy toward modern industrial society," which was a core feature of the world view of the followers of Stefan George (1868–1933) whom he met in Heidelberg.[21] Indeed, Becker's paradigm of an Islamic civilization was firmly embedded in the German intellectual context of his times.[22]

Colonialism: Islam as a Means of the German Civilizing Mission in Africa

Carl Heinrich Becker shared not only this German intellectual background, but also the political worldview associated with it. In chapter three of this book, I defined this worldview as a kind of liberal bourgeoise German nationalism. Like Max Weber, Becker advocated for Germany to take on a greater imperial role as a European great power. At the beginning of the First World War, Becker's German nationalist stance became more than clear in the dispute with his Dutch counterpart Christiaan Snouck Hurgronje. The dispute between the two scholars broke out after the Ottoman Sultan Mehmet V (1909–1918) declared jihad against the Entente nations on 11 November 1914. Two weeks earlier, the Ottoman Empire had joined the central powers Germany and Austria in the First World War. The proclamation of a "holy war" in this context was an attempt to rally the world's Muslim population behind the war aims of the central powers.[23] Given the high numbers of Muslims among British and French colonial troops, as well as in the Russian army, this seemed, at first glance, to be a useful war strategy. However, the voice of the Ottoman Sultan did not really resonate among Muslims, and the strategy ultimately failed (Trumpener 1968, 117–119). Instead, this historically last official proclamation of jihad by a Sultan-Caliph stirred a dispute within the international community of orientalists, especially as the origin of this war strategy was in Berlin rather than in the Ottoman capital, Istanbul. Evidently, it had been developed at the *Nachrichtenstelle für den Orient* (*Intelligence Bureau for the Orient*) of the German foreign ministry (Schwanitz 2003). There, a group around Max von Oppenheim (1860–1946), an adventurer, archaeologist, ethnologist, and traveling scholar, had the task of producing and disseminating German war propaganda for Muslims in the Middle East and India.[24]

Snouck Hurgronje and many of his colleagues shared a suspicion that the jihad proclamation had originated in Germany and that the country's leading orientalist scholars had played a role in it (Hagen 2004, 145). In an essay titled "The Holy War 'Made in Germany,'" Snouck Hurgronje accused Becker of apparently having been "swept away by the incredible Jihad-craze, which at present possesses German statesmen" (Snouck Hurgronje

1915a, 274, see also 1915b). He perceived Becker and Martin Hartmann as the "chief representatives of the science of Islam in Germany" (1915a, 279), who now supported a kind of war propaganda that was based on a ridiculous atavist medieval Islamic religious doctrine.[25] For Snouck Hurgronje, this proclamation of an Ottoman–German jihad was a "politico-religious mixture of deceit and nonsense" that aimed to unleash religious fanaticism, which could also harm the successful educational policies of the Dutch colonial administration in the East Indies (1915a, 283, 291). Against his better knowledge as a scholar, Snouck Hurgronje argued, Becker was participating in triggering Pan-Islamist sentiments that were based on a "worn-out, flagrantly impracticable program of world conquest by Islam" (1915a, 266). In the eyes of Carl Heinrich Becker and Martin Hartmann, Snouck Hurgronje's article clearly violated Dutch neutrality in the war. Theodor Nöldeke considered the essay to be an "unacceptable attack" against Germany by his former Dutch student. He agreed with Ignaz Goldziher that the governments of Germany and the Ottoman Empire had the right to use all possible means in this "struggle for existence" (Simon 1986, 373–376).[26] Given the serious accusations against him, it was Becker who claimed the right to respond in the name of German orientalists (Hanisch 1992, 82–83).

In his reply, Becker basically endorsed Snouck Hurgronje's judgment of jihad as an outdated medieval doctrine, as a remnant of traditional Islam not able to survive in modern times. But why not try to employ it as a possible means in times of existential conflict, Becker asked (Becker 1915a, 288). From a scholarly perspective, Becker would not have supported this strategy. As a means of implementing Germany's Islam politics amid Europe's violent imperialist power struggle, however, he supported this proclamation of jihad against France, Great Britain, and Russia. In the given historical context, Becker described Snouck Hurgronje's essay as the unrealistic comment of an armchair scholar erudite in Islamic law. In the context of existential warfare, Pan-Islamism is not a medieval doctrine, but an anti-colonial political ideology. Therefore, Becker declared the Ottoman proclamation of jihad to be a sign of the national awakening of Asian peoples, albeit under an essentially outdated religious bond (1915a, 298). The dispute between Becker and Snouck Hurgronje can be read as a kind of boundary negotiation between science and politics in which the logic of nationalist and imperial political agendas overruled the scholarly insights of the two protagonists. To a certain extent, this episode among European orientalists is an example of the explosion of nationalist hatred at the beginning of the First World War that Stefan

Zweig (1881–1942) so aptly described in *Die Welt von Gestern* (subsequently published in English as *The World of Yesterday*; see Zweig 1942). Nationalist and imperialist sentiments also divided the previously so closely knit networks of European orientalists. Once intimate scientific communities became divided by nationalist politics.

In this exchange with Snouck Hurgronje, Carl Heinrich Becker clearly identified with Germany's war strategies. This complete endorsement of German imperial politics, however, was not always the case when it comes to Becker as the representative of applied Islamic studies. In his scholarly advice regarding Germany's imperial aspirations, Becker normally based his opinion on his academic knowledge.[27] In that context, it was first the scholar and then the politician who spoke. To be sure, also Becker emphasized in his lectures and articles on German colonialism the "civilizing mission" of Europe. The aforementioned role of Germany as schoolmaster in Turkey's educational reforms is an excellent example for a German version of this colonialist ideology. Becker shared Snouck Hurgronje's position of conducting colonial policies as a historical and moral task based on solid knowledge about the Islamic practices and local customs in the colonies.[28] In his essay *Die Araber als Kolonisatoren* (*The Arabs as Colonizers*), Becker stressed Germany's right to establish colonies in Africa. In drawing a parallel between the expansion of Arab rule in the Middle Ages and European colonialism, Becker interpreted certain features of Arab governance as anticipations of what he termed "positive modern colonial thought" (1914a, 7). He mentioned the formation of an aristocratic ruling elite, the separation of the "master race" from the colonized subjects, and the prohibition of the concubinage with indigenous people in order to prevent their assimilation into the colonizing upper class (Becker 1914a, 7). In this article, first published in *Jahrbuch über die deutschen Kolonien* (*Yearbook on the German Colonies*), Becker presented himself as a strong supporter of Germany's colonial ambitions. The position at the Colonial Institute in Hamburg had definitely made an impression on him.

In many of his writings, as in the above on Arabs as colonizers, Becker expressed a certain respect for Arab and Islamic culture. In his lecture on "Islampolitik" (Islam politics), he described Islam as a morally high-ranking religion (1915b, 323). This respect, however, stands in sharp contrast to the disdain with which he often described the indigenous population of Africa. Becker spoke of the "slavish mentality of the negro" and the "primitive mindset" of Africans that "excludes them from the higher forms of the Christian religion and European civilization" (1910b, 195). Therefore, he declared the efforts of Christian missionaries to be in vain. Becker simply denied the inhabitants of Africa the right to self-determination (1915b, 330). Becker frequently resorted to racist vocabulary when describing African peoples. In this context, Becker's tone sometimes resonated with the disparaging quality that is met in the writings of Ernest Renan. Joseph van Ess argued that Becker employed the term "race" in the same vein as "people" or in the way that the word "society" was used in post-Second World War language (van Ess 1980, 48–49). To be sure, the mere usage of the term in the early twentieth century does not necessarily indicate that an author is racist in the political sense of the word. Moreover, Becker applied "race" almost synonymous with other terms for human collectivities such as "nation" or "ethnic group." Yet his studies on Germany's colonial politics were built on the premise of a cultural hierarchy of different peoples and religions. Becker clearly treated black Africans as inferior to Arabs and these in turn inferior to Europeans. In terms of religion, he applied an evolutionary hierarchy from paganism to Christianity in which Islam ranked below the Christian faith (Marchand 2009, 365). Despite his increasing critique of European capitalist modernity, for Becker, Muslims did not live up to the standard of European civilization, as his elaborations on the educational problems of Turkey show. When it comes to his public lectures, then he employed arguments couched in racially judgmental terms drawn from popular discourse on other cultures.

Finally, there is Becker's position vis-à-vis religion, which becomes evident in his attitude toward Christian missionary movements. In his critique of German missionary activities in Africa, his personal anti-clerical stance merged with some of his theoretical assumptions. In Becker's reasoning, the evolutionary process of transforming "primitive races" toward modernity initially needed to be assisted by the spread of advanced forms of [monotheist] religions. With respect to the German colonies in Africa, he thus suggested instrumentalizing Islam in the process of "morally civilizing" the African peoples. In Becker's opinion, while Islamic influences had a positive impact on them, the teachings of Christian missionaries were not understood by the local population. Consequently, it was Islam and not Christianity as a form of advanced religion that was making headway in sub-Saharan Africa (Becker 1910b, 196). According to Becker, only after the transition from so-called primitive to orthodox religion could the further transformation from traditional religion to religiosity, understood as a necessary aspect of modern, individualized human experience, become possible (Waardenburg 1962, 276). In Becker's analysis, even in Europe this modern form of religiosity could only make progress by increasingly "dechurching" (*Entkirchlichung*) modern European civilization (1910c, 205). Playing off individual religious subjectivities against orthodox forms of organized religion in modernizing societies (van Ess 1980, 44), Becker completely shared the anti-clerical and anti-orthodox positions that characterized many of his orientalist peers. In applying the above evolutionary ideas, the scholar Becker positioned himself against the political support that German politicians generally afforded to Christian missionary activities.

The collected essays of Carl Heinrich Becker on Africa and the Ottoman Empire present him as a scholar of colonialism. He "embroiled himself, deeply and willingly, in the colonial politics of the Reich" (Marchant 2009, 367). The argumentation evident in Becker's lectures endorsed German policies regarding Berlin's territorial colonies in Africa and its imperial aspirations vis-à-vis the Ottoman Empire. As we saw in chapter one of this book, whereas the German colonial administration relied on brutal military force to subjugate the populations in its African colonies, German imperial aspirations with regard to Turkey were framed as a partnership and a form of developmental assistance. Reflecting these contrasting imperial strategies, Becker employed racist terminology to describe African peoples, while portraying Germany as "Turkey's friend and mentor" in his speech on the occasion of the birthday of Emperor Wilhelm II in 1916 (1916a, 363). In Becker's view, the Orient policy of Germany was based on different principles to those of Great Britain and France because it was not directed toward the acquisition of Ottoman territories. He understood Germany's approach to Turkey as "a purely economic policy" in which the national interest of the two countries were largely aligned (Becker 1915b, 328). His thesis concerning the shared cultural origins of Islam and Europe evidently also reflected the political attitude of Imperial Germany toward the Ottoman Empire.

Conclusions: The New Scientific Community of Islamic Studies and Colonialism

In his book on Carl Heinrich Becker and the foundation of Islamic studies in Germany, Alexander Haridi concluded that Becker was instrumental in establishing the new discipline in Germany and contributed to it with new lines of inquiry and explicatory approaches. However, Haridi suggests that the real effect of Becker's own studies on the discipline was rather limited (2005, 179).[29] Presumably, Becker's break with classical orientalism was overly resolute for his colleagues at the beginning of the twentieth century. On the one hand, mainstream orientalists were not yet ready to embrace his introduction of social-scientific approaches and methods to the study of Islam. The scholarly community to which Becker addressed his work was also still dominated by the centuries-old reign of philology.[30] On the other hand, the limited reception of Becker's work may reflect the fact that it bears the profound stamp of his times. From 1908, when he took up his position at the Colonial Institute in Hamburg, he dealt largely with contemporaneous issues closely related to Germany's then current colonial politics embedded in the context of European Imperialism.[31] After the First World War and the complete failure of Germany's imperial aspirations, these issues and his concept of "applied Islamic studies" became irrelevant. Moreover, the theoretical and philosophical underpinnings of Becker's framing of Islam as a holistic civilization increasingly lost their academic appeal. As such, what were the lasting effects of Becker's work on the study of Islam?

First of all, and together with Goldziher and Snouck Hurgronje, Becker defined – in the words of Kuhn – research on Islam as the "new scientific specialty" for an emerging community of scholars (Kuhn 1970, 177). These three founding fathers of Islamic studies forged a new academic discipline with Islam as its core research object. They laid the foundations for a group of scientific practitioners who underwent similar educational paths with a focus on Islam as a distinct historical, political, religious, and social phenomenon. With the founding of *Der Islam*, Becker further provided an academic journal for this community. Thus, all three of them played a key role in the separation of Islamic studies from nineteenth-century orientalism. In Kuhn's language, Becker, Goldziher, and Snouck Hurgronje introduced a new paradigm to the emerging global system of science, the paradigm of Islam as an independent object of academic study.[32] In addition and according to Kuhn's theory, the introduction of this new paradigm was also due to non-scientific circumstances. In the case of Islamic studies, this applies to the role of Islam in international politics and the way in which European colonial rule was conducted. Against this background, the careers of Christiaan Snouck Hurgronje and Carl Heinrich Becker were inseparably connected to the colonial politics of the Netherlands and Germany. Interestingly, these two scholars and their specific national political backgrounds almost escaped Edward Said's attention, although they would have represented exemplary cases for testing his thesis on the connection between colonial politics and oriental studies.

The case studies on Snouck Hurgronje and Becker reveal the boundary negotiation between science and politics that strongly impacted on their lives and works. In the biography of Ignaz Goldziher, however, we still see the struggle between the imperatives of religious and scientific communication that molded the careers of those scholars I investigated in the second part of this book. Goldziher, too, combined his scholarly work with an engagement in religious reform. In addition, as he was a Hungarian Jew, European colonialism only had a peripheral impact on his career, mostly through the political attitudes and conflicts of his academic peers. In his case, politics impacted his life in the form of anti-Semitism, making him the victim of Europe's "internal colonialism." The academic works of Snouck Hurgronje and Becker, by contrast, thrived due to the opportunities offered by their political environment. The war in Aceh, the so-called Indian Mutiny (1857–1858), the Islamic ideological rhetoric of Sultan Abdülhamid II, and the Ottoman Empire's increasing embroilment in the European power struggle put Islam on the international political agenda. The ruling elite in Europe became haunted by the "ghost of Pan-Islamism" (Landau 1990). European politicians perceived Islam increasingly as a threat in both moral and military terms (Hourani 1991, 301). The examples of Snouck Hurgronje and Becker illustrate the way in which the prevailing political climate became an opportunity structure that facilitated their research on Islam. The ethnographic studies of Snouck Hurgronje would not have been possible without the support afforded by political interests. Likewise, Becker's chair in Hamburg and therewith his institutional platform to launch a new understanding of oriental/Islamic studies was inherently linked to Germany's imperial political ambitions. Both scholars taught students who were to become staff for the colonial administration of the Netherlands and Germany. Knowledge of Islam and Muslims became a power resource with respect to international politics. The careers of Snouck Hurgronje and Becker clearly show a historically specific nexus of power and knowledge in the times of high imperialism. It is this nexus facilitating their careers that categorically separates the two scholars from Renan, Robertson Smith, Wellhausen, and Goldziher. To what extent did this nexus leave an imprint on Islamic studies?

There is little doubt that Snouck Hurgronje's research on Aceh was intended to generate knowledge to aid the military suppression of the local insurrection against Dutch colonial rule. Carl Heinrich Becker's work also allowed him to influence colonial politics; however, his impact on the formulation of German colonial policies appears to have been far more limited than that of his Dutch counterpart. Yet Marchand's judgment on Becker's involvement in colonial politics is equally applicable to both: she observed that Becker "did not believe himself compromising science in serving the state" (Marchand 2009, 367). While Becker and Snouck Hurgronje legitimized colonialism based on their conviction in Europe's civilizing mission, this did not mean the complete and uncritical endorsement of the colonial politics of their respective governments. On the contrary. They frequently positioned themselves against the political mainstream and, at least concerning the Middle East and Islam, grounded their policy recommendations not in racist but in educationalist reasoning. In this respect, sweeping postcolonial accusations of racism against the discipline appear to be overly reductive. Significantly, all three founding fathers of Islamic studies did not claim that there were "ontological and epistemological differences" between East and West (Said 1978, 96). When they employed the "orientalist" topoi of stagnation, for instance, they clearly defined it in non-essentialist but historical terms. In their different ways, Becker, Goldziher, and Snouck Hurgronje expressed sympathy for Muslims and did not construct them as entirely external to European cultural frameworks. Theodor Nöldeke, therefore, once criticized Snouck Hurgronje's view that "Orientals" and "Occidentals" should be considered as equal (Maier 2021, 182).[33] Moreover, the three founding fathers of Islamic studies considered the modernization of the Muslim parts of the world to be a matter of historically contingent circumstances. The radical kind of otherness that constitutes a core feature of Said's "orientalist" stereotype was not part of their scholarly worldview, although in Becker's and Snouck Hurgronje's case, they were indeed embroiled in colonial politics.

In making Islam the object of study, Becker, Goldziher, and Snouck Hurgronje defined and shaped the emerging scientific community of Islamic studies. At the same time, this new focus strengthened the idea that the history of the Muslim regions of the world should be written as a unified history of Islam. Despite their insistence on explaining Islamic history in terms of non-religious factors, the very foundation of Islamic studies as an independent discipline contributed to the perception that this history contained an essentially "Islamic component" (Owen 1973,

295). Against this background, it is not surprising that the study of Islamic law based on the critical reading of classical texts became the discipline's primary focus. In this regard, Ignaz Goldziher's approach came to serve as the model to follow. Furthermore, the historical critical reading of Islamic traditions and *fiqh* established a line of continuity with their predecessors who had initiated the separation of the study of Islam from the broader orientalist field.

Snouck Hurgronje's ethnography of Muslim practices and everyday life almost disappeared, as did Becker's approach of working "on a larger canvas" (Marchant 2009, 362). His speculative portrayal of an image of an Islamic civilization embedded in world history did not find much resonance. With regard to Islamic law, all three scholars advanced the thesis that *fiqh* constituted the major obstacle to the modernization of Muslim peoples. They associated the "orientalist" understanding of Islamic history as a history of stagnation and decline with the progressive orthodoxification and dogmatization of the shariʿa. This thesis, moreover, matched their personal stance toward religion, in which they conceived of religiosity in the modern age as an individual affair. If Muslims could free themselves from the normative straitjacket of Islamic jurisprudence, this would allow a modern Muslim culture to emerge. In this sense, their diagnosis of stagnation was not of an essentialist character. In fact, they understood the perceived "inferiority" of Muslim culture that prevailed at the time to be historically conditioned and saw modern education as the principal means of overcoming it.

Notes

1 We take "Both scholars were also Becker's friends. However, the relationship between him and Snouck Hurgronje, as we will see in the conclusions of this chapter, was put to the test during the First World War. Becker was connected with Goldziher through a frequent exchange of letters between the years 1899 and 1920 (Bourel 2011, 66).

2 Becker wrote this letter on 20 May 1916. The letter is partly quoted in Trüper (2014, 183).

3 For a detailed account of Becker's work and thought on higher education, see Müller (1991). Lisa Medrow describes Becker's educational thought in the colonial context (2018, 198–211) and with respect to his growing critical attitude toward "Western" modernization (2018, 353–367).

4 In the references, I refer to these two volumes only as "Islamstudien."

5 According to Giovanni Morrone, in his years in Heidelberg, Becker even collaborated on editing the *Archive* (Morrone 2021, 373). Many of Becker's articles and book reviews were published in the *Archive.*

6 It is worth noting that Marianne Weber did not mention Becker in her portrait of Max Weber's life. Apparently, the young Becker was of a comparatively low status in the hierarchy of the participants at Weber's *jour fix*. After Max Weber's death and her return from Munich to Heidelberg, Marianne Weber continued the weekly gathering, with scholars such as Norbert Elias, Karl Mannheim, and Talcott Parsons as guests (Derman 2012, 33).

7 The Tulunid dynasty, named after its founder Ahmad ibn Tulun (835–884), achieved factual independence from the Abbasid Empire in ruling over parts of Egypt and Greater Syria (Nagel 1987, 132).

8 Regarding von Melle and the establishment of the Colonial Institute in Hamburg, see also chapter two in this book.

9 It is worth noting that Becker also gave extremely well-attended lectures to a broad audience of interested bureaucrats, entrepreneurs, teachers, theologians, and traders. His public lecture on the major problems of oriental politics, for instance, attracted as many as 400 people (Müller 1991, 66).

10 In the version published in 1932, the veneration of the Emperor, at the beginning and the end of the text was deleted.

11 In 1913, Becker's colleague Martin Hartmann founded *Die Welt des Islams* (*The World of Islam*) in Berlin, which as a second German journal became a major publication venue for the new scientific community of Islamic studies.

12 One of Becker's core critiques of Christian missionaries in Africa was their focus on religion when explaining the "backwardness" of African culture. They completely disregarded the impact of "race, climate, and history" on regional culture (Becker 1912b, 119).

13 Later, Becker also argued that Islam had become Asianized (*Asiatisierung*) without precisely defining its meaning (Becker 1915b, 310).

14 In his argumentation, Becker appears to have borrowed from Ernst Troeltsch's thesis on the rise of modern European culture, yet included Islam in it. Troeltsch argued that modern individualism and autonomy had their origins in Christianity and the Jewish prophets. Christianity, then, incorporated Platonism and Stoicism, in this way renewing the dying spirit of antiquity. Finally, Protestantism liberated European culture from its linkage to the hierarchical organization of the medieval church (Troeltsch 1928, 21). Consequently, Protestantism played a key role in the evolution of modern individualism and therefore in the modern world in general (1928, 23).

15 On this contradiction in Becker's thought, see also Haridi (2005, 30–35).

16 The article was first published in 1912 in the third volume of "*Die Religion in Geschichte und Gegenwart, Handwörterbuch in gemeinverständlicher Darstellung*" by Verlag J. C. B. Mohr in Tübingen.

17 Apparently, he continued to rely on Wellhausen in this context, while Becker deviated from Wellhausen's view, which—I would assume—fitted Weber's own study better.

18 For a contemporary state-of-the-art handbook on the life and legacy of Muhammad, see Brockopp (2010).

19 In a letter to Erich Wede on 31 July 1921, Becker described Weber's sociology of religion as "a wonderful book," which he had apparently read in preparation for his presentation "Der Islam im Rahmen einer allgemeinen Kulturgeschichte" at the *Deutscher Orientalistentag* in Leipzig in September 1921 (Müller 1991, 345).

20 As we have seen in the previous chapters, this certainly was not only a feature of German thought but of European intellectuals in general.

21 The Webers appear to have been sympathetic to the George circle's critique of capitalist bourgeoise society, but they completely rejected George's solutions and in particular the personality cult that had built up around him and his followers (Derman 2012, 21–22). Guido Müller emphasized how strongly Becker's understanding of humanism was based on the ideals of George's aesthetic-irrational world of thought (Müller 1991, 390). To a certain extent, Becker shared the critique of "Western" rationality with Weber and George. While Weber did not see any possible escape from this "iron cage," George advocated a form of irrational escapism, which Becker seems to have increasingly adopted toward the end of his life.

22 The Islamic studies of Carl Heinrich Becker clearly reflect some of the core assumptions, concepts, and questions of the discussions of the *Eranos* and Weber's *jour fix* in Heidelberg. These circles also influenced his thought through neo-Kantian philosophy, which is visible in Becker treating Islam as an integrated whole based on a kind of abstract logical construction (Batunsky 1981, 300). The conceptual thought of Max Weber was strongly influenced by the philosophy of value of Heinrich Rickert (1863–1936), who belonged to the Southwest German school of neo-Kantianism. Rickert emphasized the distinction between the humanities and the natural sciences. He applied Kant's reduction of reason to the realm of possible experience to the cultural fields, which must cope with the problem of the historicity of human reason (Schnädelbach 2000, 50–60; 1984, chapter six). This distinction between historical experience on the one hand and its analytical understanding through abstract concepts on the other was also a methodological fundament in Ernst Troeltsch's work. In his study on the relationship between Protestantism and modernity, for instance, he stated that a singular historical investigation would be impossible without the application of general concepts (Troeltsch 1928, 6). It was within this epistemological atmosphere that Becker developed his concept of Islamic civilization.

23 Jihad is often translated as "holy war," which would make sense in this case. However, the meaning of this technical term in Islam is highly complex, so describing it as holy war is often misleading, see Jung (2016).

24 For the biography of Oppenheimer, see: https://max-von-oppenheim.foundation/max-von-oppenheim/biography/.

25 While they did indeed both support the fatwa, they were presumably not directly involved in the case. Martin Hartmann translated the proclamation but wrote in the introduction to the text that he did not actually know what exactly had taken place (Hartmann 1916, 2).

26 Ignaz Goldziher never really engaged in the imperial politics of Europe. In his letters, however, we can observe a tendency to support Germany's imperial aspirations.

27 Important to mention is that he derived this knowledge of Germany's colonial estates in Africa and German collaboration with the Ottoman Empire merely from secondary sources. Therefore, Sabine Mangold-Will rightly argued that Becker's lectures and publications on Turkey were hardly of a scholarly nature and did not entail personal experience (2013, 262). This lack of "being there" clearly distinguished Becker's colonial advice on the Ottoman Empire and Africa from the "imperial knowledge" that Christiaan Snouck Hurgronje applied in his Islam politics in the Dutch East Indies.

28 This is Becker's basic argumentation in his essay from 1909: "Ist der Islam eine Gefahr für unsere Kolonien" ("Is Islam a Threat to our Colonies?").

29 Haridi's judgment evidently does not apply to all of Becker's works. Jürgen Paul showed the impact of Becker's article on the development of the European feudal system in comparison to the Orient (Becker 1914b). Paul argues that Becker's article was the standard study on this subject for about fifty years (Paul 2018, 53). Even more important, Becker's thesis concerning the lack of contractual elements in the socio-economic relations of Islamic empires also entered into conceptual elaborations of the social sciences, in particular through Max Weber's adaptation of Becker's "deficiency thesis" in the construction of the ideal types in his sociology of domination (2018, 54–57).

30 The way in which Becker himself applied sociological concepts, however, was extremely unsystematic and occurred in a non-reflecting, eclectic, often even contradictory way. Becker did not understand sociology as a methodologically elaborated rational academic discipline, but rather in terms of a generalizing philosophical manner of thought (Müller 1991, 348).

31 In addition, Becker wrote a host of book reviews on all kinds of then current orientalist literatures. Altogether, however, his scholarly work by no means reaches the breath and quantity of Goldziher's and Snouck Hurgronje's.

32 Looking at the institutional establishment of Islamic studies at German universities, however, shows that this was a rather slow process. After the First World War, only two full chairs for Islamic studies were established at the universities of Munich and Breslau. In Austria, Vienna University established Islamic studies in 1939 (Wokoeck 2009, 169). The clear institutional separation from orientalist subjects such as Semitic languages was instead a post-Second World War development. However, Islamic studies often appeared prior to this in combined chairs for Semitic languages and Islamic history.

33 As Maier showed in his article, Nöldeke clearly advocated a kind of cultural supremacy of Europe, however, excluding Irish and Polish peoples in this view (Maier 2021).

Epilogue

My account of the rise of Islamic studies ends here. I began part one with a brief discussion of *Orientalism* and the field of postcolonial studies that evolved in part from Edward Said's thesis. Although it faced much criticism, Said's narrative attained a measure of hegemony in shaping younger generations' perception of European oriental scholarship within the social sciences and the humanities. Despite positioning myself against this hegemonic narrative, I also question some assumptions made by the critics of *Orientalism*, particularly concerning their emphasis on Said's neglect of German scholarship. I stress the importance of German orientalism too. But this is due to the eminent position of German scholarship in both biblical criticism and orientalist scholarship as such, not to a supposed absence of colonial interests in the country's knowledge production. I underpinned this argument with a brief assessment of the history of German colonialism at the end of the first chapter. Having set the scene for my story in the current state of research, in the second chapter I outlined my theoretical approach. In my recourse to social theory, I defined the modern social systems of religion and science against the background of a more general theory of modernity. Moreover, based on this theoretical framework, chapter two provided a short history of German oriental scholarship in the nineteenth century. The third chapter, then, ventured into the work and life of one of the classical theoreticians of modernity: Max Weber. I critically assessed postcolonial scholars' reductive classification of the German sociologist as a racist and imperialist. In addition, I drew parallels between Weber's sociology and the studies of some of those orientalists who appear in the following chapters. My argument in this context emphasized that their works exhibit a mutual reliance.

The subsequent six chapters were divided into two parts. The chapters in part two investigated the first phase of the emancipation of Islamic studies from the broader context of orientalist scholarship. To this end, the biographies and works of Julius Wellhausen, William Robertson Smith, and Ernest Renan served me as case studies. The core argument in all three of these case studies is that their life stories are closely knit into social negotiations about religious and scientific truths, about the status of religion and science in modern society. In these social and historical contexts, the emancipation of Islamic studies from orientalism was a process of both the internal differentiation of modern sciences and the impact of external social forces related to much larger social developments. National politics played a role in these developments, however, only a minor one when it comes to colonialism. In my analysis, all three life stories disprove the main assumption of *Orientalism* that orientalist scholarship was inextricably entwined with colonial interests. This finding holds true for all three scholars, irrespective of their national backgrounds, German, British, and French alike. Their shift away from biblical studies to Islam, I contend, cannot be understood in terms of colonial politics. Such, at least, is my interpretation of their biographies.

The conclusion regarding the three scholars addressed in part three, however, was different. These three chapters examined the cases of Ignaz Goldziher, Christiaan Snouck Hurgronje, and Carl Heinrich Becker. This younger generation of scholars represented a crucial stage in the emergence of Islamic studies as an independent discipline of the humanities. There is no doubt that the colonial policies of the Netherlands and imperial Germany played an important role in the careers and works of Snouck Hurgronje and Becker. Here, we can indeed detect colonial interests connected to orientalist scholarship. Yet many of the "orientalist" stereotypes described by Said, such as the complete and immutable "othering" of Muslims, are not evident in the work of these founding fathers of Islamic studies. Furthermore, Snouck Hurgronje and Becker largely shared their historicist views on Islam with Goldziher. The Jewish-Hungarian scholar of Islam, however, had no connection to imperialist interests. In his case, colonial ambition did not play any role at all. These findings clearly show that the establishment of European studies on Islam cannot be reduced to the colonial ventures of European states alone. This process was much more complex than Said suggested. Thus, in what ways does my narrative differ from *Orientalism*?

To begin with, this book should not be read as a polemic. Admittedly, I wrote this study with a critical edge as far as Said and his postcolonial followers were concerned. But this does not mean that it was written with anger against them. My story is first and foremost intended to complement the postcolonial narrative. I wish to correct the—in my assessment—often narrow and partly misleading portrayal of European oriental studies that has its origin in *Orientalism*. My narrative is guided by analytical purposes that clearly supersede my own normative positioning. Second, while following Said's methodological suggestion of looking more closely at individuals, I choose a group of scholars who did not feature prominently in *Orientalism*. With the exception of Ernest Renan, my protagonists figure only marginally in Said's book. This, however, is not the case regarding their role in the formation of Islamic studies. Five out of the six orientalists in my case studies are considered to be instrumental in the emancipation of Islamic studies from the much broader field of orientalist scholarship. Ironically, Ernest Renan is the sole exception to this. His work was largely irrelevant for the development of Islamic studies. In Said's book, however, he appears as a kind of mastermind behind the "orientalist" project in the nineteenth century. By contrast, the groundbreaking work of Julius Wellhausen does not even bear a mention in *Orientalism*. When it comes to academic orientalism, Said's thesis is insufficiently supported by evidence from a wider range of sources. The case studies presented here expose this deficiency in *Orientalism*.

The third way in which my work differs from Said's account lies in the distinct theoretical perspective I employed in my biographical analyses of these six scholars. I positioned their construction of Islamic studies in the social context of the specifically modern separation of political, religious, and scientific spheres of society. I analyzed their life and work through the lenses of macro-sociological theory. Concepts from Niklas Luhmann's abstract Modern Systems Theory served as prisms for my empirical observations at the micro level. In his sociology, individuals are defined as psychic systems and do not belong to the social realm. Society for Luhmann is an all-comprising structure internally differentiated by social subsystems. In my study, the relevant social subsystems are politics, religion, and science. Luhmann described these subsystems as self-referential social systems based on specific codes of communication. Significantly, he rejects any hierarchy among these subsystems of modern society. In Luhmann's theoretical design, no realm of communication dominates another: subsystems remain entirely separate from their environment. My study, however, applying Luhmann's concepts as an observational framework, comes to a different conclusion. At both the individual and institutional levels, the case studies reveal certain historical hierarchies among modern subsystems. In tracing the rise of Islamic studies, I observe shifting patterns of domination among politics, religion, and science. In the field's emancipation from classical orientalism, scientific logics increasingly came to govern religious logics. During the nineteenth-century boundary negotiations between religion and science, scientific truths appear to have gradually asserted superiority over revealed knowledge. This becomes apparent, for instance, in ideas such as the replacement of religion by science in modern society. However, at the beginning of the twentieth century, in the period when Islamic studies was emerging as an independent discipline, political communication increasingly came to dominate the status of science. At the micro level, this dynamic is evident in the careers of Christiaan Snouck Hurgronje and Carl Heinrich Becker, where the central tension appears to be less about the differences between science and religion than between science and politics.

The core variable of my study, as mentioned before, was the involvement of orientalist scholars in the boundary negotiations between the social subsystems of religion and science. In these negotiations, methods of historical biblical criticism played a key role. My protagonists employed biblical criticism as the means through which they pursued boundary negotiations as individual social actors. At the same time, Old Testament scholars transferred these methods from Protestant theology via orientalist scholarship into the emerging study of Islam. In this process, I treated the political subsystem—namely, the formation of nation states and European colonialism—as an intervening variable. Part two of the book illustrated that colonial politics only played a minor role in the initial emancipation of the study of Islam from classical orientalism. My analysis shows that negotiations of colonial interests were clearly subordinate to both religious and scientific communication. In this period, all three scholars that featured in the relevant case studies largely struggled with differentiating between science and religion in both their individual faith and the specific institutional and social environments in which they lived. I argued that the most significant forces impacting their orientalist scholarship were individual and institutional struggles between religious and scientific imperatives and not the impact of colonialism.

However, specific national political interests in the context of European imperialism eventually did become an important factor in the establishment of Islamic studies as an independent academic discipline, as the biographies of Snouck Hurgronje and Becker reveal. In their writings the design of "Islam politics" formed an integral part of their scholarly work, blurring the lines between scientific inquiry and political agendas. Their research clearly displays the impact of colonial concerns, with questions of colonial governance shaping the very process by which Islam became the object of a new academic discipline. Yet this transformative historical, and social dynamic in the formation of Islamic studies as a scholarly community is almost entirely effaced in Said's account.

Colonial interests undoubtedly contributed to the establishment of the new discipline, but scholarship on Islam was never reducible to those interests alone.

Throughout the six subsequent case studies in this book, I addressed my central question concerning the ways in which European imperialism influenced the academic study of Islam. As I did so, I attempted to do justice to the historical complexities surrounding the relationship between oriental scholarship and colonialism. In sum, I would argue that colonialist interests increasingly acted as a facilitator of politically relevant scholarship, thereby contributing to the construction of Islam as an object of academic study. Colonialism thus played a role in the formation of Islamic studies as a scholarly community. Yet at the micro level, I do not discern any "colonial conspiracy" in the choice of oriental and/or Islamic studies as a field of inquiry. For the six orientalists discussed in this book, colonialism was not a decisive factor in their choice to enter this scholarly field. They undoubtedly shared a broadly Eurocentric worldview, but this should not be conflated with an unqualified endorsement of European colonialism. This applies in particular to the implementation of colonial policies as a means of exploitation, which even Snouck Hurgronje and Becker frequently criticized. Wellhausen and Goldziher certainly did not conduct their research in the interests of colonialism. Robertson Smith and Renan expressed support for the colonial policies of Great Britain and France, but this support did not govern the thrust of their academic work.

Generally speaking, Eurocentrism provided the intellectual framework within which all of these scholars, Weber included, conducted their research. Yet, within this shared context, each interpreted and applied this framework differently. In my case studies we can observe different historical, intellectual, personal, and national dispositions at work. Of the six, only Renan fully embodied the "orientalist" stereotype, portraying Islam as a culture defined by ontological differences to European culture and fundamentally incompatible with modern life. Even here, however, Renan's critique was not confined to Islam but extended to Catholicism as well. Nonetheless, he was the only one of my protagonists to treat Islam itself as the "independent variable" for understanding the social and historical life of Muslims. In this respect, he aligned most closely with the "orientalist" stereotype later defined by Said. Yet this stereotype does not apply to the other five scholars discussed in my book. They all emphasized the contingencies of Islamic history and Muslim social practices rather than reducing this history to religion alone. Most importantly, Renan was the only one to articulate his denigrating judgments on Islam in specifically racist terms. By contrast, racism—at least toward Muslims—was not an argumentative device used in the writings of the others. Thus, the sweeping accusations of racism that some postcolonial scholars level against European orientalist scholarship overlook the complexities of orientalist thought. Substantiating such claims would require them to study and carefully document cases that go beyond the example of Renan.

Future studies of orientalist scholarship and "orientalism" would benefit particularly from two directions. First, my case studies demonstrated that the agency and thought of Muslim intellectuals played a significant role in shaping the modern knowledge of Islam. This contribution is completely absent in *Orientalism*, where not a single "subaltern" voice is heard. In my view, it is precisely postcolonial scholars who should address this glaring omission. This is where the postcolonial perspective could indeed make a difference. Yet, regrettably, much postcolonial writing continues to focus primarily on literature produced in the languages of the colonizers. The journal *al-manār* was read by a number of the founding fathers of Islamic studies, and their encounters with leading Muslims thinkers such as Jamal al-Din al-Afghani, Muhammad Abduh, and Namık Kemal clearly left an imprint on their work. This influence presumably also extended to the exchange of letters between Arab reformers and Heinrich Leberecht Fleischer, just as it did to Snouck Hurgronje's and Goldziher's correspondence with Muslim intellectuals. In particular Snouck Hurgronje's long-standing collaboration with Raden Aboe Bakar Dajajadiningrat and Sayyid Uthman b. Abd Allah al-Alawi formed a core foundation for the Dutch orientalist's studies of Islam. In this way, European orientalists constructed the modern image of Islam through a dialogue with Muslim intellectuals—albeit an asymmetrical one. Here, a shift from the habitual reiteration of nineteenth-century Eurocentric assumptions to focus on the tangible impact of Islamic thought on orientalist scholarship would offer a refreshing alternative. A significant asymmetry remains between studies deconstructing European thought and those examining the entanglement of Western intellectuals with figures from the colonial peripheries.

Second, contemporary research on European orientalism should make greater use of intersectional approaches, applying them not only to the societies of the colonized but also to those of the colonizers. Modern knowledge of Islam emerged within European societies that were themselves deeply structured by multiple forms of oppression. The lives of the scholars examined in this book were shaped by these asymmetrical power relations and by historically prevalent categories of class, gender, nation, and race. As representatives of their societies, these scholars reflected these social hierarchies in their own perspectives. Accordingly, it is crucial to broaden the intersectional lens to encompass both the center and the periphery of the colonial world. Let me briefly outline what I mean.

When it comes to race, this category had a profound impact on the life of Goldziher, though in ways very different from the postcolonial framing. His scholarship on Islam was intimately intertwined with the discrimination faced by the Jewish population in Hungary. The influence of Europe's "internal colonialism" and the social forces of anti-Semitism in shaping orientalist knowledge remains an important avenue for future research. A similar gap exists regarding the gender dimension, which only appears in the margins of secondary literature on European orientalists. In the case of Weber, the significant role of his wife, Marianne Weber, in shaping his work and ensuring its sociological legacy, especially in preserving his scattered publications, is well documented. Likewise, Renan's sister, Henriette, contributed to his education and eventual break with Catholicism, and played a crucial role in editing his writings, as did his wife Cornélie.

In contrast, little is known of the ways in which Goldziher's wife may have supported him in his studies. Similarly, despite scattered evidence in their correspondence, Robertson Smith and Wellhausen revealed very little about the influence of women on their careers. Overall, the impact of mothers and wives on the lives and works of these scholars appears only marginally in the available literature. This is at least the impression I gained from the wide range of primary and secondary materials that I consulted for this book.

Finally, my account does not offer a thorough examination of the socio-economic background of the scholars who shaped orientalist and Islamic studies. They all came from European middle and upper middle classes. In the chapters on Becker and Weber, I analyzed their German bourgeoise background in some detail, but without fully exploring how socio-economic variables may have influenced their scholarship. There is no doubt that oriental and Islamic studies had a distinctly bourgeoise character. But how exactly did this social milieu shape the production of knowledge on Islam? I have not sufficiently addressed this question. In sum, I must acknowledge that although I had an intersectional approach in mind, I did not fully apply it. The result is a restricted sociology of knowledge. My book remains primarily a work of intellectual history. Hopefully, it will nonetheless motivate younger scholars to pursue more comprehensive accounts of the emergence of European studies on Islam. Scholarship, after all, is a collective endeavor. While Said's *Orientalism* remains foundational, future research on the history of the discipline and the formation of modern knowledge of Islam must move decisively beyond it.

References

Abu-Lughod, Ibrahim. 1963. *Arab Rediscovery of Europe: A Study in Cultural Encounters*. Princeton: Princeton University Press.

al-Afghani, Jamal al-Din. 1883. Answer of Jamal ad-Din to Renan. In *An Islamic Response to Imperialism*. Edited by Nikki R. Keddie. Berkeley: University of California Press [1993].

Ahmad, Aijaz. 1991. Between Orientalism and Historicism. In *Orientalism: A Reader*. Edited by Alexander L. Macfie. Edinburgh: Edinburgh University Press: 87–103 [2000].

Alatas, Syed Farid. 2002. Eurocentrism and the Role of the Human Sciences in the Dialogue among Civilizations. *The European Legacy* 7 (6): 759–770.

Aldenhoff-Hübinger, Rita. 2004. Max Weber's Inaugural Address of 1895 in the Context of the Contemporary Debates in Political Economy. *Max Weber Studies* 4 (2): 143–156.

Ammerman, Nancy T. (ed.). 2007. *Everyday Religion: Observing Modern Religious Lives*. Oxford and New York: Oxford University Press.

Armayanto, Harda, Adib Fatttah Suntoro, Zen Anwar Saeful Basyari, and Nurul Aminah Mat Zain. 2023. Snouck Hurgronje and the Tradition of Orientalism in Indonesia. *Tasfiyah: Jurnal Pemikiran Islam* 7 (2): 263–287.

Arnold, Thomas Walker. 1896. *Preaching Islam: A History of the Propagation of the Muslim Faith*. Westminster: Archibald Constable.

Asad, Talal. 1986. *The Idea of an Anthropology of Islam*. Washington, DC: Center for Contemporary Arab Studies, Georgetown University.

Asad, Talal. 1993. *Genealogies of Religion: Discipline and Reasons of Power in Christianity and Islam*. Baltimore: Johns Hopkins University Press.

Ascher, Abraham. 1961. "Radical" Imperialists within German Social Democracy, 1921–1918. *Political Science Quarterly* 76 (4): 555–575. https://doi.org/10.2307/2146541

Ashcroft, B., G. Griffiths, and H. Tiffin (eds.). 1995. *The Post-Colonial Studies Reader*. London and New York: Routledge.

Aydin, Cemil. 2007. *The Politics of Anti-Westernism in Asia: Visions of World Order in Pan-Islamic and Pan-Asian Thought*. New York: Columbia University Press.

al-Azm, Sadik Jalal. 1981. Orientalism and Orientalism in Reverse. *Khamsin* 8: 5–26.

Baird, William. 1992. *History of New Testament Research. Volume One: From Deism to Tübingen*. Minneapolis: Fortress Press.

Ballantyne, Tony. 2002. *Orientalism and Race: Aryanism in the British Empire*. Houndsmill: Palgrave Macmillan.

Barbieri, William A. 2015. Sechs Facetten der Postsäkularität. In *Postsäkularismus: Zur Diskussion eines umstrittenen Begriffs*. Edited by Matthias Lutz-Bachmann. Frankfurt am Main and New York: Campus: 41–78.

Batunsky, Mark. 1981. Carl Heinrich Becker: From Old to Modern Islamology. Commemorating the 70th Anniversary of "Der Islam als Problem." *International Journal of Middle East Studies* 13 (3): 287–310. https://doi.org/10.1017/S0020743800053435

Baumann, Zygmunt. 2007. *Liquid Times: Living in an Age of Uncertainty*. Cambridge: Cambridge University Press.

Becker, Carl Heinrich. 1902. *Beiträge zur Geschichte Ägyptens unter dem Islam: Erstes Heft*. Strassburg: Verlag von Karl J. Trübner.

Becker, Carl Heinrich. 1903. *Beiträge zur Geschichte Ägyptens unter dem Islam: Zweites Heft*. Strassburg: Verlag von Karl J. Trübner.

Becker, Carl Heinrich. 1904. Panislamismus. In *Islamstudien: Zweiter Band*. Leipzig: Quelle & Meyer: 231–251 [1932].

Becker, Carl Heinrich. 1907. *Christentum und Islam*. Tübingen: Mohr.

Becker, Carl Heinrich. 1909. Ist der Islam eine Gefahr für unsere Kolonien? In *Islamstudien: Zweiter Band*. Leipzig: Quelle & Meyer: 156–186 [1932].

Becker, Carl Heinrich. 1910a. Der Islam als Problem. *Der Islam* 1 (1): 1–21. https://doi.org/10.1515/islm.1910.1.1.1

Becker, Carl Heinrich. 1910b. Der Islam und die Kolonisierung Afrikas. In *Islamstudien: Zweiter Band*. Leipzig: Quelle & Meyer: 187–210 [1932].

Becker, Carl Heinrich. 1912a. Abriss der islamischen Religion. In *Islamstudien: Erster Band*. Leipzig: Quelle & Meyer: 331–385 [1924].

Becker, Carl Heinrich. 1912b. Ein Missionar über den Islam in Deutsch-Ostafrika. In *Islamstudien: Zweiter Band*. Leipzig: Quelle & Meyer: 116–121 [1932].

Becker, Carl Heinrich. 1912c. Islam. *Archiv für Religionswissenschaft* 15: 530–602.

Becker, Carl Heinrich. 1914a. *Die Araber als Kolonisatoren*. In *Islamstudien: Zweiter Band*. Leipzig: Quelle & Meyer: 1–15 [1932].

Becker, Carl Heinrich. 1914b. Steuerpacht und Lehnswesen: Eine historische Studie über die Entwicklung des islamischen Lehnswesens. *Der Islam* 5 (1): 81–92. https://doi.org/10.1515/islm.1914.5.1.81

Becker, Carl Heinrich. 1915a. Die Kriegsdiskussion über den Heiligen Krieg. In *Islamstudien: Zweiter Band*. Leipzig: Quelle & Meyer: 281–309 [1932].

Becker, Carl Heinrich. 1915b. Islampolitik. In *Islamstudien: Zweiter Band*. Leipzig Quelle & Meyer: 310–332 [1932].

Becker, Carl Heinrich. 1916a. *Das türkische Bildungsproblem*. In *Islamstudien: Zweiter Band*. Leipzig: Quelle & Meyer: 363–384 [1932].

Becker, Carl Heinrich. 1916b. *Islam und Wirtschaft*. In *Islamstudien: Erster Band*. Leipzig: Quelle & Meyer: 54–65 [1924].

Becker, Carl Heinrich. 1918a. *Julius Wellhausen*. *Islamstudien: Zweiter Band*. Leipzig: Quelle & Meyer: 474–480 [1932].

Becker, Carl Heinrich. 1918b. Der Islam als Weltanschauung in Vergangenheit und Gegenwart. In *Islamstudien: Erster Band*. Leipzig: Quelle & Meyer: 40–53.

Becker, Carl Heinrich. 1920. Martin Hartmann. *In Islamstudien: Zweiter Band.* Leipzig: Quelle & Meyer: 481–490 [1932].

Becker, Carl Heinrich. 1922. Ignaz Goldziher. *Der Islam* 11: 214–222.

Becker, Carl Heinrich. 1924. *Islamstudien: Erster Band.* Leipzig: Quelle & Meyer.

Becker, Carl Heinrich. 1932. Ernst Nöldeke. In *Islamstudien: Zweiter Band.* Hildesheim: Georg Olms: 514–522.

Becker, Sascha O. and Erik Hornung. 2020. The Political Economy of the Prussian Three-Class Franchise. *The Journal of Economic History* 80 (4): 1143–1188. https://doi.org/10.1017/S0022050720000443

Beckford, James. 2003. *Social Theory and Religion.* Cambridge: Cambridge University Press.

Beidelman, Thomas. 1974. *W. Robertson Smith and the Sociological Study of Religion.* Chicago: University of Chicago Press.

Benda, Harry J. 1972. *Continuity and Change in Southeast Asia: Collected Journal Articles of Harry J. Benda.* New Haven: Yale University Press.

Bergsträsser, Arnold. 1957. Max Webers Antrittsvorlesung in zeitgeschichtlicher Perspektive. *Vierteljahreshefte für Zeitgeschichte* 5 (3): 210–219.

Bergunder, Michael. 2020. Umkämpfte Historisierung. Die Zwillingsgeburt von "Religion" und "Esoterik" in der zweiten Hälfte des 19. Jahrhunderts und das Programm einer globalen Religionsgeschichte. In *Wissen um Religion: Erkenntnis—Interesse: Epistemologie und Episteme in Religionswissenschaft und interkultureller Theologie.* Edited by Klaus Hock. Leipzig: Evangelische Verlagsanstalt: 47–132.

Berman, Russell A. 2011. Colonialism, and No End: The Other Continuity Theses. In *German Colonialism. Race, the Holocaust, and Postwar Germany.* Edited by Volker Langbehn and Mohammad Salama. New York: Columbia University Press: 164–189.

Besier, Gerhard. 1990. Kulturkampf. In *Theologische Realenzyklopädie* XX: 209–230.

Beyer, Peter. 2006. *Religions in Global Society.* London and New York: Routledge.

Bhambra, Gurminder K. 2011. Historical Sociology, Modernity, and Postcolonial Critique. *The American Historical Review* 116 (3): 653–662. https://doi.org/10.1086/ahr.116.3.653

Bhambra, Gurminder K. 2014. *Connected Sociologies.* London and New York: Bloomsbury.

Bhambra, Gurminder K. 2023. *Rethinking Modernity: Postcolonialism and the Sociological Imagination.* Second Edition. Cham: Springer/Palgrave MacMillan.

Biazitov, Ataulla. 1883. Eine Erwiderung auf Ernest Renans Rede "Der Islam und die Wissenschaft." In *Moderne Muslime. Ernest Renan und die Geschichte der ersten Islamdebatte 1883.* Edited by Birgit Schäbler. Stuttgart: Ferdinand Schöningh: 205–230.

Black, John Sutherland and George Chrystal. 1912. *The Life of William Robertson Smith.* London: Adam & Charles Black.

Blinkenberg, Andreas. 1923. *Ernest Renan: Bidrag til belysning af hans filosofiske-religiøse ungdomskrise.* Copenhagen: Engelsen and Schrøder.

Boatcă, Manuela. 2016. "From the Standpoint of Germanism": A Postcolonial Critique of Weber's Theory of Race and Ethnicity. In *Postcolonial Sociologies: A Reader*. Edited by Julian Go. Leeds: Emerald Publishing: 51–76.

Booth, Gordon. 2002. The Fruits of Sacrifice: Sigmund Freud and William Robertson Smith. *The Expository Times* 113 (8): 258–264. https://doi.org/10.1177/001452460211300803

Boschwitz, Friedemann. 1938. *Julius Wellhausen: Motive und Maßstäbe seiner Geschichtsschreibung*. Marburg: Philipps-Universität.

Bošković, Aleksandar. 2021. *William Robertson Smith*. New York and Oxford: Berghahn.

Bourel, Dominique. 2011. De Berlin á Budapest: Carl Heinrich Becker et Ignác Goldziher. In *Ignáz Goldziher: Un autre orientalisme*? Paris: Paul Geuthner: 63–72.

Bowen, John R. 2012. *A New Anthropology of Islam*. Cambridge: Cambridge University Press.

Brennan, Timothy. 2000. The Illusion of a Future: "Orientalism" as Travelling Theory. *Critical Inquiry* 26 (3): 558–583. https://doi.org/10.1086/448978

Brennan, Timothy. 2014. Subaltern Stakes. *New Left Review* 89: 67–87. https://doi.org/10.64590/tzz

Breuer, Stephan. 2006. *Max Weber's tragische Soziologie: Aspekte und Perspektiven*. Tübingen: Mohr/Siebeck.

Brockelmann, Carl. 1922. Die morgenländischen Studien in Deutschland. *Zeitschrift der Deutschen Morgenländischen Gesekllschaft* 76 (1): 1–17.

Brockopp, Jonathan E. (ed.). 2010. *The Cambridge Companion to Muhammad*. Cambridge: Cambridge University Press.

Bruckmayr, Philipp. 2024. Facing Mecca from Java: Two Treaties on the Establishment of the *qibla*, and their Scholarly and Social Context. *Islamic Law and Society* 31: 102–135.

Burkitt, Francis Crawford. 1894. William Robertson Smith. *The English Historical Review* 9 (36): 684–689. https://doi.org/10.1093/ehr/IX.XXXVI.684

Buskens, Léon and Jean Kommers. 2022. Mekka as an Ethnographic Text: How Christiaan Snouck Hurgronje Lived and Constructed Daily Life in Arabia. In *Scholarship in Action: Essays on the Life and Work of Christiaan Snouck Hurgronje (1857–1936)*. Edited by Léon Buskens and Jan Just Witkam with Annemarie van Sandwijk. Leiden and Boston: Brill: 168–259.

Buskens, Léon and Annemarie van Sandwijk. 2022. Chris, Christiaan, Snouck, Snouck Hurgronje, 'Abd al-Ghaffar, the Master: Images of a Scholar in Action. In *Scholarship in Action: Essays on the Life and Work of Christiaan Snouck Hurgronje (1857–1936)*. Edited by Léon Buskens and Jan Just Witkam with Annemarie van Sandwijk. Leiden and Boston: Brill: 3–50.

Carvalho, Christina. 2010. *Christiaan Snouck Hurgronje: Biography and Perception*. MA Thesis, Graduate School for Humanities, Universiteit van Amsterdam.

Cashdollar, Charles D. 1889. *The Transformation of Theology, 1830–1890: Positivism and Protestant Thought in Britain and America*. Princeton: Princeton University Press.

Chalcraft, David J. and Austin Harrington (eds.). 2001. *The Protestant Ethic Debate: Max Weber's Replies to His Critics, 1907–1910*. Translated by Austin Harrington and Mary Shields. Liverpool: Liverpool University Press.

Chandler, Nahum D. 2006. The Possible Form of an Interlocution: W. E. B. Du Bois and Max Weber in Correspondence, 1904–1905. *The New Centennial Review* 6 (3): 193–239. https://doi.org/10.1353/ncr.2007.0015

Chapman, Mark. 2001. *Ernst Troeltsch and Liberal Theology: Religion and Cultural Synthesis in Wilhelmine Germany*. Oxford: Oxford Scholarship.

Cheyne, Alec C. 1995. Bible and Confession in Scotland: The Background to the Robertson Smith Case. In *William Robertson Smith: Essays in Reassessment*. Edited by William Johnstone. Sheffield: Sheffield Academic Press: 24–40.

Collins, Jo and John Jervis (eds.). 2008. *Uncanny Modernity: Cultural Theories, Modern Anxieties*. London: Palgrave Macmillan.

Colpani, Gianmaria, Jamila M. H. Mascat, and Katrine Smiet. 2022. Postcolonial Responses to Decolonial Interventions. *Postcolonial Studies* 25 (1): 1–16. https://doi.org/10.1080/13688790.2022.2041695

Conrad, Lawrence. 1990. The Near East Study Tour Diary of Ignaz Goldziher. *Journal of the Royal Asiatic Society* 1: 105–126.

Conrad, Lawrence. 1993. The Pilgrim from Pest: Goldziher's Study Tour to the Near East (1873–1874). In *Golden Roads, Migration, Pilgrimage and Travel in Medieval and Modern Islam*. Edited by Ian Richard Netton. Richmond: Cruzon Press: 110–148.

Conrad, Sebastian. 2024. Anklage eines Ansatzes. In Den postkolonialen Forschungen war Israel lange marginal: Warum gelten sie jetzt weithin als antisemitisch? *Frankfurter Allgemeine Zeitung*, Nr. 38, 14 February.

Coogan, Michael D. 2008. *The Old Testament: A Very Short Introduction*. Oxford: Oxford University Press.

Coogan, Michael D. 2012. *A Brief Introduction to the Old Testament: The Hebrew Bible in Its Context*. Second Edition. Oxford and New York: Oxford University Press.

Dahrendorf, Ralf. 2006. Max Weber and Modern Social Science. In *Max Weber and His Contemporaries*. Edited by Wolfgang J. Mommsen and Jürgen Osterhammel. London: Routledge: 574–580.

Daniel, Norman. 1960. *Islam and the West: The Making of an Image*. Edinburgh: Edinburgh University Press.

Davis, Stacy. 2021. Unapologetic Apologetics: Julius Wellhausen, Anti-Judaism, and Hebrew Bible Scholarship. *Religions* 12 (8): 560. https://doi.org/10.3390/rel12080560

de Beauvoir, Simone. 1949. *The Second Sex*. New York: Vintage.

Dejung, Christof. 2019. From Global Civilizing Missions to Racial Warfare: Class Conflicts and the Representation of the Colonial World in European Middle-Class Thought. In *The Global Bourgeoisie: The Rise of the Middle Classes in the Age of Empire*. Edited by Christof Dejung, David Motadel, and Jürgen Osterhammel. Princeton: Princeton University Press: 170–183.

Deringil, Selim. 1998. *The Well-Protected Domains: Ideology and the Legitimation of Power in the Ottoman Empire, 1876–1909*. London: I. B. Tauris.

Derman, Joshua. 2012. *Max Weber in Politics and Social Thought: From Charisma to Canonization*. Cambridge: Cambridge University Press.

de Vries, Anton. 2011. Christiaan Snouck Hurgronje: History of Orientalist Manipulation of Islam—Analysis. *New Civilization*, 14 September.

de Vries, Simon John. 1968. *Bible and Theology in the Netherlands: Dutch Old Testament Criticism under Modern and Conservative Auspices, 1850 to World War 1*. Wageningen: H. Veenman & Zonen N.V.

Dhahir, Sanna. 2023. What it Means to be Black in Saudi Arabia: Slavery and Racial Discrimination in Saudi Women's Fiction. *Arabica* 70 (1–2): 113–156. https://doi.org/10.1163/15700585-12341655

Dipper, Christof. 2014. Religion in modernen Zeiten: Die Perspektive des Historikers. In *Moderne und Religion: Kontroversen um Modernität und Säkularisierung*. Edited by Ulrich Willems, Detlef Pollack, Helene Basu, Thomas Gutmann, and Ulrike Spohn. Bielefeld: transcript: 262–293.

Dirksen, P. B. and A. van der Kooij (eds.). 1993. *Abraham Kuenen (1828–1891): His Major Contributions to the Study of the Old Testament*. Leiden: Brill.

Dohm, Hedwig. 1876. *Der Frauen Natur und Recht: Zur Frauenfrage zwei Abhandlungen über Eigenschaften und Stimmrecht der Frauen*. Berlin: Wedkind & Schweiger.

Dörfler-Dierken, Angelika. 2001. *Luthertum und Demokratie: Deutsche und amerikanische Theologen des 19. Jahrhunderts zu Staat, Gesellschaft und Kirche*. Göttingen: Vandenhoeck & Ruprecht.

Dozy, Reinhart. 1864. *De Israëliten te Mekka: Van Davids Tijd Tot in de Vijfde euw Onzer Tijdrekening*. Haarlem: A. C. Kruseman.

Drewes G. W. J. 2022. Snouck Hurgronje and the Study of Islam. In *Scholarship in Action: Essays on the Life and Work of Christiaan Snouck Hurgronje (1857–1936)*. Edited by Léon Buskens and Jan Just Witkam with Annemarie van Sandwijk. Leiden and Boston: Brill: 519–534.

Drori, Gili S., John W. Meyerm, Francisco Ramirez, and Evan Schofer. 2003. *Science in the Modern World Polity: Institutionalization and Globalization*. Stanford: Stanford University Press.

Durkheim, Émile. 1898. L'individualisme et les intellectuals. *Revue Bleue* 4 (10): 7–13.

Durkheim, Émile. 1922. *De la division du travail social*. 4th Edition. Paris: Allcan.

Durkheim, Émile. 1995. *The Elementary Forms of Religious Life*. New York: The Free Press.

Dussaud, René. 1951. *L'Oeuvre scientifique d'Ernest Renan*. Paris: Librairie Orientaliste Paul Geuthner.

Eckl, Andreas. 2008. The Herero Genocide of 1904: Source-Critical and Methodological Considerations. *Journal of Namibian Studies* 3: 31–61.

Eisenstadt, Shmuel N. 2000a. Multiple Modernities. *Daedalus* 129 (1): 1–29.

Eisenstadt, Shmuel N. 2000b. The Reconstruction of Religious Arenas in the Framework of 'Multiple Modernities'. *Millenium: Journal of International Studies* 29 (3): 591–611. https://doi.org/10.1177/03058298000290031201

Eisenstadt, Shmuel N. 2001. The Civilizational Dimension of Modernity: Modernity as a Distinct Civilization. *International Sociology* 16 (3): 320–340. https://doi.org/10.1177/026858001016003005

El-Hani, Charbel N. and Sami Philström. 2002. Emergence Theories and Pragmatic Realism. *Essays in Philosophy* 3 (1): Article 3.

Enderwitz, Sabine. 1997. Shuʿūbiyya. *The Encyclopaedia of Islam.* New Edition. Volume IX. SAN – SZE. Leiden: Brill: 513–516.

Eriksen, Thomas Hylland. 2022. Review Article. *Anthropological Journal of European Cultures* 31 (1): 118–120.

Ette, Ottmar. 2009. *Alexander von Humboldt und die Globalisierung: Das Mobile des Wissens.* Frankfurt am Main: Insel Verlag.

Euchner, Walter. 1996. Nation und Nationalismus: Eine Erinnerung an Ernest Renans Rede "Was ist eine Nation?" In Ernest Renan: *Was ist eine Nation? Rede am 11.* März 1882 an der Sorbonne. Stuttgart: Europäische Verlagsanstalt.

Fähndrich, Hartmut. 1988. Orientalismus und Orientalismus: Überlegungen zu Edward Said, Michel Foucault und westlichen "Islamstudien." *Die Welt des Islams* 28: 178–186. https://doi.org/10.1163/9789004659827_015

Farris, Sara R. 2010. An "Ideal Type" Called Orientalism. *Interventions* 12 (2): 265–284. https://doi.org/10.1080/1369801X.2010.489701

Fayolle, Azélie. 2019. La science contre la foi. Portrait de Renan en séminariste. *Revue d'Histoire littéraire de la France* 119 (2): 279–288.

Feldt, Jakob Egholm. 2019. Immanuel Wolf (1799–1847): Outlining a Program for the Scientific Study of Judaism. *History of Humanities* 4 (2): 251–256. https://doi.org/10.1086/704811

Findley, Carter Vaughn. 1998. An Ottoman Occidentalist in Europe: Ahmed Midhat Meets Madame Gülnar, 1889. *The American Historical Review* 103 (1): 15–49. https://doi.org/10.1086/ahr/103.1.15

Fine, David J. 1997. Solomon Schechter and the Ambivalence of Jewish Wissenschaft. *Judaism* 46 (1): 3–24.

Fitzgerald, Timothy. 2007. *Discourse on Civility and Barbarity: A Critical History of Religion and Related Categories.* Oxford: Oxford University Press.

Fowden, Garth. 2011. Book Review. *The English Historical Review* CXXVI (518): 209–212. https://doi.org/10.1093/ehr/ceq407

Fraisse, Ottfried. 2016. From Geiger to Goldziher: Historical Method and its Impact on the Conception of Islam. In *Modern Jewish Scholarship in Hungary: The "Science of Judaism" between East and West.* Edited by Tamás Turán and Carsten Wilke. Oldenbourg: De Gruyter: 203–222.

Franke, Patrick. 2010. Review: "Das Paradigma der 'Islamischen Zivilisation'" by Alexander Haridi. *Die Welt des Islams* 50 (1): 169–171. https://doi.org/10.1163/157006010X496551

Freitag, Ulrike. 2003. Der Orientalist und der Mufti: Kulturkontakt im Mekka des 19. Jahrhunderts. *Die Welt des Islams* 43 (1): 37–60. https://doi.org/10.1163/157006003763317777

Freitag, Ulrike. 2022. Urban Life in Late Ottoman, Hashemite, and Early Saudi Jeddah, as Documented in the Photographs in the Snouck Hurgronje Collection in Leiden. In *Scholarship in Action: Essays on the Life and Work of Christiaan Snouck Hurgronje (1857–1936)*. Edited by Léon Buskens and Jan Just Witkam with Annemarie van Sandwijk. Leiden and Boston: Brill: 139–167.

Freriks, Kester. 2021. Book Review: Wim van den Doel, Snouck: Het volkommen geleerdenleven van Chrsitiaan Snouck Hurgronje. *History of Humanities* 6 (2): 707–709. https://doi.org/10.1086/715963

Fück, Johann W. 1955. *Die arabischen Studien in Europa: Bis in den Anfang des 20. Jahrhunderts*. Leipzig: Otto Harrassowitz.

Fück, Johann W. 1962. Islam as an Historical Problem in European Historiography since 1800. In *Historians of the Middle East*. Edited by Bernard Lewis and P. M. Holt. London: Oxford University Press: 315–329.

Fuhrmann, Malte. 2003. DEN ORIENT DEUTSCH MACHEN: Imperiale Diskurse des Kaiserreiches über das Osmanische Reich. *Kakanien Revisted*, 2 September.

Fuhrmann, Malte. 2006. *Der Traum vom deutschen Orient: Zwei Deutsche Kolonien im Osmanischen Reich 1851–1918*. Frankfurt and New York: Campus.

Gadamer, Hans-Georg. 1960. *Wahrheit und Methode: Grundzüge einer philosophischen Hermeneutik*. Gesammelte Werke Bd. 1. Tübingen: J. C. B. Mohr (Paul Siebeck) [1990].

Geiger, Abraham. 1833. *Was hat Mohammed aus dem Judenthume aufgenommen?* Leipzig: Lazarus Goldschmidt [1902].

Geiger, Abraham. 1970. *Judaism and Islam*. New York KTAV Publishing House.

Gerdmar, Anders. 2009. *The Roots of Theological Anti-Semitism: German Biblical Interpretation and the Jews, from Herder and Semler to Kittel and Bultmann*. Boston and Leiden: Brill.

Gibb, H. A. R. and J. H. Kramers. 2001. *Concise Encyclopaedia of Islam*. Fourth Impression. Leiden and Boston: Brill.

Girard, René. 1972. *La violence et le sacré*. Paris: Grasset.

Glover, Willis B. 1954. *Evangelical Nonconformists and Higher Criticism in the Nineteenth Century*. London: Independent Press LTD.

Goitein, Shelomo Dov. 1979. Review of "Ignaz Goldziher Tagebuch" edited by Alexander Schreiber. *Jewish Social Studies* 41 (3–4): 323–327.

Goldziher, Ignaz. 1876. *Der Mythos bei den Hebräern und seine geschichtliche Entwicklung*. Leipzig: F. A. Brockhaus.

Goldziher, Ignaz. 1879. Universitäts-Moschee el-Azhar. In *Gesammelte Schriften*. Band VI. Edited by Joseph Desomogyi. Hildesheim: G. Olms [1973]: 44–61.

Goldziher, Ignaz. 1884. *Die Zairiten: Ihr Lehrsystem und ihte Geschichte. Ein Beitrag zur Geschichte der muhammedanischen Theologie*. Hildesheim: G. Olms [1967].

Goldziher, Ignaz. 1886a. Muhammedanisches Recht in Theorie und Wirklichkeit. In *Gesammelte Schriften.* Band II. Edited by Joseph Desomogyi. Hildesheim: G. Olms [1968]: 353–370.

Goldziher, Ignaz. 1986b. Über Gebärden- und Zeichensprache bei den Arabern. In *Gesammelte Schriften.* Band II. Edited by Joseph Desomogyi. Hildesheim: G. Olms [1973]: 155–172.

Goldziher, Ignaz. 1887. Review of Kingship and Marriage in Early Arabia. *Literatur-Blatt für orientalische Philologie* 3: 19–28.

Goldziher, Ignaz. 1888a. *Muhammedanische Studien.* Erster Teil. Hildesheim G. Olms [1971].

Goldziher, Ignaz. 1888b. *Muhammedanische Studien.* Zweiter Teil. Hildesheim: G. Olms [1971].

Goldziher, Ignaz. 1893. *Renan als Orientalist: Gendenkrede am 27 November 1893.* Aus dem Ungarischen übersetzt von Peter Zalán. Bearbeitet, mit einer Einleitung versehen und herausgegeben von Friedrich Niewöhner. Zürich: Spur Verlag [2000].

Goldziher, Ignaz. 1896. *Abhandlungen zur arabischen Philologie.* 2 Bände in 1 Band (1896–1899). Hildesheim: G. Olms [1982].

Goldziher, Ignaz. 1897. Real-Encyklopädie des Islam. In *Gesammelte Schriften.* Band IV. Edited by Joseph Desomogyi. Hildesheim: G. Olms [1970]: 129–132.

Goldziher, Ignaz. 1904. Heinrich Leberecht Fleischer. In *Gesammelte Schriften.* Band VI. Edited by Joseph Desomogyi. Hildesheim: G. Olms [1973]: 190–200.

Goldziher, Ignaz. 1910. *Vorlesungen über den Islam.* Zweite umgearbeitete Auflage. Heidelberg: Carl Winters Universitätsbuchhandlung.

Goldziher, Ignaz. 1914. Katholische Tendenz und Partikularismus im Islam. In *Gesammelte Schriften.* Band V. Edited by Joseph Desomogyi. Hildesheim: G. Olms [1970]: 285–312.

Goldziher, Ignaz. 1920. *Die Richtungen der islamischen Koranauslegung: An der Universität Upsala gehaltene Olaus-Petri Vorlesungen.* Leiden: Brill [1952].

Goldziher, Ignaz. 1978. *Tagebuch.* Edited by Alexander Schreiber. Leiden: Brill.

Goldziher, Ignaz. 2007. *The Ẓāhirīs: Their Doctrine and their History. A Contribution to the History of Islamic Theology.* Leiden: Brill.

Gottheil, Richard. 1922. Ignaz Goldziher. *Journal of the American Oriental Society* 42: 189–193. https://doi.org/10.2307/593621

Graf, Friedrich W. 1982. *Kritik und Pseudo-Spekulation: David Friedrich Strauss als Dogmatiker im Kontext der positionellen Theologie seiner Zeit.* München: CHR. Kaiser Verlag.

Graf, Friedrich W. 1987. Max Weber und die protestantische Theologie seiner Zeit. *Zeitschrift für Religions- und Geistesgeschichte* 39: 122–147. https://doi.org/10.1163/157007387X00291

Graf, Friedrich W. 1990. Kulturprotestantismus. In *Theologische Realenzyklopädie* XX: 231–243.

Graf, Friedrich W. 1993. Die Spaltung des Protestantismus: Zum Verhältnis von evangelischer Kirche, Staat und "Gesellschaft" im frühen 19. Jahrhundert.

In *Religion und Gesellschaft im 19. Jahrhundert*. Edited by Wolfgang Schieder. Stuttgart: Klett-Cotta: 157–180.

Gründer, Horst. 1991. *Geschichte der deutschen Kolonien*. 2. Auflage. Tübingen: UTB Schönigh.

Gu, Ming Dong. 2020. What is "Decoloniality"? A Postcolonial Critique. *Postcolonial Studies* 23 (4): 596–600. https://doi.org/10.1080/13688790.2020.1751432

Guettel, Jens-Uwe. 2012. The Myth of the Pro-Colonialist SPD: German Social Democracy and Imperialism before World War I. *Central European History* 45: 452–484. https://doi.org/10.1017/S0008938912000350

Guizot, François. 1828. *Cours d'histoire moderne—Histoire général de la civilization en Europe*. Paris: Pichon et Didier.

Gumbrecht, Hans Ulrich. 2003. *The Powers of Philology: Dynamics of Textual Scholarship*. Urbana and Chicago: University of Illinois Press.

Haarmann, Ulrich. 1974. Die islamische Moderne bei den deutschen Orientalisten. In *Araber und Deutsche: Begegnungen in einem Jahrtausend*. Edited by Friedrich H. Kochwasser and Hans R. Roemer. Tübingen and Basel: Horst Erdmann Verlag: 56–91.

Haber, Peter. 2004. Bruchstellen einer ungarisch-jüdischen Symbiose: Ignaz Goldziher. In *Herausforderung Osteuropa. Die Offenlegung stereotyper Bilder*. Edited by Thede Kahl, Elisabeth Vyslonzil, and Alois Wondan. Wien: Verlag für Geschichte und Politik: 69–80.

Haber, Peter. 2006a. *Zwischen jüdischer Tradition und Wissenschaft: Der ungarische Orientalist Ignác Goldziher 1850–1921*. Köln: Böhlau Verlag.

Haber, Peter. 2006b. Sprache, Rasse, Nation. Der ungarische Turkologe Ármin Vámbery. In *Jüdische Identität und Nation, Fallbeispiele aus Mitteleuropa*. Edited by Peter Haber, Erik Petry, and Daniel Wildmann. Köln and Wien: Böhlau Verlag: 19–49.

Hagen, Gottfried. 2004. German Heralds of the Holy War: Orientalists and Applied Oriental Studies. *Comparative Studies of South Asia, Africa and the Middle East* 24 (2): 145–162.

Halliday, Fred. 1993. Orientalism and Its Critics. *British Journal of Middle Eastern Studies* 20 (2): 145–163. https://doi.org/10.1080/13530199308705577

Hamburger, Peter. 2022. Orientalist or Master Spy: The Career of Christian Snouck Hurgronje. In *Scholarship in Action. Essays on the Life and Work of Christiaan Snouck Hurgronje (1857–1936)*. Edited by Léon Buskens and Jan Just Witkam with Annemarie van Sandwijk. Leiden and Boston: Brill: 546–570.

Hanisch, Ludmila (ed.). 1992. *Islamkunde und Islamwissenschaft im Kaiserreich: Der Briefwechsel zwischen Carl Heinrich Becker und Martin Hartmann (1900–1918)*. Leiden: Rijksuniversiteit Leiden.

Hanisch, Ludmila (ed.). 2000. *Machen Sie doch unseren Islam nicht gar zu schlecht: Der Briefwechsel der Islamwissenschaftler Ignaz Goldziher und Martin Hartmann 1894–1914*. Wiesbaden: Harrassowitz Verlag.

Hanisch, Ludmila. 2003. *Die Nachfolger der Exegeten: Deutschsprachige Erforschung des Vorderen Orients in der ersten Hälfte des 20. Jahrhunderts*. Wiesbaden: Harrassowitz.

Hanna, Daniel. 2015. Defending Divinity: A Teresian Carmelite Responds to Ernest Renan's Vie de Jésus. *Women in French Studies* 23: 23–38. https://doi.org/10.1353/wfs.2015.0008

Haridi, Alexander. 2005. *Das Paradigma der "islamischen Zivilisation"—oder die Begründung der deutschen Islamwissenschaft durch Carl Heinrich Becker (1876-1933). Eine wissenschaftsgeschichtliche Untersuchung*. Würzburg: Ergon Verlag.

Harris, Horton. 1975. *The Tübingen School*. Oxford: Clarendon Press.

Hartmann, Martin. 1909. *Der Islam: Geschichte—Glaube—Recht. Ein Handbuch*. Leipzig: Verlag von Rudolf Haupt.

Hartmann, Martin. 1912. Das Seminar für Orientalische Sprachen in Berlin. Zum 25 jährigen Bestehen. *Internationale Wochenschrift für Wissenschaft, Kunst und Technik* 1: 858–866.

Hartmann, Martin. 1916. Die fünf heiligen Fetwas (Rechtsgutachten). *Die Welt des Islams* 3 (1): 1–23.

Hartmann, Richard 1922. *Ignaz Goldziher. Zeitschrift der Deutschen Morgenländischen Gesellschaft* 76: 285–290.

Hartwig, Dirk. 2009. Die Wissenschaft des Judentums und die Anfänge der kritischen Koranforschung. Perspektiven einer modernen Koranhermeneutik. *Zeitschrift für Religions- und Geistesgeschichte* 61: 234–256. https://doi.org/10.1163/157007309788620647

Hassan, Waïl S. 2002. Postcolonial Theory and Modern Arabic Literature: Horizons of Application. *Journal of Arabic Literature* 33 (1): 45–64. https://doi.org/10.1163/15700640252955487

Hatem, Mervat. 2009. MESA Presidential Address 2008: Power and Knowledge Revisited in Middle East Studies. *Review of Middle East Studies* 43 (1): 3–10. https://doi.org/10.1017/S2151348100000045

Hawes, James. 2017. *Den korte historie om Tyskland*. Copenhagen: Bilgrav.

Heinrichs, Wolfgang. 2000. *Das Judenbild im Protestantismus des Deutschen Kaiserreichs. Ein Beitrag zur Mentalitätsgeschichte des deutschen Bürgertums in der Krise der Moderne*. Köln: Rheinland-Verlag.

Henningsen, Bernd. 2021. *Die Welt des Nordens. Zwischen Ragnarök und Wohlfahrtsutopie: Eine kulturhistorische Dekonstruktion*. Berlin: BWV.

Hennis, Wilhelm. 1996. *Max Webers Wissenschaft vom Menschen: Neue Studien zur Biographie des Werks*. Tübingen: Mohr/Siebeck.

Hennis, Wilhelm. 2003. *Max Weber und Thukydides: die "hellenische Geisteskultur" und die Ursprünge von Webers politischer Denkart*. Göttingen: Vandenhoeck und Ruprecht.

Hennis, Wilhelm, Brisson Ulrike, and Roger Brisson. 1994. The Meaning of "Wertfreiheit" on the Background and Motives of Max Weber's "Postulate." *Sociological Theory* 12 (2): 113–125. https://doi.org/10.2307/201858

Henry, John. 2010. Religion and the Scientific Revolution. In *The Cambridge Companion to Science and Religion*. Edited by Peter Harrison. Cambridge: Cambridge University Press: 39–58. https://doi.org/10.1017/CCOL9780521885386.003

Heschel, Susannah. 1998. *Abraham Geiger and the Jewish Jesus*. Chicago and London: Chicago University Press.

Heschel, Susannah. 2018. *Jüdischer Islam: Islam und jüdisch-deutsche Selbstbestimmung*. Berlin: Matthes & Seitz.

Heschel, Susannah. 2019. The Rise of Imperialism and the German Jewish Engagement in Islamic Studies. In *Modern Jewish Scholarship on Islam in Context: Rationality, European Borders, and the Search for Belonging*. Edited by Ottfried Fraisse. Berlin and Boston: De Gruyter: 61–92.

Hirschler, Konrad. 2006. Review: "Das Paradigma der 'islamischen Zivilisation'" by Alexander Haridi. *Bulletin of the School of Oriental and African Studies* 69 (2): 321–322. https://doi.org/10.1017/S0041977X0624014X

Hjelde, Sigurd. 2000. "Introduction." In *Man, Meaning, Mystery. 100 Years of History of Religions in Norway: The Heritage of W. Brede Kristensen*. Edited by Sigurd Hjelde. Leiden: Brill.

Hobson, John M. 2012. *The Eurocentric Conception of World Politics: Western International Theory, 1760–2010*. Cambridge: Cambridge University Press.

Holland, John H. 1998. *Emergence: From Chaos to Order*. Oxford: Oxford University Press.

Holloway, Steven W. 2000. Reviewed Work(s): Lectures on the Religion of the Semites: Second and Third Series by William Robertson Smith and John Day. *Journal of Near Eastern Studies* 59 (2): 137–140.

Hölscher, Lucian. 1993. Bürgerliche Religiosität im protestantischen Deutschland des 19. Jahrhunderts. In *Religion und Gesellschaft im 19. Jahrhundert*. Edited by Wolfgang Schieder. Stuttgart: Klett-Cotta: 181–215.

Holtzmann, Livnat and Miriam Ovadia. 2024. Ignaz Goldziher: The Founding Father of Gesture Studies in Arabic and Islamic Studies. In *Building Bridges: Ignaz Goldziher and His Correspondents*. Edited by Hans-Jürgen Becker, Kinga Dévényi, Sebastian Günther, and Sabine Schmidkte. Leiden: Brill: 79–138.

Holzer, Boris. 2011. Die Kontingenz der Moderne und die Modernität der Kontingenz. *Soziologische Revue* 34 (2): 153–162. https://doi.org/10.1524/srsr.2011.0010

Honigsheim, Paul. 2000. *The Unknown Max Weber*. New Brunswick and London: Transaction Publishers.

Honold, Alexander. 2002. Nach Bagdad und Jerusalem: Die Wege des Wilhelminischen Orientalismus. In *Kolonialismus als Kultur: Literatur, Medien, Wissenschaft in der deutschen Gründerzeit*. Edited by Alexander Honold and Oliver Simons. Tübingen und Basel: A. Francke Verlag: 143–164.

Honold, Alexander and Oliver Simons (eds.). 2002. *Kolonialismus als Kultur: Literatur, Medien, Wissenschaft in der deutschen Gründerzeit*. Tübingen und Basel: A. Francke Verlag.

Hourani, Albert. 1966. Islam and the Philosophers of History. *Middle Eastern Studies* 3 (3): 206–268. https://doi.org/10.1080/00263206708700074

Hourani, Albert. 1991. *A History of Arab Peoples*. London: Faber and Faber.

Houtman, Cornelis. 2000. Abraham Kuenen and William Robertson Smith Their Correspondence. *Nederlands archief voor kerkgeschiedenis* 30 (2): 221–240. https://doi.org/10.1163/187124000X00124

Howell, Alison and Melanie Richter-Montpetit. 2020. Is Securitization Theory Racist? Civilizationism, Methodological Whiteness, and Antiblack Thought in the Copenhagen School. *Security Dialogue* 51 (1): 3–22. https://doi.org/10.1177/0967010619862921

Hübinger, Gangolf. 1994. *Kulturprotestantismus und Politik: Zum Verhältnis von Liberalismus und Protestantismus im wilhelminischen Deutschland.* Tübingen: Mohr.

Huff, Toby E. and Wolfgang Schluchter (eds.). 1999. *Max Weber and Islam.* New Brunswick: Transaction.

Hull, Isabel V. 2005. *Absolute Destruction. Military Culture and the Practices of War in Imperial Germany*. Ithaca and London: Cornell University Press.

Hurgronje, Christiaan Snouck. 1880. *Het Mekaansche Feest.* Leiden: Brill.

Hurgronje, Christiaan Snouck. 1885a. Der Mahdi. In *Verspreidede Geschriften van C. Snouck Hurgronje, I.* Leiden: Brill: 145–182 [1923].

Hurgronje, Christiaan Snouck. 1885b. Aus Arabien: Verschenen in Münchener Allgemeine Zeitung van 16. November 1885, Nr. 318. In *Verspreidede Geschriften van C. Snouck Hurgronje, III.* Leiden: Brill: 1–14 [1923].

Hurgronje, Christiaan Snouck. 1887a. Über eine Reise nach Mekka. In *Verspreidede Geschriften van C. Snouck Hurgronje, III.* Leiden: Brill: 47–63 [1923].

Hurgronje, Christiaan Snouck. 1887b. Een Rector der Mekaansche Universiteit (Met Aanhangsel). In *Verspreidede Geschriften van C. Snouck Hurgronje, III.* Leiden: Brill: 65–122 [1923].

Hurgronje, Christiaan Snouck. 1888. *Mekka: Die Stadt und ihre Herren.* Haag: Martinus Nijhoff.

Hurgronje, Christiaan Snouck. 1889. *Mekka: Aus dem heutigen Leben.* Haag: Martinus Nijhoff.

Hurgronje, Christiaan Snouck. 1898. Besprechung von Eduard Sachaus: Mohammedanisches Recht nach Schafiitischer Lehre. *Zeitschrift der Deutschen Morgenländischen Gesellschaft* 53: 125–67.

Hurgronje, Christiaan Snouck. 1906a. *The Achehnese.* Volume I. Leiden: Brill.

Hurgronje, Christiaan Snouck. 1906b. *The Achehnese.* Volume II. Leiden: Brill.

Hurgronje, Snouck Christiaan. 1911. Politique musulmane de la hollande. *Revue du Monde Musulman XIV* (6).

Hurgronje, Christiaan Snouck. 1915a. The Holy War "Made in Germany." In *Verspreidede Geschriften van C. Snouck Hurgronje, III.* Leiden: Brill: 257–284 [1923].

Hurgronje, Christiaan Snouck. 1915b. Deutschland und der Heilige Krieg. In *Verspreidede Geschriften van C. Snouck Hurgronje, III*. Leiden: Brill: 285–292 [1923].

Hurgronje, Christiaan Snouck. 1916. *Islam: Origin Religious and Political Growth and Its Present State*. Reprint of "Mohammedanism. Lectures on Its Origin, Its Religious and Political Growth and Its Present State" (New York: G. P. Potnam's Sons). New Delhi: Mittal Publications [1995].

Hurgronje, Christiaan Snouck. 1921. Goldziher. In *Verspreidede Geschriften van C. Snouck Hurgronje, VI*. Leiden: Brill: 453–464 [1927].

Hurgronje, Christiaan Snouck. 1922. L'Islam et le problème des races. In *Verspreidede Geschriften van C. Snouck Hurgronje, I*. Leiden: Brill: 413–430 [1923].

Hurgronje, Christiaan Snouck. 1931. Theodor Nöldeke. *Zeitschrift der Deutschen Morgenländischen Gesellschaft* 10: 239–281.

Hurgronje, Christiaan Snouck. 2006. *Mekka in the Latter Part of the 19th Century: Daily Life, Customs and Learning. The Moslims of the East-Indian Archipelago*. Leiden and Boston: Brill.

Illies, Florian. 2018. *1913: Was ich unbedingt noch erzählen wollte*. Frankfurt am Main: Fischer.

Irwin, Robert. 2006. *For the Lust of Knowing: The Orientalists and their Enemies*. London: Penguin Books.

Jaspers, Karl. 1949. *Vom Ursprung und Ziel der Geschichte*. Zürich: Artemis.

Jepsen, Alfred. 1956. Wellhausen in Greifswald: Ein Beitrag zur Biographie Julius Wellhausens. In *Festschrift zur 500-Jahrfeier der Universität Greifswald, 17.10.1956*. Band II. Universität Greifswald: 48–55.

Jervis, John. 2004. *Exploring the Modern: Patterns of Western Culture and Civilization*. Oxford: Blackwell.

Joas, Hans. 2015. *Die Sakralität der Person: Eine neue Genealogie der Menschenrechte*. Frankfurt am Main: Suhrkamp.

Jung, Dietrich. 2011. *Orientalists, Islamists, and the Global Public Sphere: A Genealogy of the Modern Essentialist Image of Islam*. Sheffield: Equinox.

Jung, Dietrich. 2014. The "Ottoman-German Jihad": Lessons for the Contemporary "Area Studies" Controversy. *British Journal of Middle Eastern Studies* 2014: 1–19.

Jung, Dietrich. 2015. Sociology, Protestant Theology, and the Concept of Modern Religion: William Robertson Smith and the "Scientification" of Religion. *Journal of Religion in Europe* 8 (3–4): 335–364. https://doi.org/10.1163/18748929-00804006

Jung, Dietrich. 2016. Understanding the Multiple Voices of Islamic Modernities: The Case of Jihad. *Temenos* 52 (1): 61–85. https://doi.org/10.33356/temenos.52712

Jung, Dietrich. 2021. Islamism, Islamic Modernism and the Search for Modern Authenticity in an Imaginary Past. *Religions* 12 (11): 1005. https://doi.org/10.3390/rel12111005

Jung, Dietrich. 2023. *Islamic Modernities in World Society: The Rise, Spread, and Fragmentation of a Hegemonic Idea*. Edinburgh: Edinburgh University Press.

Jung, Dietrich. 2024. Negotiating the Boundaries between Religion and Science in the Abbasid Empire. In *Historicizing Secular-Religious Demarcations. Interdisciplinary Contributions to Differentiation Theory*. Edited by Monika Wohlrab-Sahr, Daniel Witte, and Christoph Kleine. Sonderband der Zeitschrift für Soziologie. Berlin and Boston: De Gruyter: 105–124.

Jung, Dietrich and Florian Zemmin (eds.). 2024. *Postcolonialism and Social Theory in Arabic*. New York: Palgrave MacMillan.

Jung, Martin H. 2000. *Der Protestantismus in Deutschland von 1815 bis 1870*. Leipzig: Evangelische Verlagsanstalt.

Jung, Martin H. 2002. *Der Protestantismus in Deutschland von 1870 bis 1945*. Leipzig: Evangelische Verlagsanstalt.

Jung, Martin H. 2008. *Christen und Juden: Die Geschichte ihrer Beziehungen*. Darmstadt: Wissenschaftliche Buchgesellschaft.

Juynboll, G. H. A. 1993. Muslim al-Hadjdjadj. In *The Encyclopaedia of Islam*. New Edition. Volume VII. MIF – NAZ: 691–693.

Kaesler, Dirk. 2014. *Max Weber: Eine Biographie*. München: C. H. Beck.

Kallai, Zecharia. 2009. Biblical Narrative and Historical Method. In *Homeland and Exile: Biblical and Ancient Near Eastern Studies in Honour of Bustenay Oded*. Edited by Gershon Galil, Mark Geller, and Alan Millard. Leiden and Boston: Brill: 455–468.

Kalmar, Ivan. 1987. The Völkerpsychologie of Lazarus and Steinthal and the Modern Concept of Culture. *Journal of the History of Ideas* 48 (4): 671–690. https://doi.org/10.2307/2709693

Kaptein, Nico. 2014. *Islam, Colonialism and the Modern Age in the Netherlands East Indies: A Biography of Sayyid Uthman (1822-1914)*. Leiden and Boston: Brill.

Karachouli, Regina. 1994. Vermutungen über das Orientbild des Leipziger Arabisten: Heinrich Leberecht Fleischer (1801–1888). In *Gedenkschrift Wolfgang Reuschel*. Edited by Dieter Bellmann. Stuttgart: Franz Steiner: 175–184.

Käsler, Dirk. 1995. *Max Weber: Eine Einführung in Leben, Werk und Wirkung*. Frankfurt am Main: Campus.

Katz, Jacob. 1998. *A House Divided. Orthodoxy and Schism in Nineteenth-Century Central European Jewry*. Hanover and London: Brandeis University Press.

Kaube, Jürgen. 2020. *Max Weber: Ein Leben zwischen den Epochen*. Fünfte Auflage. Berlin: Rowohlt.

Kemal, Namık. 1962. *Renan Müdafaanamesi (İslamiyet ve Maarif)*. Ankara: Milli Kültür Yayınları.

Kemal, Namık. 2016. Die Verteidigung des Islam gegen Renan. In *Moderne Muslime: Ernest Renan und die Geschichte der ersten Islamdebatte 1883*. Edited by Birgit Schäbler. Stuttgart: Ferdinand Schöningh: 167–202.

Kerr, Malcom. 1980. Orientalism – Book Review. *International Journal of Middle East Studies* 12 (4): 544–547. https://doi.org/10.1017/S0020743800031342

Kippenberg, Hans G. 1993. Max Weber im Kreise von Religionswissenschaftlern. *Zeitschrift für Religons- und Gesellschaftsgeschichte* 45 (1): 348–366.

Klimkeit, Hans-Joachim. 1997. Friedrich Max Müller (1823–1900). In *Klassiker der Religionswissenschaft: Von Friedrich Schleiermacher bis Mircea Eliade*. Edited by Axel Michaels. München: C. H. Beck: 29–40.

Knöbl, Wolfgang. 2007. *Die Kontingenz der Moderne: Wege in Europa, Asien und Amerika*. Frankfurt am Main and New York: Campus.

Knöbl, Wolfgang. 2014. Aufstieg und Fall der Modernisierungstheorie und des säkularen Bildes moderne Gesellschaften. Versuch einer Historisierung. In *Moderne und Religion: Kontroversen um Modernität und Säkularisierung*. Edited by Ulrich Willems, Detlef Pollack, Helene Basu, Thomas Gutmann, and Ulrike Spohn. Bielefeld: transcript: 75–116.

Kohl, Karl-Heinz. 1997. Edward Burnett Tylor (1832–1917). In *Klassiker der Religionswissenschaft: Von Friedrich Schleiermacher bis Mircea Eliade*. München: C. H. Beck: 41–59.

Kołodziejczyk, Dariusz and Igor Iwo Chabrowski. 2023. Unobvious Parallels: Christiaan Snouck Hurgronje, Waclaw Sieroszewski, and their Role in Gathering Imperial Knowledge in Sumatra and Yakutia in the 1890s. *Journal of World History* 34 (1): 47–76. https://doi.org/10.1353/jwh.2023.0002

Kopf, David. 1980. Hermeneutics versus History. *Journal of Asian Studies* 39 (3): 496–506. https://doi.org/10.2307/2054677

Kopp, Kristin. 2011. Arguing the Case for a Colonial Poland. In *German Colonialism: Race, the Holocaust, and Postwar Germany*. Edited by Volker Langbehn and Mohammad Salama. New York: Columbia University Press: 146–163.

Kramer, Martin (ed.). 1999. *The Jewish Discovery of Islam*. Tel Aviv: Tel Aviv University.

Kratz, Reinhard G. 2009. Eyes and Spectacles: Wellhausen's Method of Higher Criticism. *Journal of Theological Studies* 60 (2): 381–402.

Kraus, Hans-Joachim. 1982. *Geschichte der historisch-kritischen Erforschung des Alten Testaments*. Dritte erweiterte Auflage. Neukirchen-Vluyn: Neukirchener Verlag.

Krieken, Gerard van. 2022. Snouck Hurgronje and Pan-Islamism. In *Scholarship in Action: Essays on the life and Work of Christiaan Snouck Hurgronje (1857–1936)*. Edited by Léon Buskens and Jan Just Witkam with Annemarie van Sandwijk. Leiden and Boston: Brill: 260–278.

Küenzlen, Gottfried. 1980. *Die Religionssoziologie Max Webers*. Berlin: Duncker & Humblot.

Kuhn, Thomas S. 1970. *The Structure of Scientific Revolutions*. Second Edition. Chicago: University of Chicago Press.

Kuitert, Lisa. 2023. De "vlijmende klewang"' van Snouck Hurgronje. Groniek. *Historisch Tijdschrift* 231: 149–166. https://doi.org/10.21827/groniek.231.39878

Kundus, Birthe. 2011. German Colonialism: Some Reflections on Reassessments, Specificities, and Constellations. In *German Colonialism: Race, the Holocaust, and Postwar Germany*. Edited by Volker Langbehn and Mohammad Salama. New York: Columbia University Press: 29–47.

Kuper, Adam. 2016. Anthropologists and the Bible. In *Local Knowledge, Global Stage: Histories of Anthropology*. Annual 10. Nebraska: University of Nebraska Press.

Kurtz, Paul Michael. 2015. The Way of War: Wellhausen, Israel, and Bellicose Reiche. *Zeitschrift für die alttestamentliche Wissenschaft* 127 (1): 1–19.

Laffan, Michael F. 2003. Writing from the Colonial Margin: The Letters of Aboe Baker Djajadiningrat to Christiaan Snouck Hurgronje. *Indonesia and the Malay World* 31 (91): 356–380.

Lahme, Tilmann. 2025. *Thomas Mann: Ein Leben*. München: dtv.

Landau, Jacob M. 1990. *The Politics of Pan-Islamism*. Oxford: Clarendon Press.

Langbehn, Volker Max and Mohammad R. Salama. 2011. Introduction. In *German Colonialism: Race, the Holocaust, and Postwar Germany*. Edited by Volker Langbehn and Mohammad R. Salama. New York: Columbia University Press: vi–xxxi.

Lapidus, Ira. 2002. *A History of Islamic Societies* (Second Edition). Cambridge: Cambridge University Press.

Larson, Göran. 2005. Ignaz Goldziher on the shuʿūbiyya. *Zeitschrift der Morgenländischen Gesellschaft* 155 (2): 365–372.

Lash, Scott. 1987. Modernity or Modernism? Weber and Contemporary Social Theory. In *Max Weber, Rationality and Modernity*. Edited by Scott Lash and Sam Whimster. London: Allen & Unwin: 355–377.

Lasserre, Pierre. 1926. *La jeunesse d'Ernest Renan: Histoire de la crise religieuse au xix siècle. De Tréguier à Saint-Sulpice*. Paris: Librairie Garnier Frères.

Lassner, Jacob. 1999. Abraham Geiger: A Nineteenth-Century Jewish Reformer on the Origins of Islam. In *The Jewish Discovery of Islam*. Edited by Martin Kramer. Tel Aviv: The Moshe Dayan Center for Middle Eastern and African Studies: 103–135.

Lazarus, Neil. 2002. The Politics of Postcolonial Modernism. *The European Legacy* 7 (6): 771–782. https://doi.org/10.1080/1084877022000029055

Lee, David C. J. 1996. *Ernest Renan: In the Shadow of Faith*. London: Duckworth.

LeGouis, Catherine. 1997. *Positivism and Imagination: Scientism and Its Limits in Emile Hennequin, Wilhelm Scherer, and Dimitri Pisarev*. Cranbury and London: Associated University Press.

Lehne, Jakob. 2010. Max Weber and Nationalism—Chaos or Consistency? *Max Weber Studies* 10 (2): 209–234. https://doi.org/10.1353/max.2010.a808823

Leistle, Bernhard. 2010. Representation of the Other: Reading Orientalism through Phenomenology. In *Counterpoints: Edward Said's Legacy*. Edited by May Telmissany and Stephanie Tara Schwartz. Newcastle: Cambridge Scholar Publishing: 211–225.

Lessing, Eckhard. 2000. *Geschichte der deutschsprachigen evangelischen Theologie von Albrecht Ritschl bis zur Gegenwart. Band 1: 1870–1918*. Göttingen: Vandenhoeck & Ruprecht.

Levine, Baruch. 1997. Review of Lectures on the Religion of the Semites. Second and Third Series. *Journal of the American Oriental Society* 117 (3): 617. https://doi.org/10.2307/605293

Lewis, Bernard. 1968. The Pro-Islamic Jews. *Judaism* 17 (4): 391–404.

Lewis, Bernard. 1993. The Question of Orientalism. In *Orientalism. A Reader*. Edited by Alexander L. Macfie. Edinburgh: Edinburgh University: 249–271.

Libson, Gideon. 1998. Hidden Worlds and Open Shutters: S. D. Goitein between Judaism and Islam. In *The Jewish Past Revisited: Reflections on Modern Jewish Historians*. Edited by David N. Myers and David B. Ruderman. New Haven and London: Yale University Press: 163–198.

Littman, Enno. 1918. Erinnerungen an Julius Wellhausen. *Zeitschrift der Deutschen Morgenländischen Gesellschaft* 106: 18–22 [1956].

Littman, Enno. 1936. Christiaan Snouck Hurgronje. *Zeitschrift der Deutschen Morgenländischen Gesellschaft* 90: 445–458.

Livingstone, David N. 2004. Public Spectacle and Scientific Theory: William Robertson Smith and the Reading of Evolution in Victorian Scotland. *Studies in History and Philosophy of Biological and Biomedical Sciences* 35: 1–29.

Livingstone, David N. 2015. Finding Revelation in Anthropology: Alexander Winchell, William Robertson Smith and the Heretical Imperative. *British Journal of Historical Studies* 48 (3): 435–454. https://doi.org/10.1017/S0007087415000035

Locher-Scholten, Elsbeth. 1994. Dutch Expansion in the Indonesian Archipelago Around 1900 and the Imperialist Debate. *Journal of Southeast Asian Studies* 25 (1): 91–111.

Lombard, Maurice. 1992. *Blütezeit des Islams: Eine Wirtschafts- und Kulturgeschichte 8.–11. Jahrhundert*. Frankfurt am Main: Fischer.

Löwith, Karl. 1989. *Mein Leben in Deutschland vor und nach 1933: Ein Bericht*. Frankfurt am Main: Fischer Taschenbuch Verlag.

Luhmann, Niklas. 1986. *Ökologische Kommunikation: Kann die moderne Gesellschaft sich auf ökologische Gefährdungen einstellen?* Opladen: Westdeutscher Verlag.

Luhmann, Niklas. 1990. The World Society as a Social System. In *Essays on Self-Reference*. New York: Columbia University Press: 175–190.

Luhmann, Niklas. 1992. Kontingenz als Eigenwert der modernen Gesellschaft. In *Beobachtungen der Moderne*. Opladen: VS Verlag: 93–128.

Luhmann, Niklas. 2002. *Religion der Gesellschaft*. Frankfurt an Main: Suhrkamp.

Luhmann, Niklas. 2017. *Einführung in die Systemtheorie*. Edited by Dirk Baecker (7th edition). Heidelberg: Carl Ayer Verlag.

Lukes, Steven. 1985. *Emile Durkheim: His Life and Work. A Historical and Critical Study*. Stanford: Stanford University Press.

Lutfi al-Sayyid, Afaf. 1968. *Egypt and Cromer: A Study in Anglo-Egyptian Relations*. London: John Murray.

Macdonald, Duncan Black. 1902. *Development of Muslim Theology, Jurisprudence and Constitutional Theory*. Beirut: Khayats [1965].

Machinist, Peter. 2009. The Road Not Taken: Wellhausen and Assyriology. In *Homeland and Exile. Biblical and Ancient Near Eastern Studies in Honour of Bustenay Oded*. Edited by Gershon Galil, Mark Geller, and Alan Millard. Leiden and Boston: Brill: 469–532.

Mahner, Martin and Mario Bunge. 2001. *Function and Functionalism: A Synthetic Perspective*. Stanford: Stanford University Press.

Maier, Bernhard. 2008. From Pietism to Totemism: William Robertson Smith and Tübingen. *Journal of Scottish Thought* 1 (2): 25–51. https://doi.org/10.57132/jst.111

Maier, Bernhard. 2009. *William Robertson Smith: His Life, His Works and His Times*. Tübingen: Mohr Siebeck.

Maier, Bernhard. 2016. William Robertson Smith, Solomon Schechter and Contemporary Judaism. *Jewish Historical Studies* 48: 64–73. https://doi.org/10.14324/111.444.jhs.2016v48.026

Maier, Bernhard. 2021. Der Orientalist als Kommentator des Zeitgeschehens: Theodor Nöldeke über Politik, Religion und Gesellschaft. In *Deutschland und der Orient: Philologie, Philosophie, historische Kulturwissenschaften*. Edited by Edoardo Massimilla und Giovanni Morone. Hildesheim: Georg Olms Verlag: 177–192.

Makdisi, Ussama. 2002. After 1860: Debating Religion, Reform, and Nationalism in the Ottoman Empire. *International Journal of Middle East Studies* 34 (4): 601–617. https://doi.org/10.1017/S0020743802004014

Manasse, Ernst Moritz. 1947. Max Weber on Race. *Social Research* 14 (2): 191–221.

Mangold, Sabine. 2004. *Eine "weltbürgerliche Wissenschaft"—Die deutsche Orientalistik im 19. Jahrhundert*. Stuttgart: Frank Steiner Verlag.

Mangold, Sabine. 2011. Ignác Goldziher et Ernest Renan—Vision du monde et innovation scientifique. In *Ignác Goldziher. Un autre Orientalisme?* Paris: Libraire Orientaliste Paul Geuthner: 73–88.

Mangold-Will, Sabine. 2013. *Begrenzte Freundschaft: Deutschland und die Türkei 1918–1933*. Göttingen: Wallenstein Verlag.

Mangold-Will, Sabine. 2021. Deutsch-Jüdischer Orientalismus: Das Werden der Islamwissenschaft und die Selbstverortungen Deutsch-jüdischer Orientalisten. In *Deutschland und der Orient: Philologie, Philosophie, historische Kulturwissenschaften*. Edited by Edoardo Massimilla und Giovanni Morone. Hildesheim: Georg Olms Verlag: 47–68.

Mani, Lata and Ruth Frankenberg. 1985. The Challenge of Orientalism. *Economy and Society* 14 (2): 174–192. https://doi.org/10.1080/03085148500000009

Mann, Golo. 1992. *Deutsche Geschichte des 19. und 20. Jahrhunderts*. Frankfurt am Main: Fischer.

Mannathukkaren, Nissim. 2015. Postcolonialism and Modernity: A Critical Realist Critique. *Journal of Critical Realism* 9 (3): 299–327. https://doi.org/10.1558/jcr.v9i3.299

Manuel, Frank E. 1962. *The Prophets of Paris*. Cambridge: Harvard University Press.

Marchand, Suzanne L. 2009. *German Orientalism in the Age of Empire: Religion, Race, and Scholarship*. Cambridge: Cambridge University Press.

Martin, Richard C. 2010. Islamic Studies in the American Academy: A Personal Reflection. *Journal of the American Academy of Religion* 78 (4): 896–920.

Masuzawa, Tomoko. 2005. *The Invention of World Religions*. Chicago and London: University of Chicago Press.

Mayer, J. P. 1944. *Max Weber and German Politics: A Study in Political Sociology*. London: Faber and Faber.

McCarthy, Conor. 2010. *The Cambridge Introduction to Edward Said*. Cambridge: Cambridge University Press.

McCleery, Alistair. 2007. William Robertson Smith (1846–94). In *Edinburgh History of the Book in Scotland. Volume 4: Professionalism and Diversity 1880-2000*. Edited by David Finkelstein and Alistair McCleery. Edinburgh: Edinburgh University Press: 298–301.

McCutcheon, Russel T. 1997. *Manufacturing Religion: The Discourse on Sui Generis Religion and the Politics of Nostalgia*. Oxford and New York: Oxford University Press.

McFate, Montgomery. 2019. Useful Knowledge: Snouck Hurgronje and Islamic Insurgency in Aceh. *Orbis* 63 (3): 416–439. https://doi.org/10.1016/j.orbis.2019.05.005

McGuire, Meredith B. 2008. *Lived Religion: Faith and Practice in Everyday Life*. Oxford and New York: Oxford University Press.

McLeod, Hugh. 1982. Protestantism and the Working Class in Imperial Germany. *European Studies Review* 12 (3): 323–344. https://doi.org/10.1177/026569148201200305

Medrow, Lisa. 2018. *Moderne Tradition und religiöse Wissenschaft: Islam, Wissenschaft und Moderne bei I. Goldziher, C. Snouck Hurgronje und C. H. Becker*. Stuttgart: Ferdinand Schöningh.

Menczer, Béla. 1939. Joseph Eötvös and Hungarian Liberalism. *The Slavonic and East European Review* 17 (51): 527–538.

Michaelis, Paul. 1913. *Philosophie und Dichtung bei Ernest Renan*. Berlin: Verlag von Emil Ebering.

Mignolo, Walter D. 2020. On Decoloniality: Second Thoughts. *Postcolonial Studies* 23 (4): 612–618. https://doi.org/10.1080/13688790.2020.1751436

Millepierres, François. 1961. *La vie d'Ernest Renan sage d'Occident*. Paris: Libraire Marcel Rivière.

Miller, Michael L. 2025. Kaufmann, David. *The YIVO Encyclopedia of Jews in Eastern Europe*. https://encyclopedia.yivo.org/article/1598

Miller, Patrick D. Jr. 1982. Wellhausen and the History of Israel's Religion. *Semeia* 25: 61–73.

Minear, Richard H. 1980. Orientalism and the Study of Japan. *The Journal of Asian Studies* 39 (3): 507–517. https://doi.org/10.2307/2054678

Missbach, Antje. 2010. The Aceh War (1873–1913) and the Influence of Christiaan Snouck Hurgronje. In *Aceh. History, Politics, Culture*. Edited by Arndt Graf, Susanne Schröter, and Edwin Wieringa. Singapore: Institute for Southeast Asian Studies: 40–62.

Mitchell, Timothy. 1989. The World as Exhibition. *Comparative Studies in Society and History* 31 (2): 217–236. https://doi.org/10.1017/S0010417500015802

Mittwoch, Eugen. 1926. Das Seminar für Orientalische Sprachen and der Universität zu Berlin. In *Weltpolitische Bildungsarbeit and Preussischen Hochschulen*. Berlin: Verlag von Reimar Hobbing: 12–22.

Moaddel, Mansoor. 2002. The Study of Islamic Culture and Politics: An Overview and Assessment. *Annual Review of Sociology* 28: 359–386. https://doi.org/10.1146/annurev.soc.28.110601.140928

Mommsen, Wolfgang J. 1959. *Max Weber und die deutsche Politik 1890-1920*. Tübingen: Mohr/Siebeck.

Mongia, Padmini (ed.). 1996. *Contemporary Postcolonial Theory: A Reader*. London and New York: Arnold.

Morrone, Giovanni. 2021. Carl Heinrich Becker: Zwischen Epigenese und Essentialismus. In *Deutschland und der Orient: Philologie, Philosophie, Historische Kulturwissenschaften*. Edited by Edoardo Massimilla und Giovanni Morone. Hildesheim: Georg Olms Verlag: 373–392.

Mortimer, Mildred. 2004. Tribute to Edward Said. *Research in African Literatures* 35 (1): 6–8. https://doi.org/10.1353/ral.2004.0020

Motzki, Harald. 2000. *The Origins of Islamic Jurisprudence: Meccan Fiqh before the Classical Schools*. Leiden: Brill.

Motzki, Harald. 2014. *Wie glaubwürdig sind die Hadithe: Die klassische islamische Hadith-Kritik im Licht moderner Wissenschaft*. Springer Essentials. Wiesbaden: Springer VS.

Motzki, Harald, with Nicolet Boekhoff-van der Voort and Sean W. Anthony (eds.). 2013. *Analysing Muslim Traditions. Studies in Legal, Exegetical and Maghāzī Ḥadīth*. Leiden: Brill.

Müller, Guido. 1991. *Weltpolitische Bildung und akademische Reform: Carl Heinrich Beckers Wissenschafts- und Hochschulpolitik 1908-1930*. Köln, Weimar, and Wien: Böhlau Verlag.

Mutman, Mahmud. 1992–1993. Under the Sign of Orientalism: The West vs. Islam. *Cultural Critique* 23: 165–197. https://doi.org/10.2307/1354194

Nagel, Tilman. 1987. Das Kalifat der Abbasiden. In *Geschichte der Arabischen Welt*. Edited by Ulrich Haarmann. München: C. H. Beck: 101–165.

Nallino, Carlo Alfonso. 1922. Ignaz Goldziher. *Rivista degli studi orientali* 9 (1/2): 236.

Nash, Geoffrey. 2022. *Religion, Orientalism and Modernity: Mahdi Movements of Iran and South Asia*. Edinburgh: Edinburgh University Press.

Nelson, Benjamin. 1976. On Orient and Occident in Max Weber. *Social Research* 43 (1): 114–129.

Nicholson, Ernest. 1998. *The Pentateuch in the Twentieth Century: The Legacy of Julius Wellhausen*. Oxford: Clarendon Press.

Nietzsche, Friedrich. 1902. *Friedrich Nietzsches gesammelte Briefe, zweiter Band*. Edited by Elisabeth Förster-Nietzsche und Fritz Schöll. Berlin und Leipzig: Schuster and Löffler.

Niewöhner, Friedrich. 2000. Kritik und Liebe: Einleitung von Friedrich Niewöhner. In *Renan als Orientalist: Ignaz Goldziher 1893*. Zürich: Spur Verlag: 5–18.

Niewöhner, Friedrich. 2004. Ignaz Goldziher (1850–1921) oder: Der Mythos als Apologie. In *Religious Apologetics—Philosophical Argumentation*. Edited by Yossef Schwartz and Volkhard Krech. Tübingen: Mohr Siebeck: 175–184.

Nipperdey, Thomas. 1988. *Religion im Umbruch: Deutschland 1870-1918*. München: C. H. Beck.

Nipperdey, Thomas. 1990. *Nachdenken über die deutsche Geschichte*. Essays. München C. H. Beck.

Nirenberg, David. 2013. *Anti-Judaism: The Western Tradition*. New York and London: W. W. Norton & Company.

Nöldeke, Theodor. 1860. Geschichte des Qorāns. Göttingen: Verlag der Dieterichschen Buchhandlung.

Nöldeke, Theodor. 1886. Review of Kinship and Marriage in early Arabia by W. Robertson Smith. *Zeitschrift der Deutschen Morgenländischen Gesellschaft* 40 (1): 148–187.

Nöldeke, Theodor. 1892. *Orientalische Skizzen*. Berlin: Verlag von Gebrüder Paetel.

Noronha-DiVanna, Isabel. 2010. *Writing History in the Third Republic*. Newcastle: Cambridge Scholars Publishing.

Nowak, Kurt. 1998. Symbolisierung des Unendlichen: Ernest Renan und sein Verhältnis zum Protestantismus. *Zeitschrift für Kirchengeschichte* 109 (1): 59–79.

Olender, Maurice. 1992. *The Languages of Paradise: Race, Religion, and Philology in the Nineteenth Century*. Cambridge: Harvard University Press.

Osterhammel, Jürgen. 1997. Edward W. Said und die "Orientalismus"-Debatte. Ein Rückblick. *Asien Afrika Lateinamerika* 25: 597–607.

Osterhammel, Jürgen. 2011. *Die Verwandlung der Welt: Eine Geschichte des 19. Jahrhunderts*. München: C. H. Beck.

Otterspeer, Willem. 2022. Snouck Hurgronje and the Indonesian Students in Leiden. In *Scholarship in Action: Essays on the Life and Work of Christiaan Snouck Hurgronje (1857-1936)*. Edited by Léon Buskens and Jan Just Witkam with Annemarie van Sandwijk. Leiden and Boston: Brill: 503–516.

Owen, Roger. 1973. Studying Islamic History. *Journal of Interdisciplinary History* 4 (2): 287–298. https://doi.org/10.2307/202268

Palonen, Kari. 2001. Was Max Weber a "Nationalist"? A Study in the Rhetoric of Conceptual Change. *Max Weber Studies* 1 (2): 196–214.

Paret, Rudi. 1968. *Arabistik und Islamkunde and deutschen Universitäten: Deutsche Orientalisten seit Theodor Nöldeke*. Wiesbaden: Steiner.

Pasto, James. 1998. Islam's "Strange Secret Sharer": Orientalism, Judaism, and the Jewish Question. *Comparative Studies in Society and History* 40 (3): 437–474. https://doi.org/10.1017/S0010417598001364

Patai, Raphael. 1987. *Ignaz Goldziher and His Oriental Diary: A Translation and a Psychological Portrait*. Detroit: Wyne University Press.

Patke, Rajeev S. 2002. Back to the Future: The Post- in the Colonial. *The European Legacy* 7 (6): 693–696. https://doi.org/10.1080/1084877022000028984

Paul, Jürgen. 2003. Max Weber und die "Islamische Stadt." In *Max Webers Religonssoziologie in interkultureller Perspektive*. Edited by Hartmut Lehmann and Jean Martin Quédraogo. Göttingen: Vandenhoeck und Ruprecht: 109–137.

Paul, Jürgen. 2018. Carl Heinrich Beckers "Lehenswesen"-Aufsatz von 1914 und seine Wirkung. In *Islam in der Moderne, Moderne im Islam: Eine Festschrift für Reinhard Schulze zum 65. Geburtstag*. Edited by Florian Zemmin, Johannes Stephan, and Monica Corrado. Leiden and Boston: Brill: 41–60.

Pedersen, Johannes. 2022. The Scientific Work of Snouck Hurgronje [First in 1957]. In *Scholarship between Europe and the Levant. Essays in Honour of Alastair Hamilton*. Edited by Jan Loop and Jill Kraye. Leiden and Boston: Brill: 535–544.

Pels, Peter. 1997. The Anthropology of Colonialism: Culture, History, and the Emergence of Western Governmentality. *Annual Review of Anthropology* 26: 163–183.

Perrine, Simon-Nahum. 2007. *Revue d'histoire intellectuelle* 25 (1): 61–74. https://doi.org/10.3917/mnc.025.0061

Peyre, Henri. 1969. *Renan*. Paris: Presses Universitaires de France.

Philsooph, Hushang. 1995. A Reconsideration of Frazer's Relationship with Robertson Smith: The Myth and the Facts. In *William Robertson Smith: Essays in Reassessment*. Edited by William Johnstone. Sheffield: Sheffield University Press: 331–342.

Pickering, W. S. F. 1984. *Durkheim's Sociology of Religion: Themes and Theories*. London: Routledge and Kegan Paul.

Pietsch, Walter. 1999. *Zwischen Reform und Orthodoxie: Der Eintritt des ungarischen Judentums in die moderne Welt*. Berlin: Philosophische Verlagsanstalt.

Pitt, Alan. 2000. The Cultural Impact of Science in France: Ernest Renan and the Vie de Jésus. *The Historical Journal* 42 (1): 79–101. https://doi.org/10.1017/S0018246X99008948

Plé, Bernhard. 1996. *Die "Welt" aus den Wissenschaften: Der Positivismus in Frankreich, England und Italien von 1848 bis ins zweite Jahrzehnt des 20. Jahrhunderts, eine wissenssoziologische Studie*. Stuttgart: Klett-Cotta.

Plietzsch, Susanne. 2019. Hermeneutik des Konkreten: Die Propheten als Repräsentanten Israels bei Julius Wellhausen und Abraham Geiger. In *Deutsch-jüdische Bibelwissenschaft: Historische, exegetische und theologische Perspektiven* (Europäisch-Jüdische Studien 40). Edited by Daniel Vorpahl, Sophia Kähler, and Shani Tzoref. Oldenbourg: De Gruyter: 25–40

Poggi, Gianfranco. 1975. Review Article. *The British Journal of Sociology* 26 (2): 245–247. https://doi.org/10.2307/589594

Poliakov, Léon. 1974. *The Aryan Myth: A History of Racist and Nationalist Ideas in Europe*. London: Sussex University Press.

Pouchepadass, Jacques. 2004. Que reste-t-il des Subaltern Studies? *Critique internationale* 24 (juillet): 67–79. https://doi.org/10.3917/crii.024.0067

Prakash, Gyan. 1995. Orientalism Now. *History and Theory* 34 (3): 199–212. https://doi.org/10.2307/2505621

Preisendörfer, Bruno. 2023. *Als Deutschland erstmals einig wurde: Reise in die Bismarckzeit.* Köln: Kiepenheur & Witsch.

Preissler, Holger. 1995. Die Anfänge der Deutschen Morgenländischen Gesellschaft. *Zeitschrift der Deutschen Morgenländischen Gesellschaft* 145 (2): 241–327.

Preißler, Holger. 2008. Les contacts entre orientalistes francais et allemands dans les années 1820 et 1830, d'après la correspondance de Heinrich Leberecht Fleischer (1801–1888). *Revue germanique internationale* 7: 93–108. https://doi.org/10.4000/rgi.399

Priest, Robert D. 2015a. *The Gospel According to Renan: Writing, and Religion in Nineteenth-Century France.* Oxford: Oxford University Press.

Priest, Robert D. 2015b. Ernest Renan's Race Problem. *The Historical Journal* 58 (1): 309–330. https://doi.org/10.1017/S0018246X14000181

Quinn, Riley. 2017. *An Analysis of Edward Said's Orientalism.* London and New York: Routledge.

Rabault-Feuerhahn, Pascale and Céline Trautmann-Waller. 2008. Introduction. *Revue germanique internationale* 7: 5–8. https://doi.org/10.4000/rgi.223

Randeria, Shalini. 2002. Entangled Histories of Uneven Modernities: Civil Society, Caste Solidarities and Legal Pluralism in Post-Colonial India. In *Unravelling Ties—From Social Cohesion to New Practices of Connectedness.* Edited by Y. Elkana, I. Kratev, E. Malcamo, and S. Randeria. Frankfurt am Main and New York: Campus: 284–311.

Rash, William. 2012. Luhmann's Ontology. *Revue internationale de philosophie* 1 (259): 85–104. https://doi.org/10.3917/rip.259.0085

Raz, Josepha. 2023. *The Poetics of Prophecy: Modern Afterlives of a Biblical Tradition.* Cambridge: Cambridge University Press.

Renan, Ernest. 1851. Mahomet et les origines de l'islamisme. *Revue des Deux Mondes* 12 (6): 1063–1101.

Renan, Ernest. 1858. *Histoire générale et système comparé des langues sémitiques. Première partie. Histoire général des langues sémtitiques.* Paris: L'Imprimerie Impériale.

Renan, Ernest. 1860. De l'avenir religieux des sociétés modernes. *Revue des Deux Mondes* 29 (4): 761–797.

Renan, Ernest. 1862a. De la part des peuples sémitiques dans l'histoire de la civilisation. Discours d'ouverture du cours de langues hébraïque, chaldaïque et syriaque au Collège de France prononcé le 21 févier 1862. In *Ernest Renan: Qu'est-ce qu'une nation? Et autres essais politiques.* Edited by Joël Roman. Paris: Presses Pocket: 182–200.

Renan, Ernest. 1862b. Bulletin mensuel de L'Académie des Inscriptions: Mois d'avril et de mai. Mission de Phénicie troisième rapport á l'Empereur. *Revue Archéologique.* Nouvelle Série 5: 394–408.

Renan, Ernest. 1863. *The Life of Jesus (La Vie de Jésus)*. Amherst: Prometheus Books [1991].

Renan, Ernest. 1872. *La Réforme intellectuelle et moral*. Paris: Michel Lévy Frères.

Renan, Ernest. 1882. Qu'est-ce qu'une nation? In *Ernest Renan: Qu'est-ce qu'une nation? Et autres essais politiques*. Edited by Joël Roman. Paris: Presses Pocket: 37–56.

Renan, Ernest. 1883. *L'Islamisme et la Science: Conférence faite à la Sorbonne le 29 mars 1883*. Paris: Ancienne Maison Michel Lévy Frères.

Renan, Ernest. 1886. Les origines de la Bible: Histoire et Légende (première partie). *Revue des Deux Mondes* 74 (1): 5–27.

Renan, Ernest. 1890. *L'Avenir de la science. Pensées de 1848*. Paris: Calmann-Lévy.

Renan, Ernest. 1936. *Souvenirs d'enfance et de jeunesse*. Paris: Calmann-Lévy and Nelson.

Renan, Ernest. 1992. Lettres à Strauss avec lettres de Strauss. In *Ernest Renan. Qu'est-ce qu'une nation? Et autres essais politiques*. Edited by Joël Roman. Paris: Presses Pocket: 107–163.

Reuter, Astrid. 2014. *Religion in der verrechtlichten Gesellschaft: Rechtskonflikte und öffentliche Kontroversen um Religion als Grenzarbeiten am religiösen Feld*. Göttingen: Vandenhoeck & Ruprecht.

Rich, Jennifer. 2007. *An Introduction to Modern Feminist Theory. Philosophy Insights*. Tirril: Humanities-Ebooks.

Riesen, Richard Allan. 1985. *Criticism and Faith in Late Victorian Scotland: A. B. Davidson, William Robertson Smith, and George Adam Smith*. Lanham, New York, and London: University Press of America.

Ring, Max. 1872. *Ein Besuch in Barackia: Berliner Lebensbild*. Leipzig: Verlag von Ernst Keil.

Ringer, Fritz. 1992. *Fields of Knowledge: French Academic Culture in Comparative Perspective 1890–1920*. Cambridge: Cambridge University Press.

Ringer, Fritz. 2000. *Toward a Social History of Knowledge: Collected Essays*. New York and Oxford: Berghahn Books.

Ringer, Fritz. 2002. Max Weber's Liberalism. *Central European History* 35 (3): 379–395. https://doi.org/10.1163/15691610260426506

Ritschl, Otto. 1896. *Albrecht Ritschls Leben: Zweiter Band, 1864–1889*. Freiburg: Mohr.

Ritter, Hellmut. 1937. Carl Heinrich Becker als Orientalist. *Der Islam* 24 (2): 175–185. https://doi.org/10.1515/islm.1937.24.2.175

Ritter, Hellmut. 1963. Dem Andenken an Carl Heinrich Becker den Begründer dieser Zeitschrift. *Der Islam* 38: 272–282.

Rivière, Peter. 1995. William Robertson Smith and John Ferguson McLennan: The Aberdeen Roots of British Social Anthropology. In *William Robertson Smith: Essays in Reassessment*. Edited by William Johnson. Sheffield: Sheffield Academic Press: 293–302.

Robertson, J. M. 1924. *Ernest Renan*. London: Watts & Co.

Robertson, Roland. 1992. *Globalization, Social Theory and Global Culture*. London: Sage.

Robertson, Roland. 2011. S. N. Eisenstadt: A Sociological Giant. *Journal of Classical Sociology* 11 (3): 303–311. https://doi.org/10.1177/1468795X11406029

Robertson Smith, William. 1868. Prophecy and Personality: A Fragment. In *Lectures and Essays of William Robertson Smith*. Edited by John Sutherland Black and George Chrystal. London: Adam and Charles Black [1912]: 97–108.

Robertson Smith, William. 1869. Christianity and the Supernatural. In *Lectures & Essays of William Robertson Smith*. Edited by John Sutherland Black and George William Chrystal. London: Adam and Charles Black: 109–136.

Robertson Smith, William. 1874. What History Teaches Us to Seek in the Bible? In *Lectures and Essays of William Robertson Smith*. Edited by John Sutherland Black and George Chrystal. London: Adam and Charles Black [1912]: 207–234.

Robertson Smith, William. 1875. Bible. *Encyclopedia Britannica Ninth Edition* (3): 634–648.

Robertson Smith, William. 1876. Two Lectures on Prophecy. In *Lectures and Essays of William Robertson Smith*. Edited by John Sutherland Black and George William Chrystal. London: Adam and Black: 341–366.

Robertson Smith, William. 1879. Wellhausen's Geschichte Israels. In *Lectures and Essays of William Robertson Smith*. Edited by John Sutherland Black and George Chrystal. London: Adam and Charles Black [1912]: 601–607.

Robertson Smith, William. 1880. Animal Tribes in the Old Testament. In *Lectures and Essays of William Robertson Smith*. Edited by John Sutherland Black and George Chrystal. London: Adam and Charles Black [1912]: 455–483.

Robertson Smith, William. 1881a. *The Old Testament in the Jewish Church: Twelve Lectures on Biblical Criticism*. Edinburgh: Adam and Charles Black.

Robertson Smith, William. 1881b. A Journey in the Hejaz. In *Lectures and Essays of William Robertson Smith*. Edited by John Sutherland Black and George Chrystal. London: Adam and Charles Black [1912]: 484–597.

Robertson Smith, William. 1882. *The Prophets of Israel and Their Place in History*. New Brunswick and London: Transaction Publishers [2002].

Robertson Smith, William. 1887. *Histoire du Peuple d'Israël. In Lectures and Essays of William Robertson Smith*. Edited by John Sutherland Black and George Chrystal. London: Adam and Charles Black [1912]: 608–622.

Robertson Smith, William. 1892. *The Old Testament in the Jewish Church: A Course of Lectures on Biblical Criticism*. Second edition. New York: D. Appleton and Co.

Robertson Smith, William. 1903. *Kinship and Marriage in Early Arabia*. New Edition. London: Adam and Charles Black.

Robertson Smith, William. 1927. *Lectures on the Religion of the Semites: The Fundamental Institutions*. Third Edition. London: A. & C. Black.

Robin, Christian. 2011. La mission d'Ernest Renan en Phénicie. In *Histoire et archéologie méditerranées sous Napoléon III*. Edited by André Laronde, Pierre Toubert et Jean Leclant. Paris: Diffusion de Boccard: 125–154.

Robson, J. 1979. Al-Bukhari, Muhammad B. Ismail. In *The Encyclopaedia of Islam*. New Edition. Volume I. A–B: 1296–1297.

Rodinson, Maxime. 1966. *Islam et capitalisme*. Paris: Ed. du Seuil.

Rodinson, Maxime. 1988. *Europe and the Mystique of Islam*. London: I. B. Tauris.

Rodríguez, Encarnación Gutiérrez. 2010. Decolonizing Postcolonial Rhetoric. In *Decolonizing European Sociology: Transdisciplinary Approaches*. Edited by Encarnación Gutiérrez Rodríguez, Manuela Boatcă, and Sérgio Costa. London and New York: Routledge: 49–67.

Rogerson, J. W. 1995. *The Bible and Criticism in Victorian Britain. Profiles of F. D. Maurice and William Robertson Smith*. Sheffield: Sheffield University Press.

Rohde, Achim. 2005. Der Innere Orient: Orientalismus, Antisemitismus und Geschlecht im Deutschland des 18. bis 20. Jahrhunderts. *Die Welt des Islams* 45 (3): 370–411. https://doi.org/10.1163/157006005774774820

Rohls, Jan. 1997. *Protestantische Theologie der Neuzeit I*. Tübingen: J. C. B. Mohr.

Rohmana, Jajang A. 2018. Rereading Christiaan Snouck Hurgronje: His Islam, Marriage and Indo-European Descents in the Early Twentieth-Century. *Priangan Walisongo: Jurnal Penelitian Sosial Keagamaan* 26 (1): 35–66. https://doi.org/10.21580/ws.26.1.2148

Rösel, Hartmut N. 2009. The Book of Joshua and the Existence of a Hexateuch. In *Homeland and Exile: Biblical and Ancient Near Eastern Studies in Honour of Bustenay Oded*. Edited by Gershon Galil, Mark Geller, and Alan Millard. Leiden and Boston: Brill: 559–570.

Rudolph, Kurt. 1982. Wellhausen als Arabist. *Semeia* 25: 111–155.

Rudolph, Kurt. 1983. *Wellhausen als Arabist*. Berlin: Akademie-Verlag.

Rürup, Reinhard. 1987. *Emanzipation und Antisemitismus: Studien zur "Judenfrage" der bürgerlichen Gesellschaft*. Frankfurt am Main: Fischer.

Said, Edward. 1978. *Orientalism*. New York: Vintage.

Said, Edward. 1980. Islam, the Philological Vocation, and French Culture: Renan and Massignon. In *Islamic Studies: A Tradition and its Problems*. Edited by Malcom Kerr. Malibu: Undena Publications: 53–72.

Said, Edward. 1983. *The World, the Text, and the Critic*. Cambridge: Harvard University Press.

Said, Edward. 1994. Afterword. In *Orientalism*. New York: Vintage: 329–352.

Said, Edward. 1999. *Out of Place: A Memoir*. London: Granta Publications.

Said, Edward. 2000. My Encounter with Sartre. *The London Review of Books* 22 (11), 1 June.

Salusinszky, Imre. 2002. *Criticism in Society*. London and New York: Routledge.

Scarborough, William J. 2018. Introduction: New Developments in Gender Research: Multidimensional Frameworks, Intersectionality, and Thinking Beyond the Binary. In *Handbook of the Sociology of Gender*. Edited by Barbara. J. Risman, Carissa M. Froyum, and William J. Scarborough. Cham: Springer Nature: 3–18.

Schäbler, Birgit. 2016. *Moderne Muslime: Ernest Renan und die Geschichte der ersten Islamdebatte 1883*. Stuttgart: Ferdinand Schönigh.

Schaper, Joachim. 2008. William Robertson Smith's Early Work on Prophecy and the Beginnings of Social Anthropology. *Journal of Scottish Thought* 1 (2): 13–23.

Scheffler, Thomas. 1997. Linker Orientalismus? August Bebels Buch "Die Mohamedanisch-Arabische Kulturperiode." *Asien, Afrika, Lateinamerika* 25: 99–109.

Schimanck, Uwe. 2005. *Differenzierung und Integration der modernen Gesellschaft: Beiträge zur akteurzentrierten Differenzierungstheorie*. Wiesbaden: VS Verlag.

Schlichte, Klaus. 2023. Indien gibt es nicht. Die Vernachlässigung Osteuropas steht für ein größeres Problem der deutschen Sozialwissenschaft. *Soziologie* 52 (3): 415–424.

Schmiedel, Ulrich. 2016. The Politics of Europeanism. "God" in Ernst Troeltsch's War and Post-War Writings. *Journal for the History of Modern Theology* 22 (2): 231–249. https://doi.org/10.1515/znth-2016-0004

Schmitt, Rüdiger. 2014. Olshausen, Justus. *Encyclopedia Iranica*, online edition, 18 March [2000]. https://www.iranicaonline.org/articles/olshausen-justus/

Schnädelbach, Herbert. 1984. *Philosophy in Germany 1831-1933*. Translated by Eric Matthews. Cambridge: Cambridge University Press.

Schnädelbach, Herbert. 2000. *Philosophie in der modernen Kultur*. Frankfurt am Main: Suhrkamp.

Schölch, Alexander. 1987. Der arabische Osten im neunzehnten Jahrhundert 1800–1914. In *Geschichte der arabischen Welt*. Edited by Ulrich Haarmann. München C. H. Beck: 365–431.

Schorsch, Ismar. 2016. Beyond the Classroom: The Enduring Relationship between Heinrich L. Fleischer and Ignaz Goldziher. In *Modern Jewish Scholarship in Hungary: The "Science of Judaism" between East and West*. Edited by Tamás Turán and Carsten Wilke. Oldenbourg: De Gruyter: 119–156.

Schwanitz, Wolfgang G. 2003. Djihad "Made in Germany": Der Streit um den heiligen Krieg 1914–1915. *Sozial.Geschichte* 18 (2): 7–34.

Schwartz, Eduard. 1938. Julius Wellhausen. In *Gesammelte Schriften*. Erster Band. Berlin: Walter De Gruyter: 326–361.

Schweitzer, Albert. 1913. *Die Geschichte der Leben Jesu Forschung*. Tübingen: Mohr.

Scott, David. 2004. *Conscripts of Modernity: The Tragedy of Colonial Enlightenment*. Durham: Duke University Press.

Scott, David. 2006. The Trouble of Thinking: An Interview with Talal Asad. In *Powers of the Secular Modern: Talal Asad and His Interlocutors*. Edited by David Scott and Charles Hirschkind. Stanford: Stanford University Press: 243–303.

Sellheim, Rudolf. 2007. Theodor Nöldeke (1836–1930): Begründer der modernen Orientalistik. *Die Welt des Orients* 37: 135–144.

Seth, Sanjay. 2021. *Beyond Reason*. Oxford: Oxford University Press.

Seyhan, Ahmet Emin. 2024a. Ignaz Goldziher'in Hadislerin Kitabetiyle İlgili İddiaları Üzerine Bir Değerlendirme (An Evaluation on Ignaz Goldziher's Claims About the Composition of Hadith). *Kocatepe İslami İlimler Dergisi* 7 (1): 213–237. https://doi.org/10.52637/kiid.1444713

Seyhan, Ahmet Emin. 2024b. Ignaz Goldziher'in İslam'ın Evrenselliğiyle İlgili Düşünceleri Üzerine Bir Değerlendirme (An Evaluation of Ignaz Goldziher's

Thoughts on the Universality of Islam). *Burudur İlahiyat Dergisi* 8: 20–52. https://doi.org/10.59932/burdurilahiyat.1460756

Sharot, Stephen. 2001. *A Comparative Sociology of World Religions: Virtuosos, Priests, and Popular Religion*. New York: New York University Press.

Shaw, Wendy M. K. 2003. *Possessors and Possessed: Museums, Archaeology and the Visualization of History in the Late Ottoman Empire*. Berkeley: University of California Press.

Shiel, Judith B. 1995. William Robertson Smith in the Nineteenth Century in the Light of His Correspondence. In *William Robertson Smith: Essays in Reassessment*. Edited by William Johnstone. Sheffield: Sheffield Academic Press: 78–85.

Silberman, Lou H. 1982. Wellhausen and Judaism. *Semeia* 25: 75–82.

Simon, Robert. 1986. *Ingnác Goldziher: His Life and Scholarship as Reflected in His Works and Correspondence*. Leiden: Brill.

Simonsen, Jørgen Bæk. 2016. Johannes Pedersen og dansk islamforskning i mellemkrigstiden. *Tidskrift for Islamforskning* 10 (1): 149–164.

Sivan, Emmanuel. 1985. *Interpretations of Islam: Past and Present*. Princeton: Darwin Press.

Sivaramakrishnan, K. 1995. Situating the Subaltern: History and Anthropology in the Subaltern Studies Project. *Journal of Historical Sociology* 8 (4): 395–429. https://doi.org/10.1111/j.1467-6443.1995.tb00173.x

Skovgaard-Petersen, Jakob. 2010. DET GLEMTE HØJDEPUNKT: Den internationale orientalist-kongres i København 1908. In *Det fremmede som historisk drivkraft. Danmark efter 1742: Festskrift til Hendes Majestæt Dronnings Margrethe II ved 70-års-fødselsdagen den 16. april 2010*. Edited by Marita Akhøj. København: Det Kongelige Danske Videnskabernes Selskab: 245–252.

Smend, Rudolf. 1981. Wellhausen in Greifswald. *Zeitschrift für Theologie und Kirche* 78 (2): 141–176.

Smend, Rudolf. 1982. Wellhausen und das Judentum: In dankbarer Erinnerung an Isac Leo Seeligmann (1907–1982). *Zeitschrift für Theologie und Kirche* 79 (3): 249–282.

Smend, Rudolf. 1988. 1897—die Universität in Preußen. In *Stationen der Göttinger Universitätsgeschichte 1737—1787—1837—1887—1937*. Edited by Bernd Moeller. Göttingen: Vandenhoeck and Ruprecht: 68–90.

Smend, Rudolf. 1995. William Robertson Smith and Julius Wellhausen. In *William Robertson Smith: Essays in Reassessment*. Edited by William Johnstone. Sheffield: Sheffield Academic Press: 226–242.

Smend, Rudolf (ed.). 2013. *Julius Wellhausen Briefe*. Tübingen: Mohr Siebeck.

Smend, Rudolf. 2021. The Graf—Kuenen—Wellhausen School. *The Oxford Handbook of the Pentateuch*. Edited by Joel S. Baden and Jeffrey Stackert. Oxford: Oxford University Press: 143–164.

Sommer, Anders Urs. 2008. Nietzsche und die Bibel: Forschungen und Desiderate. *Jahrbuch Internationale Germanistik* 40 (1): 49–63. https://doi.org/10.3726/82030_49

Southern, R. W. 1962. *Western Views of Islam in the Middle Ages*. Cambridge: Harvard University Press.

Spivak, Gayatri C. 1985. Subaltern Studies: Deconstructing Historiography. In *Subaltern Studies IV: Writings on South Asian History and Society*. Edited by Ranajit Guha. Delhi: Oxford University Press: 330–363.

Spivak, Gayatri C. 1997. Poststructuralism, Marginality, Postcoloniality and Value. In *Contemporary Postcolonial Theory: A Reader*. Edited by Padmini Mongia. London and New York: Arnold: 198–222.

Spivak, Gayatri C., Gianmaria Colpani, and Jamila M. H. Mascat. 2022. Epistemic Daring: An Interview with Gayatri Chakravorty Spivak. *Postcolonial Studies* 25 (1): 136–141. https://doi.org/10.1080/13688790.2022.2030600

Steenbrink, Karel. 1993. *Dutch Colonialism and Indonesian Islam: Contacts and Conflicts 1596–1950*. Amsterdam and Atlanta: Rodopi.

Stefani, Claudio de. 2021. Von Sylvestre De Sacy zur Leipziger Schule: Heinrich Leberecht Fleischer. In *Deutschland und der Orient: Philologie, Philosophie, historische Kulturwissenschaften*. Edited by Edoardo Massimilla und Giovanni Morone. Hildesheim: Georg Olms Verlag: 19–46.

Steinmetz, George. 2006. Decolonizing German Theory: An Introduction. *Postcolonial Studies* 9 (1): 3–13. https://doi.org/10.1080/13668250500488793

Steinmetz, George. 2016. Neo-Bourdieusian Theory and the Question of Scientific Autonomy: German Sociologists and Empire, 1890s–1940s. In *Postcolonial Sociologies: A Reader*. Edited by Julian Go, Emerald Publishing: 145–206.

Steinthal, Hermann. 1857. Zur Sprachwissenschaft. *Zeitschrift der Deutsch Morgenländischen Gesellschaft* 11 (3): 396–426.

Sternhell, Zeev. 2010. *The Anti-Enlightenment Tradition*. New Haven and London: Yale University Press.

Stichweh, Rudolf. 1984. *Zur Entstehung des modernen Systems wissenschaftlicher Disziplinen: Physik in Deutschland 1740–1890*. Frankfurt am Main: Suhrkamp.

Stoler, Ann Laura. 2009. *Along the Archival Grain: Epistemic Anxieties and Colonial Common Sense*. Princeton: Princeton University Press.

Strazzeri, Victor. 2022. *The Young Max Weber and German Social Democracy: The Labour Question and the Genesis of Social Theory in Imperial Germany (1884–1899)*. Leiden and Boston: Brill.

Surburg, Raymond F. 1979. Wellhausenism Evaluated after a Century of Influence. *Concordia Theological Quarterly* 43 (2): 78–95.

Swatos, William H. and Peter Kivisto. 1991. Max Weber as "Christian Sociologist." *Journal for the Scientific Study of Religion* 30 (4): 347–362. https://doi.org/10.2307/1387273

Sylvester, Christine. 1999. Development Studies and Postcolonial Studies: Disparate Tales of the "Third World." *Third World Quarterly* 20 (4): 703–721. https://doi.org/10.1080/01436599913514

Tagliacozzo, Eric. 2000. Kettle on a Slow Boil: Batavia's Threat Perceptions in the Indies Outer Islands 1870–1910. *Journal of Southeast Asian Studies* 31 (1): 70–100.

al-Tahtawi, Rifaʿa R. 2011. *An Imam in Paris: al-Tahtawi's Visit to France 1826-1831*. Reprint edition. London: Saqi Books.

Thadden, Rudolf von. 1988. 1837—die Universität im Königreich Hannover. In *Stationen der Göttinger Universitätsgeschichte 1737—1787—1837—1887—1937*. Edited by Bernd Moeller. Göttingen: Vandenhoeck and Ruprecht: 46–67.

Theilhaber, Amir. 2020. *Friedrich Rosen: Orientalist Scholarship and International Politics*. Berlin and Boston: De Gruyter.

Tiryakian, E. A. 1966. A Problem of Sociology of Knowledge: The Mutual Unawareness of Émile Durkheim and Max Weber. *European Journal of Sociology* 7 (2): 330–336. https://doi.org/10.1017/S0003975600001478

Tolan, John V. 2019. *Faces of Muhammad: Western Perceptions of the Prophet of Islam from the Middle Ages to Today*. Princeton: Princeton University Press.

Toral, Isabel. 2025. The Abbasid Capital Baghdad as a Boom Town, Trade Hub, and Stage of Consumption. In *The Routledge Handbook of Global Islam and Consumer Culture*. Edited by Birgit Krawietz and Francois Gauthier. London and New York: Routledge: 98–107.

Trautmann-Waller, Céline. 2008. Du "caractère des peoples sémitiques" à une "science de la mythologie hébraïque" (Ernest Renan, Heymann Steinthal, Ignác Goldziher). *Revue germanique internationale* 7: 169–184. https://doi.org/10.4000/rgi.408

Treiber, Hubert. 1999. Zur Genese des Askesekonzepts bei Max Weber. *Saeculum* 50 (2): 247–297. https://doi.org/10.7788/saeculum.1999.50.2.247

Treiber, Hubert. 2020. Max Weber in Heidelberg (1897–1918). Hochschullehrer, Privatgelehrter und "etablierter Außenseiter." *Soziopolis: Gesellschaft beobachten*.

Troeltsch, Ernst. 1928. *Die Bedeutung des Protestantismus für die Entstehung der Modernen Welt* 5. Auflage. München und Berlin: Verlag von R. Oldenbourg.

Trüper, Henning. 2014. Matte farbige Schatten: Zugehörigkeiten des Gelehrtenpolitikers Carl Heinrich Becker. *Österreichische Zeitschrift für Geschichtswissenschaften* 25 (3): 177–211.

Trüper, Henning. 2020. *Orientalism, Philology, and the Illegibility of the Modern World*. London: Bloomsbury.

Trumpener, Ulrich. 1968. *Germany and the Ottoman Empire 1914-1918*. Princeton: Princeton University Press.

Tulloch, John. 1876–1877. Progress of Religious Thought in Scotland. *Contemporary Review* 29 (Dec. 1876: May 1877): 535–551.

Turán, Tamás. 2023. *Ignaz Goldziher as a Jewish Orientalist: Traditional Learning, Critical Scholarship, and Personal Piety*. Berlin and Boston: De Gruyter.

Turki, Abdel-Magid. 2002. Al-Ẓāhiriyya. In *The Encyclopaedia of Islam*. New Edition. Volume XI. W – Z. Leiden: Brill: 394–396.

Turner, Bryan. 1974. *Weber and Islam: A Critical Study*. London: Routledge.

Turner, Bryan. 2016. Max Weber and the Sociology of Islam. *Revue Internationale de Philosophie* 70 (2): 213–229. https://doi.org/10.3917/rip.276.0213

Tyrell, Hartmann. 1990. Worum geht es in der protestantischen Ethik? Ein Versuch zum besseren Verständnis Max Webers. *Saeculum* 41 (2): 130–177. https://doi.org/10.7788/saeculum.1990.41.2.130

Ullendorff, Edward. 1979. Review of Alexander Schreiber, Ingaz Goldziher: Tagebuch. *Bulletin of the School of Oriental and African Studies* 42 (3): 553–555. https://doi.org/10.1017/S0041977X00135827

van den Doel, Wim. 2022. Snouck Hurgronje and the Colonial Administration of the Dutch East Indies. In *Scholarship in Action: Essays on the Life and Work of Christiaan Snouck Hurgronje (1857-1936)*. Edited by Léon Buskens and Jan Just Witkam with Annemarie van Sandwijk. Leiden and Boston: Brill: 281–311.

van der Heyden, Ulrich. 2011. Christian Missionary Societies in the German Colonies, 1884/85–1914/15. In *German Colonialism. Race, the Holocaust, and Postwar Germany*. Edited by Volker Langbehn and Mohammad Salama. New York: Columbia University Press: 215–253.

van der Meij, Dick. 2022. Book Review: Wim van den Doel, SNOUCK; Het volkomen geleerenleven van Christiaan Snouck Hurgronje. *Wacana* 23 (2): 519–521. https://doi.org/10.17510/wacana.v23i2.1306

van der Zande, Daniël. 2022. The Correspondence between Nöldeke and De Goeje on Christiaan Snouck Hurgronje. In *Scholarship in Action: Essays on the Life and Work of Christiaan Snouck Hurgronje (1857-1936)*. Edited by Léon Buskens and Jan Just Witkam with Annemarie van Sandwijk. Leiden and Boston: Brill: 117–138.

van Dijk, Kees. 2022. The Scholar and the War-Horse: The Aceh War, Snouck Hurgronje, and Van Heutsz. In *Scholarship in Action. Essays on the Life and Work of Christiaan Snouck Hurgronje (1857-1936)*. Edited by Léon Buskens and Jan Just Witkam with Annemarie van Sandwijk. Leiden and Boston: Brill: 326–373.

van Ess, Josef. 1980. From Wellhausen to Becker: The Emergence of Kulturgeschichte in Islamic Studies. In *Islamic Studies: A Tradition and Its Problems*. Edited by Malcom Kerr. Malibu: Undena Publications: 27–51.

van Koningsveld, Pieter Sjoerd. 1985a. *Orientalism and Islam: The Letters of C. Snouck Hurgronje to Th. Nöldeke*. Rijksuniversiteit Leiden.

van Koningsveld, Pieter Sjoerd. 1985b. *Scholarship and Friendship in Early Islamwissenschaft. The Letters of C. Snouck Hurgronje to I. Goldziher*. Rijksuniversiteit Leiden.

van Koningsveld, Pieter Sjoerd. 2016. Conversion of European Intellectuals to Islam: The Case of Christiaan Snouck Hurgronje alias ʿAbd al-Ghaffār. In *Muslims in Interwar Europe: A Transcultural Historical Perspective*. Edited by Bekim Agai, Umar Ryad, and Mehdi Sajid. Leiden and Boston: Brill: 88–104.

van Oostrum, Anne. 2012: Arabic Music in Western Ears: An Account of the Music of the Hejaz at the Turn of the Twentieth Century. *Quaderni die Studi Arabi* (Nuova Serie) 7: 127–144.

Varsányi, Orsolya. 2024. Ignaz Goldziher and His Correspondents. *Ephemeris Hungarologica* 2024 (2): 99–104. https://doi.org/10.53644/EH.2024.2.99

Vierhaus, Rudolf. 1963. Review Article. *Vierteljahrschrift für Sozial- und Wirtschaftsgeschichte* 50 (2): 273–277.

Virchow, Rudolf. 1852. *Die Noth im Spessart: Eine Medicinisch-Geographisch-Historische Skizze*. Würzburg: Verlag der Stahel'schen Buchhandlung.

Vlekke, Bernhard H. M. 1945. *The Story of the Dutch East Indies*. Cambridge: Harvard University Press.

vom Bruch, Rüdiger, Friedrich Wilhelm Graf, and Gangolf Hübinger (eds.). 1989. *Kultur und Kulturwissenschaften um 1900: Krise der Moderne und Glaube an die Wissenschaft*. Stuttgart: Frank Steiner Verlag.

von Kremer, Alfred. 1868. *Geschichte der herrschenden Ideen des Islams: Der Gottesbegriff, die Prophetie und Staatsidee*. Hildesheim, Zürich, and New York: Georg Olms Verlag [1984].

von Melle, Werner. 1923. *Dreißig Jahre Hamburger Wissenschaft 1891-1921: Rückblicke und persönliche Erinnerungen von Werner von Melle*. Hamburg: Kommissionsverlag von Broschek & Co.

von Moltke, Helmuth. 1987. *Briefe: Über Zustände und Begebenheiten in der Türkei aus den Jahren 1835-1839*. Edited by Helmut Arndt. Nördlingen: Franz Greno.

von Strandmann, Hartmut Pogge. 2011. The Purpose of German Colonialism, or the Long Shadow of Bismarck's Colonial Policy. In *German Colonialism: Race, the Holocaust, and Postwar Germany*. Edited by Volker Langbehn and Mohammad Salama. New York: Columbia University Press: 193–214.

von Stuckrad, Kocku. 2014. *The Scientification of Religion: An Historical Study of Discursive Change (1800-2000)*. Berlin and The Hague: De Gruyter.

Vrolijk, Arnoud. 2001. The Leiden Edition of Tabari's Annals: The Search for the Istanbul Manuscripts as Reflected in Michael Jan de Goeje's Correspondence. *Quaderni di Studi Arabi* 19: 71–86.

Waardenburg, Jacques. 1962. *L'Islam dans le miroir de l'Occident*. The Hague: Mouton and Co.

Waardenburg, Jacques. 1988. Muslim Enlightenment and Revitalization. *Die Welt des Islams* 28: 569–584.

Wagner, Falk. 1998. Rothe, Richard (1799–1867). In *Theologische Realenzyklopädie*. Vol. 29. Berlin and New York: De Gruyter: 436–440.

Wagner, Peter. 2001. *Theorizing Modernity: Inescapability and Attainability in Social Theory*. London, Thousand Oaks, and New Delhi: Sage.

Wagner, Peter. 2008. *Modernity as Experience and Interpretation: A New Sociology of Modernity*. Cambridge: Cambridge University Press.

Wanning, Frank. 1999. *Gedankenexperimente: Wissenschaft und Roman im Frankreich des 19. Jahrhunderts*. Tübingen: Max Niemeyer Verlag.

Warburg, Margit. 1989. William Robertson Smith and the Study of Religion. *Religion* 19 (1): 41–61. https://doi.org/10.1016/0048-721X(89)90076-6

Wardman, H. W. 1964. *Ernest Renan: A Critical Biography*. London: The Athlone Press.

Weber, Eugene. 1976. *Peasants to Frenchmen: The Modernization of Rural France, 1870-1914*. Stanford: Stanford University Press.

Weber, Marianne. 1975. *Max Weber: A Biography*. New York: John Wiley and Sons.

Weber, Max. 1895. The Nation State and Economic Policy (Inaugural Lecture). In *Weber. Political Writings*. Edited by Peter Lassman and Ronald Spiers. Cambridge: Cambridge University Press [1994]: 1–28.

Weber, Max. 1904. "Objectivity" in Social Science and Social Polity. In *The Methodology of the Social Sciences*. Translated and edited by Edward A. Shils and Henry A. Finch. New York: The Free Press: 49–112.

Weber, Max. 1910. Weber's First Reply to Rachfahl, 1910. In *The Protestant Ethic Debate. Max Weber's Replies to His Critics, 1907-1910*. Edited by David J. Chalcraft and Austin Harrington. Translated by Austin Harrington and Mary Shields. Liverpool: Liverpool University Press (2001): 61–88.

Weber, Max. 1915a. The Social Psychology of the World Religions. In *From Max Weber: Essays in Sociology*. Edited by H. H. Gerth and C. Wright Mills. London and New York: Routledge [1991]: 267–301.

Weber, Max. 1915b. *Religious Rejections of the World and Their Directions*. Translated and edited by H. H. Gerth and C. Wright Mills. London and New York: Routledge [1991]: 323–362.

Weber, Max. 1919. Science as Vocation. In *From Max Weber: Essays in Sociology*. Edited by H. H. Gerth and C. Wright Mills. London and New York: Routledge [1991]: 129–156.

Weber, Max. 1921. *Gesammelte Aufsätze zur Religionssoziologie III*. Tübingen: Paul Siebeck.

Weber, Max. 1972. *Wirtschaft und Gesellschaft: Grundriss der Verstehenden Soziologie*. Fünfte revidierte Auflage, besorgt von Johannes Winckelmann. Tübingen: Paul Siebeck.

Weber, Max. 1978. *Economy and Society: An Outline of Interpretive Sociology*. Edited by Guenther Roth and Claus Wittich. Berkeley: University of California Press.

Weber, Max. 2001. *The Protestant Ethic and the Spirit of Capitalism*. Translated by Talcott Parsons. Routledge Classics. London and New York: Routledge.

Wehler, Hans-Ulrich. 1970a. Einleitung. In *Imperialismus*. Edited by Hans-Ulrich Wehler. Köln und Berlin: Kiepenheuer & Witsch: 11–38.

Wehler, Hans-Ulrich. 1970b. Bismarcks Imperialismus 1862–1890. In *Imperialismus*. Edited by Hans-Ulrich Wehler. Köln und Berlin: Kiepenheuer & Witsch: 259–288.

Wehler, Hans-Ulrich. 1995. *Deutsche Gesellschaftsgeschichte. Dritter Band: Von der "Deutschen Doppelrevolution" bis zum Beginn des Ersten Weltkrieges 1849-1914*. München: C. H. Beck.

Weikart, Richard. 1993. The Origins of Social Darwinism in Germany, 1859–1895. *Journal of the History of Ideas* 54 (3): 469–488. https://doi.org/10.2307/2710024

Weil, Gustav. 1843. *Mohammed der Prophet, sein Leben und seine Lehre: aus handschriftlichen Quellen und dem Koran geschöpft und dargestellt*. Stuttgart: Metzler.

Weinberg, Kurt. 1958. "Race" et "races" dans l'oeuvre d'Ernest Renan. *Zeitschrift für französische Sprache und Literatur* 68 (3/4): 129–164.

Wellhausen, Julius. 1882. *Muhammad in Medina: Das ist Vakidi's Kitab al-Maghazi in verkürzter Deutscher Wiedergabe*. Berlin: G. Reimer.

Wellhausen, Julius. 1883a. Mohammedanism. In *Encyclopedia Britannica*, Volume 16, Men–Mos, 9th edition. Edinburgh: Adam and Charles Black: 545–565.

Wellhausen, Julius. 1883b. *Prolegomena zur Geschichte Israels*. Sechste Ausgabe. Berlin und Leipzig: Walter De Gruyter [1927].

Wellhausen, Julius (comp. and ed.). 1887. *Reste Arabischen Heidentums*. Berlin und Leipzig: De Gruyter [1927].

Wellhausen, Julius. 1889. *Die Composition des Hexateuchs und der historischen Bücher des Alten Testaments*. Zweiter Druck. Berlin: Verlag von Georg Reimer.

Wellhausen, Julius. 1902. *Das Arabische Reich und sein Sturz*. Berlin: Verlag von Georg Reimer.

Wellhausen, Julius (trans. and ed.). 1903. *Das Evangelicum Marci*. Berlin: Verlag von Georg Reimer.

Wellhausen, Julius (trans. and ed.). 1904. *Das Evangelium Matthaei*. Berlin: Verlag von Georg Reimer.

Wende, Erich. 1959. *C. H. Becker: Mensch und Politiker. Ein biographischer Beitrag zur Kulturgeschichte der Weimarer Republik*. Stuttgart: Deutsche Verlagsanstalt.

Wertheim, W. F. 1972. Counter-insurgency Research at the Turn of the Century—Snouck Hurgronje and the Acheh War. *Sociologische gids* 19 (5–6): 320–328.

Wheeler-Barclay, Marjorie. 1993. Victorian Evangelicalism and the Sociology of Religion: The Career of William Robertson Smith. *Journal of the History of Ideas* 54 (1): 59–78. https://doi.org/10.2307/2709860

Whitelam, Keith W. 1995. William Robertson Smith and the So-called New Histories of Palestine. In *William Robertson Smith: Essays in Reassessment*. Edited by William Johnstone. Sheffield: Sheffield Academic Press: 180–189.

Williams, Patrick. 2013. Postcolonialism and Orientalism. In *Postcolonialism and Islam*. Edited by Geoffrey Nash, Kathleen Kerr-Koch, and Sarah Hackett. London and New York: Routledge: 48–61.

Winant, Howard. 2000. Race and Race Theory. *Annual Review of Sociology* 26: 169–185. https://doi.org/10.1146/annurev.soc.26.1.169

Winder, Bayly. 1981. Orientalism—Review Article. *The Middle East Journal* 35 (4): 615–619.

Witkam, Jan Just. 2021. Snouck Hurgronje's Consular Ambitions. In *Scholarship between Europe and the Levant: Essays in Honour of Alastair Hamilton*. Edited by Jan Loop and Jill Kraye. Leiden and Boston: Brill: 349–374.

Witkam, Jan Just. 2022. Christian Snouck Hurgronje: Lives and Afterlives. In *Scholarship in Action: Essays on the Life and Work of Christiaan Snouck Hurgronje (1857–1936)*. Edited by Léon Buskens and Jan Just Witkam with Annemarie van Sandwijk. Leiden and Boston: Brill: 73–116.

Wokoeck, Ursula. 2009. *German Orientalism: The Study of the Middle East and Islam from 1800 to 1945*. London: Routledge.

Wrzecionko, Paul. 1964. *Die philosophischen Wurzeln der Theologie Albrecht Ritschls: Ein Beitrag zum Problem des Verhältnisses von Theologie und Philosophie im 19. Jahrhundert*. Berlin: Verlag Alfred Töpelmann.

Wucher, Albrecht. 1956. *Theodor Mommsen: Geschichtsschreibung und Politik*. Göttingen: Musterschmidt Verlag.

Wulf, Andrea. 2015. *The Invention of Nature: The Adventures of Alexander von Humboldt. The Lost Hero of Science*. London: John Murray.

Wulf, Andrea. 2022. *Fabelhafte Rebellen: Die frühen Romantiker und die Erfindung des Ich*. München: C. Bertelsmann.

Yazıcı, Hafize. 2020. Yahudi Oryantalizminim´n Tarihi Temelleri Üzerine Bir Araştırma: Ignaz Goldziher Örneği (A Study on the Historical Foundations of Jewish Orientalism: The Example of Ignaz Goldziher). *Hadith* 5: 105–147.

Yegenoglu, Meyda. 1998. *Colonial Fantasies: Towards a Feminist Reading of Orientalism*. Cambridge: Cambridge University Press.

Young, Robert J. C. 2003. *Postcolonialism: A Very Short Introduction*. Oxford: Oxford University Press.

Zachhuber, Johannes. 2011. Albrecht Ritschl and the Tübingen School. A Neglected Link in the History of 19th Century Theology. *Journal for the History of Modern Theology* 18 (1): 51–70. https://doi.org/10.1515/znth.2011.004

Zachhuber, Johannes. 2013. *Theology as Science in Nineteenth-Century Germany: From F. C. Baur to Ernst Troeltsch*. Oxford: Oxford University Press.

Zantop, Susanne N. 1999. *Kolonialphantasien im vorkolonialen Deutschland (1770–1870)*. Berlin: Erich Schmidt Verlag.

Zimmerman, Andrew. 2001. *Anthropology and Antihumanism in Imperial Germany*. Chicago: Chicago University Press.

Zimmerman, Andrew. 2006. Decolonizing Weber. *Postcolonial Studies* 9 (1): 53–79. https://doi.org/10.1080/13668250500488827

Zweig, Stefan. 1942. *Die Welt von Gestern: Erinnerungen eines Europäers*. Stockholm: Bermann-Fischer Verlag.

Index of Names

Index of Subjects

www.ingramcontent.com/pod-product-compliance
Lightning Source LLC
LaVergne TN
LVHW050508100826
845148LV00002B/265

* 9 7 8 1 8 0 0 5 0 8 6 7 5 *